LESSONS AND LEGACIES XIII

LESSONS AND LEGACIES XIII

New Approaches to an Integrated History of the Holocaust: Social History, Representation, Theory

Edited and with an introduction
by Alexandra Garbarini and Paul B. Jaskot

NORTHWESTERN UNIVERSITY PRESS EVANSTON, ILLINOIS

Northwestern University Press
www.nupress.northwestern.edu

Holocaust Educational Foundation
of Northwestern University
Founded by Theodore Zev and Alice R. Weiss

Printed in the United States of America

10 9 8 7 6 5 4 3 2 1

ISBN 978-0-8101-3767-7 (cloth)
ISBN 978-0-8101-3766-0 (paper)
ISBN 978-0-8101-3768-4 (ebook)

Cataloging-in-Publication data are available from the Library of Congress.

To all the wonderful professors all over the world
who teach about the Holocaust
(Theodore Zev Weiss)

Contents

Theodore Zev Weiss

Foreword

IT IS MY PLEASURE ONCE AGAIN TO THANK THOSE WHO HAVE MADE the publication of another volume in the Lessons and Legacies series possible. This is the thirteenth volume of the series of scholarly papers to be published as an outgrowth of Lessons and Legacies Conferences that the Holocaust Educational Foundation in parnership with major centers of higher learning has sponsored for more than three decades. These publications have established themselves as a very important contribution to Holocaust study and research.

The Holocaust Educational Foundation sponsors a multitude of programs that promote the teaching and study of the Holocaust: from organizing conferences and seminars throughout the United States, Europe, and Israel to providing grants to young scholars working on their graduate degrees in Holocaust studies. We are assisting, promoting, and working with hundreds of academics and educational institutions around the globe. Our primary objective is to encourage and support scholars and future scholars, and to ensure that Holocaust education is included in as many schools, colleges, and universities as possible throughout the United States and other nations and continents.

The Lessons and Legacies publication series, born out of our conferences of the same name, includes the work of top scholars in the field of Holocaust studies, as well as up-and-coming academicians nationally and internationally. Professors Alexandra Garbarini and Paul Jaskot devoted a great deal of time and energy to editing this fine volume. They also served as co-chairs of the 2014 Lessons and Legacies Conference, and I want to express my heartfelt thanks for all the meticulous preparation and hard work they put into providing a wonderful and memorable learning experience for all in attendance.

I would also like to express my deepest appreciation to Florida Atlantic University and to Professor Alan Berger for hosting the conference.

As always, I draw great strength from my wife, Alice, and my children, Deborah and Gabriel, and Danny and Jodi, and my grandchildren, Tamar, David, Matthew, Benjamin, Jacob, and Zoey.

Acknowledgments

OVER THE COURSE OF PREPARING THIS VOLUME, WE HAVE BENEFITED greatly from the support and input of several colleagues in particular. We want them to know how much we appreciate their time and wise counsel.

Earlier versions of the thirteen articles that appear in this volume were first delivered by their authors in 2014 at the Lessons and Legacies Conference, hosted by Florida Atlantic University and organized by the Holocaust Educational Foundation (HEF) at Northwestern University. Our thanks go to Alan Berger and Heather Coltman of Florida Atlantic University for their local hospitality. Several colleagues' generosity with their time and expertise impressed us greatly and contributed in important ways to the conference. We want to express our appreciation in particular to Hilary Earl, Doris Bergen, Dagmar Herzog, and Wendy Lower for their help in organizing the workshops and the special sessions which added much to the intellectual exchange. The success of that conference was due in no small measure as well to the energy and attentiveness of Benjamin Frommer, then director of HEF, and Alexandra Israel, HEF's assistant director. As co-organizers of that conference, we were lucky to have been able to work with them closely and share responsibility for the myriad tasks that went into the conference planning and execution. We are grateful to HEF's current director, Sarah M. Cushman, for her support during the editorial and publishing process of this volume. We are also deeply appreciative of Zev and Alice Weiss. We hope that their vision of Holocaust Studies is honored by the serious work of the scholars in these pages.

It has been a pleasure to move the manuscript through the publication process at Northwestern University Press with Gianna Francesca

Mosser and Maggie Grossman. We owe a special thanks to Anne E. Gendler and Lori Meek Schuldt for their attentive editorial work.

Finally, our thanks to our spouses (and Zeke Singer!) for all of their patience and support during this long process. We, of course, couldn't have done it without you.

—*Alexandra Garbarini and Paul B. Jaskot*

LESSONS AND LEGACIES XIII

Alexandra Garbarini and Paul B. Jaskot

Introduction: Integrated Histories of the Holocaust

IN HOLOCAUST SCHOLARSHIP AT THE PRESENT MOMENT, A CONSENSUS on the dominant intellectual paradigm for the field seems to have emerged, however short-lived it may prove to be. It is not the first time this has happened. In the 1980s the intentionalist/functionalist debate was the key question to which most historians, at least, addressed themselves directly or indirectly. The particular intellectual problem that has come to constitute the current consensus in the field is the concept introduced by Saul Friedländer of an "integrated history" of the genocide.[1]

Friedländer's paradigm is deceptively simple: an integrated history of the Holocaust is one that takes the social history of the European Jews as seriously as it does the political and ideological history of the German perpetrators. While scholars of the Holocaust may have acknowledged this point previously, Friedländer's work awakened most of us to how shockingly little attention we had given to a *serious* integration of the two groups in our work. On the one hand, one set of scholars focused on individual Jewish experiences, social histories of communities, representational strategies, and post–World War II projects of memorialization—all significant work in which, however, the perpetrator's position was too often an abstract cipher against which these microhistories and literary/cultural studies played out. On the other hand, studies of perpetrators investigated the deep political and bureaucratic history of the National Socialist state, its pursuit of genocide, and the institutional or structural conditions that might explain how seemingly normal people could engage in crimes of such violence and scope. In the latter much larger category of scholarly works, Jews were present, but usually as a demographic group that was little distinguished or analyzed. Generally and somewhat schematically speaking, Friedländer's intervention demanded that microhistorical perspectives be linked significantly and analytically to macrohistorical approaches.

As scholars continue to grapple with this desideratum, it has become clear that any attempt at a truly integrated history of the Holocaust requires at a minimum three levels of engagement: deep archival knowledge of the Nazi period and also of its postwar impact (since what we know about the past is necessarily shaped by how we have come to know about the past); attention to the individual narratives and self-representations of both Jewish and non-Jewish participants (since, historically speaking, these individuals and groups did not exist in isolation from the others, and ethically speaking, we must engage with them all as historical subjects and human beings); and theorization of the whole, especially as such theorization posits a connection of the individual to the systemic (since a century of work in the social sciences and humanities has taught us that the self and society are connected in complex ways that challenge older conceptions of the self as autonomous subject or as the mere object of social forces). That is to say, an integrated history worth its name requires careful engagement with sources, social history, and theory.

Our selection of contributions from the thirteenth biennial Lessons and Legacies Conference of the Holocaust Educational Foundation exemplifies the new insights and knowledge to be gained about the Holocaust from the consideration in tandem of social history and theory. We have chosen for inclusion studies that focus on the most intimate scale—on the individual or on a particular locale—which can, in turn, be related to other, broader studies of the war or postwar order. Complementing those works are theoretical investigations that make us think anew about individual agency, moral judgment, and the construction of meaning and memory in the study of the victims of the Holocaust and in our understanding of society as a whole. Taken together, these articles mark the contemporary scholarly landscape, incorporating history, film and literary studies, philosophy, and religious studies (among other disciplines). Read in relation to one another, they push our understanding of the Holocaust forward in critical and ambitious ways. They reinforce the notion that the particulars matter and take on all the more significance when set in relation to broader frameworks.

An integrated approach to the study of the Holocaust requires, at its best, not only attention to the nodes of agency and structure but also to the mediation between them and to the ruptures and continuities in their mediation. How are individuals and systems brought together and how have their interconnections changed over time? Where have perpetrators, victims, and bystanders come together in history? What impact did wartime relationships have on the postwar world? How can a theoretical model tell us something about both ourselves and the horrific deeds of the Nazi past? These subquestions about interconnections and change are crucial to the construction of integrated histories, and they have in turn demanded new approaches by scholars in the field.

In terms of the current volume, such questions are clearly referenced by our contributors. Several scholars, for example, expand the geography of the Holocaust. Indeed, no transformation to Holocaust studies has been perhaps clearer than this expansion and (literal) movement of the focus of study. Highlighting events in the East at the level of small communities indicates the fluidity of Nazi institutional power. Bringing into focus events in the South, at the ports of departure for refugees, points to the antisemitism at the margins. Moreover, these studies reveal moments of agency and reaction from perpetrators and victims alike. In so doing, they show the workings of power structures at the local level, at the level of specific individual and social groups, thus modeling the very essence of integrated history.

Just as important, the expanded range of questions about mediation points to different kinds of sources and different readings of sources. Attending to testimonies as sources has influenced Holocaust studies equally as profoundly as the geographic expansion of scholars' focus. By their very nature, testimonies combine the personal reflections of individuals as mediated by their personalities, backgrounds, experiences of genocide, prevalent forms of narrative, and conceptions of truth telling and bearing witness. Testimonies are neither simply the product of an individual nor of a culture but rather a complicated mediation between the two. In the twenty-first century, overshadowing all uses and discussions of Holocaust testimony has been the Visual History Archive (VHA) of the Shoah Foundation, a collection of more than fifty-two thousand video testimonies that has become digitally searchable by scholars. The accessibility of this archive has dovetailed with a historiographical interest in other kinds of testimony, such as diaries, accounts collected by the Jewish historical commissions in the immediate aftermath of the war, trial transcripts, autobiographical artistic responses, and documentaries (both before and after Claude Lanzmann's landmark *Shoah* [1985]). Several of the scholars in this volume make significant use of this broader array of testimonies to probe their limits and possibilities for critically approaching the Holocaust. The idea that "testimony" could also include the works of postwar scholars in constructing a distorted picture of the fascist past is one of the darker conclusions advanced by one of our authors, a cautionary tale that points all too clearly to the importance of paying strict attention to the mediation of our sources.

At the nub of integrated history resides a strong ethical component. Discussion on what basis scholars can—and whether they ought to—judge the actions of perpetrators, victims, postwar communities, and other scholars has excited renewed interest, especially as more scholars have attempted to extrapolate lessons of the Holocaust in relation to other genocides or contemporary politics. Ethics at its core implies a concept of normative standards, actions taken in accordance with or in opposition to such standards, and the ability to judge those actions. Many of the contributions in this volume draw on these core principles explicitly or implicitly.

The articles in this volume draw on these themes and subthemes to varying degrees, and, as a whole, they represent new interests in the field that contribute to the ongoing work of researching and writing integrated histories of the Holocaust. Part 1, on social history, begins with three articles that bring into focus aspects of the experiences of Jewish victims—and in particular Central European, primarily German Jewish victims—that have received little scholarly attention before now. Dana Smith's study of German Jews in the 1930s shifts our attention away from the German capital, Berlin, to Bavaria, and specifically to the Munich branch of the Jewish cultural association, the *Kulturbund*, that was established under Nazi auspices in response to the "Aryanization" of cultural production in the Third Reich. Smith reminds us of the importance of not painting all German Jewry with the brush of Berlin and the fluidity of German Jewish identity in the years between the two world wars. Marion Kaplan's examination of German Jewish experiences shifts our geographic focus outside the Reich altogether to explore the experiences of Jews who reached Lisbon, Portugal. Unlike the standard historical treatments of refugees, which focus on state actors and policies or, more recently, on the actions of international aid organizations, Kaplan examines the experiences of refugees themselves, as individuals and as a collective of individuals. Among those relatives left behind were Jewish patients with disabilities who were not able to emigrate. Lutz Kaelber's article brings to light what happened to Jews who were categorized as "disabled" and were killed by the Nazi regime as part of the "Euthanasia" program. Kaelber most pointedly poses the question that is raised in all three of these articles about why such victims and victim experiences have been overlooked for so long.

The second cluster of articles in part 1 examines life during the Holocaust in Eastern Europe, in Slovakia and Poland. In her "dark" social history of popular attitudes toward Jews in Slovakia, Hana Kubátová's article brings into focus the inadequacy of the term "bystander" for categorizing many of the people who lent their support to the removal of Jews from their societies. Kubátová's is a study of popular attitudes toward the removal of Jews from the Slovakian economy, from Slovakian society, and, ultimately, from Slovakia itself, to death camps in Poland. Analyses of local dynamics in Eastern Europe are possible because of the new archival research that scholars have been able to conduct in recent years, and Martin Dean's article is another example of how much our understanding of the social history of the Holocaust has changed thanks to the transformation of the archival landscape. Dean's article showcases the research he has been able to conduct using the International Tracing Service (ITS) records, and also his attentiveness to story lines that do not fit the standard narratives we have been telling and retelling about Jewish pathways to survival. He traces a story of survival in rural Eastern Galicia: several hundred Jews escaped liquidations of ghettos in the summer and fall of 1943 and continued to escape subsequent raids and hunts for Jews by Germans and Ukrainians in the region. Jan Grabowski carries forward the exploration of Jewish survival strategies in his microhistory of the destruction of the Jewish population in Węgrów County, a rural district approximately fifty miles from Warsaw. Here, Grabowski carefully reconstructs the "*Liquidierungsaktion*" of the Jews in the Węgrów Ghetto and surrounding area, in which they were violently rounded up to be executed in the local Jewish cemetery or gassed in Treblinka. This microgeographic study of killing in one locale reveals how little—and how much—knowledge it is possible to gain on the basis of existing source material about what happened that day and about the narrow scope of action available to Jews as they tried by various means to escape the genocidal action.

Part 2 of this volume, on representation, brings together four essays that analyze particular representations of the Holocaust, their reception, and the ways in which both representations and their reception have changed over time. Simone Gigliotti's article explores a topic that has attracted much scholarly attention in recent years—the history of Jews as displaced persons, or DPs, after the war—but here in the guise of a little-studied and genre-breaking film: *The Illegals*, produced over the course of six months in 1947 and 1948 by the Jewish journalist and writer Meyer Levin. A different politics of representation emerges in Pedro Correa Martín-Arroyo's article. His work traces the political instrumentalization of narratives about the Holocaust in postwar Spain under Generalissimo Francisco Franco, including the propagation of the story about Franco as a friend of Jewish refugees and Sephardic Jews under Nazi occupation when his regime's actual actions and decrees were designed to prevent Jews, even those who were Spanish citizens, from reaching Spanish soil. In the case of the "Franco myth," the narrative has proven so effective that it still has an impact on contemporary historiography. Jonathan Druker and Brad Prager analyze more familiar sources, but they do so in unfamiliar ways. Druker returns us to the short stories of Tadeusz Borowski from the volume *This Way to the Gas, Ladies and Gentlemen*, but by way of Walter Benjamin's concept of a "real state of emergency," helping to reveal new dimensions of Borowski's work on Auschwitz. Prager likewise returns us to well-known postwar representations, in this case Claude Lanzmann's *Shoah* and the testimonies of survivor-witnesses during the trial of the Nazi leader Adolf Eichmann for war crimes. However, Prager does so through the lens of the less widely viewed documentary from 1979, *Kitty: Return to Auschwitz*. In the process, he complicates our understanding of the performativity of testimony and the valuation of testimony over time, particularly with respect to gender.

Part 3 of this volume, on theory, brings together three essays, each of which, in its own way, explores a dimension of Holocaust victims' experiences. They reflect three distinct disciplinary approaches (religious studies and Jewish thought; philosophy; and comparative literature and critical theory). Yet all three raise sharp moral issues that cause us to question our received wisdom about appropriate critical vantage points for the study of Holocaust victims. Gershon Greenberg challenges us to recognize how limited scholars' engagement has been with trying to understand the perspectives of the people who constituted the largest proportion of Jewish Holocaust victims—namely, the Orthodox and ultra-Orthodox Jews of Eastern Europe. Greenberg maps the range of Jewish theological responses, as the genocide was still unfolding, to the destruction of Jewish life. Lissa Skitolsky challenges us to abandon what has become a moral truism, articulated most profoundly by Primo Levi, that we cannot judge the actions of the Jewish members of the *Sonderkommando*. Contrary to previous readings of Levi's moral proscription, Skitolsky maintains that suspending judgment is implicitly passing judgment, a judgment that is premised on and reaffirms the Socratic denigration of choosing "life" over the "good life" that underpins morality in the Western philosophical tradition and was shared by Levi. The volume closes with Dorota Glowacka's incisive reflection on Holocaust memory, testimony, and history, and how feminist thought brings into view people, experiences, and behaviors that have been heretofore neglected. Understanding the reasons for our collective blindness proves to be of tremendous significance for bringing such subjects to light.

Our separation of the articles into three discrete, analytical parts is an approximate move. In part 1 on social histories, for example, we have set contributions that focus on the daily life and experiences of European Jews alongside analyses of such understudied social groups as disabled youth (Jewish and non-Jewish) and Christian neighbors implicated in various ways in Jewish killings in Eastern Europe. "Social" for us is thus more a matter of understanding the Holocaust as a series of individual actions or reactions that took place within institutional constraints, certainly, but that nevertheless occurred to, between, and within distinct social groups. In a similar fashion, our presentation of representation in part 2 foregrounds a wide range of sources and analyses of culture. Documentary films based on survivor testimony and autobiographical writing are no stranger to this category. By contrast, questions about how a state represents itself in relation to the Holocaust or what it means for a film to blur the line between documentary and narrative film traditions point to understandings of Holocaust representation that carry us from the individual to the social in complex ways. And, finally, our part 3 category of theory: this too takes us in new directions. All too often, postwar theory has avoided engaging with real Jews, deploying the Jew as a trope to develop arguments about political identity, morality, and meaning in the wake of the Holocaust. Theoretical discussions in this volume lead from the challenge presented to the moral framework underpinning Western philosophical thought by serious consideration of the circumstances and choices of victims during the Holocaust; to the difficult task of research and comprehension for secular scholars seeking to understand the range of Orthodox and ultra-Orthodox Jewish theological responses to the destruction of Jewish life; to the importance of paying heed to Holocaust victims—frequently women victims—who have long been ignored, forgotten, excluded, or worse, for developing a critical feminist understanding of violence and society. Such philosophical and theoretical interventions call our attention to the benefits that can derive from the interpolation of theory with social history and from the engagement of theoreticians with a range of representational sources. Taken together, these articles represent a way of thinking about the Holocaust that is at once theoretically sophisticated and attuned to issues of representation while simultaneously grounded in the social realities of the historical participants.

NOTES

1. See in particular the introductions to Saul Friedländer, *Nazi Germany and the Jews*, Vol. 1, *The Years of Persecution, 1933–1939* (New York: HarperCollins Publishers, 1997), and Saul Friedländer, *Nazi Germany and the Jews*, 1939–1945, *The Years of Extermination* (New York: HarperCollins, 2007). For a recent volume with various reflections on the impact of Friedländer's work on the field of Holocaust studies, see Christian Wiese and Paul Betts, eds., *Years of Persecution, Years of Extermination: Saul Friedländer and the Future of Holocaust Studies* (London: Continuum Publishers, 2010).

I. S•O•C•I•A•L H•I•S•T•O•R•I•E•S

Dana Smith

Munich's Jewish Marionette Theater, *Moses*, and the Jewish Cultural League in Bavaria

IN JANUARY 1935 A GROUP OF JEWISH ARTISTS BASED IN MUNICH PERformed the story of one of Judaism's most important prophets on the marionette stage. As a local review in Munich's Jewish newspaper asked, "A play about Moses at the Puppet Theater?"[1] The combination of a major Jewish religious text performed through a comedic and oftentimes subversive folk medium was, at least initially, a surprising endeavor.[2] Unlike the early crib plays of Roman Catholicism, there was no connection between Judaism and puppetry. In addition, the National Socialist regime referred to the marionette stage as "no more and no less than the Theatre of the Volk."[3] The emotional connection to the marionette stage was particularly high in Bavaria; a 1933 letter of denunciation mailed to the Bavarian Ministry of Education and Culture claimed that "Munich, the oldest Marionette City [*Marionettenstadt*]," should not allow the continued professional success of Jewish artists on the marionette stage.[4]

And yet an adaptation of August Strindberg's *Moses* was the inaugural performance of Munich's Marionette Theater of Jewish Artists (München Marionettentheater Jüdischer Künstler), a locally based marionette theater established under the administrative domain of the Jewish Kulturbund in Bavaria.[5] Munich's Jewish marionette theater was comprised entirely of Jewish artists who performed self-described "Jewish" themed plays for a Jewish audience. And these artists performed this "Jewish" theater through a medium they imbued with a strong local "Bavarian" cultural meaning and tradition.[6]

Munich's Jewish marionette theater reflected the diversity of German Jewish self-conceptualizations and self-representations. Its programming should be understood as a "projection of willed identity."[7] Indeed, constructing a cultural program is not a haphazard or thoughtless endeavor. Its performances, particularly in early seasons when state censorship was most lax, reflected the ways its artists chose to stage their own understandings of what it meant, to them, to be "Jewish" at that time and in that place. In this way, the creation of a "Jewish" cultural program in Bavaria can be understood as the conscious construction of local leadership and artists.[8] The inaugural performance of *Moses* in early 1935 was undoubtedly chosen as representative of the troupe's ideals and vision of their own "Jewishness"—a hybrid creation of German, Bavarian, and Jewish traditions; it reflected varied, perhaps even conflicting, forms of local Jewish self-representations, social negotiations, and coming to terms with their contemporary experiences. While the Bavarian Kulturbund and Munich's Marionette Theater of Jewish Artists speak to the details of a specific Bavarian Jewish self- or communal understanding, they also speak to the need for further study on the role of regional identification among German Jewish communities. The regional and local deepen and sharpen our understanding of the complexities of Jewish life under National Socialism. There was no singular German Jewish experience.

Scholarship on Kulturbund cultural production in 1930s Germany has remained entrenched in a worn German-Jewish "assimilationist" tradition; it overlooks the multifaceted ways "German" and "Jewish" forms of cultural expression were intertwined in Jewish self-representation under Nazism. The maintenance of this assimilationist paradigm is based almost entirely on cultural expression originating from the Kulturbund in Berlin. What has developed is an interpretation of Jewish cultural production under Nazism that portrays it as aligned with traditional "German" or Western European humanist traditions until it was forced by the National Socialist regime into a more "Jewish" (i.e., Eastern European) repertoire in the late 1930s—which is generally interpreted as an unwelcome development. Herbert Freeden, a former dramaturge for the Berlin Kulturbund and an early author on the Kulturbund, wrote of the Kulturbund that it was a "Jewish Cultural League without Jewish culture [*Jüdischer Kulturbund ohne jüdische Kultur*]."[9] A more recent publication on the Kulturbund orchestra in Berlin follows this same path, claiming that "Jewish" cultural expression was "in fact merely a sideline activity or tangential experiment."[10]

Yet Jewish artists did actively engage with "Jewish" cultural themes, particularly in communities outside of Berlin. Extending scholarship beyond the capital can serve to broaden our understanding of Jewish experiences during National Socialism. Local Bavarian Kulturbund leaders and artists published articles debating the possible forms of "Jewish" music already in 1934.[11] Bavaria's Kulturbund lecture series, which existed throughout the entirety of the organization's tenure from 1934 until 1938, exclusively featured issues relating to Jewish history, Jewish artists, Jewish authors, or contemporary Jewish concerns. Bavaria's visual arts department featured a marionette theater, a self-described "specifically Jewish endeavour" that performed self-defined "Jewish" art.[12]

Further, pitting "Western European" or "German" art traditions against "Jewish" art traditions sustains the notion of two cultural absolutes that did not, perhaps even could not, overlap, as if individuals were either "German" or "Jewish." Maintaining such categorical rigidity is not useful as an interpretative tool, at least not in the Bavarian case. Sharon Gillerman's research regarding the impulses of Jewish social reformers in the Weimar years is a useful framework for examining the Bavarian Kulturbund program: "a new expression of Jewish particularism did not depend on the surrender of their Germanness."[13] The belief that one could be both German and Jewish, that "to be German did not negate the possibility of being Jewish," was, as Philip Bohlman has stated, "a particularly twentieth-century realization" that gained credence during the Weimar years.[14]

In Bavaria, the Jewish Kulturbund program was constructed from multiple conceptual frameworks; it represented human experiences expressed during a span of political and social turbulence, and human experiences can rarely be divided into neat ideological boxes. Munich's Marionette Theater of Jewish Artists is just one example of such cultural blending. The local artists employed a self-described "German" and "Bavarian" folk medium to perform "Jewish" art for adult Jewish audiences. Furthermore, the theater reflected varied, perhaps even conflicting, forms of local Jewish self-representations, social negotiations, and internal attempts at coming to terms with their contemporary experiences. The 1935 *Moses* performance sought to make sense of the community's current political and social situation. Maria Luiko, a young Jewish visual artist from Munich, and her fellow artists blended various cultural traditions and motifs to present a link between the ancient Israelites and the contemporary Bavarian Jewish community. It was a fluid maneuvering between disparate times and spaces that were nonetheless linked by a shared communal "Jewish" experience, that of Jewish suffering and persecution.

ORGANIZED JEWISH CULTURAL LIFE IN NAZI GERMANY

In the summer of 1933, Joseph Goebbels's Ministry of Public Enlightenment and Propaganda granted official approval for a Jewish cultural organization in Berlin: the Cultural League of German Jews (Kulturbund deutscher Juden). This new Jewish Kulturbund, headed by the neurologist and conductor Dr. Kurt Singer[15] and the young stage director Kurt Baumann, consisted entirely of Jews—from its various advisory and executive boards, dramaturges, stage directors, performers, and support staff, to its audience members. According to its founders, Berlin's Kulturbund was designed to remedy unemployment, create a sense of community, and enrich Jewish cultural and theatrical life in the German capital.[16] Furthermore, the Kulturbund had support from a wide range of influential members of Berlin's Jewish community, including Leo Baeck, Max Lieberman, Martin Buber, and Jacob Wasserman.[17]

Oversight of Singer's new Jewish cultural endeavor was vested in Hans Hinkel, an "old fighter" and underling of Goebbels in the Ministry of Public Enlightenment and Propaganda.[18] Hinkel's office passed a number of guidelines in an effort to regulate Kulturbund activity to the ministry's needs. State stipulations required that performance proposals be submitted to Hinkel's office for approval at least two weeks in advance of the performance. Such a deadline allowed state officials time to read the proposal and censor any aspects they deemed contrary to the Reich-wide National Socialist anti-Jewish cultural policy. In principle, this anti-Jewish cultural policy was meant to limit the Kulturbund program to non-"German," nonpolitical, and "Jewish" performances: theater performances were limited to "Jewish" scripts and themes; concerts were to feature "Jewish" music; lectures were to focus on "Jewish" topics and concerns.[19] In practice, the idea of "Jewish" and non-"German" cultural forms was never well enough defined to result in a clear process of censorship. Added to this, National Socialist anti-Jewish cultural policy was only haphazardly enforced, often with event limitations being subjected to the knowledge base or whims of the individual censor. The issue of maintaining a cohesive censorship standard was made more difficult as Jewish cultural organizations developed in the provinces. In Bavaria, the Bavarian Ministry of Education and Culture, the Bavarian Political Police, and local city police forces were all responsible for enforcing the censorship decrees coming from the country's capital. As in Berlin, local Bavarian censorship was undertaken by a rotating cast of individual censors, many of whom had little to no background in the arts. In addition, Kulturbund event advertisements were limited to the Jewish press. Finally, Kulturbund performances were closed events, which meant that audience members were limited to Jews.[20]

Despite these restrictions, successes came quickly for Berlin's Kulturbund. The *Nürnberg-Fürther Israelitisches Gemeindeblatt*, the main Jewish newspaper for Franconia, concluded, "within its two weeks of activities [the Kulturbund] has far exceeded expectations."[21] Membership in Berlin increased throughout the autumn of 1933. In November 1933 its membership list registered 19,744 individuals, approximately 12 percent of the city's Jewish population.[22] Berlin's successes encouraged the development of numerous other Kulturbund branch locales between late 1933 and mid-1934, including the regional Kulturbund Rhein-Ruhr and the Kulturbund Rhein-Main in Frankfurt. Singer consolidated these regional branches under the administrative control of his Berlin Kulturbund over the course of 1934.[23] By the early spring of 1935, Singer oversaw Jewish cultural life in sixty-one German cities.[24] A small number of Jewish cultural organizations remained outside of Berlin's administrative domain until the state required the creation of a nationalized Jewish Kulturbund structure in April 1935.[25] The largest of these regional and autonomous branches was the Jewish Kulturbund in Bavaria.

Bavarian Jewish communities were, on the whole, more conservative and traditional, particularly in comparison to the Jewish community in Berlin.[26] Still, this leaning varied from location to location. In 1933, Munich, the lone Kulturbund branch in Upper Bavaria, was the home of the state's largest Jewish community; approximately 9,005 Jews lived in the Bavarian capital.[27] Munich was also home to the Bavarian Kulturbund's central office, which operated under the bureaucratic control of the Bavarian Jewish Community (Bayerische Israelitische Kultusgemeinde); the majority of Munich's Jewish elite had a religious background in the liberal strand of Judaism.[28] However, the majority of Bavarian Jews, approximately 60 percent, lived in Franconia.[29] The Franconian Jewish communities were, again in general, more conservative than in Munich. Nuremberg, which boasted the largest Jewish community in Franconia as well as the second largest in Bavaria, was home to 7,502 Jews. Würzburg had a Jewish community of 2,145 individuals, while Fürth, the neighboring community in close proximity to Nuremberg, consisted of 1,990 members.[30] Of these six Franconian locales, three (Würzburg, Aschaffenburg, and Bad Kissingen) were located in Lower Franconia—the "bastion" of Orthodox Judaism.[31]

The late Weimar era saw an increased interest in Jewish community cultural activity in Bavaria, particularly in Munich. In 1927, Franz Kleinbauer and Heinrich Lamm, two youths from Munich, founded the Jewish Chamber Orchestra in Munich (Jüdisches Kammerorchester München). This was the first "Jewish" orchestra in the Bavarian capital. According to its founders, the Jewish Chamber Orchestra was to facilitate a process of community building through cultural participation, to "bring together a Jewish circle," and to foster a "collegium musicum."[32] There were also "Hebrew Theatre Evenings" with theatrical and musical performances in Hebrew and Yiddish, although the details of these performances are currently unknown.[33] However, the scope and purview of organized Jewish cultural activity was forced to expand under National Socialism.

Jewish composer and conductor Erich Erck (legal name: Erich Eisner)[34] submitted an initial proposal to create the Jewish Cultural League in Bavaria [Jüdischer Kulturbund in Bayern] to the Bavarian State Ministry of Education and Culture and the Bavarian Political Police in October 1933. Artistic events were divided into three categories: adult education (mainly a lecture series), visual arts, and music. According to Erck's proposal, the main purpose of the Kulturbund in Bavaria was to provide employment for out of work Jewish artists and academics. He explained, writing:

> As a result of the provisions of the Restoration Law of the Civil Service in all areas of public life, a large number of Jewish artists and academics find any practice of their career impossible. In the vast majority of cases, finding an alternative occupation is not feasible given the long-term economic situation and because of advanced age.[35]

Erck suggested that these social and financial burdens facing the Jewish community be assuaged through the creation of a Jewish cultural organization for Bavaria. The Bavarian Kulturbund eventually grew to serve ten Bavarian cities: Munich, Nuremberg, Würzburg, Fürth, Augsburg, Regensburg, Bamberg, Bad Kissingen, Aschaffenburg, and Memmingen. During the 1935–1936 season, the first season that required a membership registration in order to attend events, 4,710 Bavarian Jews were Kulturbund members, ranging from approximately one-third of the Jewish populations in Munich and Nuremberg to two-thirds of Jews living in Regensburg.[36]

Although modeled on the Berlin example, Erck pointed to important differences between the two. First and foremost, the Bavarian Kulturbund was established under the jurisdiction of the Bavarian Jewish Community and was not, as in Berlin, a separate institutional organization. As such, there was no separate Kulturbund membership structure; rather, all members of the Bavarian Jewish Community could purchase an event ticket from the community's administrative offices or from certain Jewish-owned stores. Erck defended this decision to operate the Kulturbund within the *Gemeinde* (community) structure due to the "oppressive financial situation" facing Bavarian Jews. Further, the Bavarian Jewish Community itself was responsible for maintaining the Kulturbund's daily operations. In the first season, it provided an initial financial backing of one thousand reichsmarks.[37]

Yet the differences between the Berlin and Bavarian Kulturbund organizations extended beyond the internal operating guidelines. Unlike the situation in Berlin, Zionists held key positions in the Bavarian Kulturbund already in 1934. In Berlin, Kulturbund supporters were divided along Zionist and non-Zionist lines. Members of the Berlin leadership, who were decidedly not Zionists, strove to maintain a Western European and "German"-oriented cultural program. The German capital's Zionist ranks, however, urged the Kulturbund to steer the league toward a "Jewish" program.[38] In Berlin, therefore, the Zionist minority was a disruptive force in the Jewish cultural sphere. Indeed, the Zionists initially withheld their full support of the Berlin Kulturbund after it became clear that the Berlin offices were not going to willingly engage with "Jewish" art on the Jewish stage.[39]

The situation was markedly different in Bavaria. In September 1934 Dr. Alfred Perlmutter was elected the chair of the Bavarian

Kulturbund; he held this position until the Bavarian league was dissolved in November 1938. Not only was Perlmutter the Bavarian Kulturbund chair, he was also a board member of the Bavarian Jewish Community and "counted among the most committed Zionists in Munich" due to his leadership role in Munich's local Zionist group.[40] In addition, other local Zionists, such as Maria Luiko, were active participants from the regional Kulturbund's inception. Instead of fissure and division, Zionists and non-Zionists worked side by side in the Bavarian Kulturbund, perhaps hastening the speed and depth with which the Bavarian Kulturbund grappled with issues of "Jewish" cultural performance and artistic forms.

Not only did Bavarian Kulturbund officials and artists create a "Jewish" cultural program, but this program also had a certain "Bavarian" bent. The Bavarian Kulturbund's identification with regional pride was particularly apparent in its visual arts department. Often, however, this regional pride was conflated with a sense of Munich's civic pride stemming from the city's nineteenth-century reputation as the German City of Art (Kunststadt). By the fin de siècle, Munich had emerged as a leading city in the art world; its contributions to exhibitions and the art trade were at the time incomparable.[41] Munich was one of the top cities for art in the world, its atmosphere one of "convivial bohéme."[42] As author Thomas Mann famously noted in his 1902 novella *Gladius Dei*, "Munich glowed."[43] However, less than a decade into the twentieth century, Munich's glowing reputation had dimmed and the city lost the claim to its former title. Cultural and political conservatism swept the Bavarian capital while Berlin, the new German capital, became the focal point of political, economic, and cultural growth. Still, segments of the educated and culturally inclined strove to regain their city's former glory.[44] Indeed, articles published in the local Jewish press continued to invoke the local Kunststadt traditional mythos when describing Kulturbund events, particularly Munich's Jewish marionette theater.

MUNICH'S MARIONETTE THEATER OF JEWISH ARTISTS

On January 30, 1935, the Bavarian Kulturbund's Jewish marionette theater—Munich's Marionette Theater of Jewish Artists—opened in the *Gemeinde*-owned *Museumsaal* (museum hall) on Promenadestrasse 12 (now Kardinal-Faulhaber-Strasse in central Munich) at 8:00 P.M.

The troupe debuted with an evening billing of two plays: an adaptation of August Strindberg's *Moses* followed by Jacques Offenbach's *Das Mädchen von Elizondo*. Over the course of the next four seasons, the Jewish marionette theater was consistently praised in the local Jewish press as one of the region's most popular Jewish cultural undertakings. Berthold Wolff, cofounder and financial backer of the theater, described the Bavarian Kulturbund's Jewish marionette theater as a "specifically Jewish endeavor" that performed "Jewish" art. He further explained, writing in Munich's Jewish newspaper, that "all works either have to be written by a Jewish author or have to contain an easily identifiable Jewish theme, and all acting and technical work is to be exclusively in Jewish hands."[45]

The Munich Kulturbund's marionette theater was founded by a "handful of idealistic collaborating artists" led by Wolff and Maria Luiko and Wolff.[46] Wolff was a middle-aged, middle-class Jewish businessman who had served in the German armed forces prior to World War I.[47] Luiko was a then thirty-year-old artist who was born, raised, and educated in Munich. She was under Gestapo surveillance due to her (supposed, later refuted) Socialist and (known) Zionist activities.[48] Luiko and Wolff stressed that their theater was not a Kasperl-theater (similar to the English Punch and Judy tradition, often meaning a lowbrow comedic theater) but rather an experimental theater with a high artistic standard. Plays began in the evening, often at eight o'clock, which meant that performances were oriented toward an adult audience.[49] The visual aspects (e.g., marionettes, props, stage backdrops) were designed and created by Luiko and Rudolf Ernst, both highly regarded Munich-based artists. Vocal roles were filled by professionals—such as Dr. Paul Kuhn, Walter Reis (both formerly of the Munich's National Theater), and Elisabeth Springer—or by skilled amateurs such as Sonja Ziegler.

The Kulturbund's marionette theater was not the first Jewish marionette theater in the Bavarian capital. Two preexisting Jewish marionette theaters developed in Munich during the first years of the 1930s: Alfons Rosenberg's short-lived, single-person puppet stage and Bimath-Buboth, a "biblical-experimental stage."[50] Rosenberg performed one play, *Golem*, in the autumn and winter of 1934 in Frankfurt am Main and Munich. Rosenberg acted alone and appeared to have had limited and simple props.[51] Bimath-Buboth, on the other hand, was a more extensive artistic undertaking. Like the

Kulturbund theater, Bimath-Buboth ("Puppet Theater" in Hebrew) was under the artistic direction of Luiko with assistance from Ernst. Local Munich author Fritz Rosenthal (who later changed his name to Schalom Ben-Chorin) wrote or adapted the scripts. From 1933 until 1935 Bimath-Buboth staged three original plays based on the Bible or Yiddish folk stories: *Das Buch Esther*, *Megillath Ruth*, and *Hersch Ostropoler wird Kalendermacher*.[52] Bimath-Buboth performed in front of Jewish audiences, often for the Zionist youth group and on Jewish holidays, until Rosenthal's immigration to Jerusalem in 1935. Despite the links between Bimath-Buboth and the Kulturbund's marionette theater—not only in artistic personnel but also in the actual marionettes and stage props shared between the two groups—the local Jewish press never made mention of Bimath-Buboth when reviewing the Kulturbund's marionette performances.

Various trends collided in the Bavarian Kulturbund's Jewish Marionette Theater: the cultural search for a supposedly "authentic," "German" folk art tradition; the search for a supposedly "authentic," "Jewish" cultural tradition; and the concomitant process of German-Jewish cultural dissimilation. The marionette stage was a medium imbued with centuries-old German folk traditions; the Jewish press praised the theater for its maintenance of "German" and "Bavarian" traditions. The marionette stage had no traditional connection to Judaism, particularly when performed outside of Purim. Instead, it originated in the crib plays of medieval Christianity, particularly within Roman Catholic Mariology.[53]

Indeed, marionettes were especially popular in Catholic Munich, which was still known at the time as the "center of puppetry [*klassischen Boden der Puppenspielpflege*]."[54] By the early twentieth century, the marionette stage in Bavaria had recently turned from the supposedly primitive pastime of the provincial backwaters to a serious art form performed in the city. The cultural turn toward neo-Romanticism established at the end of the previous century had ushered in a revival of folk traditions; this resulted in a widespread rebirth of popularity for the marionette theater, particularly in southern Germany.[55] In the late 1920s, the German art historian Max von Boehn declared in his book *Puppen und Puppenspiele* that there had been a "renaissance of the puppet theater in Germany."[56] The marionette stage was no longer considered a means of cheap popular entertainment for the village but rather a medium for serious artistic expression.[57]

At the same time, however, this theater's plots and marionettes (as physical objects) distanced the Bavarian Kulturbund's Jewish marionette theater from the traditional realm of local and regional puppetry. The Kulturbund's marionette theater was introduced in the local Jewish press as bringing "something new to Munich, namely drama of purely Jewish forms"[58]—with "Jewish forms" here referring to biblical themes or stories originating from the Yiddish-speaking artistic circles of Eastern Europe. These dramas were paired with comedies written by authors of Jewish heritage, the most often performed author being Jacques Offenbach. Furthermore, the visual appearance of the theater's marionettes was not oriented toward a traditional "German" marionette aesthetic but was instead influenced by the experimental style of the Habima theatrical productions of the 1920s.[59]

Indicative of this cultural blending was the group's adaptation of *Moses* for the marionette stage. The medium rooted the theater in a certain local cultural tradition. Yet the marionettes and stage elements incorporated a visual representation of contemporary "Jewish" forms. The decision to stage the story of Moses—one of the most important figures in Judaism—situated the performance within the purview of a contemporary notion of Jewish Orientalism. The staging also had important contemporary sociopolitical parallels to a persecuted Jewish community: Moses is, ultimately, a redemptive figure. His story is one of hope, as the once-enslaved Jewish people overcome their oppression and find freedom.

MOSES ON THE MARIONETTE STAGE IN 1935

Set in Egypt, Strindberg's *Moses* follows the biblical narrative of the prophet. *Moses* begins with a dream sequence whereby a high priest orders Pharaoh to kill all the male Jewish children. The plot thus begins with Pharaoh's edict to drown all newborn Israelite boys in the Nile, which in turn causes Moses's mother to hide him on the banks of the river, in effect saving his life. Events in the production stayed true to the biblical narrative, with Pharaoh's daughter finding the hidden Moses along the Nile and then adopting the child as her own son. Moses grows into adulthood as a member of the Egyptian royal family. However, after killing an Egyptian slave master for abusing an Israelite, Moses is forced to cross the Red Sea and flee Egypt. It is then that Moses encounters the God of Israel through the form of the burning bush; God calls Moses to return to Egypt to free the Israelites from slavery and lead them to the Promised Land. Pharaoh initially refuses Moses's demands, and his refusal is followed by the Ten Plagues. It is only then that Pharaoh allows Moses to lead the Israelites from their Egyptian bondage. However, once at the border of Egypt, the situation changes as Pharaoh and his army descend on the Israelites. In an act of strength, the God of Israel decimates Pharaoh and his army at the Red Sea, and the play approaches its resolution as Moses finally leads the Israelites to Mount Sinai, where the prophet receives the Ten Commandments.[60]

The cultural critic for the Jewish press was not impressed with the performance. The Moses character was described as both monotonous and unheroic—and indeed, it was the Moses figure that received the most negative attention from the local Jewish critic Ba. (79, 82). As Ba. wrote, the complex story of Moses is a story of great heroism: "He must, against all odds, prepare his Volk for their mission" (79, 82). Unfortunately, the review continued, the marionette Moses did not fulfill the heroic mission of the biblical Moses: "Moses as a marionette must present to the viewer all the psychological developments [of the biblical figure]. When attached to a rigid mask, we cannot see the flashing of his triumphant soul; the immutability of the puppet condemned him to monotony" (82). True to his misgivings about the limits of the Moses figure—which had been previously used as the King Ahasuerus character in Bimath-Buboth's production of *Das Buch Esther*—the reviewer did suggest that subtle changes could improve the overall performance, mostly by creating a Moses puppet with a more "supernatural" facial expression (82). The marionette Moses, it seems, was too common in appearance.

Despite these negative aspects, Ba.'s review did praise the overall artistic work of the *Moses* drama. Luiko's stage design was noted as "tasteful" and "exemplary." The puppets themselves (other than the Moses figure) were said to have made a strong personal impression (82). What, then, was the problem with the "problematic" *Moses* play? Despite the review's claim that the figure of Moses presented onstage did not represent the heroic nature of the biblical Moses, the same review praised the visual aspects of the performance. And despite the earlier complaint that the "monotony" of Moses was also apparent in the character's voice, the review ended with a favorable description of the "strength of the vocal performers in the Moses-Drama" (82). Thus, the technical aspects of the performance were, by the reviewer's own admission, sound.

The general "problem" with the *Moses* play was perhaps in the reviewer's inability to reconcile the traditions of the marionette stage with an overtly biblical story. An element of dissonance existed between the biblical theme of the Moses drama and the traditionally comedic and satirical nature of the marionette stage. The presentation of serious "Jewish" religious themes in a traditionally "German" satirical form challenged preexisting expectations about the medium. For the critic Ba., the general problem with the *Moses* play was seemingly a conceptual issue. Ba. wrote, "Can, however, a fundamental question be raised, can a Puppet Theater be concerned with religious motifs?" (79). Marionettes were, according to the critic, the realm of the "*heimisch*" (local or regional) *Volk* drama, as well as comedies and political satire (79). On the surface, *Moses* did not fit this model. Indeed, Ba. argued that the *Moses* performance was a stark departure from this purview of "German" marionette traditions. The review ended by stating, "We all have confidence that Mr. Wolff and his colleagues will find the ways and the means to create a distinctive *Heimstätte*-styled *Kleinkunst* [small-scale performance art of regional importance]" (82). The implication of this sentence is that *Moses*, the so-called problematic piece, did not yet fall within these "*Heimstätte*" boundaries.

While the critical reception of the inaugural performance of *Moses* suggested general success, albeit with room for improvement, the popular reception of the Jewish marionette theater was strong. The event sold out more than two weeks prior to its performance. Additionally, two separate articles noted the strong applause at the end of the evening. An encore evening performance was scheduled in Munich for late February due to its popularity.[61]

MUNICH'S *MOSES* MARIONETTES AND A "JEWISH" VISUAL CULTURE

The Kulturbund's marionettes were made from easy-to-find materials, likely due to the deteriorating financial situation facing German Jews by the middle of the 1930s. The marionettes' clothing and accessories were made from fabric remnants, glass beads, and paper leftovers; bodies were made from wooden frames shaped with paper and painted, legs from wood and wire, and heads from papier-mâché casts. Their heights ranged from forty to fifty centimeters (roughly sixteen to twenty inches), depending on the importance of the character.

Visually, Luiko's *Moses* marionettes were conceptualized within group frameworks, with shared visual cues signifying group membership. Such similarities in size and clothing made the figures easily identifiable, an exaggerated technique common in puppetry.[62] The Israelites from *Moses* resembled one another and used a similar visual language, which also constituted an allusion to Luiko's visual notion of a collective Jewish community described by Luiko herself as being representative of "the biblical Hebrews."[63] The marionette Israelite men were dressed in simple, plain dark costumes (dark earth tones). Moses himself wore a dark underlayer with only a red cloak on top to distinguish his dress from the group. The Israelite men and the Moses figure were uniform in basic shape (head, torso, legs). The importance of Moses was only denoted by his height—he was a full ten centimeters (four inches) taller than the others—although the rest of his physical appearance reflected that of the group. Luiko's Jewish figures had large, dark eyes and angular facial features that appeared evocative and highly emotional. Finally, the puppets had large, sharply angled hands.[64] Likewise, Luiko's Egyptians from *Moses* shared a collective visual language that situated the individual figures into the group dynamic. The Egyptians were dressed alike in white with colorful adornment (golden embroidery and blue beads).[65]

The visual language evident in the *Moses* play was evocative of the theatrical techniques popularized in the 1920s by the Habima Theater. The Habima Theater is a Hebrew-language theater first established in Bialystok in 1912 and then reestablished in Moscow in 1918; it later relocated to Tel Aviv in 1928, eventually becoming the national theater of Israel, which it remains to the present day.[66] It was the first professional Hebrew dramatic art theater.[67] During the late 1920s, the theater embarked on multiple tours that took it to Bavaria, performing in Munich in 1928, 1929, and 1930, and a somewhat infamous performance in Würzburg in 1930.[68] According to the art historian Diana Oesterle, Luiko was inspired by the stage elements of Habima's productions in her own choices of sharp earth tone color combinations and highly evocative and emotional facial expressions (although the aforementioned review from Ba. suggests that the contemporary critic disagreed with this interpretation as it pertained to the face of the Moses figure).[69] Utilizing these techniques placed Luiko's Kulturbund marionette theater within the broader tradition of modern Jewish theater; she was effectively creating a cultural link between her local marionette theater, the Jewish theater of Eastern Europe, and the Yishuv in Palestine.

Lending further support to this point, Munich's Jewish Marionette Theater's *Moses* performance was rooted in contemporary discourses that presented the image of an idealized Eastern Jewry, what would today be termed Jewish Orientalism. In this particular instance, the marionette's *Moses* performance combined a portrayal of the ancient biblical Jewish community with a visual technique oriented toward contemporary Palestinian motifs and Luiko's own representations of Munich's Eastern European Jewish community. By the mid-1930s, the Jews of Eastern Europe—a group that, on the whole, was less acculturated and more traditional than German Jews—became representative of a supposedly "authentic" vision of a seemingly more "pure" Judaism untouched by the modern world.[70] Such a view was problematic; it was highly romanticized and, at times, utopian in nature while also being patronizing and paternalistic.[71] It looked both backward and forward, combining the idealized times of the ancient Israelites with a contemporary vision of the generally more religious and traditional Jewish communities of Eastern Europe.

Luiko's decision to create what she considered a clearly stated "Jewish" visual was not surprising;[72] Luiko was an active member of Munich's Zionist organization and often performed biblically inspired marionette plays for the city's Zionist youth groups with the same collection of marionettes. Yet Luiko made the conscious decision to cast her Jewish figures—figures that were, to an extent, meant to exemplify a foreign and idealized Jewry—in an entirely familiar, specifically Central European, German, and Bavarian, folk medium. In addition, the physical attributes apparent in her puppets—the large hands, angular faces, dark eyes—were the same physical markers found in her artwork on Munich's Eastern European Jewish community.[73] This shared visual effect spanned vast amounts of time and geographic locations, suggesting that, at least to Luiko, there was the possibility of an "authentic" Jewishness in the local context. The ancient Israelites portrayed on the marionette stage became *Einheimisch*—that is, the foreign became local. Munich's *Moses* production was, then, a textual and visual combination of the Other and the familiar. This combination suggests that, at least to Luiko, there was the possibility of an "authentic" expression of Judaism within the local (Bavarian and German) context.

Staging the Moses story in 1935 was thus wrought with sociopolitical importance. Munich's Kulturbund marionette theater's performance combined a long-standing Bavarian folk medium with a self-described "Jewish" purpose. One of the most important religious texts in Judaism became intertwined with a local folk tradition, and the ancient Israelite community of the biblical past became intertwined with the audience's contemporary Bavarian community. Indeed, the audience would have recognized, and drawn parallels to, the themes of Jewish persecution and slavery in Egypt and their own persecution in Nazi Germany—and, for some Jews who were also political opponents of the regime, their imprisonment in the nearby Dachau concentration camp (Dachau is a suburb of Munich; the camp opened in 1933).

As the former Bavarian Kulturbund member Werner Cahmann wrote, Jewish cultural performance in Bavaria under Nazism was a vehicle of "self-knowledge" and "self-consciousness."[74] The *Moses* performance is just one example of Bavarian Jews' efforts to grapple with the meaning of their "Jewishness" under state persecution. Such efforts were not clear-cut. Munich's Marionette Theater of Jewish Artists was described in the Jewish press as "bringing something new to Munich, namely a drama of a purely Jewish milieu"[75] while also lauded as being of "the best Munichish [*münchnerische*] tradition"[76]—thus Moses, the great figure of Jewish history and religious thought, being portrayed as a marionette. It was a performance that blended the old and new, the familiar and foreign, and the "Bavarian" and "Jewish." Further, this performance, as well as the Bavarian Kulturbund cultural program more generally, represented a serious mode of internal community self-reflection, self-definition, and self-representation as the local Jewish community sought actively to redefine itself during a period of social and political uncertainty.

NOTES

1. All translations from German are my own. Ba., "Marionettenvorstellung in Jüd. Kulturbund: 'Moses' von Strindberg-Wolff—'Das Mädchen

von Elizondo von Offenbach,'" *Bayerische Israelitische Gemeindezeitung*, February 15, 1935, 79.

2. Henryk Jurkowski, *A History of European Puppetry: The Twentieth Century* (Lewiston, N.Y.: Edwin Mellen Press, 1996), 227.

3. *Das deutsche Puppenspiel: Einsatz, Erfolge und Zielsetzung* (Berlin: Verlag der Deutschen Arbeitsfront, 1939), 51.

4. Georg Deininger to Hans Schemm, "VII 40423 II," August 24, 1933, 4. MK 41101, Bayerisches Hauptstaatsarchiv München (BHStAM).

5. The Jewish Kulturbund in Germany, founded in Berlin in the spring of 1933, was the lone state-approved Jewish cultural organization in Nazi Germany. Local Kulturbund branches inspired by the Berlin example were established in more than eighty German cities. The Bavarian Kulturbund's München Marionettentheater Jüdischer Künstler performed throughout Bavaria from January 1935 until late 1937. During its tenure, it maintained a seven-play repertoire and was praised in the Bavarian Jewish press as one of the Bavarian Kulturbund's most popular cultural undertakings. Despite offers from Berlin, Munich's Jewish marionette theater never performed outside Bavaria. The *Moses* adaptation was followed by a rendition of Jacques Offenbach's *Das Mädchen von Elizondo*—although this chapter will focus only on the evening's *Moses* performance.

6. Berthold Wolff, "Zur Aufführung des Marionetten-Theaters," *Bayerische Israelitische Gemeindezeitung*, January 15, 1935, 31.

7. Lily E. Hirsch, *A Jewish Orchestra in Nazi Germany: Musical Politics and the Berlin Jewish Cultural League* (Ann Arbor: University of Michigan Press, 2012), 62.

8. These representations were either embraced or rejected by the viewing audience. However, as will be addressed shortly, the role of performance reception is difficult to gauge. As a result, the majority of the thesis focuses much more extensively on the ideas represented in the performances themselves.

9. Herbert Freeden, "Jüdischer Kulturbund ohne 'jüdische' Kultur," in *Geschlossene Vorstellung: Der Jüdische Kulturbund in Deutschland 1933–1941*, ed. Akademie der Künste (Berlin: Akademie der Künste, 1992), 55.

10. Dr. Kurt Singer looked back on his early work and reflected, "Without a constructive idea of Jewish art did we wake up from our depression and isolation, and grope our way like blind men towards Jewish spiritual values." Quoted in Hirsch, *Jewish Orchestra*, 44 and 62; see also Freeden, "Jüdischer Kulturbund," 55; Herbert Freeden, "A Jewish Theater under the Swastika," *Leo Baeck Institute Yearbook* 1 (1956): 147.

11. The Bavarians defined "Jewish" music as music by a composer of Jewish heritage (regardless of whether the composer self-identified as Jewish;

the famous example being the complicated relationship between Felix Mendelssohn and his Jewish heritage), liturgical music, or folk music.

12. Wolff, "Zur Aufführung," 31.

13. Sharon Gillerman, *Germans into Jews: Remaking the Jewish Social Body in the Weimar Republic* (Stanford, Calif.: Stanford University Press, 2009), 4.

14. Philip V. Bohlman, *"The Land Where Two Streams Flow": Music in the German-Jewish Community of Israel* (Chicago: University of Illinois Press, 1989), xii.

15. Singer was born in Koblenz in 1885. He settled in Berlin after initially moving to the German capital for university. In addition to his medical career, Singer was an established member of Berlin's musical circles. See Gabriele Fritsch-Vivié, *Gegen alle Widerstände: Der Jüdische Kulturbund 1933–1941* (Berlin: Hentrich and Hentrich, 2013), 29–33; Adam Sacks, "Kurt Singer's Shattered Hopes," *Leo Baeck Institute Yearbook* 48 (2003): 191–203.

16. The league's founding occurred as a reaction to the recent purging of Jewish artists from the "German" cultural sphere through the passing of the Law for the Restoration of the Professional Civil Service (April 1933) and the creation of the Reich Chamber of Culture (September 1933). Rebecca Rovit, "Jewish Theater: Repertory and Censorship in the Jüdischer Kulturbund, Berlin," in *Theater under the Nazis*, ed. John London (Manchester, U.K.: Manchester University Press, 2000), 188.

17. The entirety of its first honorary leadership council consisted of: Leo Baeck, Martin Buber, Ismar Elbogen, Arthur Eloesser, Georg Hermann, Leonid Kreutzer, Max Liebermann, Max Obsorn, Franz Oppenheimer, and Jacob Wasserman. "Ehrenpräsidium," (Honorary Presidium) September 6, 1933. Fritz Wisten Archiv 74/86/128, Akademie der Künste (AdK).

18. Hinkel first joined the National Socialist movement in 1921 as a university student in Munich (NSDAP membership number 287); by 1925 he was a key party organizer in southern Germany. In April 1933 he was named the head of the Prussian Theater Commission and oversaw the monitoring of artistic personnel in all Prussian theaters, opera companies, and orchestras. After the Jewish Kulturbund was established in the summer of 1933, Hinkel's control expanded to include all cultural life in Prussia, encompassing both "German" and non-"German" (i.e., Jewish) cultural undertakings. In mid-1935 he was appointed a "Reichskulturwalter" of the Reich Chamber of Culture and was named the "Special Commissioner for the Supervision and Monitoring of the Cultural and Intellectual Activity of All Non-Aryans Living in the Territory of the German Reich." Reinhard Bollmus, *Das Amt Rosenberg und seine Gegner: Studien zum Machtkampf im nationalsozialistischen Herrschaftssystem* (Munich: Oldenbourg, 2009), 27;

see also Alan E. Steinweis, "Hans Hinkel and German Jewry, 1933–1941," *Leo Baeck Institute Yearbook* (1993): 209–19. For further information on Hinkel's role in National Socialist Judenpolitik after the Kulturbund, see Dan Michman, *The Emergence of Jewish Ghettos during the Holocaust* (New York: Cambridge University Press, 2011), 63–64.

19. Bayerisches Staatsministerium für Unterricht und Kultus, "Beilagen: Gesuch um Genehmigung eines Jüdischen Kulturbund in Bayern," February 9, 1934, MK 15382, BHStAM; Gestapo, "Richtlinien für die Tätigkeit des Reichverbandes der jüdischen Kulturbünde in Deutschland, B. Nr. 18484/35 I 1 B," August 29, 1935, Gestapo 65, Staatsarchiv München (StAM).

20. Rebecca Rovit, *The Jewish Kulturbund Theater Company in Berlin* (Iowa City: University of Iowa Press, 2012), 188.

21. E.D., "Ein Abend im Theater des jüdischen Kulturbundes in Berlin," *Nürnberg-Fürther Israelitisches Gemeindeblatt*, November 1, 1933, 127.

22. Kurt Singer, "Vertraulich: Orientierungs-Bericht II," November 1933, 5, Fritz Wisten Archiv 74/86/5000, AdK.

23. Kurt Singer to Hans Hinkel, January 22, 1934; Kurt Singer to Hans Hinkel, March 18, 1934; Kurt Singer to Hans Hinkel April 23, 1934; Doc 575 Reel 54/30/IV, Wiener Library.

24. *Almanach Kulturbund Deutscher Juden* (Berlin: Verlag Kulturbund Deutscher Juden, 1935).

25. Jüdischer Kulturbund in Deutschland, "Protokoll der Tagung der jüdischen Kulturbünde Deutschlands am Sonnabend, den 27. April und Sonntag, den 28. April 1935," April 1935, AR 166 MF 341, Leo Baeck Institute, New York (LBINY).

26. Jacob Borut, "Struggles for Spaces: Where Could Jews Spend Free Time in Nazi Germany?" *Leo Baeck Institute Yearbook* 56 (2011): 344.

27. Werner J. Cahnman, "The Decline of the Munich Jewish Community, 1933–1938," in *Jewish Social Studies* 3 (July 1941): 285.

28. Edith Raim, "Die Verfolgung und Vernichtung der Fränkischen Juden in der NS-Zeit," in *Die Juden in Franken*, ed. Michael Brenner and Daniela F. Eisenstein (Munich: Oldenbourg, 2012), 199; Steven M. Lowenstein, "Alltag und Tradition: Eine Fränkisch-Jüdische Geographie," in Brenner and Eisenstein, *Die Juden in Franken*, 17; Anthony Kauders, *Democratization and the Jews: Munich, 1945–1965* (Lincoln: University of Nebraska Press, 2002), 39.

29. Raim, "Die Verfolgung und Vernichtung der Fränkischen Juden," 199.

30. The statistics in this paragraph are taken from Falk Wiesemann, "Judenverfolgung und nichtjüdische Bevölkerung 1933–1944," in *Bayern*

in der NS-Zeit, Bd. 1: Soziale Lage und politisches Verhalten der Bevölkerung im Spiegel vertraulicher Berichte, ed. Martin Broszat, Elke Fröhlich, and Falk Wiesemann (Munich: De Gruyter, 1977), 427–86, at 428.

31. Lowenstein, "Alltag und Tradition," 17.

32. "Das Jüdische Kammerorchesters," *Bayerische Israelitische Gemeindezeitung*, May 23, 1927, 163; "Das Jüdische Kammerorchester München," *Bayerische Israelitische Gemeindezeitung*, December 13, 1927, 377.

33. Samuel Taubes, "Hebräischen Theaterabend," *Bayerische Israelitische Gemeindezeitung*, March 15, 1929, 87; "Das hebräische Theater in München," *Münchener N.N.*, 1928, 41A.

34. Erck began his professional musical career after serving in World War I. In 1930 he returned to Munich after nearly a decade's absence and emerged as an active figure in the city's musical scene. In 1931 Erck took over leadership of Munich's Jewish Chamber Orchestra. Erck, like many others, was forced into unemployment in April 1933. "Nachlass Erich Eisner und Notenmaterial der 'Cantata Bolivia'." 2002/38; 2004/236; R-2003/118–120, 128–131; R-2004/25; BIB/287–288, JMB; P 10243, Jüdisches Museum Berlin (JMB); "Gestapo 65," StAM; Waldemar Bonard, *Die gefesselte Muse: Das Marionettentheater im Jüdischen Kulturbund 1935–1937* (Munich: Buchendorfer Verlag, 1994), 46.

35. Erich Erck, "Gesuch um Genehmigung eines Jüdischen Kulturbunds in Bayern als vordringliche Aktion der sozialen Winterhilfe," October 10, 1933, MK 15382, BHStAM.

36. M. Ltz., "Regensburg," *Bayerische Israelitische Gemeindezeitung*, January 15, 1937, 32; "Aus den Gemeinden: Nürnberg," *Israelitisches Familienblatt*, July 22, 1937, 15; "Konzerte und Vorträge: Nürnberg-Fürth," *Central Verein Zeitung*, December 30, 1937; "Jüdisches Leben in Nürnberg: Kulturbund," *Israelitisches Familienblatt*, October 20, 1938, 10.

37. Erck, "Gesuch um Genehmigung," 2.

38. Hirsch, *Jewish Orchestra*, 43–44.

39. Rovit, *Jewish Kulturbund Theater*, 10, 39, 41–42, 46.

40. Reinhard Weber, *Das Schicksal der jüdischen Rechtsanwälte in Bayern nach 1933* (Munich: Oldenbourg Verlag, 2006), 144; Werner J. Cahnman, "The Jews of Munich: 1918–43," in *German Jewry: Its History and Sociology, Selected Essays by Werner J. Cahnman*, ed. Joseph B. Maier, Judith Marcus, and Zoltán Tarr (New Brunswick: Transaction, 1989), 137.

41. Winfried Nerdinger, "Die 'Kunststadt' München," in *Die Zwanziger Jahre in München*, ed. Cristoph Stoelzl (Munich: Münchner Stadtmuseum, 1979), 93–119; Maria Makela, *The Munich Secession: Art and Artists in Turn of the Century Munich* (Princeton, N.J.: Princeton University Press, 1991).

42. Ilse Macek, *Schwabing und Schwabinger Schicksale 1933 bis 1945: Ausgegrenzt—entrechtet—deportiert* (Munich: Volk Verlag, 2008), 19–28,

471; Paul Mendes-Flohr, *Divided Passions: Jewish Intellectuals and the Experience of Modernity* (Detroit: Wayne State University Press, 1991), 77.

43. "München leuchtete." Thomas Mann, *Gladius Dei; Schwere Stunde* (Berlin: Fischer Verlag, 1903), 1.

44. Douglas Klahr, "Munich as Kunststadt, 1900–1937: Art, Architecture, and Civic Identity," *Oxford Art Journal* 34 (2011): 179–201.

45. Wolff, "Zur Aufführung," 31.

46. Ibid.

47. Berthold Wolff (1876–1945) came from a well-known local business family. His business, Firma Gebrüder Wolff GmBH, operated in Munich and Regensburg for thirty-five years, until it was "Aryanized" in 1936. He and his family emigrated to Brazil. Bonard, *Die gefesselte Muse*, 51.

48. Polizeidirektion München, 7015, StAM.

49. Wolff, "Zur Aufführung," 31, 34.

50. "Das Buch Esther auf der Marionettenbühne," *Israelitisches Familienblatt*, March 1, 1934, 22.

51. Photographs of Rosenberg's *Golem* puppets and props were included in the *Israelitisches Familienblatt* insert on Luiko's Bimath-Buboth performance of the Ruth story. See "Megillath Ruth auf der Marionettenbühne," *Israelitisches Familienblatt*, November 1, 1934.

52. Ibid.; "Megillath Ruth;" "Heiterer Purimabend am 23. März," *Bayerische Israelitische Gemeindezeitung*, March 15, 1935, 135; "Purimfeier der Zionistischen Ortsgruppe," *Bayerische Israelitische Gemeindezeitung*, April 1, 1935, 152.

53. John McCormick and Bernie Pratasik, eds., *Popular Puppet Theater in Europe, 1800–1914* (Cambridge: Cambridge University Press, 1998).

54. "Megillath Ruth."

55. Jurkowski, *History of European Puppetry*, 268.

56. Max von Boehn, *Puppen und Puppenspiele* (Munich: F. Bruckmann, 1929); Reinhard Valenta, *Franz von Poccis Münchener Kulturrebellion: Alternatives Theater in der Zeit des bürgerlichen Realismus* (Munich: Ludwig, 1991), 157.

57. Jurkowski, *History of European Puppetry*, 4–5.

58. Berthold Wolff, "Marionetten-Aufführung," *Bayerische Israelitische Gemeindezeitung*, December 15, 1935, 549.

59. An exception to this statement would be Luiko's 1937 Kasperl-figure puppets, which were created in the form of the traditional style popularized throughout Bavarian puppet stages.

60. Ba., "Marionettenvorstellung in Jüd. Kulturbund," 79, 82. Parenthetical page numbers in text that follows are from this source.

61. "Wiederholdung der Marionetten-Vorstellung am 25. Februar im Museum," *Bayerische Israelitische Gemeindezeitung*, February 15, 1935, 82.

62. McCormick and Pratasik, *Popular Puppet Theater.*

63. Maria Luise Kohn to Schalom Ben-Chorin, September 6, 1935, 2 Judaica Varia, StadtAM.

64. Diana Oesterle, *"So süßlichen Kitsch, das kann ich nicht": Die Münchener Künstlerin Maria Luiko (1904–1941)* (Munich: Oldenbourg Verlag, 2009).

65. Luiko's marionettes are housed at the Munich City Museum in central Munich. A few of her puppets are shown in the permanent display on Munich during National Socialism, while the remaining puppets are held in the museum archive.

66. Vladislav Ivanov, "Habima and 'Biblical Theater,'" in *Chagall and the Artists of the Russian Jewish Theater*, by Susan Tumarkin Goodman et al. (New Haven, Conn.: Yale University Press, 2009), 27.

67. Benjamin Harshav, "Habima and Goset: An Illustrated Chronicle," in Goodman et al., *Chagall and Russian Jewish Theater*, 90.

68. On November 19, 1930, Habima staged its second performance of the year in Würzburg, performing *Der Dybuk*. Habima's return, and ultimately its popularity during its first stop in the Franconian city, agitated local National Socialist members, particularly leader Otto Hellmuth. In the days leading up to the November performance, the local NSDAP group littered the town with leaflets condemning the group's upcoming performance. Local NSDAP members gathered a group of nearly one thousand individuals, who congregated at the door of Würzburg's City Theater, hoping to block audience members from entering the building. They remained in front of the building until after the play began, banging on the doors, beating on the walls with fists and sticks, and screaming racial slurs. After the play finished, audience members were followed home and accosted in the street. Lowenstein, "Alltag und Tradition," 20; Michael Wildt, *Hitler's Volksgemeinschaft and the Dynamics of Racial Exclusion: Violence against Jews in Provincial Germany, 1919–1939* (New York: Berghahn Books, 2011), 65–66; Roland Flade, *Juden in Würzburg 1918–1933* (Würzburg: Freunde Mainfränkischer Kunst und Geschichte, 1985), 341–49; Robert Gellately, *The Gestapo and German Society: Enforcing Racial Policy, 1933–1945* (New York: Oxford University Press, 1991), 92–93.

69. Oesterle, *"So süßlichen Kitsch,"* 125.

70. Michael Brenner, *The Renaissance of Jewish Culture in Weimar Germany* (New Haven, Conn.: Yale University Press, 1996), 130–31.

71. Steven E. Ascheim, *Brothers and Strangers: The East European Jew in Germany and German Consciousness, 1800–1923* (Madison: University of Wisconsin Press, 1982).

72. Wolff, "Zur Aufführung," 31.

73. Oesterle, *"So süßlichen Kunst,"* 41–109.

74. Werner Cahnman, "The Jews in Munich: 1918–1943," in Maier, Marcus, and Tarr, *German Jewry*, 137.

75. Berthold Wolff, "Marionetten-Aufführung," December 15, 1935, *Bayerische Israelitische Gemeindezeitung*, 549.

76. Ca., "Marionettentheater in München," *Central Verein Zeitung*, January 9, 1936, 7.

Marion Kaplan

Sites of Anxiety and Hope: Jewish Refugees in Lisbon, 1940–1945

IN THE OPENING SCENE OF *CASABLANCA*, RELEASED IN 1942 AND RANKED one of the top two "greatest movies of all time," the camera zooms in on a map of Casablanca in relation to Portugal.[1] The refugees in Casablanca "wait and wait and wait" for visas to get to Lisbon, "the great embarkation point" for the "freedom of the Americas."[2] At the end of the film, its heroes fly off to Lisbon. But what happened before and after refugees arrived in Lisbon? Between 1940 and 1945, about eighty thousand to one hundred thousand Jewish refugees, "the largest number of Jews to escape the Nazis during the war by flight to the west," reached Lisbon, escaping by train, car, or foot through France, Spain, and Portugal.[3] Most moved on within weeks, but between ten thousand and fourteen thousand remained far longer than they had anticipated, some as many as years, for lack of proper visas and ship tickets or due to expired visas. Many of them had already suffered social death and violence in their homelands. As they discovered that their new European "host" nation did not want them, either, nor did many other safe havens, these rejections added one more link to the chain of dehumanization they bore. Their frightening odysseys from impending doom to fragile safety, their fearful wait in an oddly peaceful purgatory, and their grateful surprise at the reactions of Portuguese citizens linked up with their other personal, private agonies.

This article offers an emotional history of fleeing, a neglected perspective for analyzing the Jewish refugee crisis of the Nazi era. By concentrating on their feelings, we can more deeply understand how historical events affected individuals at the grassroots, while they were on the run, seeking a safe haven.[4] Generally political history has dominated the historiography of refugee crises: Which political regimes drove them out? Who turned them away? Who accepted them—reluctantly or willingly? In addition, we have learned about numbers, the millions of displaced people. In these cases and others, historians have left emotions or "emotionality" to studies of premodern, female, and nonwhite groups, "whereas normative bourgeois masculinity was defined by the ability to control and repress emotions even in moments of great personal danger."[5] Although cultural anthropologists and recent historians have challenged these preconceptions,[6] few have turned their attention to the historical experiences of refugees: what it felt like—viscerally or emotionally—to have lost everything, to climb mountains in order to enter countries illegally, or to beg for mercy on foreign turf, never knowing what the future would hold.

Often this kind of history fell through the cracks, not just due to patriarchal traditions that valued ostensibly "rational" politicians and generals, but also because the sources took time to emerge. Most refugees in Lisbon did not realize what had happened to other Jews in Nazi-occupied Europe until they got out or until the war ended. Then, in contrast to the Holocaust, these refugees felt they were "fine," simply because they had not been murdered. And when they began to reflect, they gave precedence to the distress they had felt as Nazi persecution grew "at home" and to the difficulties of adjusting to new lands as immigrants. Lisbon took second or third place in their narratives. Often decades passed before these former refugees dealt with their flight and the "in between" weeks, months, or years of waiting. Addressing their feelings allows us to revalue the kinds of experiences they endured during this liminal moment when former social hierarchies had dissolved, former customs were disrupted, and futures, once taken for granted, appeared doubtful.[7]

How did Jewish refugees experience their physical and emotional lives while heading toward Portugal and later, while there? How did the contingencies of World War II and the ambiguities of Portuguese policies affect them? To answer these questions, I describe emotionally heightened spaces that they traversed. They might not even have noticed these locations in normal times. Geographers refer to these spaces as "geographies of emotional life" or "emotional geographies"[8] and examine the interplay between emotions and place at particular moments—for example, the way a home can feel safe but then turn frightening. Experiences shaped feelings about simple sites: once, a mountain path leading to Spain, a line at a ticket office, or a café in the center of Lisbon could have meant a vacation, but in these years it could become a matter of life and death. Conversely, feelings also shaped experiences at these same sites.

Refugees from Nazi Europe to Lisbon encountered just such sites of anxiety and hope. They faced dangerous border crossings as they headed to Portugal, a country whose government did not want them to remain for any length of time but whose people overwhelmed them with their hospitality. Visits to the offices of Portugal's secret police, however, terrified the refugees. In addition, the refugees endured long, frustrating lines and interactions at American and other consulates, at post offices, and at shipping agencies. These locations induced feelings of angst or relief—often both—and they served as sites where refugees had to face their loss of a past and their fears for the future. Finally, Portugal's cafés, filled to the brim with refugees, became settings that could assuage some of these strains, raise morale, and offer the opportunity to participate in meaningful, if transient, communities of waiting.

1933–1939: PORTUGAL AND EARLY REFUGEES

Before the war, Jewish refugees from Germany and Austria sought safety from the growing Nazi threat in neighboring countries, especially France and Holland, or in the United States and Palestine.[9] The vast majority did not consider Portugal—a poor, agricultural country under another dictatorship—an option, even though, until 1938, German citizens could enter Portugal without a visa.[10] Several hundred did arrive between 1933 and the fall of France in June 1940. Most settled in Lisbon, the capital and a lively port city of about six hundred thousand, where the majority of Portugal's four hundred Jewish families, comprising about two thousand people, lived.[11] The refugees of the 1930s—some intending to stay, others hoping to wait until the Nazis lost power—brought some money with them to start small enterprises. They set up businesses as importers, manufacturers, doctors, engineers, and merchants, or they represented German or American companies.[12]

Portugal's visa policy changed in 1938, the year of the fruitless Evian Conference, assembled to solve the refugee crisis, and the November pogrom, also known as Kristallnacht. That October, Portugal sought to limit refugees entering the country by issuing its *Circular 10*, allowing only thirty-day tourist visas to persons who could document that they already had visas to overseas destinations and could show proof of ship tickets and the ability to pay expenses in Portugal. This new policy barred "aliens and Jews" from *settling* in Portugal. Since Jews made up virtually all refugees, this decision affected them almost exclusively.[13] Then in November 1939, Portugal issued *Circular 14*, intended to block the entry of foreigners, Russians, and "Jews expelled from the country of their nationality or from those they come from."[14] Still, refugees came, and the fall of France triggered a stampede.

BORDER CROSSINGS AFTER JUNE 1940: FRANCE, SPAIN, AND PORTUGAL

Border crossings emerged not only as a "traumatic parting" from one's homeland but also as "one of the central" emotional experiences of flight.[15] From the ninth to the fifteenth of June 1940, as Germany successfully invaded France, Jewish and non-Jewish refugees fled Paris, "crawl[ing] along roads by day and night, bombers overhead, accidents by the way."[16] In its armistice with Germany, signed on June 22, 1940, France agreed to "surrender on demand" individuals named by the German government.[17] Thus, German and German Jewish refugees faced particular risks. Refugees in France found themselves in an emotional purgatory, "jittery with fear at the idea of staying and paralyzed with fear at the idea of leaving."[18]

Adding to their dilemma, the acquisition of legal papers proved an arduous and frustrating feat, hard enough in normal times but heartbreaking and terrifying during war. For example, individuals fleeing from France to the United States would need a U.S. visa. Once lucky enough to secure it, they had to stand in long lines in front of consulates asking for transit visas from Portugal and then Spain, and then an exit visa from France, in that exact sequence. Every country handled the visas in reverse order, since no country would give permission to pass through its borders until refugees showed proof that another country would allow them to enter.[19] Often, by the time one had acquired the last visa, the first had expired.[20] Those who had made it legally to Portugal generally had ship tickets, but many—especially those who had entered illegally—had none. Purchasing these tickets often took so long that their American and/or Portuguese visas expired and they had to start all over again. That summer of 1940, Varian Fry, of the (American) Emergency Rescue Committee in Marseille, noted the emotional fragility of those refugees who had made it to that town: hungry, sleep deprived, and destitute, their "badly frayed nerves" had given way altogether as they succumbed to breakdowns.[21]

Borders no longer meant simply traversing from one place to another, exchanging money, and casually showing one's passport.[22] Borders carried terrifying consequences: freedom, jail, even death if one had to turn back. Formerly "normal" sites in the refugees' previous lives—even sites that might have caused happy anticipation—suddenly meant danger. Refugees faced the terror of being arrested or turned back, since many of their visas were "quasi-legal."[23] In his book's chapter "Forgery Is a Fine Art," Varian Fry writes how he put refugees in touch with excellent forgers around Marseille.[24] Fry was hardly the only one doing this.[25] Indeed, having arranged illegal escapes over the Pyrenees, Fry thought of "illegal emigration as the normal, if not the only way to go."[26] Even those with legal papers approached borders with great apprehension.

Refugees and their helpers thought that the French, Spanish, and Portuguese border guards enforced the rules randomly. Although France officially refused to give refugees exit visas, it did provide some at first, or its frontier guards allowed refugees possessing overseas visas to pass into Spain. But the French quickly hardened their stance.[27] Moreover, Gestapo pressure at the borders increased over time.[28] During the fall 1940, Spain, too, "opened and closed the frontier again and again," making it "hard to imagine a crueler way of torturing human beings."[29] For some, this unpredictability proved fatal. The philosopher and literary critic Walter Benjamin faced this situation as he crossed the mountains by foot into Spain with several companions in September 1940. He had his boat ticket, U.S. entrance permission, and both transit visas through Portugal and Spain. At Portbou, guards—possibly under Gestapo surveillance—refused to let him pass since he could not produce a French exit visa. He took his life that night.[30] The next morning, the guards let his companions continue on. The Portuguese border generally (although not always) proved more hospitable, at least for those with visas. Most refugees with proper papers faced nothing more onerous than long waits, sometimes overnight, as they crossed the popular border at Vilar Formoso.

Those without the precious visa came over borders by themselves or hired human traffickers. Nadia Gould's family, for example, trying to flee to Portugal, did not have the correct papers. They hired traffickers: "Our guides . . . were real smugglers who only occasionally took people like us across the river into Portugal. They preferred to smuggle merchandise which was a more lucrative and less risky venture." They met at midnight but had to wait another day due to a full moon. The smugglers "were annoyed with my father who had conveniently forgotten to tell them there would be children in our group."[31] An offer of extra money calmed the situation. The smugglers knew the routines of the border police but nervously eyed the two-year-old and fed her caramels so that she remained silent.[32]

Overall, fearful refugees withstood scrutiny, begged for mercy, or learned to bribe guards or sneak in. Thus people continued to slip by and arrive in Lisbon. Leaders of the Portuguese government felt overrun.

PORTUGAL: THE GOVERNMENT, ITS PEOPLE, AND THE SECRET POLICE

Portugal's dictator, Dr. António de Oliveira Salazar, who ruled from 1932 until 1968, stressed Portugal's neutrality during the war. Portugal attempted to balance the interests of the Allies and the Germans for a variety of economic and political reasons, including opportunism.[33] More specifically, Portugal had an alliance with England dating back to the fourteenth century (1373, 1386) and a centuries-old commercial relationship.[34] Portugal also depended on American oil, iron, and steel, among other supplies.[35] Neutrality "paid handsome dividends" and helped the Portuguese economy.[36] Both warring sides relied on Portuguese tungsten, necessary for hardening steel for military production.[37] Indeed, some Portuguese feared a German invasion to take over the tungsten mines. The Germans paid with looted gold and used bribes and smugglers, but in the end, they received less tonnage than the Allies did.[38] The Portuguese Azores, too, caused tension.[39] Ultimately—and late—Portugal tipped toward the Allies.[40]

On a covert level, the Allies and the Axis played roles inside Portugal that could make for a spy thriller. The British secret service, MI5 and MI6, infiltrated the Portuguese secret police, and the Germans established several German-paid and Portuguese-staffed spy networks.[41] Ian Fleming's novel *Casino Royale* and its hero, James Bond, emerged out of Fleming's experience as a spy for the British Royal Navy stationed in Portugal.[42]

In Lisbon, Jewish refugees nervously read mixed messages. They saw both British and Nazi newspapers on the stands and feared that the Gestapo roamed Lisbon. They also knew of *Circulars 10* and *14*. Yet Portugal admitted tens of thousands of transmigrants with the slimmest evidence, including useless visas to Curaçao and Costa Rica, places that could not be reached from Lisbon, since the consuls of transit hubs, such as the United States or Mexico, refused to issue transit visas.[43] Moreover, even after the Portuguese government placed restrictions on immigrants, it still welcomed Jews with capital or businesses.[44]

Salazar himself did not evince overt antisemitism. Within the boundaries of Portugal itself, citizenship for him meant political and legal status, not a racial category.[45] The government, for example, restricted only the actions of non-Portuguese Jews, such as denying them the right to work and prohibiting some from living in Lisbon, not of its own Jewish citizens.[46] Further, Salazar's minuscule circle of friends and advisers included Professor Moses Amzalak, a prominent economist from a well-known Lisbon Jewish family and a leader of the Jewish community.[47] Whereas Salazar regularly opposed "liberals," "republicans," and "communists"—terms that could be interpreted as stand-ins or code words for "Jews"—he did not openly discuss Jews.[48] In addition, individual Portuguese consuls, such as Aristides de Sousa Mendes, courageously came to the aid of thousands of refugees—often against the desires of the government.[49] On the ground, American officials considered the Portuguese government "generous" toward the refugees as well as "cooperative" with American organizations.[50] Even the German embassy—probably to its consternation—noted the absence of antisemitism in Portugal.[51] Indeed, the Portuguese would likely have offered temporary visas far more readily, since Portugal officially accepted transmigrants, had the United States acted expeditiously instead of purposely slowing down its acceptance of refugees.

Because of the combination of Portugal's relatively liberal practices and the success of refugees entering Portugal illegally, a flood of harried refugees arrived in Lisbon with and without papers.[52] By July 1940, Lisbon had emerged as the best way station for Jews to escape continental Europe for North and South America. In October 1940, a Jewish refugee wrote, "New émigrés from France and from German occupied territories arrive constantly. One hardly hears any

Portuguese. . . . Lisbon is sold out."[53] While tens of thousands soon continued their exodus by boat or plane, more refugees continued to enter, especially after Germany invaded southern France in 1942.[54]

As they arrived "flat broke,"[55] the refugees appreciated the compassion and generosity of the Portuguese.[56] When Alma Mahler-Werfel tried to pay her hotel bill, the clerk "seemed to sense that it would leave me short of cash. 'Never mind paying the bill,' he said. 'I'll advance it for you, and you can send me the money from New York.'"[57] One woman, on a train heading to Lisbon and obviously starving, eyed a young girl eating bread. The conductor noticed and offered her a whole loaf of bread. He also gave her a place to lie down in first class.[58] The poor, too, welcomed refugees at the borders, offered them soup and fruits and did not expect payment.[59] Miriam Stanton, a penniless refugee herself, commented, "The Portuguese people were so good to refugees. They would even go up to someone in the street . . . and ask if any help was needed." Many gave their names and addresses to the refugees and told them "to call if there was anything they could do. These were people in all walks of life—doctors, business people, laborers, etc."[60]American philanthropies also recognized the friendliness of the Portuguese.[61] How can we explain such generosity from people who themselves had very little and toward refugees who often faced rejection as they flooded into lands unwilling or unready to take them in? After refusing payment for the room (his master bedroom) and meals he had offered a couple, a villager explained, "The people of Portugal are poor—very poor. But they have a deep understanding and compassion for those who are more miserable than they. Always will we share bread with strangers who need it."[62]

The refugees, however, were caught in a bind: they praised the Portuguese for their extraordinary hospitality and kindness, but they feared the Portuguese police, whom they experienced as xenophobic, anti-immigrant, and antisemitic. The police harassed them to move on, threatened them with jail, and sometimes imprisoned them.[63] Miriam Stanton, who had to extend her transit visa, appeared at police headquarters, where they took her passport away. Frantic, she agonized, "Why do these officials have to take our passports away . . . ? This is not peacetime, not a normal time. To get these passports . . . we had spent a great amount of money and money which we could not afford. . . . These passports mean life to us, to the refugees, and yet . . . officials just take them away and say 'you can collect it in a few days. . . .' How do they think that a refugee can sleep at night if that precious passport . . . is lost? It is not only the money, it is our lives. . . . Yet these officials do not seem to realize our worries."[64]

WAITING IN LISBON: TAKING STOCK OF THEIR LIVES

A roller coaster of emotions accompanied and often shaped the ways in which refugees coped as they waited to journey on. Their previous ordeals and the continuing hardships of family and friends back home reverberated. As they tried to make sense of their new environment, they did not appear aware of the attractions or attractiveness of the city or villages. Bewildered, frustrated, and fearful, they felt physically—but also psychologically—in transit. Most saw Portugal as a way station.

The newcomers did feel relief, focusing on "freedom and peace. . . . The 'new world' seemed to begin here," one refugee recalled. "Only one more step and Europe with its oppression and hatred lay behind us."[65] Another refugee described Lisbon as the "first place that was normal . . . in two years."[66] Still another refugee found himself "stuck in this most pleasant city. . . . The whole town had become an enormous rooming house."[67]

This sunny, peaceful, and relatively safe site, however, did not generate a sense of comfort, even though they had left persecution, war, and narrow escapes behind them. Instead, many refugees confronted the extent of their losses: their intense psychological dislocation, their crisis of identity, and their steep, drastic, downward mobility. For the most part, they had already lost their middle-class existence, including their homes, jobs, and previous daily lives: "We lost touch with the soil, we were cut from the security of bourgeois life—with no work, no home, no homeland"[68] (or *Heimat*—a sentimentally charged word in German). Their languages—the medium in which they expressed quotidian needs and their deepest feelings—no longer served them in their new environments. They needed Portuguese for their daily interactions and English for the aid organizations. Hannah Arendt explained, "We lost our language, which means the naturalness of reactions, the simplicity of gestures, the unaffected expression of our feelings."[69] Many years later, Arendt reflected, "I write in English, but I have never lost a feeling of distance from it. There is a tremendous difference between your mother tongue and another language."[70] In addition, friends and relatives remained behind, resulting in increased anxiety. Many also suddenly realized that their relationship to their homelands had proven illusory. Now they stood unprotected by citizenship and also bereft of psychological belonging.[71]

These wounds festered, as did the economic dislocations of refugee status. A few of the more fortunate quickly sold whatever they managed to carry along with them.[72] But most had nothing to sell, having fled with little of value or having spent whatever they had while racing toward Portugal. Many depended on philanthropies. Local and international aid organizations, such as the American Friends Service Committee (the Quakers) and the Unitarian Service Committee but especially Jewish ones, took on these tasks. The Jewish organizations—HIAS, HICEM, the American Jewish Joint Distribution Committee, and the World Jewish Congress, among others—supported refugees in a spirit of solidarity with Jews in trouble, and also to prevent them from burdening the state or antagonizing its citizens.[73] The various aid organizations provided food and shelter and helped find ship tickets. Additionally, they advocated for the refugees with the Portuguese and the American governments.[74] The tiny Portuguese Jewish community of Lisbon also worked closely with American Jewish committees[75] and used its own political influence to protect refugees.[76] Moreover, it found doctors and provided clothing for refugees and set up a soup kitchen that served 250 meals per day.[77]

The refugees had become supplicants. Many refugees' "bewildered looks and the condition of their clothes" announced their plight.[78] Still, "crumbling clothes" proved the least difficult problem to address.[79] Crucially, they had lost a sense of self. Arendt, in Lisbon in the spring of 1941, captured this moment: "Once we were somebodies about whom people cared, we were loved by friends, and even known by landlords as paying our rent regularly."[80] She saw "parables of increasing self-loss" among refugees, and she realized the impossibility of finding a new identity under conditions of flight.[81] Arendt summed up the frustrations of a middle-aged man who had appeared before countless committees and finally exclaimed in exasperation, "Nobody here knows who I am!"[82] Evincing shame at his role as an indigent, pride at what he had once achieved, and impotent anger that the bureaucrats and strangers he now dealt with did not respect him, he mourned for his previous identity and his former place in the world. Clinging to one's old status while watching it disappear caused grave disorientation, frustration, and sadness. Were men more prone to this reaction because they had previously held public or economically respected positions? Is this particular trauma gendered? Probably, but more data are needed. There were also significant generational differences. Young people, children, and young adults appear to have been more open to adventure and new surroundings and eager to get on with their lives.

These identity crises sometimes merged with what later generations have called post-traumatic stress disorder (PTSD).[83] Even when they did not suffer the extremes of PTSD, many refugees, unable to work and "supported and guided like children," felt despondent.[84] Aid workers, such as Howard Wriggins of the Quakers, agonized about the fragility of these appellants.[85] Some refugees, suffering emotionally driven, physiological symptoms, accepted "the pills for anxiety and . . . sleeplessness" that local doctors prescribed.[86] Driven to despair, some resorted to suicide. Arthur Koestler tried to take his own life there, and another refugee recalled suicides when the American consul turned people down.[87] Jan Lustig believed many of the refugees were "often close to suicide."[88]

Fears of a spreading war ranked highest among their worries. The thought that Hitler might invade Portugal gnawed at terrified Jews in stages between June 1940 and November 1942. Kurt Israel, for example, had a straightforward analysis: "After all, Portugal is also Europe."[89] Like many in Lisbon, Hans Sahl believed that the feeling of safety "was deceiving. . . . Hitler had occupied almost all of Europe. Why should he spare Portugal? We had to hurry. We had to ensure a passage before it was too late."[90] Both Jews and Portuguese showed relief only when the Allies landed in North Africa in November 1942 and they believed the war had tilted in their favor.[91]

LINES AND MORE LINES

For the refugees, life felt as though it had been reduced to an unending series of lines in which they had to queue up: for food, shelter, and visas; for letters at the post office; and finally for tickets on a ship out.

Lining up for Food, Shelter, and Visas

Tormented by fears related to the war's expansion and their uncertain future, refugees found that simply getting through the day took determination. Refugees prioritized the search for basic shelter and food. They lined up at aid organizations, waiting patiently and sometimes irritably as social workers processed their cases. Reliance on these organizations provided relief but also exasperation. Gratitude clashed with frustration similar to the resentments and mistrust that often complicate relations between social welfare organizations and their clients. Hannah Arendt, for example, bitterly resented appearing as a supplicant over and over again: "I do not know how long we will have to stay here. We have no transportation at the moment and I will have to hassle with HICEM, which hasn't gotten nicer with time."[92] The social workers themselves felt overwhelmed. A community aide, Yvette Davidofe, recalled, "Many problems were so huge that we could not solve them. During the first few weeks, I cried at home every night."[93] Lodgings ran the gamut from small, run-down rooms in boardinghouses or with private families to apartments in which rooms could be rented to other refugees and refugee women did the housekeeping for small sums. Memoir writers remembered many versions of sardine dinners "because that was the main affordable food."[94] Those with insufficient incomes or who stayed in rooms where they could not cook trekked up the Lisbon hills at noon to receive a free hot lunch from the Jewish community, subsidized by the Joint Distribution Committee.[95]

Thereafter, the paper chase began. Carla Pekelis recalled that: "there were things that were now in our blood like a sort of poison. They were called . . . 'residence permits,' 'identity cards' and . . . 'temporary safe conduct' . . . 'exit visas,' and 'transit visas,' and 'entry visas.' "[96] To acquire proper papers, Pekelis and her husband, Alex, turned their room into an office. While Alex went out to "visit consulates, police commissioners, travel agencies . . . in search of a million things: travel permits, proofs of citizenship, money exchange, ship passage . . . and so on . . . [Carla] pounded out letters on the typewriter addressed to friends and relatives, especially in New York, with requests that went from a simple testimonial, authenticated by a notary, to the all-important 'affidavit' that would place the responsibility for our future on the shoulders of whoever acted as our guarantor."[97] These repetitive errands to consulates—major sites of anxiety—demanded time, attention, and perseverance. Refugees waited in endless lines.[98] Suddenly, lines did not simply progress toward an attainable goal—a desired purchase, an anticipated entertainment—but might stymie an escape. One woman walked for eight minutes to reach the end of the line at the police office for foreigners. The line at the American legation seemed to have "no end at all."[99] The lucky ones made it into the waiting rooms of various consulates, "those vestibules of heaven and hell."[100] Finally in front of the American consul, Kurt Israel felt himself "trembling and shaking."[101] The Pekelis couple beseeched the American consul but also tried to acquire visas for Brazil, Panama, and Costa Rica.[102] And as consuls turned them away after long and arbitrary delays, refugees stood bewildered and heartbroken, disoriented and at a complete loss as to the next steps to take. Alex Pekelis commented, "One day someone will tell the story of these 'waiting rooms.'"[103] Carla summed up: "It would have taken the pen of a Kafka . . . to depict the world of visas in all its surrealistic absurdity; that of a Dostoyevsky to render the nightmare of the petitioners' struggle for survival."[104]

Post Office Lines: Waiting for Letters from Loved Ones

After days of wrestling with consuls and charities, refugees waited in lines at the post office, another site of trepidation. They anxiously awaited letters from loved ones or cables with news about affidavits, visas, and money. Although they visited the central post office daily, their *thoughts* revolved around it "continually. . . . People came here morning or evening, many came both morning and evening," Alfred Dőblin recalled.[105] They located the general delivery (*poste restante*) windows, "pressed to the wall as we ourselves were."[106] Observing other refugees as he approached these windows, Dőblin wrote, "many of them asked their questions numbly and then numbly left. They had been asking them for a long time."[107]

Refugees and loved ones poured their angst, exasperation, and love into letters. These fragile threads held families and friends together, providing news from Nazi-occupied Europe as well as from safe lands.[108] The former induced grave anxiety, as the sojourners in Lisbon learned about the persecutions through hints or cries for help.[109] Fearing Nazi censorship, letter writers described daily life, forced labor, and removal from their homes in understated or somewhat coded language. Hunger was a different issue. Letters urgently and straightforwardly pleaded for food packages from Lisbon.[110] That the writers faced serious hunger in German-occupied lands, given severely limited rations, hard labor, and restricted shopping hours, could not have been plainer. Moreover, in ghettos and concentration camps, people starved. Individual Jewish refugees as well as the Lisbon Jewish community did send packages of food, especially sardines, chocolate, canned goods, and preserves.[111] In Terezin, Ruth Bondy writes that the packages "strengthened those who received them, both physically and mentally, gave them a few hours of happiness, and provided them with hope."[112] These packages may have even brought relief to Jews in Portugal—representing the only action they could take to make the suffering of loved ones more bearable.

Letters from occupied Europe can also help historians understand the kinds of information gleaned, the suspicions and worries aroused, and the emotional connections felt by refugees in Portugal. The refugees in Portugal knew that many of their correspondents coped with forced labor and cramped housing and confronted impossible hurdles to get out of Europe or out of internment or concentration camps. They followed the war as closely as they could through these censored letters and the censored news. They may have sensed an impending catastrophe through letters, without comprehending the escalating genocide.

Children, friends, and relatives who had made it out of Europe also wrote letters. These letters assuaged fears—but created longing. The expression "children turned into letters" (*aus Kindern wurden Briefe*) revealed the despair of parents who had sent their children ahead and now ached for word from them.[113] Parents lost daily—even monthly—contact, given the slowness of international postal services during the war.[114] The Quakers in Lisbon wrote to an agency in New York in March 1943, asking that the addresses where children had been placed be cabled to them as soon as possible: "The parents on this end are most anxious for this information and will continue to besiege us until we have [it]."[115]

Ship Tickets: Lining up for One Last Hurdle

As soon as a refugee secured the coveted visa, repetitive errands to shipping agencies quickly ensued.[116] The entire process of emigration from Lisbon reminded Hannah Arendt of the German children's game *Mensch ärgere Dich nicht!*[117] akin to the American board game *Sorry!* Just as one's playing piece neared the goal, someone could bump it back to "start." When the Romanian writer Valeriu Marcu approached clerks in the steamship company to buy a ticket for passage to the United States in February 1941, they "looked at me in surprise, as though I had come to ask for their daughters' hands. I want something quite normal and I am regarded as a madman."[118] As prices of tickets "sky rocketed" and "every second Portuguese businessman became a shipping agent broker," the refugees found themselves "at the mercy of every little agent."[119] Some desperately wrote to friends in the United States asking for their intervention: on March 4, 1941, Siegfried Kracauer wrote that he was happy to arrive in Lisbon but had learned that, despite his paid ship tickets, HICEM would make him wait months, because others, whose U.S. visas would expire shortly, had priority over him. He begged friends in New York to pressure agencies there, because he would otherwise lose the job that awaited him.[120] Many refugees, already familiar with Jewish philanthropies, now beseeched them to pay for the costs of tickets and, often, to actually help find spots for them aboard the few ships sailing from Lisbon. Hannah Arendt noted that "a true battle rages over places on the ship."[121] In April 1941, *Life* magazine displayed photos of refugees jamming into the American Export Line office although tickets had been sold out until February 1942.[122]

SHARING SPACE, SHARING FEELINGS: THE CAFÉ

After refugees finished their recurring visits to consulates, post offices, aid organizations, and shipping offices, forbidden from working, they sat in cafés sharing their fears for loved ones and for themselves.[123] There they constructed temporary spaces, communities, where they could evoke the one milieu that might make them feel better—a café culture in which they could exchange impressions and feelings with others going through the same upheavals. They also bridged national, ethnic, political, and gender distinctions for the moment. These tables even bridged class differences, although the wealthiest refugees in Portugal chose the town of Estoril, a resort, for their stay. The cafés created a kind of diasporic homeland, a place to sip coffee while sharing experiences, support, and advice.

Because they had left the landscapes, urban features, and knowledge of belonging to their nations behind, they resorted to the only public space that felt private and that they could afford. The café emerged as a new transnational and temporary "home." This corner of their new urban landscape offered a setting[124] they recognized from their former lives, where "one heard more German and French . . . than Portuguese."[125] A liminal world of café identities allowed most Jews a semblance of normalcy, a place to remember who they once were and feel recognized by others from their previous worlds.

No longer simple sites of culture and sociability—although these may have been pleasant by-products—Lisbon cafés also offered indispensable locations in which to exchange advice and rumors ("the refugee telegraph") about the war, the police, American philanthropies, and possible exit visas.[126] The refugees recognized one another immediately and quickly developed relationships, talking about "problems, family . . . anxiety, what happened to other members of the family."[127] Sharing angst and empathy, they bonded quickly, creating a temporary solidarity among themselves.[128] The writer Hermann Kesten endowed the café with symbolic meaning: "In exile, the café becomes home and homeland. . . . The café becomes the only site of continuity. I sat in cafés in a dozen lands of exile and it was always the same café. . . . I only have to sit in a café and I feel at home."[129] Stretching their cups of coffee for many hours, women and men found solace among people in the same situation. Many café patrons faced the same "psychic hell,"[130] worrying about family and friends left behind, exchanging information and inferences from the letters they received. Mourning their losses, they dreaded the process of starting all over again in a new place with a new language and new rules. These table partners deeply understood one another's grief and fear.

Cafés also presented opportunities for new, if fleeting, friendships among refugees, though not with native Portuguese. They served as a temporary meeting space, a "momentary rendezvous, a passing station, on the[ir] never-ending escape through life."[131] Yet these must have been somewhat strange and strained relationships. The refugees depended on one another, but they competed for scarce visas and shipping space at the same time. Erika Mann observed that while café patrons rejoiced for a lucky woman about to embark for the United States, "all were jealous of her."[132] Commiseration vied with envy.

Obstructions notwithstanding, by mid-1942 most refugees had managed to emigrate westward.[133] Eventually, the Joint Distribution Committee chartered some ships in order to secure definite places for the refugees and also to keep prices down.[134] Yet, even on board the coveted ship, relieved to be escaping their hellish experiences in occupied Europe, countless earlier memories tempered the joy of some refugees. Fourteen-year-old Mara Vishniac felt a "deep sadness" as she realized she was "abandoning Europe."[135] Hans Sahl mourned the "words that I spoke as a child," the "music of the countryside," and the world into which he had been born.[136] Eugen Tillinger watched the port of Lisbon disappear and recalled "the most beautiful scenes from the European past, baroque and gothic. . . . I saw the towers of Prague, the sweet Austrian landscape, Paris—a whole life spent in Europe."[137]

CONCLUSION

Those refugees who were determined and lucky enough to clear the myriad hurdles between their countries of origin and the Portuguese coastline had suffered physical and mental anguish. They had endured "emotional geographies" that created intense anxieties: dangerous and unpredictable border crossings as well as long lines in Lisbon to plead for basic food, shelter, visas, mail, and ship tickets. They experienced frustration, sadness, and poverty as well as despondency about friends and families left behind, and they consoled one another in cafés. They also knew that Portugal would tolerate them only briefly, as long as they were in transit. Lisbon thus emerged as a site of temporality and transition, a "no-man's-land" between a lost past and an unpredictable future.[138]

In some ways, these refugees symbolize the plight of all refugees—embarking on dangerous escapes while fleeing persecution at home and then facing uncertainty and inhospitality abroad—but in other ways they were unique. Unlike most refugees fleeing from war today, we know in hindsight that Jews fled a methodically planned extermination. And even as they felt abandoned by most nations that limited their entry, by the time Jewish refugees arrived in Portugal, they found not only a safe haven (at least temporarily) but a variety of philanthropies willing to support them. Yet, as for many current refugees, these transitory moments dragged on from weeks to years, so that many grew increasingly frustrated, fearing that they would not be able to establish a normal life. Then and now, refugees learned that documents mattered—and matter—far more than the individual. And they all endured waiting for unseen bureaucrats to determine their fates. In the 1940s, a German political refugee spoke out for refugees then and now: "We are the victims, without rights, without passports, without a fatherland, the burdensome foreigners, whom one arrests and maligns. . . . When will this stop? When will we once again have OUR land, OUR *Heimat*, OUR laws?—We are really nothing but sand strewn by the winds of history."[139]

NOTES

1. *Casablanca* ranked second, after *Citizen Kane*. "AFI's 100 Greatest Movies of All Time," American Film Institute, accessed November 6, 2017, http://www.afi.com/100years/movies.aspx.

2. The voiceover speaks these words at the beginning of the film.

3. "Largest number" in Yehuda Bauer, *American Jewry and the Holocaust: The American Jewish Joint Distribution Committee, 1939–1945* (Detroit: Wayne State University Press, 1981), 47; estimate of one hundred thousand in "Review of the Year 5704," *American Jewish Year Book*, vol. 45 (New York: American Jewish Committee, 1943–44), 238. Varying widely, the numbers lie somewhere between Bauer's *American Jewry* estimate of forty thousand Jews passing through Portugal in 1940–41 (61) and the *American Jewish Yearbook* (vol. 45) estimate of one hundred thousand mostly Jewish refugees, a figure the same as that of the Joint Distribution Committee between 1936 and 1944: American Jewish Joint Distribution Committee archives, File 896–97, p. 365 (hereafter cited as JDC). Jewish sources however, cannot tell the whole story, since Jews also passed through Portugal on their own, without the assistance of Jewish organizations. See, e.g., Irene Flunser Pimentel, "Refugiados entre portugueses (1933–1945)," *Vértice* (November–December 1995): 103, who suggests sixty thousand to eighty thousand refugees; and Patrik von zur Mühlen, *Fluchtweg Spanien-Portugal: Die deutsche Emigration und der Exodus aus Europa 1933–1945* (Bonn: J. H. W. Dietz, 1992), who suggests eighty thousand. Zur Mühlen gives a 90 percent estimate of Jews among all refugees and states that German Jews made up about two-thirds of the Jewish refugees (*Fluchtweg*, 124,151–52).

4. The historical study of emotions has grown rapidly since the late twentieth century. For hundreds of publications since 2008, which do not even include the classics by Peter Stearns, Peter Gay, or William Reddy, or (earlier ones) by Ute Frevert, see "Institute Publications: History of Emotions (2008–)," Max Planck Institute, accessed November 7, 2017, https://www.mpib-berlin.mpg.de/en/research/history-of-emotions/publications. For an enlightening discussion, see also "Forum: History of Emotions," in *German History* 28, no. 1 (2010): 67–80.

5. Martina Kessel, "Gefühle und Geschichtswissenschaft," in *Emotionen und Sozialtheorie*, ed. Rainer Schützeichel (Frankfurt am Main: Campus,

2005) as paraphrased by Frank Biess, "Feelings in the Aftermath: Toward a History of Postwar Emotions," in *Histories of the Aftermath: The Legacies of the Second World War in Europe*, ed. Frank Biess and Robert Moeller (New York: Berghahn Books, 2010), 31.

6. Biess, "Feelings," 31.

7. Agnes Horvath, Bjørn Thomassen, and Harald Wydra, introduction to *Breaking Boundaries: Varieties of Liminality*, ed. Agnes Horvath, Bjørn Thomassen, and Harald Wydra (New York: Berghahn Books, 2015).

8. Joyce Davidson and Liz Bondi, "Spatialising Affect; Affecting Space: An Introduction," *Gender, Place and Culture* 11, no. 3 (September 2004): 373–74; Kay Anderson and Susan Smith, "Emotional Geographies," *Transactions of the Institute of British Geographers* 26, no. 1 (2001): 7–10. See also the journal *Emotion, Space and Society* at www.elsevier.com/locate/emospa. Holocaust "spaces" can help us understand the varieties of persecutions that Jews suffered. See, e.g., Anne Kelly Knowles, Tim Cole, and Alberto Giordano, eds., *Geographies of the Holocaust* (Bloomington: Indiana University Press, 2014), esp. the introduction.

9. Herbert A. Strauss, "Jewish Emigration from Germany: Nazi Policies and Jewish Responses," *Leo Baeck Institute Year Book* 25 and 26 (London: Secker and Warburg, 1980 and 1981). Until the end of 1936, Palestine attracted the most refugees from Germany.

10. This allowance for entry without a visa was based on an accord signed by the two countries in 1926 (Pimentel, "Refugiados," 103). Thanks to Hilary Kaplan (no relation), who helped me with translations from Portuguese. All translations from German are mine.

11. Augusto d'Esaguy, chairman of COMASSIS (Comissão Portuguesa de Assistência aos Judeus Refugiados), cited four hundred families, June 4, 1941: JDC, File 896 (2 of 3), Countries: Portugal general 1933; 1939–42, p. 1. The number of two thousand Jewish inhabitants of Lisbon is from *Jüdisches Nachrichtenblatt* (Berlin), December 10, 1940, 1. Zur Mühlen estimates about one thousand in Lisbon, Porto, Far, and Braganza together (*Fluchtweg*, 125).

12. Ben-Zwi Kalischer, *Vom Konzentrationslager nach Palaestina: Flucht durch die Halbe Welt* (Tel Aviv: Edition Olympia, 1946?), 151; Zur Mühlen, *Fluchtweg*, 122–23.

13. Pimentel, "Refugiados," 103; Avraham Milgram, *Portugal, Salazar, and the Jews* (Jerusalem: Yad Vashem, 2011), 66.

14. Milgram quotes *Circular 14* of November 11, 1939. "Portugal, the Consuls, and the Jewish Refugees, 1938–41," Shoah Resource Center, note 58, accessed November 26, 2012, http://www.yadvashem.org/odot_pdf/Microsoft%20Word%20-%203230.pdf. Accessed Feb. 11, 2018.

15. Marita Krauss, *Heimkehr in ein fremdes Land: Geschichte der Remigration nach 1945* (Munich: Beck, 2001), 19.

16. Waitstill and Martha Sharp, *Journey to Freedom: The First Chapter of Unitarian Service* (Boston: Unitarian Service Committee, 1940), 12.

17. Varian Fry, *Surrender on Demand* (New York: Random House, 1945), xi.

18. Ibid., 16.

19. Ernst Hofeller, "Refugee," 24, Leo Baeck Institute Archive, New York (hereafter cited as LBI).

20. Examples are shown in "Varian and Putzi: A Twentieth-Century Tale," directed by Richard Kaplan (Richard Kaplan Productions, 2004), DVD, 80 min. The film portrays Varian Fry's attempt to save Jews.

21. Fry, *Surrender on Demand*, 13, 103.

22. Passports had fallen into disuse in the thirty years prior to World War I, but this changed with the war. Michael Marrus, *The Unwanted: European Refugees in the Twentieth Century* (New York: Oxford University Press, 1985), 92–93. For an introduction to border studies, see: Alexander Diener and Joshua Hagen, *Borders: A Very Short Introduction* (New York: Oxford University Press, 2012).

23. Bauer, *American Jewry and the Holocaust*, 46.

24. Fry, "Forgery Is a Fine Art," in *Surrender on Demand*, 39–55; see also Karl Frucht, *Verlustanzeige: Ein Überlebensbericht* (Vienna: Kremayr und Scheriau, 1992), 167.

25. Klaus Mann, *Briefe und Antworten: Band II, 1937–1949*, ed. Martin Gregor-Dellin (Munich: Ellermann, 1975), 114.

26. Fry, *Surrender on Demand*, 170.

27. Ibid., 122.

28. Virginia López Enano, "The Spanish Train Station That Became a Hub for Nazis, Gold, and Spies," *El Pais*, February 9, 2018, https://elpais.com/elpais/2018/02/07/inenglish/1517999169_869596.html. Accessed June 27, 2018.

29. Fry, *Surrender on Demand*, 85; Varian Fry, *Assignment: Rescue* (New York: Four Winds Press, 1968), 95.

30. See *Who Killed Walter Benjamin?* (*Quién mató a Walter Benjamin*), directed by David Mauas (2005; Barcelona: Cameo Media, 2014), DVD, 73 min. The film raises the question as to whether he killed himself with a morphine overdose or died of a stroke or heart attack.

31. Nadia Gould Collection, RG-02.141, 4, United States Holocaust Memorial Museum, Washington, D.C. (hereafter cited as USHMM).

32. Ibid.

33. Fernando Rosas, "Portuguese Neutrality in the Second World War,"

in *European Neutrals and Non-Belligerents during the Second World War*, ed. Neville Wylie (New York: Cambridge University Press, 2002).

34. Sandro Sideri, *Trade and Power: Informal Colonialism in Anglo-Portuguese Relations* (Rotterdam: Rotterdam University Press, 1970), argues that Britain reaped far more benefit than Portugal. Glyn Stone, *The Oldest Ally: Britain and the Portuguese Connection, 1936–1941* (London: Royal Historical Society, 1994), looks at the relationship from the British diplomatic and strategic perspective.

35. Cordell Hull, *The Memoirs of Cordell Hull*, 2 vols. (New York: Macmillan, 1948); vol. 2, part 1, p. 1334, http://babel.hathitrust.org/cgi/pt?id=mdp.39015004963727;view=1up;seq=437;q1=Portugal;start=1;size=10;page=search;num=1335.

36. Perez Leshem, "Rescue Efforts in the Iberian Peninsula," in *Leo Baeck Institute Year Book* (1969), 235. Salazar's trade balance improved from a deficit of $90 million in 1939 to a surplus of $68 million in 1943. See Herbert R. Reginbogin, *Faces of Neutrality: A Comparative Analysis of the Neutrality of Switzerland and Other Neutral Nations during WW II* (Berlin: Lit Verlag, 2009), 126.

37. Douglas Wheeler, "The Price of Neutrality: Portugal and the Wolfram Question and World War II," *Luso-Brazilian Review*, Summer 1986, 108.

38. The Nazis looted the gold from the occupied territories (from national banks, private businesses, and individuals). See Neill Lochery, *Lisbon: War in the Shadows of the City of Light, 1939–1945* (New York: Public Affairs, 2011), esp. "Nazi Gold," chap. 25. Moreover, Portuguese tungsten helped prolong the war (Reginbogen, *Faces of Neutrality*, 129). U.S. Secretary of State Cordell Hull had worried about exactly this during the war (Hull, *Memoirs*, 1336).

39. Portugal ultimately leased naval and air bases to the British as of October 1943. By then, however, Germany had suffered a major defeat at Stalingrad (in January), and the Allies had already landed in Sicily (in July).

40. Douglas Wheeler, "In the Service of Order: The Portuguese Political Police and the British, German and Spanish Intelligence, 1932–1945," *Journal of Contemporary History* 18, no. 1 (January 1983): 6–9. Notwithstanding its tilt toward the Allies, Portugal ranked second to Switzerland in the amount of looted gold it received from the Nazi government. See Antonio Louça and Ansgar Schäfer, "Portugal and Nazi Gold: The 'Lisbon Connection,'" in *Portugal and Nazi Gold: The "Lisbon Connection" in the Sales of Looted Gold by the Third Reich* (North Charleston, S.C.: Createspace, 2011). See also Antonio Louça, *Nazigold für Portugal: Hitler und Salazar* (Vienna: Holzhausen, 2002); Marlise Simons, "Nazi Gold and Portugal's Murky Role," *New York Times*, January 10, 1997, http://www.nytimes.com/1997/01/10/world/nazi-gold-and-portugal-s-murky-role.html?pagewanted=all&src=pm.

41. Wheeler, "In the Service of Order," 8, 10.

42. Ronald Weber, *The Lisbon Route* (Lanham, Maryland: Ivan R. Dee, 2011), 271–72.

43. Valery Bazarov, "Racing with Death: HIAS (HICEM) Lisbon Files (1940–45)," *Avoteynu* 20, no. 4 (Winter 2004): 25.

44. *Korrespondenzblatt über Auswanderungs- und Siedlungswesen* (Berlin), August 1934, 12; September 1935, 22.

45. Portugal did make distinctions based on "race" in its colonial empire, with "color" becoming a near synonym for "race." See Patrícia Ferraz de Matos, *The Colours of the Empire: Racialized Representations during Portuguese Colonialism* (New York: Berghahn Books, 2013).

46. Pimental, "Refugiados," 109.

47. Lochery, *Lisbon*, 46. See also accusations that Amzalek believed the Nazis were defending Europe from communism and leaned toward them. Tom Segev, "How We Missed Out on the Swiss Option," *Haaretz*, November 29, 2007, http://www.haaretz.com/weekend/magazine/how-we-missed-out-on-the-swiss-option-1.234249. See also "The Jew with the Nazi Medal," May 3, 2010, produced by EszterPictures, http://www.youtube.com/watch?v=5RcQ_WzmvLA.

48. Milgram, *Portugal, Salazar, and the Jews*, 11, 43.

49. Marrus, *Unwanted*, 263.

50. Sharp, *Journey to Freedom*, 10.

51. Zur Mühlen, *Fluchtweg*, 128.

52. Fry, *Surrender on Demand*, 152 and passim. This article cannot discuss the organizations, from the OSE (Oeuvre de Secours aux Enfants) to Varian Fry's (American) Emergency Rescue Committee, that managed to smuggle refugees into Portugal from France. Obviously "many rings were involved," as observed by Debórah Dwork and Robert Jan van Pelt, *Flight from the Reich: Refugee Jews, 1933–1946* (New York: W. W. Norton, 2009), 213. These rings included criminal rings.

53. *Aufbau*, October 12, 1940, cited in Christa Heinrich, ed., *Lissabon 1933–1945: Fluchtstation am Rande Europas* (Berlin: Akademie der Künste und Haus der Wannsee Konferenz, 1995), published in conjunction with an exhibition presented at the Goethe-Institut in Lisbon.

54. Lisbon housed about eight thousand refugees in December 1940 and about fourteen thousand by June 1941. D'Esaguy, June 4, 1941, JDC.

55. Friedrich Torberg, *Eine tolle, tolle Zeit: Briefe und Dokumente aus den Jahren der Flucht, 1938–1941*, in *Gesammelte Werke*, vol. 18 (Munich: Langen-Müller, 1989), 123; Jan Lustig, *Ein Rosenkranz von Glücksfällen: Protokoll einer Flucht* (Bonn: Weidel, 2001), 66; Fry, *Surrender on Demand*, 103.

56. Lochery, *Lisbon*, 104.

57. Alma Mahler-Werfel, *And the Bridge Is Love* (New York: Harcourt, Brace, 1958), 268–69.

58. As presented in *Lisbon: Harbor of Hope*, directed by Pavel Schnabel, (Lanham, Md.: National Film Network, 1994), DVD, 70 min., at 21:20–22:15.

59. Maria Bauer, *Beyond the Chestnut Trees* (Woodstock, N.Y.: Overlook Press, 1984), 105–6.

60. Miriam Stanton, *Escape from the Inferno of Europe* (London: M. Stanton, 1996), 144–45.

61. American Jewish Committee, *American Jewish Yearbook* 43 (1941–42): 203–4, 325.

62. George Rony, *This, Too, Shall Pass Away* (New York: Creative Age Press, 1945), 253.

63. Most often, refugees without papers would be interned in "fixed residences," small towns they could leave only with police permission.

64. Stanton, *Escape from Inferno*, 146.

65. "An Octogenarian's records of his life and experience as a German Jew," Wiener Lib ref. P. II.f.No.972, recorded in 1958. 39 pp. [Author: M.M., from Freiburg I Br], 36.

66. Oral history interview with Felix Bauer, RG-50.166*0002, USHMM.

67. Hofeller, "Refugee," 29.

68. Hans Reichmann, *Deutscher Bürger und verfolgter Jude, Novemberpogrom und KZ Sachsenhausen 1937–1939* (Munich: R. Oldenbourg, 1998), 261.

69. Hannah Arendt quoted in Marc Ellis, *Encountering the Jewish Future: With Wiesel, Buber, Heschel, Arendt, and Levinas* (Minneapolis: Fortress Press, 2011), 172.

70. Hannah Arendt, "What Remains? The Language Remains: A Conversation with Günter Gaus," in *Essays in Understanding, 1930–1954: Formation, Exile, and Totalitarianism* (New York: Schocken Books, 1994), 13.

71. Adriana Nunes, *Ilse Losa, Schriftstellerin zwischen zwei Welten* (Berlin: Ed. Tranvía, 1999), 4.

72. William Bayles, "Lisbon: Europe's Bottleneck," *Life*, April 28, 1941, 80.

73. These organizations created turf wars, sometimes cooperating and other times not. Even as they alleviated dire need, some observers have criticized them for clinging to legal strategies in the face of growing knowledge of mass murder (Milgram, *Portugal, Salazar, and the Jews*). HICEM resulted from a merger in 1927 among three Jewish migration associations: the Hebrew Immigrant Aid Society (HIAS), based in New York; the Jewish Colonization Association (ICA), based in Paris; and Emigdirect, based in Berlin.

The acronym HICEM is formed from letters representing HIAS, ICA, and Emigdirect. "HICEM," Shoah Research Center, Yad Vashem, accessed November 8, 2017, http://www.yadvashem.org/odot_pdf/Microsoft%20Word%20-%206368.pdf; "Jewish Colonization Organization (ICA)," Jewish Virtual Library, accessed November 8, 2017, http://www.jewishvirtuallibrary.org/jewish-colonization-association-ica.

74. The American Friends Service Committee, the Catholic Relief Services, and the Unitarian Service Committee, among others, helped non-Jewish refugees but often Jews as well. The Quakers cared for Jews who had converted to Christianity as well as stateless people "of Jewish ancestry" who did not identify as Jews and partners in Jewish–Christian mixed marriages. William Howard Wriggins, *Picking up the Pieces from Portugal to Palestine: Quaker Refugee Relief in World War II* (Lanham, Maryland: University Press of America, 2004), 17.

75. Supported by several wealthy Jewish families, it still could not have functioned financially on its own, needing financial support from the JDC and coordination with HICEM.

76. D'Esaguy; June 4, 1941, JDC.

77. Heinrich, *Lissabon 1933–1945*, 13–14.

78. Fry, *Surrender on Demand*, 4.

79. Isaac Bitton interview, May 17, 1990, RG -50.030*0027, USHMM.

80. Arendt, "We Refugees," in *Altogether Elsewhere: Writers on Exile*, ed. Marc Robinson (Winchester, Mass.: Faber and Faber, 1994), 115.

81. Dagmar Barnouw commenting about Arendt in *Der Jude als Paria*, 44, cited in Nunes, *Ilse Losa*, 26.

82. Arendt, "We Refugees," 115. Arendt was certainly not the only refugee writer in Lisbon. Many others also waited there in 1941. See Christina Heine Teixeira in "'Warten auf das rettende Schiff'—Hanna Arendts Flucht über Lissabon," in *Neuer Nachrichtenbrief der Gesellschaft für Exilforschung*, vol. 19 (June 2002).

83. No one used this terminology then. Only in 1955 did psychologists recognize that not only concentration camp survivors but also refugees had mental health, social, and psychological problems. See Henry B. M. Murphy, *Flight and Resettlement* (Paris: UNESCO, 1955). See also Atina Grossmann, *Jews, Germans, and Allies: Close Encounters in Occupied Germany* (Princeton, N.J.: Princeton University Press, 2009), 151–53.

84. Leshem, "Rescue Efforts," 240.

85. Leshem, "Rescue Efforts," 240; Wriggins, *Picking Up*, 22.

86. Hans Sahl, *Das Exil im Exil* (Hamburg: Luchterhand-Literaturverlag, 1994), 277.

87. Hertha Pauli recollection in Daniel Blaufuks, *under strange skies*, http://www.danielblaufuks.com/webnew/film/strangeskies/english.html.

Accessed Feb. 11, 2018. Koestler information in David Cesarani, *Arthur Koestler: The Homeless Mind* (London: William Heineman, 1998), 169. See also Lilly Lewis, Shoah Foundation, no.12696, seg. 44–47.

88. Lustig, *Rosenkranz*, 91.

89. Kurt Ibson to family in the United States, August 25, 1940, private collection. Thank you to Ralph Ibson for sharing his father's letters with me. In the United States, Kurt Israel changed his last name to Ibson.

90. Sahl in Blaufuks, *under strange skies*.

91. Wriggins, *Picking Up*, 45, 54–55.

92. Hannah Arendt to Salomon Adler-Rudel, February 17, 1941. Briefwechsel in den Originalsprachen, http://www.hannaharendt.net/index.php/han/article/view/72/108, accessed Feb. 10, 2018.

93. Heinrich, *Lissabon 1933–1945*, 13–14.

94. Henri Deutsch, Shoah Foundation, no. 10463, seg. 57–65.

95. Regarding the trek, see James Reston, "Lisbon's Refugees Now Put at 8,000," *New York Times*, December 15, 1940; regarding the subsidy, see zur Mühlen, *Portugal*, 162.

96. Pekelis, *My Version of the Facts*, trans. George Hochfield (Evanston, Ill.: Marlboro Press, 2004), 324.

97. Ibid., 134–35.

98. Sol Hasson, Shoah Foundation, no. 1937, seg. 71–72.

99. Erika Mann, "In Lissabon gestrandet," 150. In *Im Fluchtgepäck die Sprache: Deutschsprachige Schriftstellerinnen im Exil*, ed. by Claudia Schoppmann (Berlin, Orlanda: 1991).

100. Pekelis, *Facts*, 134–35.

101. Ibson to family, August 25, 1940.

102. Pekelis, *Facts*, 138.

103. Ibid., 148.

104. Ibid., 149. Many refugees referred to Kafka. See also Wriggins, *Picking Up*, 30.

105. Alfred Döblin, *Destiny's Journey*, trans. Edna McCown (New York: Paragon House, 1992), 217–18.

106. Ibid., 218.

107. Ibid.

108. An eight-way correspondence across two generations makes similar points in Rebecca Boehling and Uta Larkey, *Life and Loss in the Shadow of the Holocaust: A Jewish Family's Untold Story* (Cambridge: Cambridge University Press, 2011).

109. I have used a highly unusual set of sources, a cache of 290 letters and postcards from 29 countries written at the end of 1941 and into early 1942 at the Museum of Jewish Heritage (MJH) in New York City. The letters and cards were addressed to Lisbon and Barcelona. I used only those

addressed to Portugal. Some of the letters remained unopened until the museum allowed me to see them, probably the most moving experience of my professional life. I owe thanks to Bonnie Gurewitsch and Esther Brumberg at the MJH for telling me about them.

110. Jenny Sara Goldstern, Vienna to Herr Torn, Lisbon, March 30, (probably 1942), MJH Lisbon Letter collection, no. 198.

111. MJH no. 1851.90.1–4, notebook on display at the museum, second floor permanent exhibit. Stores too advertised they would send packages of food to occupied Europe. See Pimentel, "Refugiados," 106, ad of October 5, 1940. See also postcards from Warsaw at the Jewish Historical Institute in Warsaw, Centralna Biblioteka Judaistyczna, accessed June 20, 2016, http://cbj.jhi.pl/collections/658182.

112. Ruth Bondy, writing of Terezin, in "The Miracle of the Loaves," in *Trapped: Essays on the History of the Czech Jews, 1939–1943*, trans. Chaya Naor (Jerusalem: Yad Vashem Publications, 2008), 137.

113. Marion Kaplan, *Between Dignity and Despair: Jewish Life in Nazi Germany* (New York: Oxford University Press, 1998), 117, 235.

114. Letter to US Committee for the Care of European Children, New York, July 30, 1943, German-Jewish Children's Aid (GJCA), 1933–1953, RG 249, microfilms, MKM8.14, folder 245, YIVO Archives, New York.

115. American Friends Service Committee to unknown agency, March 1943, GJCA, 1933–1953, RG 249, microfilms, MKM8.27, folder 486, YIVO Archives, New York.

116. In 1940, HIAS scrambled to get Jews onto a ship, "whatever it costs," before their visas expired. YIVO, HIAS-HICEM Archives, 245.4, file no. XII-Portugal, A-23, p. 1.

117. Hannah Arendt to Adler-Rudel, April 2, 1941, Hannah Arendt website, http://www.hannaharendt.de/documents/briefe_1.html. Accessed May 10, 2012

118. Valeriu Marcu, *"Ein Kopf ist mehr als vierhundert Kehlköpfe": Gesammelte Essays* (Constance, Germany, Hartung-Gorre: 2002), 203–4.

119. "Report of the HIAS-ICA Activities in Lisbon, July 1, 1940–Dec. 18, 1941," HIAS-HICEM Archives, series 1, file no. XII-Portugal A-2, pp. 2–3.

120. He still had to wait six weeks. Peter Jansen and Christian Schmidt, eds., *In steter Freundschaft: Leo Löwenthal-Siegfried Krakauer Briefwechsel 1921–1966* (Lüneburg: Zu Klampen, 2003), 118, 140.

121. Arendt to Adler-Rudel, April 2, 1941.

122. Bayles, "Lisbon's Bottleneck," *Life*, April 28, 1941, 77.

123. For the content in this section, see Barbara Rosenwein, "Worrying about Emotions in History," *American Historical Review* 107, no. 3 (June 2002): 842. See also "Forum: History of Emotions," 67–80. Although much

narrower in both time and space, these café relationships shared similar norms of emotional valuation and expression reminiscent of Rosenwein's "emotional community."

124. According to the German intellectual Eva Lewinski, in Pimentel, "Refugiados," 105.

125. Fred Mann, *A Drastic Turn of Destiny* (Toronto: Azrieli Foundation, 2009), 173.

126. Regarding rumors about the war, see Janina Lauterbach, Shoah Foundation, no. 1138, seg. 36–41. The "refugee telegraph" is mentioned in Wriggins, *Picking Up*, 58.

127. Bitton interview.

128. Ute Frevert, "Was haben Gefühle in der Geschichte zu suchen?" *Geschichte und Gesellschaft* 35, no. 2 (April–June 2009): 183–208.

129. Hermann Kesten, *Dichter im Café* (Vienna, Munich, Basel, 1959), 12–13.

130. Wriggins, *Picking Up*, 58.

131. Nunes, *Ilse Losa*, 60.

132. E. Mann, "In Lissabon gestrandet,"155.

133. Only about eight hundred refugees remained in Portugal (Milgram, *Portugal, Salazar, and the Jews*, 116). The police forced three hundred to live in Caldas da Rainha.

134. "Herbert Katzki: A Lifetime with JDC," *Footnotes: The Newsletter of the JDC New York Archives*, December 1999, 2, 4.

135. Mara Vishniac quoted in "Natürlich Berlin! Erinnerungen an Roman Vishniac," in *Roman Vishniacs Berlin*, ed. James Howard Fraser et.al. (Berlin: Judisches Museum Berlin / Nico, 2005), 32.

136. Sahl, *Exil*, 103–4.

137. Quoted in Irene Pimentel, "Salazar impediu os refugiados de contagiarem Portugal," *Publico*, March 18, 1995, 22–23.

138. Arthur Koestler, *Arrival and Departure* (New York: Macmillan, 1943), 19.

139. Karl O. Paetel, *Reise ohne Uhrzeit: Autobiographie*, ed. Wolfgang D. Elfe and John M. Spalek (London: World of Books, 1982), 255.

Lutz Kaelber

Jewish Children as Victims of "Euthanasia" in Nazi Germany

ERWIN SÄNGER WAS BORN INTO A JEWISH FAMILY IN HAMBURG IN 1935. He had an older brother, Jacob, whom his parents put on a *Kindertransport* to England. Erwin Sänger's mother and father, Flora and Willy Sänger, were deported to Theresienstadt in 1942 and died in Auschwitz in 1944. Curiously enough, seven-year-old Erwin was not deported along with his parents. On the very day his parents were deported, the Gestapo had him placed in the "special children's ward" at Hamburg-Langenhorn. The name "special children's ward," or, literally translated, "expert facility for pediatric care" (*Kinderfachabteilung*), suggested to the public a benevolent purpose. It was in fact a medical killing station in Hamburg's sole state-run facility for the mentally ill during World War II. Erwin received a Christian baptism and died there in April 1943, seven months after his admission, a victim of Nazi "children's euthanasia." Dr. Friedrich Knigge, as head of the special children's ward, carried out the killings of such children by administering an overdose of a barbiturate (Luminal); Erwin's "official"—that is, falsified—cause of death, as noted in his medical record, was pneumonia. His admission record had an oversized stamp on it, "Jew," and it also noted his medical disorder: "mongolism," or trisomy 21 (also known as Down syndrome).[1]

The fate of Jewish minors with disabilities like Erwin in Nazi Germany is the topic of this article. Henry Friedlander's pioneering research on the murder of Jews with disabilities revealed the patent falsity of the claim by leading representatives of the Nazi state that Jews were not included in Nazi medical killing programs,[2] and scholars such as Georg Lilienthal, Annette Hinz-Wessels, and Rael Strous recently have added to our knowledge about the subject matter. Yet their studies have not focused on children and adolescents.[3] After briefly addressing the rhetoric and policies toward German Jews with disabilities and mental illnesses in the Third Reich, this chapter analyzes how Jewish minors were murdered as part of the "T4" program and a "special action." Then it turns to killing programs specifically targeting children and Jewish minors, showing that Jewish minors were deliberately systematically segregated and murdered within Germany even before the deportations to, and murders in, the East commenced: it presents case studies of Jewish children murdered as part of the "children's euthanasia" program, which focused on children with disabilities. The concluding section addresses how minors became objects of a unique killing program at the Hadamar "mixed race ward" for minors, which targeted Jewish *Mischlinge*, or literally "cross-breeds" of the first degree (i.e., those who had two Jewish grandparents, as defined by the 1935 Nuremberg race laws and a supplementary decree).

NAZI RHETORIC AND POLICIES TOWARD JEWS WITH DISABILITIES AND MENTAL ILLNESSES

Overtly social Darwinist policies had powerful promoters with the Nazi assumption of power in 1933. Since World War I, ideas underlying such policies had circulated widely in German society, particularly around discussions of the book *Permission to Annihilate Life Unworthy of Living* by Karl Binding, a leading scholar of jurisprudence, and psychiatrist Alfred Hoche, but they had remained a minority position. The ascendance of such ideas in the Third Reich and the Nazi leaders' embrace of "racial hygiene" expressed itself in 1933 with the passage of a compulsory sterilization law targeting individuals with physical and intellectual disabilities along with mental disorders, one of the first new legal policies in the Third Reich. The law itself was not particularly original; it had a strong similarity to a model sterilization law propagated by American eugenicist Harry Laughlin in 1922. While more than thirty states in the United States had passed eugenic sterilization laws by 1933, the German federal law went beyond most American state laws in that it provided for compulsory sterilization without requirement of consent and expressly allowed sterilization of individuals not housed in state facilities.[4]

Jews became victims of Nazi sterilization policies, and those with mental illnesses and disabilities were further victimized by state policies over the course of the 1930s. Not only did Jews who fled Nazi Germany often have to leave disabled family members and relatives behind (as they were almost uniformly barred from immigration), but in 1938 Jews were also excluded from public assistance, which meant that for those in public care, their financial support fell to the Reich Association of Jews in Germany, local or regional Jewish associations, or private citizens. Discrimination also extended to excluding or removing Jewish patients from German state, and many private, hospitals.[5] This progression of discrimination occurred in the context of a general deterioration in the 1930s in the condition of the disabled and mentally ill, as public appropriations for hospitals and asylums were cut back, leading to severe shortages of medical personnel, food, equipment, and other supplies.

The case of the Jewish patient Adelheid B., diagnosed with "idiocy," at the state mental hospital in Wiesloch evinces the radicalization of views toward Jews with disabilities and mental illnesses.[6] In 1938 the physician who treated Adelheid B. noted that she was "terribly difficult and disruptive." He then entered into the record, "isn't worth living [*lebensunwert*]!" with an exclamation mark (see figure 1), a formulation used by Binding and Hoche in their treatise on death and disability. By then such a formulation had been incorporated into medical language in Nazi Germany, a perspective that saw the "value" of individuals in terms of their utility for society.[7] In addition, psychiatrists and physicians were not the only ones to subject Jewish patients to discriminatory treatment. Reported incidents of hostility from other non-Jewish patients indicate that Jewish patients were increasingly isolated within psychiatric facilities.[8] Thus public attitudes combined with discrimination in law, medicine, and economic policy to leave Jewish patients in public mental hospitals in a particularly vulnerable situation.

THE T4 PROGRAM AND THE "SPECIAL ACTION" AGAINST JEWS

Adelheid B.'s life ended in the gas chamber of Grafeneck in 1940, at a time when the wholesale extermination of Europe's Jews by Germans had not been systematically planned as such. By August 1941, under the T4 program, death in a gas chamber had become the typical fate of Jews institutionalized in mental hospitals, of whom there were an

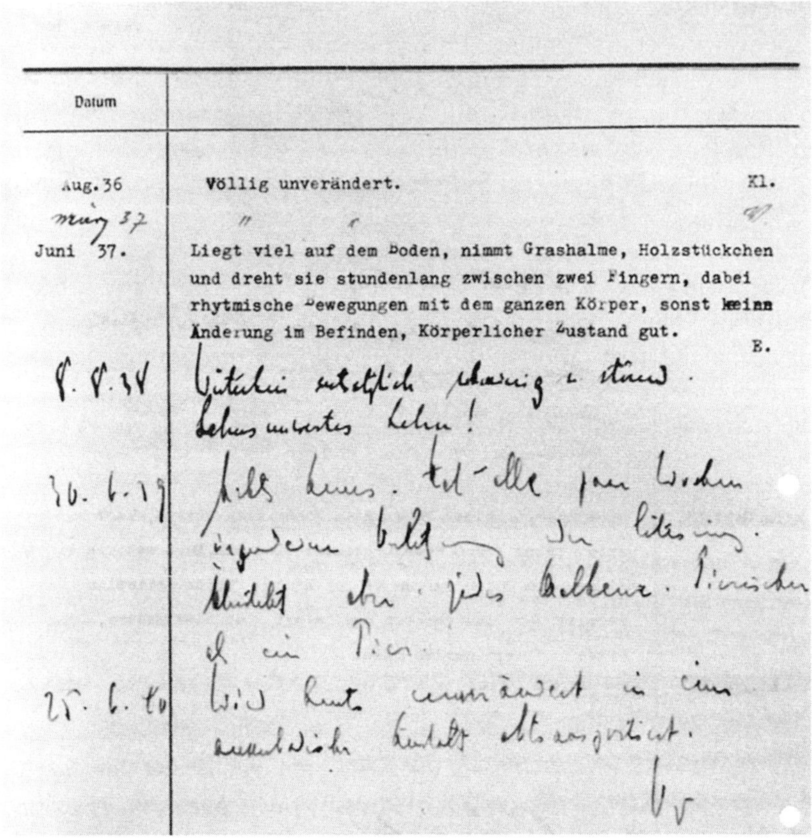

Datum	
Aug. 36	Völlig unverändert. Kl.
März 37 [uncertain]	" "
Juni 37.	Liegt viel auf dem Boden, nimmt Grashalme, Holzstückchen und dreht sie stundenlang zwischen zwei Fingern, dabei rhytmische Bewegungen mit dem ganzen Körper, sonst keine Änderung im Befinden, Körperlicher Zustand gut. B.

Figure 1. Adelheid B.'s medical record, Wiesloch facility. Source: Bundesarchiv Berlin, R179/24497.

estimated 2,500 to 5,000 in Germany, adults and children.[9] While Henry Friedlander's analysis established the inclusion of Jews in T4, new research has led to the recognition of both the extent and the administrative procedure of this "early extermination" program. A unique record, that of Klara B., can be used to illustrate this point.

Klara B. was a Jewish patient at the asylum Am Steinhof (which also housed the Spiegelgrund "special children's ward") in Vienna. Her diagnosis was given as schizophrenia, her symptoms as "personality in decline" and "fizzled out," and her ability to work as "useless." The sheet that contains this information (see figure 2) is the form that the central T4 office in Berlin sent to the individual psychiatric hospitals, with the information contained in it to be assessed by a group of T4 evaluators. This record is unique because it is the only one known to have survived with remarks in the black box at the bottom left: the actual "evaluation" by T4 physicians. The first is a red plus sign by the physician "N," who also appears to have been the one who highlighted the words "Jew" and "schizophrenia" in light red pencil in the record. The second and third physicians also entered a red plus sign, as did the chief evaluator physician who entered his mark below those of the others.[10] The "evaluated" form was sent to the gassing facility at Hartheim, Germany, on August 7, 1940, along with the patient (see the tiny stamp at the bottom left), where Klara B. was murdered the next day.

Her death is recorded in a section of the form at the top right, where information is filled in the blanks of a stamp. The stamp has four lines. On the first line the stamp uses the bureaucratic term "resolved . . . on" (*erledigt . . . am*). "C" stands for the Hartheim gassing facility. On the second line, the date of death is filled in: August 8, 1940. On the third line, the stamp sets out "certified in . . ."; and on the fourth line, there is a space for the recorded date of death, filled out with "X11" and January 7, 1941, about five months after her actual death. The X is a prefix that appears to have been applied solely to Jews. The number behind the X was likely assigned in a continuous order (of notarized death, not date of actual death). Such X numbers were used in the correspondence sent to the relatives of murdered Jewish patients, including death notices from a fictitious Cholm Lunatic Asylum in Poland, to which these patients had allegedly been sent.[11] This charade functioned as a cover for the transport of patients to the actual gassing sites, and it allowed for the extraction of money from patients' relatives until their deaths had been certified. As we see in the case of Klara B., the Reich Association of Jews was fraudulently made to pay her continued expenses for approximately five months, a period typical for murdered Jews as compared to non-Jews, for whom the period between a patient's death and the certification of a patient's death was on average two to three weeks.[12]

Klara B. was sent to Hartheim along with non-Jewish patients; at least four hundred Jews overall were murdered as part of such mixed transports. In this case, being Jewish was considered a negative factor and in itself might have been enough of a reason for an evaluator to enter a red plus sign, which then marked the patient for what

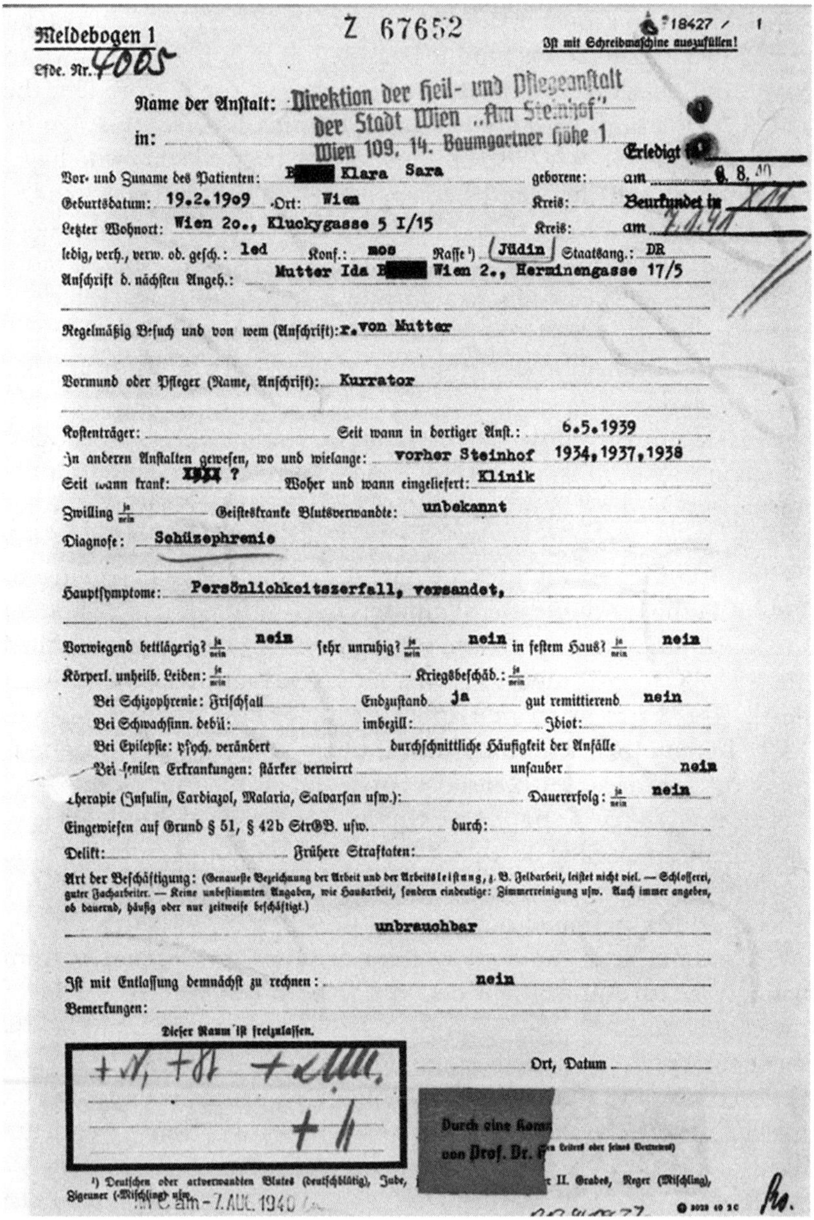
Meldebogen 1 Z 67652 18427 / 1

Ist mit Schreibmaschine auszufüllen!

Lfde. Nr. 4005

Name der Anstalt: Direktion der Heil- und Pflegeanstalt der Stadt Wien „Am Steinhof"

in: Wien 109, 14. Baumgartner Höhe 1

Erledigt

Vor- und Zuname des Patienten: B▮▮▮ Klara Sara geborene: am 8. 8. 40

Geburtsdatum: 19.2.1909 Ort: Wien Kreis: Beurkundet in XIII

Letzter Wohnort: Wien 20., Kluckygasse 5 I/15 Kreis: am

ledig, verh., verw. od. gesch.: led Konf.: mos Rasse[1]) Jüdin Staatsang.: DR

Anschrift d. nächsten Angeh.: Mutter Ida B▮▮▮ Wien 2., Herminengasse 17/5

Regelmäßig Besuch und von wem (Anschrift): r. von Mutter

Vormund oder Pfleger (Name, Anschrift): Kurrator

Kostenträger: Seit wann in dortiger Anst.: 6.5.1939

In anderen Anstalten gewesen, wo und wielange: vorher Steinhof 1934, 1937, 1938

Seit wann krank: ? Woher und wann eingeliefert: Klinik

Zwilling ja/nein Geisteskranke Blutsverwandte: unbekannt

Diagnose: Schizophrenie

Hauptsymptome: Persönlichkeitszerfall, versandet,

Vorwiegend bettlägerig? ja/nein nein sehr unruhig? ja/nein nein in festem Haus? ja/nein nein

Körperl. unheilb. Leiden: ja/nein Kriegsbeschäd.: ja/nein

Bei Schizophrenie: Frischfall Endzustand ja gut remittierend nein

Bei Schwachsinn. debil: imbezill: Idiot:

Bei Epilepsie: psych. verändert durchschnittliche Häufigkeit der Anfälle

Bei senilen Erkrankungen: stärker verwirrt unsauber nein

Therapie (Insulin, Cardiazol, Malaria, Salvarsan usw.): Dauererfolg: ja/nein nein

Eingewiesen auf Grund § 51, § 42b StrGB. usw. durch:

Delikt: Frühere Straftaten:

Art der Beschäftigung: (Genaueste Bezeichnung der Arbeit und der Arbeitsleistung, z. B. Feldarbeit, leistet nicht viel. — Schlosserei, guter Facharbeiter. — Keine unbestimmten Angaben, wie Hausarbeit, sondern eindeutige: Zimmerreinigung usw. Auch immer angeben, ob dauernd, häufig oder nur zeitweise beschäftigt.)

unbrauchbar

Ist mit Entlassung demnächst zu rechnen: nein

Bemerkungen:

Dieser Raum ist freizulassen.

Ort, Datum

Durch eine Komm... von Prof. Dr. ...

[1]) Deutschen oder artverwandten Blutes (deutschblütig), Jude, ... II. Grades, Neger (Mischling), Zigeuner (-Mischling) usw.

... am - 7. AUG. 1940

Figure 2. Klara B.'s "evaluation" on her T4 reporting form. Source: Bundesarchiv Berlin R179/18427.

was officially called "disinfection." Jewish patients, on average, were hospitalized for a shorter period and were transported more quickly than their non-Jewish counterparts. For them, other criteria such as ability to work appear to have played less of a role in determining the outcome of the "evaluation."[13]

Apart from mixed transports, a "special action" (*Sonderaktion*) was specifically set up for Jews and involved a far larger number of victims. Its implementation followed on the heels of the failed attempt in Nazi federal policy of physically separating Jewish psychiatric patients from the rest. A decree of the Reich Ministry of the Interior (RMI) of June 22, 1938, demanding such a separation could not be implemented fully, for the austerity policy toward psychiatric facilities left no funds to construct separate wards or pay for the additional costs in personnel. Existing Jewish facilities did not have space for expansion, and new construction projects were equally unfeasible. Nor were regional initiatives successful in accomplishing such a separation. In 1940 a new policy commenced, concentrating Jewish psychiatric patients in certain designated hospitals and from there transporting them collectively, irrespective of criteria such as their ability to work, to the T4 gas chambers. The "special action" included German, Polish, and stateless Jews, whereas Jews of other nationalities and so-called half Jews, or part Jews of the first degree (*Mischlinge ersten Grades*; those with two Jewish grandparents) and quarter Jews, or part Jews of the second degree (*Mischlinge zweiten Grades*; those with one Jewish grandparent) were not. In July 1940 it appears that more than 500 Jewish patients were murdered in such a "special action" at Brandenburg alone, and more than 300 more were murdered in August at Hartheim. Hadamar also participated, as did Sonnenstein/Pirna. This "special action" continued until May 1941. That not a single record of these patients has been found among the R179 records is indicative of the furtive character of this program, but a glimpse of it is provided in the pocket calendar of the Brandenburg/Havel director and gassing physician Dr. Irmfried Eberl, in which he recorded his "appointments" for personal use and off the official record. Entries in Eberl's calendar can be matched with lists of transports recorded elsewhere (see figure 3). Shown here is one such entry for two groups solely comprised of Jewish patients: 136 patients from Hamburg-Langenhorn from September 23, 1940, and 158 patients from Hanover-Wunstorf from four days later. Both transports are noted in green pencil, with a "J" for Jews. One of Eberl's

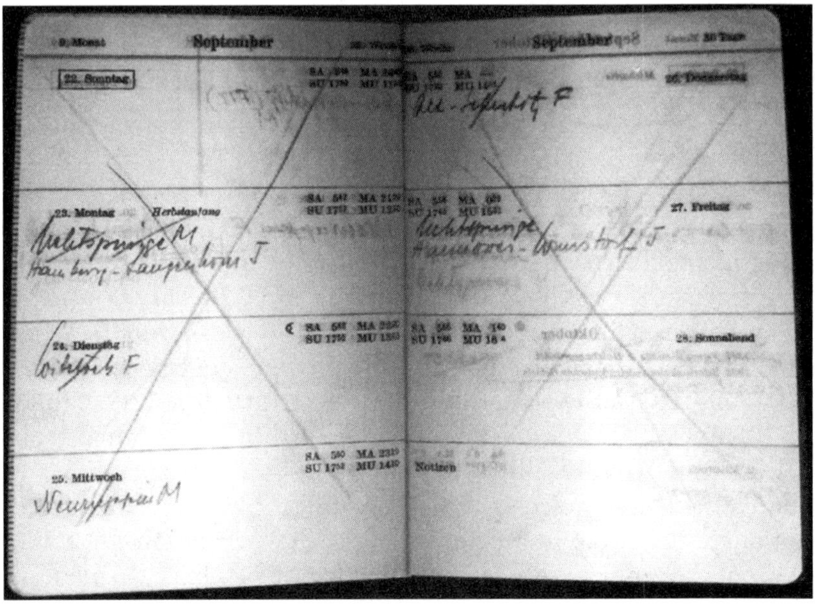

Figure 3. Dr. Irmfried Eberl's pocket calendar. Source: Brandenburg Memorial; original at the Hessisches Hauptstaatsarchiv Wiesbaden, 631a, 1611. Author's photo.

tasks was to operate the gas valve, to prune the "body of the people" of its "failed specimens."[14]

The aforementioned X-numbers assigned to Jews allow us to estimate for the first time on a reliable basis the total number of Jewish patients killed in the six T4 facilities. By February 1941, the X-numbers had exceeded 2,000, a figure that closely tracks the figure George Lilienthal calculated in his study, the most exhaustive to date, of the number of Jews murdered in the T4 gas chambers. Lilienthal counted only those Jewish victims whom he could identify by name, and arrived at a figure of more than 2,000 such victims. By July 1942, the X-numbers fictitiously notarized at Cholm had reached 2,500, most of which derived from the "special action." Considering that the Reich Association of Jews for Germany counted 2,500 Jewish patients in public care facilities in May 1940, the X-numbers attest to a systematic and near total annihilation of the Jewish psychiatric population in Germany by the summer of 1941—that is, months before Chelmno began to function as the first killing facility for the Nazis' mass murder of all European Jews. By the time Chelmno began its operation in late 1941, few German Jews (minors or adults) with psychiatric or severe developmental or mental disabilities who had been living outside of home care were still alive.[15]

Among those patients who were killed in the T4 facilities were minors with psychiatric or developmental disabilities, including Jews. Based on an analysis of the R179 records, scholars have put the percentage of minors among the more than 70,000 T4 victims overall at about 6 percent, or 4,000 to 4,500 children and youths. The predominant marker for the selection of minors in general for T4 was a diagnosed lack of "educability," considered predictive of their prospects for being a "burden" on society. In Brandenburg/Havel, 885 victims, or almost 11 percent of the total, were minors, reflective of the fact that large pediatric facilities for children and youths with mental disorders and developmental disabilities, particularly those in Uchtspringe and Brandenburg-Görden, were in its vicinity. Children as young as age two were gassed, and three Jewish children housed at Görden were among the early victims. Possibly to make room for Görden's "special children's ward," the first of its kind, several transports from there to Brandenburg/Havel consisted solely of children, including three in May 1940. The last of these transports, in October 1940, consisted of at least 59 children, apparently selected on the basis of how useful they might be for research at the Kaiser-Wilhelm Institute for Brain Research at Berlin-Buch conducted by the noted neuropathologist Professor Julius Hallervorden.[16]

The numbers of Jewish minors who became part of the "special action" are about 50 for Brandenburg/Havel, about 30 for Hartheim, and about 10 for Hadamar.[17] However, beyond being recorded in the victims' memorial book accessible at the recently expanded Brandenburg T4 memorial site, victims' identities, including those who were Jewish, have generally not been revealed to the public due to privacy concerns. For the aforementioned "special action" that included patients from Langenhorn noted in Dr. Eberl's calendar, the Memorial Book of the Federal Archives for the Victims of the Persecution of Jews in Germany lists only 100 victims or so by name, including about a dozen minors over the age of thirteen.[18]

Beyond the T4 and "special action" operations, Jews with disabilities and mental illnesses, including minors, were victimized in other ways. The Jewish hospital at Bendorf-Sayn continued to admit and house Jewish patients up to its closure in November 1942, and its designated replacement, the psychiatric station at the Jewish hospital in Berlin, was closed at the end of 1943, after its patients, like those in Bendorf-Sayn before, were deported to the killing facilities in the East. Due to the insufficient capacity of both facilities, Jews also continued to be admitted to regular psychiatric facilities, where they subsequently became victims of what was called "decentralized euthanasia."[19] Moreover, from fall 1939 onward, Jews who were residents in the many psychiatric facilities in Eastern Europe numbered among those facilities' patients who were murdered in shootings, in a stationary gas chamber at Poznan, and in gassing vans. The murders sometimes included infants and children who were not patients in such facilities. For example, in October 1940, 290 elderly, infirm, and mentally ill Jews who resided in a geriatric home in Kalisz, Poland, were killed in a gassing van, as were 214 children with disabilities in the local children's home of Jeiskk in Ukraine in October 1942 and 54 seriously ill infants in Spa-Teberda on the Crimea in January 1943.[20]

The T4 mixed transports, the "special action," and the emptying of psychiatric and other care facilities in Nazi-occupied Europe resulted in thousands of Jewish deaths, including those of minors. Commencing at the beginning of 1940, these killing actions, however, do not exhaust the Third Reich's murderous policies targeting Jews with disabilities and mental disorders. At that time, a related killing program with Jews among its victims was being implemented. It is known as "children's euthanasia," but researchers have not systematically addressed the involvement of Jewish minors in it.

JEWISH CHILDREN AND "CHILDREN'S EUTHANASIA"

The National Socialist "children's euthanasia" program operated about thirty killing facilities, or "special children's wards," between 1939 and 1945. The program was initially set up to include small children up to three years of age, but it would soon be expanded to include minors up to the age of sixteen.[21] Pediatricians, nurses, and other health practitioners reported children with disabilities, congenital illnesses, and malformations to local public health offices, which, through a reporting form, notified a benignly labeled but fictitious "Reich Committee for the Scientific Registration of Severe Hereditary Ailments" (Reichsausschuss zur wissenschaftlichen Erfassung von erb- und anlagebedingten schweren Leiden). Asylums and hospitals providing pediatric care notified the same fictitious committee. After an administrative screening of the reports, the "Reich Committee," which was actually located in a branch office of the Chancellery of the Führer in Berlin, commissioned a permanent board of three medical evaluators to determine a reported child's fate. A "positive" evaluation resulted in the child's admission to a "special children's ward" for "treatment"—that is, murder—or for further observation. To entice parents to consent to admit their children, parents were told that the ward would provide the most expert treatment to their children. If parents did not comply, they could be subjected to threats. Physicians and staff members killed the children, who were termed *Reichsausschusskinder* (Reich Committee children). They typically carried out the murder with an overdose of Luminal. Parents received notifications of their children's "sudden unexpected" death. Each case of murder was to be authorized via a formal "*Ermächtigung*" (authorization) notice from Berlin, though the authorization was not an order of murder but rather a formalized expectation thereof. Physicians participated voluntarily and had ultimate authority (but no direct obligation) to order a killing that had been preauthorized from Berlin. Of about 100,000 individuals reported on the reporting forms, at least 5,000 children were killed in this program. As historian Herwig Czech has noted, the actions taken thus did not represent indiscriminate extermination (i.e., as in the Holocaust) but rather a medicalized screening, which involved a process of deliberate observation, evaluation, selection for life or death, and murder of those who were in the latter category. Insofar as every reported and admitted minor could potentially be killed as part of a daily, deadly routine, *all* those who died can be considered victims, irrespective of whether their demise can be proved to have been brought about intentionally or was due to neglect, malnutrition, or starvation.[22]

The perfidious nature of this killing program is obvious today, but even before 1933, a belief in the right to life of an infant with a severe disability may not have been widely shared in Germany, not even among the parents of such infants. That was the import of the results of a survey taken in 1920 by Ewald Meltzer, the director of one of Saxony's oldest educational and residential facilities for disabled children. The survey asked parents of children in his facility whether they would agree to a painless curtailment of their child's life if experts established that their child suffered from incurable idiocy. To Meltzer's consternation, about three-fourths of the parents answered in the affirmative.[23] The survey results, published in 1925, became part of a larger discussion in Germany that centered on the merits of Binding and Hoche's argument. It has been suggested that such an indication of parents' latent acceptance to have their disabled children killed as an act of "mercy" could only have encouraged the Third Reich's planners of "children's euthanasia" once the political circumstances allowed the implementation of the corresponding killing program.[24] Moreover, German and American attitudes toward "euthanasia" at the time may not even have differed as much as one might expect.[25]

Complete vital records have not survived for many of the approximately thirty "special children's wards," and in at least one site of a "special children's ward," medical and administrative records that are believed to have survived have not been made accessible to researchers. Thus, the inclusion of minors with Jewish parents (including those who were considered *Mischlinge* because they had one Jewish parent) cannot be comprehensively documented here. Still, the records yield fragmentary biographies of some Jewish minors who died in "special children's wards" in Leipzig-Dösen, Schwerin, Brandenburg-Görden, Vienna, and Idstein, presented here as a panorama of previously (largely) untold individual stories and fates.

In the ward at Leipzig-Dösen (located in what today is the state of Saxony), operating between October 1940 and December 1943, about 550 deaths occurred. This number includes two Jewish girls. Elfriede Thieberg died there at age ten in 1941. Born in Poland, she had an intellectual disability and was institutionalized at Dösen at age two and then transferred to two other care facilities before returning to Leipzig-Dösen in March 1941. Her parents, Ciwie and Josef Thieberg, who had left for Belgium in 1939, were transported to Auschwitz in August 1942. A sister survived by being placed by the children's aid society Oeuvre de Secours aux Enfants in homes in France. A second Jewish victim, Ruth Kirschbaum, was murdered at age seven in November 1941, having previously been in the asylum Grossschweidnitz. She, too, had an intellectual disability, and she was considered a *Mischling* of the first degree. Divorced since 1929 from her non-Jewish husband, her mother was Jewish and remained herself a resident of a care institution until her death in 1942, possibly a victim of "decentralized euthanasia."[26]

Another teenager, Horst Ladewig, who was considered a *Mischling*, was one of about 300 children and teenagers who died in the Sachsenberg "special children's ward" in Schwerin. Horst's death was due to "nervous exhaustion in the presence of idiocy" in April 1942 at age eighteen. Being deaf-mute and having been diagnosed with an intellectual disability, he had resided in a nearby children's home since 1931 and was likely among 200 children termed "idiotic" and "at a very low level" who were transferred from there to the Sachsenberg facility in September 1941 when the "special children's ward" opened. Horst's Jewish father, Walter Ladewig, having been in prison for a conviction on "racial defilement" and other allegations, had become despondent about his son's uncertain fate and was sent to Auschwitz the same month his son died.[27]

A number of Jewish children have been identified from the psychiatric clinic Brandenburg-Görden and Vienna's Spiegelgrund facility—hardly surprising in light of the above-average residency rates of Jews in and around Berlin and Vienna. Located to the west of Berlin, Görden is notorious for several reasons. It was termed a "Reich training station" for "children's euthanasia" physicians (they attended several-week-long seminars there that very likely involved medical training in killing methods); it housed about 4,000 psychiatrically disabled or ill children and youths between 1938 and 1944, of whom almost 1,300 died, plus more than 400 who were gassed in the T4 program; it had a mortality rate of almost 90 percent among the "Reich Committee children"; and it had a research station for carrying out medical experiments on minors. Although the connection between the "special children's ward" and some of the victims still appears tenuous, records indicate the presence of Jewish children. One of them was Berto Goldstrom (figure 4). His parents, Sally and Liesbeth Goldstrom, perished at Auschwitz, as did four of his siblings, while a brother survived as the result of a *Kindertransport* to Britain. Berto was admitted to Görden at age three and died within three months, in 1941. Recent research has established the ways in which many of the "children's euthanasia" victims at Görden were also made to serve as suppliers of tissue samples used in scientific research.[28]

Between July and October 1939, four other Jewish minors (Karl C., Sara H., Manfred M., and Steffen R.) died at Görden, presumably too early for death in the "special children's ward" (historians still debate whether it had been established by late 1939 or as late as summer 1940),

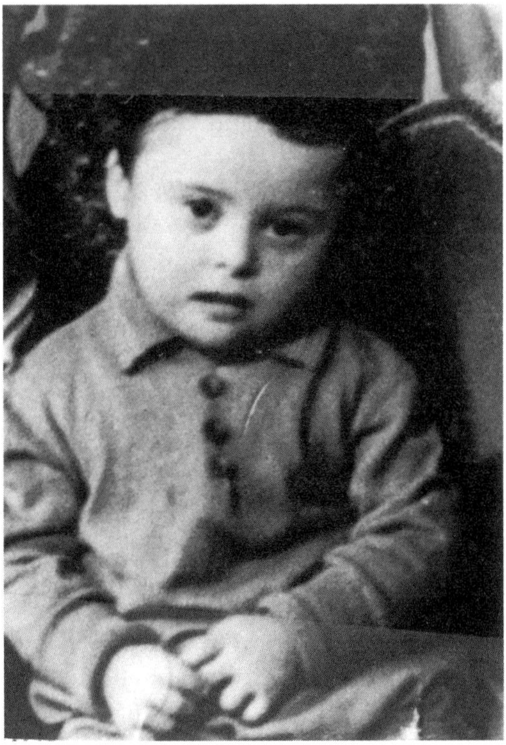

Figure 4. Berto Goldstrom. Source: Yad Vashem, Central Database of Shoah Victims' Names, http://namesfs.yadvashem.org/YADVASHEM/28031640_388_6119/238.JPG .

although it is known that mortality rates among children soared in some locations well in advance of the establishment of such a ward. Another minor, Arnold B., died in May 1940; his Jewish mother was a forced laborer in Berlin and managed to survive in hiding there. Of Arnold's father nothing further is known except that he is reported also to have been Jewish on the German supplementary census of Jews in 1939. Arnold's medical records suggest he was part of the "*Reichsausschussaktion*," even though they make no express references to it, perhaps reflective of a common practice of a "cleansing" of records before the war's end to conceal incriminating evidence.[29] Two additional Jewish minors, Hans H. and Manfred S., died in Görden at ages fourteen and nine, respectively. Nothing further is known about their parents' identity and fate at the present time. Gerd T., the son of a Jewish mother and a non-Jewish father, died in Görden at age three. Agnes Spörl, his mother, died in Bernburg's gas chamber in 1942, likely in the "14f13" action that targeted sick concentration camp inmates no longer able to work, while his (half-)brother Horst was transported to Riga (and is presumed to have been murdered there) the same year.

About 800 children died at Vienna's notorious Spiegelgrund facility. In the context of medical crimes, its name has become near synonymous with Dr. Heinrich Gross, a "child euthanasia" physician who tormented children with particular zeal.[30] Several children with Jewish parents are among the victims. For Margarethe Glaser, who died at Spiegelgrund at age fifteen, no medical records are extant, and her familial background is unknown. Wilhelm Kaposi suffered from injuries during birth and was delayed in his physical and mental development. He went through five different homes, hospitals, and institutions before ending up at Spiegelgrund, where Dr. Gross examined him on admission and from then on called him "Israel." Dr. Gross also noted typical signs of a "near-Asian race." Less than four months after his admission, the child died at age twelve from pneumonia, a common manifestation of Luminal poisoning; his father was murdered in Auschwitz in 1942.[31] Jakob Nemecinskis, too, died of pneumonia, at age eleven. Born in Lithuania, his family background is unknown.[32] Dr. Gross discovered during a physical examination upon admission that the boy was circumcised. Jakob died less than three months later. Max Reichmann developed meningitis in early childhood and became deaf and intellectually delayed. His parents fled to Australia in 1939, leaving Max behind. During his stay at Spiegelgrund, Max appeared to be starving. His case report to the Reich Committee noted that he was Jewish and unlikely ever to be able to work. He died at age fourteen in 1942. After contracting meningitis, Ilse Philippovic suffered from epilepsy and a delay in her physical and intellectual development. She died at age twelve, less than a month after being admitted. Both her parents survived until the end of the war using false papers and living in hiding. Her mother gave testimony in proceedings against Spiegelgrund physicians in 1946.[33]

Another case from Vienna is well known in existing research, but the fact that the child victim was half Jewish has mostly been overlooked. Anna Wödl's son Alfred was born in 1934. In her testimony in the proceedings against the Spiegelgrund physicians Ernst Illing, Marianne Türk, and Margarethe Hübsch in 1946, Anna Wödl noted that Alfred had not been able to speak or walk. She also stated that Alfred was a *Mischling* of the first degree since his father was Jewish and had recognized paternity, and that, once Alfred had been admitted to Spiegelgrund, he was known there as a *Mischling.* The rest of the story is well known: his mother, a practicing nurse, had gotten word of the transfer of institutionalized patients to Hartheim and was concerned that her son, then institutionalized at the facility Gugging, would soon be among them. When she courageously visited Herbert Linden, the RMI official dealing with the "euthanasia" program, she was unable to negotiate her son's release. Merely a "quick and painless" death at Spiegelgrund would be granted to him. Alfred died within two weeks after admission to the ward; pneumonia was listed as his official cause of death.[34] Another such case of a *Mischling*'s death is known for the special children's ward in Loben/Lubliniec.[35]

The Kalmenhof facility, in Idstein, also housed a "special children's ward." Founded to the south of Frankfurt with the help of Jewish philanthropists as a facility for children with intellectual disabilities and epilepsy, it had a sizable portion of Jewish residents until 1933, when it was quickly brought under National Socialist governance.[36] At Kalmenhof, a conservative estimate of the minors who died in the "special children's ward" is 350. One of them was Ruth Pappenheimer, who was reported to the Reich Committee in spite of the fact that she displayed no evidence of a disability. Her murder was apparently solely based on racial animus, and the committee used procedural legitimacy as a means of shrouding her death. Her father, Julius Pappenheimer, was probably murdered at Sobibor, while her non-Jewish mother died in 1933. Her brother, Alfred, raised by their father's brother, died at Treblinka. Ruth was alleged to be morally deviant and became a ward of the state. She ended up at Kalmenhof, where she was murdered in 1944 at age nineteen by the physician Herrmann Wesse, who was in charge of the "special children's ward" and had sought an "authorization for treatment" from Berlin, under the urging of Fritz Bernotat, one of Hesse-Nassau's senior provincial bureaucrats. The historian Martina Hartmann-Benz considers Ruth Pappenheimer a person whom welfare personnel and other authorities portrayed in accordance with the antisemitic stereotypical trope of the "beautiful Jewess," with alleged eroticized and morally corrupting features. The enduring fable of her having been killed to cover up a sexual liaison with no less a person than Bernotat himself illustrates this point.[37]

Two other *Mischlinge* at Kalmenhof encountered different circumstances. Born in 1931, Heinz H. was a child born out of wedlock to a Catholic mother and Jewish father. After both of his parents died, he was first raised by foster parents and then placed in a home. His patient record at the Kalmenhof facility contains negative remarks about his Jewishness and alleged psychopathology. Willi N. was born in the same year as Heinz H. After being placed under temporary public guardianship, he also ended up at the Kalmenhof facility. Since the hospital building housing the "special children's ward" was overcrowded, the two resided together with other children in the nearby seniors' home. The children were to be moved to the hospital later, but the two *Mischlinge* had a different fate, reflecting a division of labor between two institutions: whereas the non-Jewish children were sent to die in Kalmenhof's "special children's ward," the two Jewish *Mischlinge* were transferred to the Hadamar asylum for the same purpose. Hadamar housed a unique institution that was to become the only one of its type, specifically and solely set up for the murder of Jewish *Mischlinge*.

HADAMAR'S "MIXED-RACE WARD" (*MISCHLINGSABTEILUNG*) FOR MINORS

Hadamar was a "T4" killing site until August 1941 and in August 1942 became a site of "decentralized euthanasia" until March 1945. In spring 1943, an institution called an *Erziehungsheim* (reformatory school) was set up within it for the fictitious purpose of educating Jewish *Mischlinge*. Instead, the minors transferred there were murdered. The creation of this institution reflected the significant changes in the general policies toward *Mischlinge* after the passage of the Nuremberg Laws of 1935. Legal ambiguity allowed for varying policy implementations based on political fervor, expediency, and other considerations. In regard to *Mischling* minors, different factions in the national political leadership, the party, and local and regional administrations came to different conclusions in trying to determine whether it was possible that the "Aryan component" in minors might enable them to contribute positively to the "body of the people" despite their Jewish "racial" component. By 1943, however, public policies toward *Mischlinge* in general had become much harsher and shifted toward murder.[38] As part of this change in policy, the RMI sought to establish one or more centers with the sole purpose of housing Jewish minors in order to have them killed, but only one actually came to exist: Hadamar.

Known as the Hadamar *Mischlingsabteilung*, its beginnings and operations remain murky.[39] Information about its very beginnings derives from a transcript of a letter by the RMI, dated April 15, 1943, addressed to the administration of the regional association in Nassau. The letter refers to a decree issued by the same ministry on March 9, 1943, seeking to initiate the institutionalization of Jewish *Mischlinge* who were minors. Whether the decree focused solely on the administrative region of Nassau (where Hadamar was) or, more likely, was sent to administrations in other regions is unknown, but there is no evidence of a central plan in Berlin to carry out the killing of such minors in this way, nor of how administrations in other regions responded. The letter also referred to a report dated March 31, 1943, written by Bernotat's office, which had responded quickly and stated that such an institutionalization could take place at Hadamar.[40] In its letter of April 15, 1943, the RMI urged a quick institutionalization of such minors from the administrative regions of Nassau, Hesse, and the Rhine Province, and specified that the operation of the ward begin immediately. The minors—that is, anyone under the legal age, which was twenty-one at the time—were to be separated at Hadamar from other residents and by gender.[41]

On May 15, 1943, Bernotat wrote in a note to the Eichberg asylum that a separate reformatory school had been established at Hadamar, where all Jewish minors, including all minors considered Jewish, currently in care facilities or in *Fürsorgeerziehung* (state reformatory education) were to be quartered, and all such minors had to be reported to him within five days. Thereby Bernotat had not only turned RMI's plans to have minors quartered into an unambiguous directive but also expanded the group affected to all Jewish minors beyond *Mischlinge* who were currently placed in homes or were in *Fürsorgeerziehung*. *Fürsorgeerziehung* pertained to minors who had been removed from the care of their parents and placed in foster families or corrective institutions, but the directive for reporting minors that Bernotat gave only pertained to those in corrective institutions, not those in foster care.

The policy's vast expansion to include all Jewish minors was quickly retracted within ten days, when Bernotat and the RMI, in a follow-up letter and a decree, limited the policy's application to "Jews of the first degree (half Jews)" who were minors and not to those who were fully Jewish or Jews of the second degree. The RMI's decree of May 21, 1943, however, affirmed that to be included in the policy were, apart from those institutionalized in facilities for the psychiatrically and developmentally disabled (*Anstalten*), those in homes and in family foster care.[42] It pertained largely to those minors whose families had been torn apart by the incarceration, deportation, and murder of the Jewish spouse, or households in which the non-Jewish parent could no longer care for the minor. Racial status, not disability, made the minors the policy's target, although stereotypical allegations in their records of petty infractions in schools and in public were not uncommon and served to depict them as morally inferior, or to ascribe to them a "moral" disability.[43] Nurse Margarete Borkowski headed the ward, or section, at Hadamar, though in serious medical matters she would have deferred to the asylum's chief physician, Dr. Adolf Wahlmann, who, at admission, certified each minor as psychiatrically disabled or mentally impaired, since only such individuals could be properly admitted. Another nurse, Karl Willig, appears to have carried out the actual killings upon instruction.[44]

Graph 1 provides a chronology of admissions, with siblings shown identified with matching asterisks, and the length of the bars depicting the length of stay. The bars with a pointed end depict children who were released. The first child, EW, was admitted on February 20 and died on March 11. In light of the absence of incriminating remarks in the minor's administrative and medical records, EW likely died before the commencement of the program, although a killing in anticipation of the ward's establishment cannot be ruled out. The list shows that it was not uncommon for more than one sibling in a family to be sent to the Hadamar ward. Most *Mischlinge* were in their early teens when they were admitted, and most died within a two-month period thereafter. Save for one minor (and apart from five others who were released), none survived for more than four months. At first, almost all children came from Hesse-Nassau, possibly owing to Hadamar's notoriety as a "T4" and then "decentralized euthanasia" facility, which made some regional officials suspicious and led them to hide potential victims.[45] In the summer of 1943, children from Brunswick and Bavaria followed.

The fact that not all children and youths fell victim to the murder action at Hadamar can be attributed to the tenacious efforts of a resident of Nuremberg, GR. GR was a carpenter and a brother to JR,

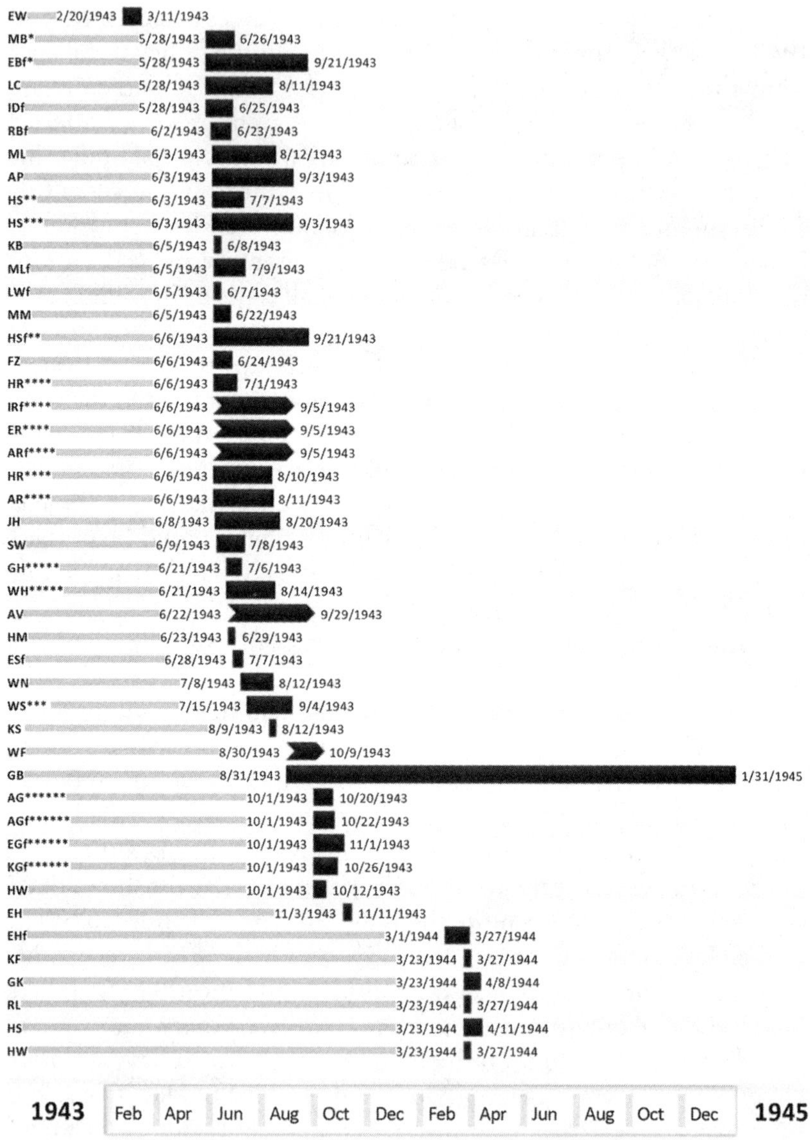

Graph 1. Admission to and Stay in the *Mischlingsabteilung* at Hadamar, 1943–1945.

who married RW in 1928. RW was Jewish and would end up surviving the Nazi period. The couple had seven children, six of whom were admitted to the Hadamar *Mischling* ward. After the two parents were sentenced to twelve and eighteen months in prison for child neglect and abuse in 1940, a court placed their children in *Fürsorgeerziehung*. Their children then lived in a children's home before being transferred to Hadamar. The uncle visited the children at Hadamar and got increasingly worried about his nieces' and nephews' well-being after the oldest had died in early July 1943. He commissioned a lawyer to petition the RMI and sought support from a Nuremberg party official ever more urgently, as two more of the siblings died.[46] The RMI's response was to allow the remaining siblings to be released into their uncle's custody while remaining in *Fürsorgeerziehung*. In another case, an equally tenacious mother whose Jewish spouse had been killed by a group of Nazis in 1933 was less fortunate. Her two children, GH and WH, were admitted to the Hadamar station after they had been dismissed from school and branded "a-social half-Jews" upon admission at a large facility for the disabled. After the mother heard that her son GH had fallen ill at Hadamar, she tried to visit him, but he was dead already. When she asked Dr. Wahlmann about his cause of death, he replied "you'll have to accept it, Mrs. H. Jewish children must be exterminated." After the mother's second son had been murdered at Hadamar, she refused work in the armament industry and was sentenced to three months in prison.[47]

On September 2, 1943, just a few days before the aforementioned three siblings' release to their uncle, the RMI promulgated a new decree, clarifying that eligibility for placement in Hadamar was limited to those who were *Mischlinge* of the first degree having been placed in *Fürsorgeerziehung*. It expressly excluded those who were not in need of being placed in a home (*anstaltsbedürftig*), especially those who still lived with their parents or grandparents.[48] As a result, Hadamar released two other youths whose profile did not fit the new decree.[49] These developments give credence to Nathan Stoltzfus's argument that government authorities, at least in 1943, were concerned not to stoke public discontent among non-Jews about the treatment of their Jewish spouses, as indicated by the Rosenstrasse protests, or about the treatment of *Mischling* family members.[50]

One former inmate of the Hadamar station, AV, later reflected on his time there, remembering a group of about ten girls and thirty boys. Graph 1 shows seven females and seventeen males to have been alive in the ward when he was admitted, a smaller number than he remembered, but it is possible that the records are incomplete and there were even more people in the ward than were recorded. For the following months, the graph shows, the number of deaths exceeded the number of admissions. "The group of children I was in was shrinking rapidly—we were now four boys and two girls," he noted.[51] By mid-September, of the children alive at the time of AV's admission, two females were indeed still alive in the station, as he had indicated, but only two other males, possibly indicative of an undercount of the actual number of males in the surviving records. WF had a similar story to tell: "there was a special section in which persons were being confined exclusively for reasons of race. In my section [for boys] there were eighteen youths, each of whom was half-Jewish. Moreover, there was a similar section for girls with about twenty of them present." He further noted that "during the six weeks I was at Hadamar, starting with my group of eighteen persons [males], many disappeared like that, and at the end there were only about seven of us left."[52] According to the records, when WF entered the Hadamar institution at the end of August, only five other males and four girls were present in the station, and only one other on the day of AV's release on September 29. WF's testimony confirms the possibility that a larger number of minors were housed there than the records indicate. August 1943 was also the approximate time period when the station as a physical unit was dissolved, and the remaining and newly admitted children were placed among psychiatrically disabled patients.[53]

As shown in graph 1, apart from GB, by early October there were a few newly admitted minors in the station, but they were all dead within a month. Given this combination of small numbers and a quick death, the presence of a separate station for the *Mischlinge* would not have made much sense. The children admitted in 1944 came from Thuringia (one in early March) and Berlin (five toward the end of March). GB, the last child in the *Mischlingsabteilung* to die there, in late January 1945, had been able to hold out for so long because he was useful in the locksmith's shop.[54] The total number of victims was about forty.

The killing of *Mischlinge* from various regions in Germany at Hadamar commencing in 1943 complemented the killing of minors institutionalized in hospitals and asylums as part of "decentralized euthanasia." It signifies a turn toward expanding the parameters of existing programs to include nondisabled and non-fully-Jewish minors as the least wanted among a larger group of children and youths considered a burden on the state because they were in *Fürsorgeerziehung*.[55]

NOTES

This article is a substantially updated and expanded version, with numerous corrections, of two articles published earlier:; "Jewish Children with Disabilities and Nazi 'Euthanasia' Crimes" in the *Bulletin of the Carolyn and Leonard Miller Center for Holocaust Studies* 17 (2013); and "The Hadamar 'Mixed-Race Ward' (*Mischlingsabteilung*) in Nazi Germany," *Bulletin of the Carolyn and Leonard Miller Center for Holocaust Studies* 18 (2014). I wish to thank the Carolyn and Leonard Miller Center for Holocaust Studies and the librarians at the Bailey-Howe library for supporting my research.

1. Hildegard Thevs, *Stolpersteine in Hamburg-Rothenburgsort* (Hamburg: Landeszentrale für politische Bildung, 2011), 146–47; Marc Burlon, "Die 'Euthanasie' an Kindern während des Nationalsozialismus in den zwei Hamburger Kinderfachabteilungen," (medical diss., University of Hamburg, 2009), 103, 170–73; for Erwin Sänger's parents, see "Memorial Book, Victims of the Persecution of Jews under the National Socialist Tyranny in Germany 1933–1945," Bundesarchiv, last updated October 13, 2017, for Flora Sänger: http://www.bundesarchiv.de/gedenkbuch/en958808; for Willy Sänger: http://www.bundesarchiv.de/gedenkbuch/en958852. Jacob Sänger changed his name and became an attorney in England.

2. Such was the declaration of Karl Brandt, Hitler's personal physician and Reich Commissioner for Health and Sanitation, and Victor Brack, chief organizer of "euthanasia" in the Chancellery of the Führer. See, for example, Paul Weindling, *Nazi Medicine and the Nuremberg Trials* (New York: Palgrave Macmillan, 2004), 253–54; and Henry Friedlander, *The Origins of Nazi Genocide* (Chapel Hill: University of North Carolina Press, 1995), 263.

3. Friedlander, *Origins of Nazi Genocide*; Rael Strous, "Extermination of the Jewish Mentally-Ill during the Nazi Era—The 'Doubly Cursed,'" *Israel Journal of Psychiatry and Related Sciences* 45 (2008): 247–56; Georg Lilienthal, "Jüdische Patienten als Opfer der NS-'Euthanasie'-Verbrechen," *Medaon* 5 (2009): 1–16; Annette Hinz-Wessels, "Antisemitismus und Krankenmord: Zum Umgang mit jüdischen Anstaltspatienten im Nationalsozialismus," *Vierteljahreshefte für Zeitgeschichte* 61 (2013): 65–92.

4. Harry Laughlin, *Eugenical Sterilization in the United States* (Chicago: Psychopathic Laboratory of the Municipal Court of Chicago, 1922); for analysis and contexts, see Paul Lombardo, *Three Generations, No Imbeciles* (Baltimore, Md.: Johns Hopkins University Press, 2010); Gisela Bock,

Zwangssterilisation im Nationalsozialismus (Opladen, W. Ger.: Westdeutscher Verlag, 1986); Stefan Kühl, *The Nazi Connection* (Oxford: Oxford University Press, 1994). On sterilizations in Vermont and other American states, see Lutz Kaelber, "Eugenics: Compulsory Sterilization in 50 American States," updated 2011,http://www.uvm.edu/~lkaelber/eugenics/.

5. Strous, "Extermination of Jewish Mentally-Ill," 248–49, notes that the percentage of Jews killed in the T4 program who had previously been sterilized was lower, not higher, than the percentage for non-Jews.

6. Her medical and administrative records were among the approximately thirty thousand records of T4 victims that survived the war and were rediscovered around 1990 (record group R179 in the Bundesarchiv Berlin).

7. It is impossible to tell whether Adelheid B.'s mental illness or developmental disability, or the fact that she was Jewish, or the coexistence of these conditions, "prompted" the physician's remark. The same physician, heading a small station dedicated to "hereditary biology" at Wiesloch at the time, trying to establish family genealogies of disease and disability, also entered a similar remark into a non-Jewish girl's medical records. I am grateful to Dr. Franz Janzowski for information. See also Gerrit Hohendorf, *Der Tod als Erlösung vom Leiden: Geschichte und Ethik der Sterbehilfe seit dem Ende des 19. Jahrhunderts in Deutschland* (Frankfurt: Wallstein, 2013), 66, for a third and a fourth patient. The facility at Wiesloch also housed a "special children's ward."

8. Hinz-Wessels, "Antisemitismus und Krankenmord," 70–73.

9. Ibid., 67. The code name "T4" was derived from the Berlin street address of the secret "euthanasia" program's headquarters, Tiergartenstrasse 4. The six T4 facilities were in the German communities of Bernburg, Brandenburg (on the Havel River near Berlin), Grafeneck, Hadamar, and Sonnenstein (near Pirna), and the Austrian town of Hartheim (along the Danube River near Linz). See "Euthanasia Program," *Holocaust Encyclopedia*, United States Holocaust Memorial Museum, accessed November 13, 2017, https://www.ushmm.org/wlc/en/article.php?ModuleId=10005200.

10. These physicians were Drs. Paul Nitsche, Theodor Steinmeyer, Friedrich Mennecke, and Werner Heyde, respectively. Bundesarchiv Berlin R179/18427.

11. All patients of the actual facility there had been murdered by SS units in early 1940.

12. Annette Hinz Wessels et al., "Zur bürokratischen Abwicklung eines Massenmords: Die 'Euthanasie'-Aktion im Spiegel neuer Dokumente," *Vierteljahrshefte für Zeitgeschichte* 53 (2005): 79–107, esp. 94–95.

13. Hinz-Wessels, "Antisemitismus und Krankenmord," 75.

14. Ibid., 84–85; Lilienthal, "Jüdische Patienten als Opfer," 8.

15. Hinz-Wessels, "Antisemitismus und Krankenmord," 77–80, 86; Astrid Ley and Annette Hinz-Wessels, *The "Euthanasia-Institution" of Brandenburg an der Havel* (Berlin: Metropol, 2012), 27; Lilienthal, "Jüdische Patienten als Opfer," 9; Annette Hinz-Wessels, "Das Schicksal jüdischer Patienten in brandenburgischen Heil- und Pflegeanstalten im Nationalsozialismus," in *Brandenburgische Heil- und Pflegeanstalten in der NS-Zeit*, ed. Kristina Hübener (Berlin: be.bra, 2002), 279. The number provided by the Reich Association of Jews does not include patients in Austria or those in private care facilities.

16. Petra Fuchs, "Zur Selektion von Kindern und Jugendlichen nach dem Kriterium der 'Bildungsunfähigkeit,'" in *Die nationalsozialistische "Euthanasie"-Aktion "T4" und ihre Opfer*, ed. Maike Rotzoll et. al. (Paderborn: Schöningh, 2010), 87–96; Thomas Beddies, "Kinder und Jugendliche in der brandenburgischen Heil- und Pflegeanstalt Görden als Opfer der NS-Medizinverbrechen," in Hübener, *Brandenburgische Heil- und Pflegeanstalten*, 129–54; Babette Reicherdt, "'Gördener Forschungskinder,'" in Rotzoll et al, *Die nationalsozialistische "Euthanasie"-Aktion "T4,"* 147–51; Ley and Hinz-Wessels, *"Euthanasia-Institution" of Brandenburg*, 24.

17. Dr. Astrid Ley, email communication to the author, July 2013.

18. "Memorial Book."

19. Lilienthal, "Jüdische Patienten als Opfer," 9–10.

20. In the annexed and occupied Polish areas, as historians have noted, "Jewish and Polish-Jewish mentally ill had no chances of survival" and were murdered "in principle." This does not mean, however, that German or non-Jewish patients in homes and asylums would be spared, as in many cases all inmates were killed indiscriminately, and any reprieve tended to be temporary. See Hans-Walter Schmuhl, *Rassenhygiene, Nationalsozialismus, Euthanasie* (2nd ed.; Göttingen: Vandenhoeck und Ruprecht, 1992), 245; Fritz Bauer, Karl Bracher, and Christiaan Rüter, eds., *Justiz und NS-Verbrechen,* vol. 37, no. 777 (Amsterdam: Amsterdam University Press, 1972–73); Volker Rieß, *Die Anfänge der Vernichtung "lebensunwerten Lebens" in den Reichsgauen Danzig-Westpreußen und Wartheland 1939/40* (Frankfurt: Lang, 1995), 362; Michael Alberti, *Die Verfolgung und Vernichtung der Juden im Reichsgau Wartheland 1939–1945* (Wiesbaden: Harrassowitz, 2006), 335–36.

21. See Lutz Kaelber, "Child Murder in Nazi Germany," *Societies* 2 (2012): 157–94.

22. Herwig Czech, "Kinder und Jugendliche als Opfer der nationalsozialistischen Medizinverbrechen in Österreich," in *Geraubte Kindheit*, ed. [Austrian] Bundesjugendvertretung (Vienna: Edition Mauthausen, 2010), 149.

23. Michael Burleigh, *Death and Deliverance* (Cambridge: Cambridge University Press, 1994), 21–23. The survey's response rate was over 80 percent.

24. This is amply discussed in the secondary literature. See, e.g., Schmuhl, *Rassenhygiene*, 106–26.

25. In the United States in 1936, Gallup asked the question, "Do you favor mercy deaths under government supervision for hopeless invalids?" to which almost half in the national sample responded affirmatively. See John Ostheimer, "The Polls: Changing Attitudes toward Euthanasia," *Public Opinion Quarterly* 44, no. 1 (1980): 125.

26. Lutz Kaelber, "[Special Children's Ward] Leipzig-Dösen," March 13, 2015, http://www.uvm.edu/~lkaelber/children/leipzigdoesen/leipzigdoesen.html; Jürgen Nitsche, "'Unter einem doppelten Fluch': Jüdische Opfer der nationalsozialistischen Krankenmordaktion in Sachsen," *Sonnenstein Hefte* 8 (2010): 47–78; Katy Hazan, *Rescuing Jewish Children during the Nazi Occupation* (Paris: Association Oeuvre de Secours aux Enfants and Somogy éditions d'art, 2008), 159. I wish to thank Dr. Jürgen Nitsche for additional information.

27. Close to 500 children and youths were committed to Sachsenberg's "special children's ward" between 1941 and 1945, of whom 300 died (Lothar Pelz, "Mecklenburgische Kinderarzte und NS-'Kindereuthanasie,'" in *Ethik und Erinnerung*, ed. Ekkehard Kumbier, Stefan J. Teipel, and Sabine C. Herpertz [Lengerich, Ger.: Pabst Science Publishers, 2009], 59–69). While Horst Ladewig's medical and administrative records do not evince a connection to the "Reichsausschuss" (Dr. Stefan Schramm, state main archive Schwerin, email communication with author, September 2014), the absence of such a connection is no proof that Horst was not killed as part of the "Reichsausschussaktion," as medical and administrative records were frequently purged of incriminating material. For information about Walter Ladewig, see Jürgen Gramenz, *Ladewig* (Plaidt, Ger.: Cardamina, 2013), 328–35.

28. Beatrice Falk and Friedrich Hauer, *Brandenburg-Görden* (Berlin-Brandenburg: be.bra, 2007), 69–132; Thomas Beddies, "Die Einbeziehung von Minderjährigen in die nationalsozialistischen Medizinverbrechen," *Praxis der Kinderpsychologie und Kinderpsychiatrie* 58 (2009): 518–29. I wish to thank Dr. Thomas Beddies and Dr. Friedrich Hauer for sharing information with me. The names of Berto Goldstrom and two other "children's euthanasia" victims were publicly identified in 2010 (see *Märkische Allgemeine, Brandenburger Kurier*, January 5, 2010).

29. This and some of the following information about locations derive from BA Lichterfelde, Bestand R 1509 (Reichssippenamt), "Ergänzungskarten für Angaben über Abstammung und Vorbildung," German Census

May 17, 1939. For the information about Arnold B.'s medical records I am indebted to Dr. Friedrich Hauer.

30. See, for example, Florian Thomas, Alana Beres, and Michael I. Shevell, "'A Cold Wind Coming': Heinrich Gross and Child Euthanasia in Vienna," *Journal of Child Neurology* 21 (2006): 342–48.

31. For this and the following, see Waltraud Häupl, *Die ermordeten Kinder vom Spiegelgrund* (Vienna: Böhlau, 2006), 250, 364, 406, 439–40, 603, 637; Wolfgang Neugebauer, "Juden als Opfer der NS-Euthanasie in Wien 1940–1945," in *Von der Zwangssterilisierung zur Ermordung*, vol. 2, ed. Eberhard Gabriel and Wolfgang Neugebauer (Vienna: Böhlau, 2002), 99–111. Additional information can be found on the website A Letter to the Stars at http://www.lettertothestars.at/. The previously reported information, derived from the website and repeated in Häupl, *Die ermordeten Kinder vom Spiegelgrund*, 250, that Wilhelm Kaposi's parents had emigrated to England is incorrect. Edmund Kaposi attempted to emigrate there and take his son with him, but his efforts came to naught.

32. According to his Lithuanian passport, his correct name was Jakovas Nemečinskis. I wish to thank Dr. Berg of the Wiener Stadt-und Landesarchiv for additional information. The book of the dead at the Spiegelgrund memorial and the honorary grave of Spiegelgrund victims in Vienna's Central Cemetery list his last name as Nemencindkis. Häupl, *Die ermordeten Kinder vom Spiegelgrund*, gives his name as Nemencinskis.

33. For excerpts from her testimony, see Samuel Totten, Williams S. Parsons, and Israel W. Charny, eds., *Century of Genocide*, 2nd ed. (New York: Routledge, 2004), 222–23.

34. Testimony of Anna Wödl on July 16, 1946 (BA Ludwigsburg B162/1546); Gerhard Fürstler and Peter Malina, "Österreichische Pflegepersonen aus der Zeit des Nationalsozialismus, Teil I: Die Wiener Krankenschwester Anny Wödl," *Österreichische Pflegezeitschrift* (March 2003), 24–27; Herwig Czech, "Nazi Medical Crimes at the Psychiatric Hospital Gugging," http://www.memorialgugging.at/pdf/Czech_MedizinverbrechenGugging_engl.pdf, 10–11.

35. The minor was Kurt P., who had a Jewish father, as noted with a thick red pencil mark in his records. His name appears in the "Luminal booklet," a booklet discovered after the war that contained the administered dosages of barbiturates (phenobarbital).

36. See Peter Sandner, *Verwaltung des Krankenmordes* (Giessen: Psychosozial-Verlag, 2003).

37. Andrea Berger and Thomas Oelschläger, "'Ich habe sie eines natürlichen Todes sterben lassen,'" in *Die Idee der Bildbarkeit*, ed. Christian Schrapper and Dieter Sengling (Weinheim: Juventa, 1988), 330–35; Sandner, *Verwaltung des Krankenmordes*, 658–63; Martina Hartmann-Menz, "Ruth

Pappenheimer" and "Julius Pappenheimer," http://www.alemannia-judaica.de/images/Images%20342/Dornheim%20GG%20Ruth_Pappenheimer.pdf and http://www.alemannia-judaica.de/images/Images%20342/Dornheim%20Julius_Pappenheimer.pdf. I wish to thank Dr. Georg Lilienthal and Martina Hartmann-Menz for additional information.

38. See Jeremy Noakes, "The Development of Nazi Policy towards the German-Jewish 'Mischlinge' 1933–1945," *Leo Baeck Institute Yearbook* 34 (1989): 291–354; Beate Meyer, *"Jüdische Mischlinge,"* 3rd ed. (Hamburg: Dölling und Galitz, 2007); James F. Tent, *In the Shadow of the Holocaust* (Lawrence: University Press of Kansas, 2003); Nathan Stoltzfus, "The Limits of Policy: Social Protection of Intermarried German Jews in Nazi Germany," in *Social Outsiders in Nazi Germany*, ed. Robert Gellately and Nathan Stoltzfus (Princeton, N.J.: Princeton University Press), 117–44.

39. For the literature on this topic, see Susanne Scholz and Reinhard Singer, "Die Kinder von Hadamar," in *Psychiatrie und Faschismus*, 2nd ed., ed. Dorothee Roer and Dieter Henkel (Frankfurt: Mabuse, 1996), 229–36; Patricia Heberer, "'Exitus heute in Hadamar': The Hadamar Facility and 'Euthanasia' in Nazi Germany" (Ph.D. diss., University of Maryland, 2001), 426–35; Sandner, *Verwaltung des Krankenmordes*, 654–70; Monica Kingreen, "Jüdische Kranke als Patienten der Landesheilanstalt Hadamar (1909–1940) und als Opfer der Mordanstalt Hadamar (1941–1945)," in *Hadamar*, ed. Uta George et al. (Marburg, Ger.: Jonas, 2006), 189–215.

40. For Bernotat's office, see Sandner, *Verwaltung des Krankenmordes*, 657. The document is printed in Scholz and Singer, "Die Kinder von Hadamar," 231.

41. HHStA Wiesbaden 461/32061, Bd. 3, Bl. 119. See also Scholz and Singer, "Die Kinder von Hadamar," 230; Heberer, "'Exitus heute in Hadamar,'" 426–27; Sandner, *Verwaltung des Krankenmordes*, 659.

42. Sandner, *Verwaltung des Krankenmordes*, 660.

43. This was couched in language of "moral degeneracy." It is discussed in the broader context of nursing in Nazi Germany in Bronwyn R. McFarland-Icke, *Nurses in Nazi Germany: Moral Choice in History* (Princeton, N.J.: Princeton University Press, 1999).

44. Heberer, "'Exitus heute in Hadamar,'" 431–32.

45. See Scholz and Singer, "Die Kinder von Hadamar," 232.

46. I wish to thank Gerhard Jochem, city archive of Nuremberg, for providing information to me.

47. Joachim Klieme, *Ausgrenzung aus der NS-"Volksgemeinschaft"* (Braunschweig: Selbstverlag des Braunschweigischen Geschichtsvereins, 1997), 204–5.

48. The decree is paraphrased in a letter to the Eichberg asylum by the state youth office (Dr. Gauhl) dated October 1, 1943 (HHStA Wiesbaden

430/1 [Eichberg files], 12557). See also Sandner, *Verwaltung des Krankenmordes*, 662.

49. See LWV-Archiv Bestand 12 (Hadamar) AN 3608 and 5031.

50. Stoltzfus, "The Limits of Policy."

51. LWV-Archiv Bestand 12 (Hadamar) AN 5031.

52. Tent, *In the Shadow of the Holocaust*, 185–88 (quotations at 186, 187). I wish to thank the author for additional information.

53. Sandner, *Verwaltung des Krankenmordes*, 658; Heberer, "'Exitus heute in Hadamar,'" 434.

54. Heberer, "'Exitus heute in Hadamar,'" 431.

55. My current research concerns the biography of the victims and the fate of their Jewish parents. Many of the parents survived the Nazi period.

Hana Kubátová

Accusing and Demanding: Denunciations in Wartime Slovakia

"RESPECTABLE MR. MINISTER OF INTERIOR," WROTE PAVOL DUBEK FROM the eastern Slovakian town of Sečovce to Alexander Mach, a man in charge of both home affairs and the Hlinka Guard (HG),[1] in his letter from February 1942.[2] Dubek had moved to eastern Slovakia from the northern Orava region when his hometown, along with a number of other villages, was demolished to make space for what, more than ten years later, became one of the largest freshwater bodies in Central Europe. In his handwritten letter, Dubek asked the minister for a state loan to buy a house. His only other option was to ask a bank for an advance, but in that case, as he openly admitted, he would need to pay interest. Dubek requested that Minister Mach reply promptly because he needed to know if he "should rely on the bank or if I can rely on you." A postscript that Dubek appended to his letter filled two additional pages. Dubek's PS was more than a mere addition, and not only because of its length. Dubek sought to reassure the minister that he "reads newspapers and insists that the Jews disappear." There are too many Jews in Sečovce, wrote Dubek, and "they are still the masters." Dubek described how difficult life had become for Catholics in this border region, and confusing his wishes for the collective with what he probably desired for himself, he insisted, "As a member of the Hlinka Guard, I can see it in their eyes that the Catholics are impoverished very much and as a member of the Hlinka Guard I want to help the poor Catholic nation by getting one Jewish room for a lease."[3]

Dubek's comments open up a range of issues concerning Slovakian attitudes toward and actions against their Jewish neighbors. This article explores denunciations in wartime Slovakia, focusing on how individuals used them to bargain with the authorities over their share in the process of "limiting Jewish influence in the social and economic life of Slovakia." This phrasing soon became a euphemism standing for a wide range of discriminatory measures, including restricting Jewish employment in certain professions; confiscating Jewish farmland and forests; liquidating and seizing Jewish businesses; and selling personal property of deported Jews, including furniture, shoes, and clothing, at auctions. The state-sponsored looting of Jewish property in Slovakia, as explored further, reached its peak in the two so-called Aryanization laws of 1940. By the end of 1941, most Jewish-owned businesses were liquidated (84 percent, 9,935 cases) and the remainder were Aryanized, taken over by non-Jewish Slovaks for what was often a below-market value (16 percent, 1,888 cases).[4] As I argue, the ease with which these and other measures against the approximately eighty-nine-thousand-member Slovak Jewish community were carried out was due in large part to the widespread acceptance of yet another aspect of the earlier quoted euphemism: that the Jewish question was to be "solved" to the benefit of the majority society.[5] The focus of this article is hence on denunciatory letters in which its writers not only *accused* but also *made demands*. In what follows, I understand denunciations in line with Sheila Fitzpatrick's and Robert Gellately's definition—that is, as "spontaneous communications from individual citizens to the state (or to another authority such as the church) containing accusations of wrongdoing by other citizens or officials and implicitly or explicitly calling for punishment."[6]

Persecution of Jews, as Frank Bajohr has shown with respect to the National Socialist dictatorship, indeed "functioned to activate an array of interests that could never have been satisfied under the rule of constitutional law. Denunciations by informers were a striking manifestation of the pursuit of such interests, because as a rule they meshed with highly personal motivations."[7] Additionally, as Tatjana Tönsmeyer has demonstrated, in Slovakia, similar to Hungary and Romania, the activation of interests was further strengthened by the fact that the administrations in Bratislava, Budapest, and Bucharest presented the distribution of Jewish property "as a 'social policy,' taking things from 'rich Jews' and handing them over to 'poor Hungarians' (and Slovaks and Romanians)."[8] With this in mind, my article aims to complicate what we know of the interactions between state and society in nondemocratic settings. It does so by exploring how individuals in Slovakia took advantage of the persecution of Jews, demanding a share of the loot while not being shy about putting pressure on the authorities. Hence, by studying denunciations, I wish to disentangle the complex web of ties between the nondemocratic regime of wartime Slovakia and its "little people," as many writers, at least in the cases I examine, called themselves.

Whether handwritten or typed, signed or anonymous, denunciatory letters that I examine here have at least three things in common. First, their authors usually requested a certain action or involvement by the state and used antisemitism in an instrumental manner to manifest their loyalty to the regime and support their case. Second, because of the authoritarian (rather than totalitarian, when compared with Nazi Germany) character of the regime, writers not only regularly complained about the corruption and incompetence of politicians and state employees on both the local and district levels, but also—what I find particularly interesting—dared to criticize the regime as such. They did so, to be clear, not because they disapproved of the regime's character or its actions against the Jews (or Czechs and Roma, for that matter) but rather because, third, they demanded that those in power keep their promise: to make the majority society benefit from the Jewish persecution.

Within wartime Slovakia, denunciations were often sent directly to party officials, especially Alexander Mach, who represented the radical wing in both the state-party and the government. My sample here consists of cases mostly from Sečovce, a town where Pavol Dubek lived, and Topoľčany, in the western part of the country. These cases are complemented by examples drawn from other parts of Slovakia.

The Slovak Jewish population was far from homogenous.[9] A sizable component of the Jewish population living in the eastern part of Slovakia was Hasidic, comprised of people who migrated to Slovakia from today's Poland and Ukraine during World War I.[10] Eastern Slovakia, in particular, was a poor region, and its Jewish population was also among the poorest in the country. The Jewish community in Sečovce, predating World War I, was one of the oldest in Slovakia, with its roots probably in the early Middle Ages. Most of its members were strictly Orthodox but not Hasidic, counting more than 1,000 Jews (about 25 percent of the general population) at the beginning of World War II.[11] Compared with the Jews of eastern Slovakia, the Jews of Topoľčany in the Nitra region were relatively well off. As

Yehoshua R. Büchler (Buechler), originally from Topoľčany himself, writes, they "had long been involved in city life, held senior positions on the town council, and made a decisive contribution to the town's economy and prosperity."[12] Almost 1,400 Jews (about 30 percent of the population) lived in Topoľčany in 1900.[13] According to the 1940 census, 2,459 Jews lived in the Topoľčany district, most of them residing in the city itself.[14] Unlike most Jewish communities in the Hungarian Kingdom, of which Slovakia was a part until 1918, there was no religious split in Topoľčany, and most of its Jews remained Orthodox.

Personal motivations rather than hatred or ideology were behind many of the individuals' "spontaneous communications" with the state. As we have encountered in the case of Pavol Dubek, he does not appear to have been so much interested in the disappearance of "the Jews," nor did he really feel concern for the "poor Catholic nation." While making numerous references to his membership in the Hlinka Guard and interspersing his letter with anti-Jewish statements, Dubek came to the point on the fourth and final page of his written plea: "We are requesting house number 454; there is enough space; and I demand that the Jews restrain themselves, one room should be plenty for them."[15] There is no indication in the files whether Dubek received an answer from Alexander Mach. About a month later, deportations of Jews from Slovakia began. The first in line were Jews from eastern Slovakia. On March 25, 1942, a thousand young women and girls were herded in freight trains and deported to Auschwitz. Altogether almost fifty-eight thousand Slovak Jews were deported between March and October 1942 in fifty-seven transports; nineteen of the trains were dispatched to Auschwitz, and thirty-eight trains were sent to the Lublin district in the General Government.[16] By the time Dubek's letter reached the office of Minister Mach, his Jewish neighbors probably were already murdered.

In April 1942, in the wake of that first deportation wave, Mach received another letter from someone calling himself (or herself) "the accuser." The otherwise anonymous writer accuses a fellow countryman of "un-Slovak, un-our, un-patriotic" behavior. The man whom the letter writer identified by both his name and his occupation allegedly was "a guardian of the Jews and received fur, money, gold, silver and other valuable things from them." This man was accused of being under "Jewish influence," of helping Jews hide their belongings, and even of conducting business with Jews at the expense of the "skilled and bold Slovaks." In return, according to this letter writer, the Jews helped him avoid military service by bribing the authorities. "The accuser" needed to remain anonymous because, as explained to Mach, he or she was afraid that the local administration was also under "their"—that is, Jewish—influence. And similar to Pavol Dubek, this writer also requested prompt action from the minister: "You will agree with me when you read this, Mr. Minister, it is immoral and unjust, and I request, I respectfully ask you, I want to say, if you could, based on your conscience and fair decision, intervene immediately and order a swift correction."[17]

Both letters quoted here are but two examples of a vast correspondence addressed to Slovak local and district authorities between 1939 and 1945; to the State Security Headquarters (Ústredňa štátnej bezpečnosti, or ÚŠB), which was modeled on the Gestapo; or personally to Minister Mach as well as other representatives of the wartime regime, including their wives. When it comes to wartime Slovakia, denunciations have largely been seen as a product of the regime's final phase, when the Germans occupied Slovakia following their suppression of the Slovak National Uprising, an armed insurrection against the Nazis and the collaborating government in Bratislava, in October 1944. For Ivan Kamenec, a pioneering historian of the Holocaust in Slovakia, what characterized this "last act of the tragedy," as he refers to the period between fall 1944 and spring 1945, was an intensification of attitudes toward the Jews. What he is pointing to is the fact that the lives of the approximately ten thousand Jews who survived the end of the war in Slovakia using false identities or staying in hiding depended, in one way or another, on assistance from the majority society. Many majority Slovaks, however, saw this "last act" of the war also as their last chance to enrich themselves at the expense of Jews, and they denounced many Jews to both German and Slovak authorities.[18] To rephrase Kamenec's observation, the intensification manifested itself not only in increased rescue activities but also in escalated looting of Jewish properties and belongings. While denunciations were particularly dangerous following the suppression of the Slovak National Uprising, they were present and actively used as a way of communication and even extortion throughout the existence of the wartime state. As I show here, denunciations became a popular means of accessing power also in the course of the subsequently examined Aryanization process.

Although no specific law existed in Slovakia ordering denunciations, state agencies encouraged and relied on information "from below." The State Security Headquarters, for example, seemed to devote the same attention to gossip and unsolicited information as it did to accounts written by its in-house detectives. No wonder, considering the relatively low number of people who worked for the Slovak version of the Gestapo. After hiring about forty new people at the end of 1940 and a few more at the beginning of the next year, in early 1941, the ÚŠB still had only 123 employees, almost a third of whom were office workers and assistants.[19] Informers such as Pavol Dubek or the anonymous "accuser" supplemented the web of confidants the ÚŠB used and misused for maintaining order and perpetuating fear in Slovak society. The main difference between informers and confidants was that while the first acted on their own initiative, confidants relied on official instructions.

The ÚŠB distinguished among three types of confidants based on their incentive and level of involvement: ideologically driven "confidants of conviction," pragmatically motivated "professional confidants," and sporadically forthcoming "occasional confidants" whose irregular delivery of information to the ÚŠB did not allow for a more detailed classification based on motivation. The "confidants of conviction" were seen as the most reliable as they were driven by "idealism and conviction." If their primary motivation was the belief that what they were doing was right, the stimulus for the second type of confidants, "professional confidants," was more down to earth: money. While this second group—also referred to as "craftsmen" for their joblike approach—was most eager to deliver information, the ÚŠB cautioned that "professional confidants" may have a tendency to report more than they actually know so as not to lose their source of income. Nevertheless, the ÚŠB did not regard confidants' reliance on some kind of compensation for their activities—whether financial or professional, by securing steady employment for the informer, for instance—as negative per se. Rather, the ÚŠB saw the relationship that developed between them and the "professional confidants" as a model that could be extended to the third group, the "occasional confidants," transforming them into those more valuable "confidants of conviction."[20]

The ÚŠB relied on "ordinary people" in composing its monthly situational reports regarding the mood and attitude of the general population. Situational reports contain numerous references to "whisper propaganda" (*šuškaná propaganda*), rumors, information learned from illegal leaflets that individuals handed over to the authorities, and anonymous letters.[21] Often those reports did not disclose their sources and were written from an omniscient point of view ("it is known" or "people think"). It appears that situational reports often presented the actual or likely views of their authors rather than the general public and, what is more, that in many cases they were entirely or partially fabricated. Nevertheless, references to a "confidant's report" suggest that the ÚŠB relied on information gained through different (spontaneous or less so) channels of communication with the public.[22]

In their public pronouncements, Alexander Mach and numerous other politicians encouraged people to notify state agencies about any wrongdoings they might have witnessed. Some authors of denunciatory letters in my sample also make direct reference to Mach's statements in this regard. Archival files of the Ministry of Interior, the State Security Headquarters, and also postwar retribution trials, to which I will turn later, are flooded with denunciations, as are newspapers and periodicals published during the six-year existence of the wartime state. Many articles in the two main periodicals *Slovák* and *Gardista* were interspersed with statements such as "We have received a letter," or "People from Bardejov ask."[23] Police reports often began with a sentence to the effect: "I have received information from a trusted source" or "according to a reliable source."[24] Denunciations were so widespread, they even became a topic of sermons. Vojtech Šulko, a parish administrator in Boleráz, a small town near Nitra, used harsh words to describe the current situation among his parishioners in one of his December 1940 sermons: "people report [on each other], slander, denounce, put [others] in jail and who knows if such a person does not end up on the gallows himself."[25] It seems probable that someone subsequently reported the parish administrator for his pronouncing those very words since, on the following Sunday, Šulko announced that he was being "discharged at his own request."[26] The omnipresent denunciations were a form of what Jan T. Gross has called the "privatization of the public domain." It gave those without any formal power the means of participating in the application of coercion and terror.[27] In Slovakia, denunciations became an almost everyday practice, a routine, nothing-out-of-the-ordinary exercise that extended well beyond the end of the war. They symbolized, to borrow the words of Sheila Fitzpatrick and Robert Gellately once again, "an *Alltag* of popular collaboration."[28]

"BALANCING" JEWISH INFLUENCE THROUGH DENUNCIATIONS

"Jews play a disproportionally large role when compared to their numbers," said Prime Minister (later President) Jozef Tiso[29] to foreign journalists in January 1939, and he elaborated on the future steps he planned to take: "It is therefore necessary to bring their participation in the economic and cultural life of Slovakia in balance with their percentage in the population."[30] From very early on, official propaganda made a strong connection between the regime, its anti-Jewish measures, and the social standing of the majority population. Work on "limiting the Jewish influence in the social and economic life of the country" began only a few weeks after the establishment of an "independent" Slovakia in March 1939. The first governmental definition of "a Jew" included provisions that restricted Jewish employment in various professions.[31] Jewish lawyers were among the first targeted groups. Their number was now not to exceed 4 percent of all members of the chamber of advocates. Jews working as physicians, pharmacists, engineers, veterinarians, and state employees were next.[32]

From a socioeconomic standpoint, as Ezra Mendelssohn and Robert Buechler suggest, Jews of Slovakia resembled their Czech rather than their sub-Carpathian counterparts in many crucial aspects but one. While many Slovak Jews, like those living in the Bohemian lands, tended to work in the nonagricultural economy (especially in the free professions, but also in handicrafts, industry, and finance), their role was much more conspicuous given the virtually nonexistent ethnic Slovak bourgeois class. Forty percent of Jews, compared with 5 percent of majority Slovaks, worked in business and finance in prewar Slovakia. Even in the late 1930s, 40 percent of doctors in Slovakia were of Jewish origin.[33] These proportions were what led Slovak political elites to "correct," or "balance," alleged Jewish influence in the country's economy.

"Balancing" Jewish influence was not the only way by which the new Slovakian leadership envisioned tackling the Jewish question. The Jewish question seemed to play a disproportionately large role in the political life of the country, at least considering the relatively small size, in numbers and from a comparative perspective, of the Jewish community in Slovakia. Disparate views on how the Jewish question should actually be "solved" divided the government and the state-party. While the conservative (or moderate) wing, including Tiso, advocated a proportionate approach, the radical wing of Alexander Mach and Vojtech Tuka looked to Nazi Germany for inspiration.

As most of Slovakia's two and a half million inhabitants were Roman Catholics, propaganda explained anti-Jewish laws as in accordance with Catholic doctrine. In May 1939, for example, a professor of theology at the Slovak (today Comenius) University, Štefan Zlatoš, justified discriminatory acts against Jews as both necessary and Christian. They were adopted, explained Zlatoš, not out of hatred but to repair old wrongs: "To correct the injustices and wrongdoings of the past, that is the duty of the authority also with regard to the Jewish question."[34] Himself a Catholic priest, President Tiso enjoyed considerable popular support. However, holding both a lay and a clerical office put Tiso in a difficult position as he tried to reconcile antisemitism with the church teaching on loving one's neighbor.[35] Tiso's dual role is crucial for explaining the Holocaust in Slovakia, especially as he relied on religious or pseudoreligious arguments to authorize the systematic discrimination of Jews. Tiso did not make many significant statements on Aryanization as such, but even in the few he did make, his message was clear. In September 1940, he proclaimed, "Moses, for example, ordered all assets to be returned to original owners after 50 years. Everything the Jew accumulated in 50 years he needed to return. But the Jews have forgotten this. They did not comply with the Law of Moses but followed the Talmud and other obscure books that they keep secret about. The Talmud praises the Jews for cheating a goy. So we will atone for their actions and take back what they stole."[36] In other words, according to Tiso's logic, discriminating against Jews was a Christian act insofar as the government was only taking back what the Jews had originally taken from the Slovak people. Such an argument was at the core of how the regime rationalized its anti-Jewish politics. Tiso used the same arguments repeatedly, injecting further theological justifications into the mix.

A significant step in the "Aryanization of Slovak life," as the propaganda dubbed the various discriminatory laws against Jews, occurred in July 1939 when the revision of trade licenses became contingent on "social reasons" or because of "public interest."[37] While the reasons given for revoking a trade license were arbitrary, official sources were more forthcoming in their articulation of the objective behind this governmental decree. As the periodical *Slovák* put it, "this decree will significantly improve the situation [. . .] for Aryan traders."[38] What Jews stood to lose, Slovaks would gain. The same twisted logic undergirded the long-awaited Aryanization law. In late March 1940, two months before the promulgation of the law itself, a six-day-long course of instruction for 150 future Aryanizers was organized by one of Bratislava's schools of higher learning. Minister of Economy Gejza Medrický took part in the opening ceremony, and he praised the initiative in his address to the crowd of eager Aryanizers: "The aim of the new government is to remove the disproportionate and undesirable involvement of Jews in the economy—the Jewish element should be replaced by a new generation of Slovak entrepreneurs."[39]

Work on the first Aryanization law had begun in October 1939 but did not take effect until June 1940. The Hlinka Slovak People's Party periodical *Slovák* welcomed its introduction with headlines "Justice for Christians" and "Slovaks Take Over Jewish Businesses."[40] Somewhat paradoxically, however, the law had to be abandoned after three months, for two main reasons. First, the mostly incompetent people entrusted with carrying out the Aryanization measures lacked an elementary understanding of business and monetary means, and they constituted a key weak spot in the process from the very beginning. Second, Aryanization was interrupted by the July 1940 German–Slovak talks that led to a reorganization of the government, the introduction of a so-called Slovak (or Christian) National Socialism, and a further radicalization of anti-Jewish politics.

Even if it had not been interrupted, the limited effect of this law could not have satisfied the hunger for Aryanization that the propaganda encouraged. On the contrary, as I have argued elsewhere, situational reports suggest that the Aryanization of Jewish property was awaited with great expectations.[41] Indeed, a more radical attempt to satisfy the Slovak population with Jewish property was in the offing. The implementation of a Slovak National Socialism was closely associated with the radicalization of anti-Jewish politics. That radicalization took the form, most explicitly, of an immediately renewed Aryanization process, as well as the introduction of the so-called Jewish Codex, a series of anti-Jewish laws adopted in September 1941, and the 1942 deportations.

A month before the more radical version of the Aryanization law was adopted in November 1940, Alexander Mach publicly admitted that the first attempt had failed because the process had been paralyzed by cheating and swindles. He was nevertheless full of optimism and promised that new guidelines would enable people "to continue fairly in the Aryanizations."[42] This second attempt at Aryanization, however, proved that membership in the Hlinka Slovak People's Party or the Hlinka Guard and political ties and influential friends were more important than skills and experience. The roughly two thousand new Aryanizers did not become the showcase of how the regime's "solving of the Jewish question" would benefit the Christian Slovaks. On the contrary, they became a symbol of corruption and incompetence.

DEMANDING A SHARE OF THE LOOT FOR THE "LITTLE SLOVAKS"

In the context of the here outlined Aryanization process, many of those approaching Minister Mach voiced their concern that the "little Slovak" was being left out when Jewish belongings were seized and redistributed. In August 1940, for example, Mach received a letter from a school caretaker, Ján Smiško, in Michalovce, a town in the vicinity of Sečovce. Smiško criticized the Aryanization process for feeding only the upper class in his hometown. He clearly saw this as both unhealthy and unfair and bluntly asked, "Wouldn't also the poorer [people] like to take over these businesses?" He and many others were putting their faith in Mach, wrote Smiško, and warned him, "People are waiting, but they need actual businesses, not promises."[43] The offense about which Smiško and others complained to Mach was that the Aryanization measures, understood here in the broadest sense as the sum of all laws that discriminated against Jews economically, were unjust. As Smiško understood it, this unfairness stemmed not from the fact that the measures were tantamount to an act of mass robbery but rather from his perception that he himself was not receiving his share of the loot.

Often when women complained to the authorities, they approached the wives of prominent Slovak politicians, including that of Alexander Mach. In one such letter from late March 1942, the twenty-three-year-old administrative assistant Margita Morbacherová complained to Alžbeta Machová, the wife of the minister, that the new regime established in 1939 had failed in its promise to give poor people who did not have anyone to pull strings for them the opportunities they so desperately needed. After explaining her family's social situation in great detail, she proceeded to the objective of her letter and asked Machová for clothes to wear during the upcoming Easter holiday: "I hear that they are taking many things from the Jews nowadays and I am sure this includes women's suits, underwear and coats, and I would like to ask [that you] take something of this kind from one rich Jewish woman and give it to a poor but brave clerk who will appreciate this greatly and forever pray for the humanitarian who helped save her from her poverty."[44] As Morbacherová's letter shows, both men and women resorted to denunciations, adjusting their language and carefully picking the addressee of their petition to maximize their chances of getting what they wanted.

What letters addressed to the Slovak authorities and those to their wives had in common was not only that they included indignant outbursts about how the regime had left out poor Slovaks who actually "needed" Jewish belongings and instead given those belongings to people with political connections but also that they demanded action in this regard and, what is more, threatened to contact superior authorities if their petitions and protests did not receive proper attention. Letters addressed to Mach often included complaints that the local administration had not heard them out. When reporting a real or alleged crime, some plaintiffs threatened the addressees of their letters that they would not be afraid to contact the Germans if the Slovak authorities did not respond appropriately. In January 1943, for example, the Topoľčany district office received an anonymous letter claiming that a local wealthy man was protecting a Jewish woman by employing her under false papers. The unnamed letter writer denounced not only the Jewish woman but also numerous others, including local police who were supposedly not wise enough to get to the bottom of the issue: "Please resolve this problem in accordance with today's law because if you will not do so, we will report it to the Germans and they will deal with the matter properly and thoroughly."[45] Another anonymous letter delivered to the State Security Headquarters in July 1941, written in the name of "we the members of the Hlinka Guard and all Slovaks," denounced local Jews for behaving provocatively and being Communists, and it also denounced "white Jews" for allegedly protecting the Jews.[46] This letter also included a critique of the local administration: "What we would like, and we believe that this would be for the good of our whole country, is if you could finally settle this matter because we have already addressed the district office but nothing was done."[47] The authoritarian nature of the regime in Slovakia allowed for this harsh critique, making the denunciatory letters not only accusations but also real threats—to the Jews and to the authorities.

Many of the denunciatory letters used antisemitism to strengthen their cause. Writers often inserted anti-Jewish statements and allegations in their letters in such an arbitrary fashion that officials complained that they could not understand what the petitioner was actually protesting. In early 1942, for example, the Topoľčany district office received an unsigned letter in which the author objected to the behavior of a local stationmaster. In its official report to the stationmaster's superior at the Ministry of Transportation, the district office claimed that it could not identify the problem, as the writer accused the stationmaster of being "a hooligan, thug, a Jew-lover but also a despot to the Jews."[48]

As it turns out, the hatred and envy of many denunciatory letters was actually directed at those who had the necessary connections to take possession of Jewish businesses in the extremely corrupt Aryanization process. In May 1944, not long before the outbreak of the Slovak National Uprising, Alexander Mach received yet another denunciatory and anonymous letter.[49] The writer began his four-page letter by claiming that his objective was to "write something about the Jews and to point out that the Jewish plague is still living very nicely and comfortably and continues doing its dirty business."[50] In reality, however, this anonymous letter was reaching the interior minister after most Slovakian Jews had already been deported, which occurred between March and October 1942. Nevertheless, the writer lamented the fact that the wood-processing sector was employing the highest number of Jews. He then proceeded to outline the situation in four lumber companies located in different parts of the country, all four of which had been taken over by Christian Slovaks. This writer disclosed the names of the previous owners as well as the new Aryanizers and elaborated, in great detail, about each company, the background of the new owners, and the positions of the former Jewish owners and employees. And while he criticized the new "Aryan" owners for obtaining exemptions for the original Jewish owners, interposing this criticism with anti-Jewish sayings—"You cannot make bacon out of a dog or a mutton out of a wolf, and so a Jew will never be a Christian or a good Slovak, never!"—it does not appear that this was his main point. Rather, what the writer demanded was his share of the loot yielded by the Aryanization measures, no matter the cost. In his words, "how many good, courageous and loyal Slovaks would be even better off [if the remaining Jews disappeared]?"[51]

The motivations behind the denunciatory letters examined here may seem obvious. After all, none of them made much of an attempt to camouflage what they *really* wanted. Often they were quite specific, pointing directly to what they were after. References to their membership in the party or in the Hlinka Guard, reassurances that they stood on the "right" side, anti-Jewish statements, all constituted part of a discourse they had learned to adopt in order to advance their cause. The case of two brothers, Michal and Ján Havrila, further illustrates my point here.

In May 1942, as most Jews of eastern Slovakia were being deported, Michal Havrila had written to Alexander Mach and demanded radical measures against both the Jews and the "white Jews" who protected them: "A radical cut with the Jews was expected especially in the East but we were disappointed. Not one of those Jews who should be in the camps is there." Michal had a white-collar job in Bratislava, but his brother Ján had Aryanized a beer warehouse in Sečovce. Michal seems to have been concerned for his brother because Ján had not been able to get rid of the former Jewish owner of the warehouse, Henrich Hecht. Michal insisted that his brother did not need the man anymore, that he knew how to run the business alone. However, Hecht remained on because he had an important friend, the director of a brewery in Michalovce. The latter was a typical "white Jew," wrote Michal, who accused this man of working tirelessly in order for Hecht to keep his work permit (and thus also a chance to survive).[52] About two months later and in a similar manner, Ján Havrila approached Anton Vašek. Vašek was nicknamed "king of the Jews" for his position as chief of Department 14 in the Interior Ministry, the section of the ministry in charge of the deportations. Writing even more straightforwardly, Ján asked Vašek to approve "deporting from Sečovce the Jew Henrich Hecht, from whom I took over property, and his wife. This Jew undermined the functioning of my company, and Mr. Dr. Nosáľ, director of the brewery in Michalovce, forces me to employ him against my will. I am against the employment of a Jew and therefore please order his immediate transportation so that I can finally feel at peace."[53]

After the war, Michal Havrila was charged with collaboration.

While there is no indication in the files that Ján Havrila was prosecuted as well, the fact that Hecht remained employed in July 1942—when Ján wrote to Vašek—was probably what got Michal acquitted. In a verdict's reasoning that is hard to understand, the court found no correlation between Michal Havrila's letter to Mach and the subsequent deportation and death of Hecht and his family.[54] With similar twisted logic, Michal was acquitted also of the second charge because "the accused sent the incriminating letter by mail, not publicly, and thus it cannot be alleged that the accused publicly approved of the activities of collaborators." When questioned, Michal maintained his innocence, but considering that both his and his brother's letters were on file, he could not deny their authenticity. Michal Havrila rested his defense on the fact that he wrote the letter to save himself from the denunciations written by a district chief of the Hlinka Slovak People's Party, which accused Michal of being "a Judeo-Bolshevik, a white Jew, a Czechoslovak and that I raised my family in a Hungarian spirit."[55] In other words, Michal Havrila claimed that his letter was only a response to the fact that the district chief and the director of the brewery wanted to give Hecht's warehouse to someone else.

Interestingly, however, while refusing any responsibility for Hecht's deportation, nowhere does Michal Havrila admit that the business he sought to protect for his brother had originally been stolen from its rightful owner. And while there are many things to be learned about this case and the motivation of its actors, it seems fair to say that the main issue for the parties to the trial was a fight over loot. Henrich Hecht was not important. "The Jew" was a burdensome witness, someone over whom neither Michal nor Ján Havrila lost any sleep. What mattered was the property, not the fate of the man himself. From a postwar perspective, going already beyond the scope of this paper, it seems that not much changed in the perceptions of the two brothers.

CONCLUSION

The authoritarian regime of wartime Slovakia encouraged the majority society to inform Slovak officials about any wrongdoings they might have witnessed. The regime depended on "spontaneous communications," including denunciations, to monitor and shape the mood and attitude in the society. Denunciations became something of a national sport, a part of everyday experience, giving the "little people" a role to play in coercion and terror. For a significant part of its existence, the wartime Slovak state could rely on the rather wide loyalty of its people. Unlike in the Protectorate of Bohemia and Moravia, Slovakia's regime was largely perceived as legitimate.[56] Propaganda encouraged a vision of a state that was finally "ours," liberated from the oppressive Hungarians and Czechs. And it was this state, it promised, that would take away Jewish belongings and distribute them to Slovak non-Jews in need. Religious arguments lent further legitimacy to the fable they constructed about Aryanization as the rightful return of property to Christian Slovaks. As I argue, the strongest tie between the non-democratic regime and its majority population was the Aryanization process—or, to be more precise, the promise that people would benefit from the state-sponsored robbery of Jewish belongings. Denunciatory letters sent directly to party officials, especially Alexander Mach, show that the government's promise to feed its people with Jewish property was not only believed in but also clamored for. Additionally, as this article confirms, the persecution of Jews activated not only popular interest in getting a share of the loot but also fascination with coercion and power. The rule of government in 1939–1945 Slovakia enabled both of these interests to be acted on. In a larger context of "spontaneous communications" between society and state that took place throughout Nazi-controlled but also Nazi-allied Europe, widespread denunciations confirm that popular consensus was what bound the majority societies together.[57]

NOTES

This article was written as part of the project PRIMUS/HUM/12, "Beyond Hegemonic Narratives and Myths. Troubled Pasts in the History and Memory of East-Central & South-East Europe."

1. Officially set up in October 1938, the Hlinka Guard (Hlinkova garda) was a paramilitary organization of the Hlinka Slovak Peoples' Party (Hlinkova slovenská ľudová strana). The HG played a pivotal role in the 1942 deportations of Slovakian Jews.

2. Pavol Dubek to Alexander Mach, February 16, 1942, Slovak National Archive (SNA), Fund Ministerstvo vnútra (MV), Box 703, File 2. Translations of all quotations from sources in these archives are mine.

3. Ibid.

4. Tatjana Tönsmeyer, "The Robbery of Jewish Property in Eastern

European States Allied with Nazi Germany," in *Robbery and Restitution: The Conflict over Jewish Property in Europe*, ed. Martin Dean, Constantin Goschler, and Philipp Ther (Oxford: Berghahn Books, 2007), 81–96; Martin Dean, *Robbing the Jews: The Confiscation of Jewish Property in the Holocaust, 1933–1945* (Cambridge: Cambridge University Press, 2010), 317–24.

5. For more on how denunciations diminished the chances of rescuing Slovakian Jews, see Nina Paulovičová, "Rescue of Jews in the Slovak State (1939–1945)" (Ph.D. diss., University of Alberta, 2012), http://hdl.handle.net/10402/era.25987.

6. Sheila Fitzpatrick and Robert Gellately, "Introduction to the Practices of Denunciation in Modern European History," *Journal of Modern History* 68, no. 4 (1996): 747.

7. Frank Bajohr, "The 'Folk Community' and the Persecution of the Jews: German Society under National Socialist Dictatorship, 1933–1945," *Holocaust and Genocide Studies* 20, no. 2 (2006): 191.

8. Tönsmeyer, "Robbery of Jewish Property," 90.

9. According to the 1930 census, there were 356,830 Jews (or "Israelites," as the statistics office called those of Jewish religion) in Czechoslovakia, and 136,736 of them lived in Slovakia. As a result of the November 1938 Vienna Arbitration, Czechoslovakia lost largely Magyar-populated regions of southern Slovakia and sub-Carpathian Ruthenia to Hungary, including approximately 40,000 Jews. According to the 1940 census, approximately 89,000 Jews lived in Slovakia. See Bruno Blau, "Nationality among Czechoslovak Jewry," *Historica Judaica* 10 (1948): 147–54; Kateřina Čapková, *Czechs, Germans, Jews: National Identity and the Jews of Bohemia* (New York: Berghahn Books, 2012), 26–55; Rebekah Klein-Pejšová, *Mapping Jewish Loyalties in Interwar Slovakia* (Bloomington: Indiana University Press, 2015), 115–42; Eduard Nižňanský, *Židovská komunita na Slovensku medzi československou parlamentnou demokraciou a slovenským štátom v stredoeurópskom kontexte* (Prešov, Slovakia: Universum, 1999), 14–15.

10. Yehudah Don and Viktor Karády, *A Social and Economic History of Central European Jewry* (Piscataway, N.J.: Transaction Publishers, 1989), 210; Klein-Pejšová, *Mapping Jewish Loyalties in Interwar Slovakia*, 93–94.

11. Eugen Bárkány and Ľudovít Dojč, *Židovské náboženské obce na Slovensku* (Bratislava: Vesna, 1991), 421–24.

12. Yehoshua Robert Büchler, "Reconstruction Efforts in Hostile Surroundings—Slovaks and Jews after World War II," in *The Jews Are Coming Back: The Return of the Jews to Their Countries of Origin after WWII*, ed. David Bankier (New York: Berghahn Books; Jerusalem: Yad Vashem, 2005), 264.

13. Bárkány and Dojč, *Židovské náboženské obce na Slovensku*, 207.

14. Yehoshua Robert Büchler, *The Story and Source of the Jewish Com-*

munity of Topoltchany (Israel: Committee for Commemorating the Jewish Community for Topoltchany and Vicinity, 1976), 6.

15. Dubek to Mach.

16. Yehoshua Büchler, "The Deportation of Slovakian Jews to the Lublin District of Poland in 1942," *Holocaust and Genocide Studies* 6, no. 2 (1991): 151–66.

17. Anonymous letter addressed to Mach, April 4, 1942, SNA, MV, Box 703, File 2.

18. Ivan Kamenec, *Po stopách tragédie* (Bratislava: Archa, 1991), 274. For an English translation, see Ivan Kamenec, *On the Trail of Tragedy: The Holocaust in Slovakia*, trans. Martin Styan (Bratislava: H&H, 2007).

19. Matěj Medvecký, *Spravodajské eso slovenského štátu: Kauza Imrich Suchý* (Bratislava: Ústav pamäti národa, 2007), 28.

20. Ibid., 34–35.

21. Situational reports from Trnava and Martin, SNA, Fund Ústredňa štátnej bezpečnosti (ÚŠB), Box 773, Files 1, 3, 12.

22. Situational reports from Martin, SNA, ÚŠB, Box 773, File 12.

23. "Na Hornej Orave treba radikálne riešiť židovskú otázku!" *Slovák,* October 17, 1939, 4; "Hoden je Žid súcitu? Odpoveď pre tých, ktorým je Židov ľúto, " *Gardista,* August 26, 1939, 7. Translations of all quotations from these two periodicals are mine.

24. Anti-Jewish measures—instructions, SNA, ÚŠB, Box 865, File 5; SNA, ÚŠB, Box 715, File 43.

25. Situational reports from Trnava, SNA, ÚŠB, Box 773, File 2.

26. Ibid.

27. Jan T. Gross, "A Note on the Nature of Soviet Totalitarianism," *Soviet Studies Soviet Studies* 34, no. 3 (1982): 367–76.

28. Fitzpatrick and Gellately, "Practices of Denunciation," 756.

29. Jozef Tiso (1887–1947) held the office of the prime minister between October 1938 and October 1939, when he was elected president, a position he retained until his capture and imprisonment in April 1945. Throughout his political career, Tiso regularly celebrated Sunday masses in his parish in Bánovce nad Bebravou.

30. "Úlohy slovenskej propagandy," *Slovák*, January 27, 1939, 3.

31. *Slovenský zákonník*, 1939, governmental decree 63/1939, Sl. z.

32. Ladislav Lipscher, *Židia v slovenskom štátě: 1939–1945* (Bratislava: Print-Servis, 1992), 39–40.

33. Ezra Mendelsohn, *The Jews of East Central Europe between the World Wars* (Bloomington: Indiana University Press, 1983), 145; Robert Buechler, "The Jewish Community in Slovakia before World War II," in *The Tragedy of the Jews of Slovakia: 1938–1945 ; Slovakia and the "Final Solution of the Jewish Question,"* ed. Wacław Długoborski et al. (Oświęcim, Poland:

Auschwitz-Birkenau State Museum; Banská Bystrica, Slovakia: Museum of the Slovak National Uprising, 2002), 11–36.

34. "Kresťanská spravodlivosť a židovský zákon," *Slovák*, May 7, 1939, 4.

35. James Mace Ward, *Priest, Politician, Collaborator: Jozef Tiso and the Making of Fascist Slovakia* (Ithaca, N.Y.: Cornell University Press, 2013), 215.

36. Miroslav Fabricius and Katarína Hradská, eds., *Jozef Tiso: Prejavy a články (1938–1944)* (Bratislava: AEP, 2007), 277. Translations of all quotations from sources in this volume are mine.

37. *Slovenský zákonník*, 1939, governmental decree 40/1939, Sl. z.

38. "Revízia živnostenských licencií," *Slovák*, July 13, 1939, 1.

39. "Slováci preberú židovské podniky," *Slovák*, March 27, 1940, 4.

40. "Spravodlivosť pre kresťanov," *Slovák*, March 2, 1940, 1; "Slováci preberú židovské podniky."

41. Hana Kubátová, *Nepokradeš! Nálady a postoje slovenské společnosti k židovské otázce, 1938–1945* (Prague: Academia, 2013); Hana Kubátová, "Popular Responses to the Plunder of Jewish Property in Wartime Slovakia," *Jewish Studies at the CEU* 7 (2013): 109–26.

42. "Čoskoro vyjdú nové smernice pre arizáciu," *Gardista*, September 19, 1940, 3.

43. Ján Smiško to Alexander Mach, August 2, 1940, SNA, MV, Box 703, File 2.

44. Margita Morbacherová to Alžbeta Machová, March 30, 1942, SNA, MV, Box 703, File 2.

45. Anonymous letter addressed to the Topoľčany district office, undated, State Archive in Nitra, Topoľčany branch (SA Topoľčany), Fund Okresný úrad Topoľčany (OÚT), Box 126, File 183/43.

46. A widely used derogatory term of the period, the label "white Jew" could have been applied to any and all non-Jews who sympathized with the plight of the Jews.

47. Anonymous letter (signed as "Guardists from Michalovce") addressed to State Security Headquarters, undated, delivered on July 1, 1941, SNA, ÚŠB, Box 610, File 5.

48. Anonymous letter addressed to the Topoľčany district office, February 14, 1942, SA Topoľčany, OÚT, Box 116, File 220/42.

49. The letter itself was typed, but someone, probably the author himself (the letter is written in a masculine form), added a handwritten note on the first page: "I would be very pleased if also the renowned Mr. Minister could read this!"

50. Anonymous letter addressed to the Ministry of Interior, May 24, 1944, SNA, MV, Box 580, File 39.

51. Ibid.

52. Michal Havrila to Alexander Mach, May 1, 1942, State archive in Bratislava, Fund Okresný ľudový súd Bratislava, Box 50, File 108/47 (Michal Havrila).

53. Ján Havrila to Anton Vašek, July 21, 1942, State archive in Bratislava (SA Bratislava), Fund Okresný ľudový súd Bratislava (OĽS Bratislava), Box 50, File 108/47 (Michal Havrila).

54. While the precise date when the Hechts family was deported has not been established yet, it seems probable that they were transported to Auschwitz sometime between July and October 1942. See also "Henricht Hecht," The Central Database of Shoah Victims' Names, accessed February 13, 2018, https://yvng.yadvashem.org/nameDetails.html?language=en&itemId=371018&ind=5.

55. Michal Havrila's testimony, November 30, 1946, SA Bratislava, OĽS Bratislava, Box 50, File 108/47 (Michal Havrila)

56. Benjamin Frommer, *National Cleansing: Retribution against Nazi Collaborators in Postwar Czechoslovakia* (Cambridge: Cambridge University Press, 2005), 173–74.

57. Robert Gellately, *Backing Hitler: Consent and Coercion in Nazi Germany* (Oxford: Oxford University Press, 2001), 191–99.

Martin Dean

Jewish Survival in Forced Labor Camps for Jews: The Agricultural Camps in Czortków County of Eastern Galicia, 1942–1944

MORE THAN FIVE HUNDRED, MOSTLY YOUNGER JEWS (AGES TEN through forty-five), survived the Holocaust in a cluster of agricultural forced labor camps in Czortków County (in German, Kreis Czortkow) in Eastern Galicia.[1] Initially, these camps served as a refuge for hundreds of Jews during the brutal liquidation of the last remaining ghettos in the region in May and June of 1943. Run mostly by the Wehrmacht, the camps were permitted to exploit Jewish forced laborers, as the crop, a type of dandelion called kok-saghyz (used for the production of synthetic rubber), was viewed as vital to the German war effort. Nonetheless, German SS forces and local Ukrainian police killed hundreds of Jews in these camps in a series of organized raids in the summer and fall of 1943. Yet surprisingly, many Jews managed to evade the raids and then returned to continue working on the remaining estate camps, as it seemed to offer them the best chance of survival. The German military officials running the camps even gave assurances that the Jews would be protected and treated the Jewish workers reasonably well. In the last months of German occupation from late 1943, the main threats to the Jews were posed by the Ukrainian police and other armed groups, including local inhabitants, who raided the camps to rob and kill the inmates.

This little-known story of Jewish survival in rural Eastern Galicia challenges some assumptions about how Jews managed to survive the Holocaust. The number of Jews who survived in hiding in this area seems to have been much less than the number of those who survived by remaining in the camps. While survival through work has long been recognized as a key strategy for some of the larger ghettos and forced labor camps,[2] the way it played out in this more remote rural setting differed somewhat from the larger industrial camps in the Radom District (Distrikt Radom), or the course of events in the Łódź Ghetto. In particular, the Jews demonstrated considerable agency in arranging for their transfer to the camps, and especially in evading the police raids by a variety of counterstrategies. As examples from other forced labor camps for Jews demonstrate, such smaller rural camps and remnant ghettos played a key role in Jewish survival, even if most of these camps were dissolved or evacuated before the German retreat and Jews were not liberated directly in the camps, as happened in Tłuste.[3]

This article will first describe the establishment, functioning, and history of the approximately thirty forced labor camps for Jews (*Zwangsarbeitslager für Juden*, or ZALfJs) in Kreis Czortkow, in order to document carefully this unique story of Jewish survival. Comparisons will then be made briefly with the patterns in Silesia, Radom, and Lublin to bring out some of the key differences and similarities in the role played by the labor camps in these respective regions. In making these comparisons, two key issues will be addressed that reflect the broader implications of this case study: In what ways did the labor camps contribute to Jewish survival? And what degree of agency did the Jews have in this process?

Another key aspect of this study is that it has been made possible thanks to the abundance of new digital sources available to historians. Especially the collection of more than fifty thousand survivor testimonies by the USC Shoah Foundation, Visual History Archive (VHA), and now the availability of several hundred thousand Jewish survivor case files (T/D—Tracing and Documentation—files) in the archives of the International Tracing Service (ITS), which are searchable digitally, make it possible to analyze the path of survival through the Holocaust of a majority of those Jews who survived.

An example from one of the T/D files can be seen in figure 1, which describes in shorthand the camp path of Paulina Sibner, who left the Czortków Ghetto in December 1942 and passed through ZALfJs Swidowa, Szypowce, and Lisowce, before being liberated in ZALfJ Tluste on March 23, 1944. This is a fairly typical trajectory for many survivors, and for some these summaries provide monthly dates for all of the camps they passed through. As these records are based on information given by the survivors themselves several years after the

T/D 375 619

Name: S I B N E R Paulina
geb. MARGULIES

BD: 28.3.28 BP: Czortkow/Pol. Nat: isr.fr.poln.

15.7.41 - 12.42	Gh. Czortkow
12.42 - 1943	ZAL Swidow
1943 - 2.44	" Szypowce
	" Lisowce
2.44 - 23.3.44	" Tluste u.d.befr.

Reg.Bez. Amt f. Wg., Koblenz
f. Julius Simon

kr.

Figure 1. Tracing and Documentation (T/D) Index Card for Paulina Sibner, describing her specific path from Czortków Ghetto to forced labor camps for Jews in Swidowa, Szypowce, and Lisowce, before being liberated in Tłuste on March 23, 1944.

war, the dates are by no means reliable, with some also being incorrect by a whole year. However, the analysis of dozens of these self-reports can reveal important patterns in the transfers, especially when used with other survivor testimonies and war crimes investigations, to fix more accurately the dates of specific events. In the case of the Kreis Czortkow camps, the dates of the transfers from one site to another sometimes correspond with roundups for the camps or mass-killing *Aktionen*, which caused Jews to be transferred or flee from one place to the next.[4]

ZWANGSARBEITSLAGER FÜR JUDEN (ZALFJS) IN KREIS CZORTKOW

To develop this case study, first the German administration of the region will be briefly outlined. In October 1939, the German authorities established the so-called General Government (Generalgouvernement) of rump Poland, which they divided into four administrative districts (*Distrikte*): Krakau, Lublin, Radom, and Warsaw. The General Government was administered by a civil administration under General

Governor (*Generalgouverneur*) Hans Frank, based in the city of Krakau (Kraków). After the invasion of the Soviet Union by German forces in June 1941, a fifth district, the Galician District (Distrikt Galizien), was added to the General Government. Each district contained a number of counties (*Kreise*). In Distrikt Galizien there were initially seventeen (later fourteen) *Kreise*. On the southeastern tip of Distrikt Galizien was Czortków County, a mainly agricultural area with a Jewish population of more than twenty thousand.[5] The Jews lived mainly in the towns working in trade and crafts—but most were familiar with the agricultural routines they witnessed daily in the surrounding countryside.

The German administration of the region consisted of three main components: the office of the Security Police in Czortków, which coordinated the deportation and murder of the Jews in the *Kreis*; the stationary units of the Order Police (*Gendarmerie* and *Schutzpolizei*), which together with the Ukrainian police provided the main manpower for the *Aktionen* against the Jews; and the German civil administration, which oversaw the local (Ukrainian) administration of the region. In addition, older Germans, serving in the Wehrmacht, the so-called agricultural special leaders (*Sonderführer*), were assigned to oversee the network of agricultural camps clustered mainly around Jagielnica and Tłuste, assisted by local Polish and Ukrainian estate managers.[6]

For volume 2 of *The USHMM Encyclopedia of Camps and Ghettos*, some fifty ghettos were identified in Distrikt Galizien (figure 2). Many of these ghettos were not created until the final months of 1942, in accordance with orders issued by the SS and police leader (*SS- und Polizeiführer*, SSPF) in Lemberg (L'viv/Lwów), Friedrich Katzmann, that Jews were permitted to reside in just thirty Jewish Residential Areas (ghettos), or otherwise in barracks camps (ZALfJs) located at their forced labor sites.[7] This pattern contrasts somewhat with the chronology in the other four districts, where most ghettos were established before the summer of 1942—and all but a handful had then been liquidated by the fall of 1942.

For the Jews in Distrikt Galizien, the German orders to clear the ghettos and murder their Jewish inhabitants did not come as a surprise. It was the culmination of an intensifying regime of persecution, deportations, and killing dating from the summer of 1941. By the end of 1942, most Jews still alive in the ghettos and forced labor camps of Eastern Galicia realized that they were living on borrowed time. As

Figure 2. Map of ghettos in Distrikt Galizien. Source: *The United States Holocaust Memorial Museum Encyclopedia of Camps and Ghettos, 1933–1945*, vol. 2, *Ghettos in German-Occupied Eastern Europe*, ed. Martin Dean (Bloomington: Indiana University Press in association with USHMM, 2012), 749.

the Bełżec extermination camp had ceased operation by January 1943, the remaining ghettos were cleared mainly by brutal mass shootings, involving the Ukrainian Police and the German Order Police, as well as the Security Police, in the first half of 1943.[8]

There were five ghettos in Kreis Czortkow: in Borszczów, Kopyczyńce, Jezierzany, and Tłuste, as well as in the county seat, Czortków. More than 500 Jews managed to survive from these ghettos, for the most part due to the existence of some 30 mainly agricultural labor camps within the county, a few of which continued to operate almost until their liberation by the Red Army in March 1944. From digital searches in the ITS, the following numbers of traces for survivors of these ghettos were found. These are minimum numbers, as slight spelling variations or reports not mentioning that they were in a ghetto are not captured by these digital searches. For the Tłuste Ghetto, there were 265 survivors; Czortków Ghetto, 142; Jezierzany Ghetto, 3; Borszczów Ghetto, 144; and Kopyczyńce Ghetto, 55. Thus from these five ghettos alone, there were more than 600 Jewish survivors registered with the ITS after the war.[9]

In addition, a number of Jews from the nearby ghettos in Buczacz and Horodenka also survived in these camps. In analyzing the T/D files, people who were reported killed or missing were excluded, as were those deported away to other camps, such as the road construction camp ZALfJ Borki Wielkie, near Tarnopol. However, the vast majority of T/D files for these ghettos represent postwar compensation claims by survivors, most of whom survived in the agricultural camps around Tłuste. For example, of the 144 Jews who survived from the Borszczów Ghetto, 103 survived mainly in camps, whereas 41 Jews went into hiding from the summer of 1943 onward. To provide an analysis of the data contained in the T/D files, a sample of 200 survivors, all from the Tłuste Ghetto, was entered into a spreadsheet and examined in more detail. The main aim was to determine the paths of survival for these Jews (which camps did they pass through and when?), but other factors, such as age and gender, were looked at as well. The sample of 200 included 91 males (45.5 percent) and 109 females (54.5 percent). The age range was 61 people age nineteen or younger (30.5 percent); 99 ages twenty through forty (49.5 percent); and 42 age forty-one or older (21 percent) at the time of liberation in early 1944.

The agricultural camps around Tłuste started taking young Jewish laborers in February 1942.[10] Edith Sternberg, for example, was rounded up in the fields near Mielnica by German and Ukrainian police and sent to ZALfJ Jagielnica by train in the summer of 1942. She spent about four months in the camp. She recalled working at night with about one thousand girls picking kok-saghyz, to be sent to Germany in sacks to make rubber for Germany's war needs. She was fed horsemeat and was guarded by members of the Jewish police (*Jüdischer Ordnungsdienst*), who received better food. Only a couple of German soldiers supervised the camp. After a friend of hers was bought out of the camp with bribes, she decided to escape at night with two other girls. They managed to avoid detection by hiding in a nearby pond during the day, before making good their escape into the forests the next night.[11]

As this and other examples show, before the mass deportations from the towns and ghettos, which started in Kreis Czortkow in the late summer of 1942, Jews were sent only reluctantly to these forced labor camps. The detailed account of Zwi Fenster in the Jezierzany *yizkor* book records that by the summer of 1942, about seventy Jewish girls from "Ozieran" (Jezierzany), most of them between the ages of seventeen and nineteen, had been sent to work in the nearby village of Glemboczek (Głęboczek). They had not volunteered, as people were afraid of any form of concentration. They slept in barns and in attics in the village. They were led to work under guard. As the village was close by, they retained contact with their families in Ozieran. After the harvest season ended, most returned home, but some of the girls remained in Glemboczek and continued to work there. In this way they avoided the deportation *Aktion* from Jezierzany in late September 1942, in which about seven hundred Jews were sent to their deaths.[12]

After the deportations to Bełżec from Kreis Czortkow started in the fall of 1942, people began to think differently about the labor camps. In the first six months of 1943, the T/D files reveal that more than thirty Jews went to ZALfJ Rożanówka from the Tłuste Ghetto, many of them either shortly before or at the time of the ghetto's liquidation, in late May and early June 1943. Among them were Michael Schiller and his brother, who, sensing the approaching danger, "figured that it would be better [in the camp] than in the ghetto."[13]

Abraham Morgenstern recalls his family bribing their way into the Świdowa camp in early January 1943. He even took with him some Sherlock Holmes detective story magazines on a horse-driven carriage from Czortków. On his arrival, three barracks had been completed and several more were under construction, which also became his first task. At that time there were about 150 Jews in the camp, and its population probably rose to around 250. The camp was surrounded with barbed wire. The Jews slept in two-tiered bunk beds. In the winter of 1942–1943, it was so cold that some inmates shared a bunk at night to keep warm. Apart from growing kok-saghyz, the inmates also performed other agricultural work, including feeding animals in the barns in winter.[14]

The liquidation of the Tłuste Ghetto took place in two phases on May 27 and June 6, 1943. It was carried out by members of the Security Police from Czortków, assisted by the local Ukrainian police. On each occasion, Jews were collected from the ghetto and taken to be shot at the Jewish cemetery in Tłuste. About three thousand Jews were shot on May 27 and up to one thousand more on June 6, as many Jews had hidden in bunkers or fled into the fields during the first *Aktion*. Despite the efforts of the German and Ukrainian police, a number of Jews survived the ghetto liquidation; as Tłuste had now been declared *judenrein* (cleansed of Jews), many of the survivors who emerged from hiding now made their way to the agricultural camps in the surrounding area, where Jews were still permitted to live and work.

Not all of the forced labor camps for Jews (ZALfJ) in Kreis Czortkow were run by members of the Wehrmacht. At least three of them—the camps in Czortków, Jagielnica, and Świdowa—were run directly by the SS, being supervised by the notorious SS official Paul Thomanek, who was based in Czortków. Conditions in these camps were somewhat harsher, and they were among the first ZALfJs to be completely liquidated in the summer of 1943, when SSPF Friedrich Katzmann moved to the next phase of cleansing Distrikt Galizien of all its Jews by eliminating the last remaining ZALfJs.[15]

An *Aktion* was conducted in ZALfJ Świdowa on June 23, 1943, in which the majority of the inmates were shot by the German and local Ukrainian police, although a number, including Izaak Szwarc, managed to hide successfully and escape. Jews brought from the nearby Muchawka and Marylówka camps, and also about a dozen other Jews brought from Buczacz, were shot together with the inmates of ZALfJ Świdowa. In total, some four hundred Jews were shot by the Germans and their collaborators here.[16]

The diary of Małgorzata Bolschower captures dramatically the intense effort it took to avoid the *Aktionen* if you were caught inside one of the SS-run camps at the wrong moment. During the liquidation of ZALfJ Czortkow, also on June 23, 1943, the camp commandant Thomanek selected about fifty Jewish workers to be kept alive; the other Jews in the camp, including more than one hundred women, were loaded onto trucks and taken away to be shot. These heartrending scenes are sensitively described in Bolschower's diary, written while she was in hiding, just a short time later:

> How cruel this all was! 120 women, mostly young beautiful creations, healthy, full of an unrestrained desire to live, were arbitrarily sentenced to death, by thoughtless beastly murderers. . . .
>
> Suddenly I was gripped by an enormous desire to live. "You must save yourself," I told myself. "You must and you will!" I looked around carefully. Opposite the bath there was a tiny house, that also belonged to the camp and whose door stood open. Within me the decision ripened that I had to get into the house, and after that, I thought, I would somehow find a way. . . .
>
> When I looked around me desperately in the little house, I noticed a small, round hole in the kitchen wall. In the next seconds, I forced myself into the hole. Behind it I found a small, narrow space. The small space reached up to the low roof, and there was a tight gap. How I managed to force myself in there, although the gap was scarcely a half a meter long and finger-long nails ripped open my back, will always remain a mystery to me.[17]

In this way Bolschower managed to avoid being sent away to be shot, but the next day she emerged from her hiding place and soon realized that she had no choice but to join the group of fifty or so selected workers who remained alive inside the Czortków camp. Bolschower was unfortunate, as she was then sent from one SS-run camp to another one. Soon she managed to escape from this next camp and went into hiding with a local non-Jew, but another woman, who had escaped with her, subsequently went back into the camp, on at least one occasion, to see her friends there and take a bath. This woman's action was very unnerving for Bolschower, as she feared that it might cause her hiding place to be revealed.

After the final ghetto liquidations, which were concluded in Distrikt Galizien by July 1943, it was legal for Jews to live only in the few remaining ZALfJs. If a Jew was caught outside of a camp, he or she was to be shot on the spot. This policy created some strange situations. For example, in Skala Podolska there was a camp run by the German Customs Border Police (Zollgrenzschutzpolizei), who employed about fifty Jews working for them during the day. For a time these Jews lived together in a small camp, but by August 1943, most of them were in hiding at night and coming out during the day to work for the Germans, as this actually offered some kind of protection.

The unusual situation at the "camp" in Skala is more or less confirmed by the postwar testimony of the German customs official Richard Kümmel: "Some of the Jews were accommodated with us in outhouses; others lived in their apartments or hiding places and came to us every morning, to do their work." Meyer Blutstein notes that the Jews regularly had to pay a customs officer named Engel coins worth five rubles in order to continue working for the Zollgrenzschutz, and they received no pay or food for their work. He reckoned that thirty-three Jews worked regularly for the Customs Border Protection officers and a few more only occasionally. This unusual arrangement seems to have protected about fifty Jews almost to the end of the German occupation.[18] The "camp" in Skala is certainly an extreme case, as in its final phase it was more or less an "illegal camp."

In this respect Skala was atypical for the camps in Kreis Czortkow, as most were agricultural camps on estates run by the Wehrmacht and local estate managers, established as part of the effort to produce synthetic rubber for the German war effort. The fact of the existence of a few of these agricultural camps in Kreis Czortkow has been ascertained only recently, thanks to access to the ITS and other previously unavailable archives. This pattern also applies to the research conducted for the *USHMM Encyclopedia of Camps and Ghettos* generally, which has revealed considerably more forced labor camps for Jews in Distrikt Galizien than were previously known. The most detailed list of ZALfJs in Distrikt Galizien, prepared in 1998 by Józef Marszałek, includes 119 camps.[19] Research conducted for the *USHMM Encyclopedia of Camps and Ghettos* has so far identified at least 190 ZALfJs in the region (figures 3 and 4).

Figure 4 shows the forced labor camps for Jews around Tłuste, including those where a number of Jews survived up until liberation: in Lisowce, Rożanówka, Kozia Góra, and Tłuste.

A few of the ZALfJs in the county were remnant ghettos (such as the camps in Czortków and Kopyczyńce), at least three were run by the SS, and some were only short-lived: Dźwiniacz, for example, was closed already in 1942, while Sniatynka may have existed for less than one month in May 1943. All have been found on local prewar maps to confirm their location. Some, such as Dobranówka, were isolated farmsteads that cannot be found on modern maps at all. Detailed local maps from the 1920s and 1930s were used to identify the precise locations for many of these farms.[20]

Figure 3. Forced Labor Camps for Jews in the Eastern Galicia Region, 1941–1944. Map prepared by Shannon Kelly, Aaron Rosen, and Max Meller, with special thanks to Professor Richard Hinton, George Washington University, Washington, D.C.

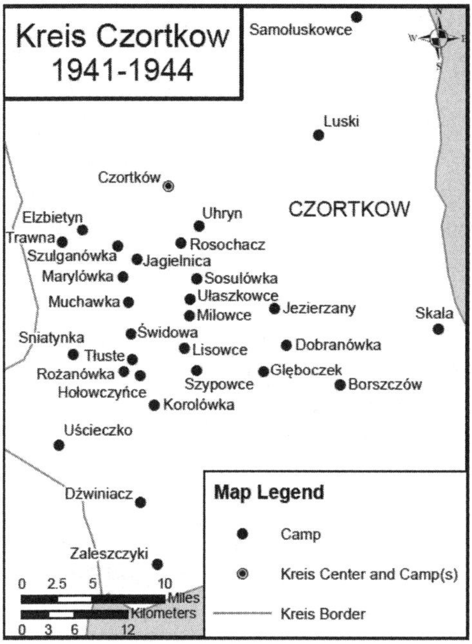

Figure 4. ZALfJ in Kreis Czortkow, Distrikt Galizien (inset from figure 3).

Only sparse information is available on the organization of the kok-saghyz camps by the German authorities. According to a personal account in the Tłuste *yizkor* book, the estates around Tłuste, which had been nationalized (and converted into state farms, or *kolkhozes*) during the brief Soviet occupation in 1939–1941, were taken over by the Germans by the beginning of 1942. Here they began to plant kok-saghyz used to make rubber. Due to the military importance of this raw material, these estates were run by a special department of the Wehrmacht. The directorate coordinating work on the various estates was based in Jagielnica.[21]

In fact, the directorate in Jagielnica reported to the Plenipotentiary for Motor Transport (Der Bevollmächtigte für das Kraftfahrwesen) within the Office of the Four Year Plan inside the Reich (rubber was desperately needed for making tires). However, this office in turn answered also to Himmler's Personal Staff Office (Persönlicher Stab Reichsführer-SS), sending him regular reports on the progress of kok-saghyz plantations throughout German-occupied Europe.

In surviving files of Himmler's Personal Staff Office, there is a brief correspondence regarding the kok-saghyz directorate in Jagielnica. In April 1943, Sonderführer Storbeck and Herrn Lobenberg visited SS-Untersturmführer Inquart, the adjutant of SSPF Katzmann, in Lemberg. They requested that 1,500 Jewish workers be released for eight weeks for the use of the estate in Jagielnica because without these workers, it would be impossible to expect any sort of harvest with the kok-saghyz plants at all, as their cultivation was very labor intensive. However, at this meeting, although it was admitted that no order had yet been received to "resettle" the local Jews there, it was explained that the orders of the SS leadership were quite clear—"under no circumstances could there be any exceptions."[22]

A subsequent letter, dated June 12, indicates that Himmler had requested Governor Wächter to alleviate the labor shortage on the Jagielnica estate through other means (presumably by making available non-Jewish laborers).[23] Historian Dieter Pohl interprets this letter as a clear denial of any further exemptions being granted for Jewish workers.[24] Jewish survivor testimony indicates, however, that the camp in Jagielnica was not liquidated until July 23, 1943, and that even after a series of *Aktionen* were conducted against various agricultural camps (including ZALfJs Milowce, Rożanówka, Szulganówka, and Trawna) by the Security Police from Czortków and its Ukrainian auxiliaries around this time, some kind of a reprieve was still granted to surviving Jews for another few months afterward.[25]

JEWISH SURVIVAL AND JEWISH AGENCY IN THE LABOR CAMPS

The accounts of survivors stress especially the role of a local German official around Tłuste, known to them simply as "Fati" or "Vati," as being decisive in assisting Jews to survive in some of these camps. One survivor states, "The administration of the estates around Tłuste was supervised by a German SA officer named 'Fati,' who had the military rank of Oberleutnant ('Oberleuter'). The administration of the estates used to requisition a number of Jews to work on the various estates via the Jewish Council. The Jews were concentrated in special labor camps ('*Arbetslagern*'). Thanks to this and also thanks in great measure to the decent conduct of our 'Oberleuter Fati,' a certain number of Jews in the labor camps in Tłuste and the surrounding area managed to save themselves and survive the general destruction of the Jews in

Poland."[26] Other sources confirm that "Fati" (aka Fathi/Vati) was the *Sonderführer* in Tłuste, who ran the Szypowce camp. He was reportedly of Dutch origin and was killed in Poland during the German retreat. Mendl Weinstock recalled that he was decent (*anständig*), and when the Jews hid in the woods during the *Aktionen*, he would come and let them know when it was safe to come out.[27]

Crucial for the survival of such a large number of Jews was a decision, announced in late July 1943, for the Jews to be taken back onto the estates again, following a series of brutal *Aktionen* carried out by the Security Police. This situation reflects the pattern of previous *Aktionen* in the ghettos, when the SS killing spree would last for a few days and then a comparative normality would reassert itself. This cyclical pattern of *Aktionen*, and also the difficulties Jews faced trying to survive in hiding or in the forests, is the context necessary for us to comprehend why Jews would return to work in these camps, just a few days after the Security Police's attempt to murder all of the Jews working there.

The Tłuste *yizkor* book states that already in 1942, the German estate administration had applied to the Gestapo in Czortków for six thousand Jewish workers to be assigned to the estates around Tłuste. However, this request was initially denied by the Gestapo offices in Czortków and Lemberg, as well as by General Governor Hans Frank in Krakau. The request was then sent up to Himmler in Berlin for a decision, but the reply came in July 1943, after the *Aktionen* against the estates had been conducted.[28] The precise details of the negotiations regarding the kok-saghyz camps cannot be determined with complete reliability from these sources. But it is clear that many of the agricultural camps continued to operate, albeit with a much diminished Jewish workforce, through the summer and fall of 1943. Numerous testimonies from various camps confirm that just a few days after the series of killing *Aktionen* in late July 1943, word spread that certain Wehrmacht-run kok-saghyz camps were permitted to retain surviving Jewish laborers. Reportedly the Wehrmacht supervisors and local estate managers still needed Jewish laborers and had negotiated for their preservation with the SS authorities. Therefore, many of the escaped Jews soon returned to the camps, including some to Rożanówka.[29]

But it was the agency of the Jews themselves that in part made it possible for some people to survive the *Aktionen*. In several camps, Jews posted on watch saw the murder squads approaching and then warned the others, so many people could hide or flee in time. For example, during the *Aktion* against the Rożanówka camp in July 1943, eighteen-year-old Michael Schiller was among the Jews on lookout duty. Although about ninety Jewish inmates were killed by the German and Ukrainian police, thanks to the warnings issued as the Ukrainian police approached, another eighty Jews managed to escape and hide successfully there.[30]

In many cases, it was only the extreme caution and foresight of the Jews that managed to save their skins. Carl Berkowitz reports, for example, that at the Szulganówka camp in the summer of 1943, his family lived in a separate building next to the house of the camp's local administrator, as this man was friends with their father, Leon Berkowitz, himself a former estate administrator. Here the Berkowitz family constructed an elaborate hiding place with a concealed entrance to the basement. During the *Aktion*, which took place probably in late July, about seventy-five Jews were found in the main barrack and were shot just behind the estate buildings. As they had seen the German and Ukrainian police arriving in trucks, the Berkowitz family of eight people was able to hide in time in their bunker. They remained undiscovered despite intense searches. When they emerged two days later, the local administrator was quite surprised to see them and advised them to leave. In response, they moved to ZALfJ Trawna, where Carl's father, Leon, also knew the local administrator, who worked for the Germans.[31]

On July 20, 1943, the Milowce camp was surrounded suddenly by SS and police forces from Czortków, which then shot fifty Jewish workers. The bodies were simply thrown into an empty well. However, more than half of the inmates managed to hide or escape during the *Aktion*, and a few days later most of the escaped Jews returned to the camp to work there. Max Schmerer, who had arrived at the Milowce camp from Tłuste just before the July *Aktion*, comments that life soon normalized once again. About forty Jews remained, who worked together in a comradely manner. However, relations with the local Ukrainian population were bad. The Ukrainian farmers, who also served as supervisors for the Germans, did not want to sell them any food and beat them during their work.[32]

Some Jews now decided to sleep nightly in the fields, so as not to be surprised by the next *Aktion*.[33] For example, Michael Hirsch, who was in the Luski camp near Kopyczyńce from June until November 1943, regularly slept in the fields at night; in this way he avoided an *Aktion* that was conducted in the camp during July 1943.[34] However, when it grew colder in the fall, Jews returned to sleep inside the camps again, but now in elaborately concealed hiding places, so as not to be taken by surprise.

Most of the agricultural camps in Kreis Czortkow were affected by at least two waves of killings by the SS and the Ukrainian police, as a second round of *Aktionen* took place in November 1943. Around Kopyczyńce, for example, the camps in Luski and on the Baworowszczyzna estate were both liquidated at this time.[35] On the Luski estate near Kopyczyńce, most of the fifteen Jews who ultimately survived from this camp report having left it in November 1943 or just before. Four survivors state explicitly that they escaped from the camp and went into hiding on November 15, 1943, thereby confirming the date of the second *Aktion* in ZALfJ Luski.[36]

In some instances local topography assisted the Jews in evading the attacks by the Ukrainian police. For example, the Ulaszkowce camp was located at a farm perched on a hill with a clear view of the surrounding area. The farm buildings were surrounded by a five-foot-high stone wall, and a peasant manned the main gate. Abraham Morgenstern recalls, however, that it was relatively easy to sneak in or out through holes in the wall. The Jewish workers were accommodated in two out of four prefabricated barracks. On November 30, 1943, Ukrainian police, under the direction of the German police in Czortków, arrived early in the morning and rounded up those Jews they could find. They shot them close to the farm. According to Soviet sources, forty-four people were shot. Morgenstern and several other Jews managed to escape from this *Aktion*, jumping from windows or hiding as the police approached. However, they soon returned to the camp, and the German director permitted them to stay a few weeks longer.[37] Jewish survivor Shmuel Finger recalled that in late 1943, after the *Aktionen* in November, word spread again around the camps that the Jews would be safe there for another three or four months, so long as they avoided the SS units until their final retreat from the region.[38]

In late 1943, another threat came from local Ukrainians, who also raided the camps at night to extort money and murder Jews. Samuel Kleiner recalled in his VHA testimony:

> During the day the [Ukrainian] police used to come in [to the Hołowczyńce camp] and just take the people and shoot them. If you give them money, they let you go. . . . At night the local people used to come in and they used to kill the people . . . sometimes by shooting, sometimes with a bayonet . . . they demanded money. . . . Local people from town would come in and say give us money for our underground.[39]

Some Jews were shot by the Ukrainian police because they had, or were suspected of having, typhus. Some camps were liquidated or closed in the winter of 1943–1944, as there was no longer a need for agricultural labor. Vlassovites and other marauding forces retreating with the Germans also killed some Jews from the camps in early 1944, whereas the retreating German army was seen by the Jews, in contrast, almost as their protector, keen to maintain a semblance of order in the rear areas.

Toward the end of the occupation, by February 1944, several hundred Jews assembled at a newly formed central camp in Tłuste, as it seemed safer there than trying to hide in the countryside. More Jews were killed in a bombing raid as the Germans finally retreated, but at least three hundred Jews survived to be liberated in Tłuste by the Red Army on March 22, 1944. As many as one hundred to two hundred more were liberated in Rożanówka, Lisowce, and at a few of the other remnant camps, including Kozia Góra. After the war, a number of Jewish survivors testified about the activities of a Ukrainian policeman in Tłuste named Schab, who participated in crimes against the Jews, including attacks on the inmates of the Lisowce camp.[40]

In addition to the many survivor testimonies used to reconstruct the history of the camps in Kreis Czortkow, a large sample of survivor documentation from the ITS (T/D files) was also examined to reconstruct their paths through the camps. Generally the data collected for the sample of two hundred survivors from the Tłuste Ghetto corroborated well the impressions gained from the survivor testimonies and other narrative sources. However, the initial impression that many Jews had managed to survive by moving from one camp to another was not confirmed for the group as a whole, but rather only for Jews in those camps that were completely liquidated or closed down in the period up to November 1943. To survive these liquidations, people both had to hide successfully during the *Aktionen* and then move on to find food and shelter in another camp that was still operating and also taking in additional Jews. By contrast, in the main survival camps close to Tłuste—that is, especially in Lisowce and Rożanówka—the bulk of survivors remained in just that one camp for the entire period from the ghetto liquidations in June 1943 or even before then. However, the analysis of survivor data clearly confirms the mass movement of many Jews to the newly established Tłuste central camp in February 1944, which at the time was viewed as a safe haven, where the German soldiers passing through the town to some extent protected them. As Reubin Prifer recalled:

> We knew we couldn't defend ourselves against the Bandera forces because of their great numbers and armaments; they were supreme in the villages and forests. Thus the camp workers resolved to go to the Tłuste farm at the head of the road to seek the protection of the German soldiers against an assault by Bandera's forces. We would position ourselves to protect against cross-fire, but it soon became apparent that the Bandera gangs had no intention of going to a place where German forces would be waiting for them! [41]

Prifer comments that although many Germans were passing through Tłuste at this time on their retreat, they were mainly from the Wehrmacht and "because they didn't know for sure if we were Jews, they greeted us warmly and even shared their medications with the wounded among us. But luckily, they did not remain for long. When one group left, another one arrived, so they didn't have time to figure out who we were. This lasted for almost a month until things quieted down."[42]

Two unexpected results emerged from analysis of the sample of T/D files as summarized in figure 5. First, that more than a dozen Jews survived by retreating with the Germans from the Tłuste area to camps in Germany and Austria is something that was not immediately apparent from a reading of many testimonies. Only in the account of Prifer, in the Horodenka *yizkor* book, is it mentioned that the German Wehrmacht official left in charge at Lisowce, Badenburg, left for Germany in early 1944, accompanied by a small group of healthy Jews to assist him on the journey.[43] Some of these Jews ended up in concentration camps, including Mauthausen in Austria, but it seems that most survived the war.

It is also quite significant that only a small number of Jews (about

ZALfJs	Total T/Ds	Tłuste Ghetto	3.44*	Known Aktionen†
Tluste	T/D x359	131	85	
Lisowce	T/D x135	60	41	6.43/23, 11.43/40 (typhus), 1.44/30
Rozanowka	T/D x44	47	27	7.43/90, 11.43/15
Swidowa	T/D x42	10	1	6.43/400(from other camps)
Czortkow	T/D x40	0		6.43/400
Dobranowka	T/D x18	0		
Jagielnica	T/D x12	1		7.43/160, 11.43/24
Kozia Gora	T/D x8	18	10	6.43/180, 1.44/7
Holowczynce	T/D x6	16	4	6.43/200, 1.44/28, 3.44/40
Szypowce	T/D x5	4		6.43/13
Dzwiniacz	T/D x5	6		
Gleboczek	T/D x4	4		
Korolowka	T/D x3	0		11.43/40
Trawna	T/D x2	6	2	7.43/100
Ulaszkowce	T/D x2	2	2	11.43/44
Marylowka	T/D x2	0		6.43/55 (to Swidowa)
Muchawka	T/D x2	0		6.43/90 (to Swidowa), 8.43/32, 11.43/15
Sniatynka	T/D x2	2		
Borszczow	T/D x2	1		8.43/360
Rosochacz	T/D x1	0		11.43/60
Jezierzany	T/D x1	1	1	
Milowce	NO T/D	2		7.43/50
Szulganowka	NO T/D	0		7.43/75, 9.43/6
Sosulowka	NO T/D	0		10.43/34
Camps in Reich		**16**		
Hiding		**11**		
Total Number of Survivors		200		

*The region was liberated in March 1944. This column shows the numbers of Jews from Tłuste Ghetto reporting that they were in the respective camp around the time of liberation.

†This column gives the dates (months in 1943 or 1944) and numbers of Jews killed for known Aktionen in the respective camps. Much of this information is derived from the Soviet Extraordinary Commission Reports, as summarized by historian Alexander Kruglov.

Figure 5. Data from 200 Jews registered as having gone through Tłuste Ghetto (roughly one-third of all survivors).

a dozen) from the sample of some two hundred claimed to have been in hiding at the time of liberation in March 1944. The actual number was probably higher, but it seems that most hid for only a short period, remaining in the camps as long as possible. The hiding narratives are often the most compelling, but they seem to represent only a small segment of those who survived from the ghettos and camps in this region. This may, in part, also reflect a certain bias in the ITS sources toward those Jews who emigrated from Poland shortly after the war, as Jews hiding with Polish families, or who adopted Polish identities, were probably more likely to remain in Poland or Ukraine after 1945. Yet other sources seem to confirm the difficulties Jews encountered trying to survive in hiding, even for the relatively short period from June 1943 to March 1944. From a group of twenty-eight Jews from the Borszczów ghetto, who hid in bunkers in the surrounding forests, only five managed to survive through to the liberation.[44] In this respect, the work of Jan Grabowski and others, focused on the survival of Jews in hiding, is complementary, as they show the many difficulties Jews faced in trying to survive in a hostile rural environment, where from the end of 1942 anyone caught giving them succor might themselves also be killed in punishment.[45]

Yad Vashem has recognized several non-Jews from Tłuste as Righteous Among the Nations for assistance given to Jews to enable them to survive in hiding. For example, Anna Domanskaya and her family hid eight Jews from the Tłuste ghetto after its liquidation, and they were joined shortly afterward by Jona Zylber, who had been working on one of the nearby farm-based camps. Yet even this account stresses the dangers from hostile neighbors and periodic searches for the Jews, which discouraged many Jews even from attempting to go into hiding.[46]

These agricultural camps are significant, as more than five hundred Jews managed to survive there, despite the brutal series of *Aktionen* conducted against them by the German and Ukrainian police during 1943. Ironically, the dispersion of the Jews among these scattered camps may have helped at least some to survive, as the German and Ukrainian police lacked the numbers to liquidate them effectively in a coordinated *Aktion*. However, the narrative sources reveal especially the agency of those Jews who managed to survive. It was not passivity or just luck that made staying in the camps a viable survival strategy, but rather a whole variety of skills deployed to navigate a path to survival. These skills ranged from bribing various individuals to get into the camp, finding secure sleeping arrangements or arranging for a lookout, maintaining good relations, especially with the farm managers, and having the right instinct as to when it was better to flee or to return to a camp that continued working after an *Aktion*. With the aid of the ITS records, it is now possible to analyze in considerable detail the paths of survivors and confirm the large scale of this event. The strategy of fleeing and hiding when the police were spotted coming down the road and then returning to work again for the Wehrmacht after the police were gone did prove successful for more than five hundred Jews.

CONCLUSION

How do these results compare with the existing historiography on the role of Jewish forced labor camps in other regions?

Bella Guterman, in her study of the "Organisation Schmelt" ZALfJs in Silesia, remarked, "In retrospect it seems that the labor camps, more than any other setting, enabled quite a few prisoners to cling to life, that is, it served them as a narrow bridge to life."[47] In Silesia, where much of the population was in any case German and many Poles were also deported to make way for ethnic Germans brought in from Eastern Europe, it was clearly quite difficult for Jews to survive in hiding. At the same time, the massive deployment of Jews to work in forced labor camps that were involved in road and railway construction, the building of factories, and textile manufacture meant that the strategy of survival through work offered some chances of success here, especially as Germany's fortunes in the war declined. As Adam Tooze has noted, "In the case of the Holocaust, ideological imperatives were clearly paramount, but [still] subject to pragmatic compromise as circumstances demanded."[48]

The "narrow bridge" concept reflects the fact that only a small percentage of the camp inmates made it through the long years of camp life, comprised of hard labor, undernourishment, and beatings, which started in Silesia in October 1940. However, there were vast differences between conditions in the various camps in the large network operated by Organisation Schmelt, which contained about two hundred ZALfJs altogether. While some camps had horrendous death rates, especially among Jews already exhausted from previous privations, there were also niches where one could build up one's strength to facilitate survival in the longer term. One such camp was ZALfJ Breslau-Güntherbrücke, which is described by several survivors as the best conditions they encountered during their own personal camp path. Chaim Roessler remarked, for example, that "Güntherbrücke was a holiday compared to [ZALfJ] Gross Masselwitz."[49] Roessler attributed his survival of subsequent concentration camps to the relative respite and recuperation that his year in Güntherbrücke provided him, after his harsh experiences in other labor camps. Some Jews even paid bribes to get sent to Güntherbrücke, as they had been told about the comparatively good conditions there. For a number of Jews, Güntherbrücke did serve as a "narrow bridge to life."[50] In contrast, other camps, such as ZALfJ Seibersdorf, had a deservedly evil reputation: according to Levie Barmhatigheid, who left Westerbork on September 7, 1942, of his group of about two hundred men, ninety-two had been buried by the time he departed Seibersdorf a few months later, headed for ZALfJ Blechhammer (Blachownia) on March 23, 1943.[51]

Research on the larger industrial camps in Distrikt Radom by Christopher Browning and Felicija Karay reflects some similar themes to the situation in Distrikt Galizien. Here there was also bribery to get into the camps, especially around the time of the mass deportations in the fall of 1942. Browning's groundbreaking work on the Starachowice slave labor camp has shown that as the deportations to the extermination camps progressed, and the available options for Jews in the ghettos diminished, "increasingly desperate Jews bought their way into their subsequent slavery as the best alternative to deportation and death."[52] Browning also stresses varying degrees of lethality during different phases of the camp, with the period of a typhus outbreak, when many sick prisoners were shot despite good chances of recovery, being the only really deadly phase for this camp. Conditions in ZALfJ Skarżysko-Kamienna were overall much worse, but this very large camp also provided niches for survival, where food and work conditions enabled Jews to remain alive.[53]

In assessing the contributory factors to Jewish survival in Starachowice, Browning concluded that Jewish agency played an important role: "Many of these factors can be attributed, at least in part, to coincidence, fate, or 'luck,' which is what most survivors invoke to account for their survival. But clearly Jewish agency played a significant role."[54] Work on the smaller camps for Jews in Distrikt Radom, such as Wolanów, just north of Radom, analyzed by Jolanta Kraemer, shows that here too Jewish agency played a vital part in increasing chances for survival, as generous bribes even facilitated the establishment of this camp in the first place, thereby sparing many Jews from deportation to the extermination camps.[55] Once inside these smaller rural camps, the Jews were then subsequently transferred to the larger industrial camps such as Pionki, which, as Raul Hilberg has shown, were not liquidated but rather evacuated into the concentration camp system in July 1944 to preserve the manpower.[56]

In his recently published book, David Silberklang poses the question of whether forced labor affected the chances of Jewish survival in Distrikt Lublin in 1942–1944. In his conclusions, he rightly stresses that less than 10 percent of the Jews were selected to stay behind temporarily in 1942, when all of the others were killed. He also notes that very few local Jews survived in the camps of Distrikt Lublin, as many of those selected had been brought there from other regions, including tens of thousands of Jews transferred from the Warsaw Ghetto in early 1943, just before the ghetto uprising. However, even though several of the main large camps for Jews in the region were liquidated during Operation Harvest Festival (Aktion Erntefest) in early November 1943, the existence of the camps could at times help Jews survive, mainly because their prospects outside of the camps were also quite bleak.[57]

In his book *Hunt for the Jews*, Jan Grabowski lists the names of eighty-nine Jewish survivors from Dąbrowa Tarnowska County, who reported to the Office of the Central Committee of Polish Jews at the end of the war (1945–1946). Of these eighty-nine, some sixty-three (71 percent) reportedly came out of hiding, and twenty-six (29 percent) had returned from a camp. These figures, based on postwar Polish sources, support the assumption that lies behind much research into Jewish survival strategies: that Jews from the ghettos mainly managed to survive by going into hiding or passing on the "Aryan" side.[58] This assumption has led researchers to focus on aspects such as the role of non-Jewish protectors or, also more recently, the difficulties Jews encountered among a largely hostile local population that had good reason to fear harsh German reprisals for aiding Jews. By contrast, not much attention has been paid to the survival of Jews in forced labor camps and in particular the extent to which this choice to work in the camps was a conscious survival strategy. Therefore, the seemingly logical assumption that Jews mainly survived the Holocaust by concealing their identities or finding a safe place to hide does not necessarily correspond with what happened on the ground. Indeed, Dieter Pohl has concluded that "probably more Jews survived in the camps than in hiding."[59] The wartime paths of Jews from Silesia, Distrikt Radom, and Distrikt Lublin, indicate that ZALfJs could provide a temporary reprieve for some able-bodied Jews after the ghetto liquidations in 1942–1943, although their ultimate chances of survival still depended on many circumstances, which varied considerably from one region, or even one camp, to another.

With regard to the agricultural camps in Kreis Czortkow, there were a number of additional local circumstances that helped more Jews survive here. The camps themselves were relatively open—some did not even have barbed wire and were scarcely guarded. Working in the fields also offered a better opportunity to escape if necessary. Added to this was the interest of the German Wehrmacht officials, who ran the camps to maximize production, in part to maintain their own jobs, away from the front lines. Not only in Eastern Galicia but also in several other regions, Jews survived in forced labor and then concentration camps right up to the end of the occupation, mainly because particular German authorities continued to exploit Jewish labor.

The relatively late liquidation of the ghettos in Distrikt Galizien meant that the Jews had to survive less than a year before liberation, and the agricultural camps helped many of the Jews bridge this gap. At the very end of the German occupation of the region, the security situation became more unstable, as German authority began to collapse. At this time, external forces, especially the Ukrainian police, marauding Vlassovite (Russian collaborationist) formations, or even the local population posed more of a threat to the surviving Jews than the retreating German military units. Ultimately the camps did not provide protection against the rural population, and many Jews headed back to the town of Tłuste for safety in numbers, even organizing their own hospital and self-defense force there.

Perhaps the most decisive evidence regarding the attitude of the Jews toward staying in the camps is given in the Borszczów *yizkor* book in a testimony entitled "The Borshchover Bande" ("The Borszczów Partisans"). On escaping from the Borszczów ghetto on June 6–7, following the liquidation *Aktion* there, a group of twenty-eight Jews fled to the forests to form a partisan unit. Soon after escaping the ghetto, the partisans sent two representatives, including the author of the testimony, B. V. Ben Barakh, into the camps in Lisowce, Dobranówka, and Jagielnica, to try to recruit Jews to come and join them in the forest. However, the Jews in these three camps refused, saying, "so long as we have a place to sleep and something to eat, why should we escape." From the Lisowce camp, one of the young Jewish men went with the partisans to take a look at how things were in the forest, but he also soon returned to ZALfJ Lisowce, as he considered that life outside the camp under such conditions was not for him.[60]

The experience of the Jewish men, women, and youths who survived in these agricultural camps in Czortków County was in many respects atypical for Holocaust survivors, but this unusual case should nevertheless cause historians to challenge some of the customary assumptions about the choices facing Jews, whose main objective was simply to try to find a way to survive. With the detailed information on the paths taken by Jewish survivors available from the records of the ITS and the testimonies of the Shoah Foundation, it now becomes possible for us to give a much clearer answer, both quantitatively and qualitatively, to the contentious question of how Jews managed to survive the Holocaust.

NOTES

The opinions stated in this article are those of the author and do not necessarily reflect those of the United States Holocaust Memorial Museum or the United States Holocaust Memorial Museum Council. Much of the information for this article was collected as part of the research for The United States Holocaust Memorial Museum's *Encyclopedia of Camps and Ghettos, 1933–1945*. Special thanks go to Alexander Kruglov, Jolanta Kraemer, Jan Lambertz, and Mark Khazanov, among others, for their invaluable help. This article is very much a work in progress, as not all relevant material could be included here.

1. Dieter Pohl, *Nationalsozialistische Judenverfolgung in Ostgalizien 1941–1944* (Munich: Oldenbourg, 1996), 361, notes that more than four hundred Jewish farm workers were still alive in Tłuste at the start of 1944. International Tracing Service (ITS) postwar documentation (mainly summaries of survivors' compensation claims) indicates that the number of Jewish survivors liberated around Tłuste in the spring of 1944 was in excess of five hundred.

2. Most infamously, this was the slogan of Mordechai Chaim Rum-

kowski, the Judenälteste of the Łódź Ghetto: "Unser einziger Weg ist—Arbeit!" See USHMM, Photo Archives, Photograph # 69721, Photographer Walter Genewein. Most recently in the literature, see Joachim Tauber, *Arbeit als Hoffnung: Jüdische Ghettos in Litauen 1941–1944* (Oldenbourg, Ger.: De Gruyter, 2015).

3. See Martin Dean, "Strategies for Jewish Survival in Ghettos and Forced Labor Camps," in *Resistance to the Holocaust*, ed. Victoria Khiterer (Cambridge: Cambridge Scholars, 2017), 38–49.

4. The term *Aktion* is found in many survivor accounts; it can be roughly translated as a police operation, including roundups both for deportation and for mass slaughter locally.

5. Bundesarchiv Aussenstelle Ludwigsburg (BA-L), B 162/5187, p. 7676, gives the figure of twenty-seven thousand Jews in Kreis Czortkow; it is not clear on what sources this is based.

6. On the institutions of occupation in Distrikt Galizien, see especially Pohl, *Nationalsozialistische Judenverfolgung*, 74–96.

7. Polizeiverordnung des HSSPF Krüger über die Errichtung jüdischer Wohnbezirke, November 10, 1942, *Verordnungsblatt des Generalgouvernements*, November 11, 1942, published in *Faschismus, Getto, Massenmord: Dokumentation über Ausrottung und Widerstand der Juden in Polen während des zweiten Weltkrieges*, ed. Tatiana Berenstein et. al. (Berlin: Rütten und Loening, 1961), 344–45.

8. On the deportations and killing *Aktionen* in Kreis Czortkow up until June 1943, see especially Thomas Sandkühler, *"Endlösung" in Galizien: Der Judenmord in Ostpolen und die Rettungsinitiativen von Berthold Beitz 1941–1944* (Bonn: Dietz, 1996), 249–56. For an overview of the ghettos in Distrikt Galizien, see *The United States Holocaust Memorial Museum Encyclopedia of Camps and Ghettos 1933–1945*, vol. 2, *Ghettos in German-Occupied Eastern Europe*, ed. Martin Dean (Bloomington: Indiana University Press in association with the United States Holocaust Memorial Museum, 2012), 744–48.

9. These results were achieved by keyword searches in the ITS digital database (0.1) for "Gh. Tluste," "Gh. Czortkow," "Gh. Borszczow," "Gh. Jezierzany," and "Gh. Kopyczynce."

10. ITS, 6.3.3.2, T/Ds 472199, 471772–471773, 481646, all reported being sent to the Hołowczyńce camp in February 1942.

11. USC Survivors of the Shoah, Visual History Archive (VHA), # 07803, testimony of Edith Sternberg.

12. ITS, 1.2.7.5, Folder 5, p. 249, report of Zwi Fenster (translated from Hebrew into German).

13. VHA, # 32925, testimony of Michael Schiller. The number of thirty Jews is derived from the analysis of T/D files for "Gh. Tluste."

14. Abraham Morgenstern, *Chortkov Remembered (The Annihilation of a Jewish Community)* (Dumont, N.J.: A. Morgenstern, 1990), 60.

15. The infamous Katzmann Report has been republished by Andrzej Żbikowski, ed., Friedrich Katzmann, *Lösung der Judenfrage in Distrikt Galizien* (Warsaw: IPN, 2001). The agricultural camps in Kreis Czortkow are not listed among the remaining ZALfJs in Distrikt Galizien in this report as of late June 1943, see p. 14.

16. Archives of the Jewish Historical Institute in Warsaw (AŻIH), 301/327, testimony of Izaak Szwarc; State Archives of the Russian Federation in Moscow (GARF), 7021-75-107, pp. 30, 31, 324–26.

17. AŻIH, 302/50, Diary of Małgorzata Bolschower (translated by the author of this article from the German original).

18. USHMM, RG-14.101M, Folders 1236–39, 1343–45, 1360–69 (BA-L, B 162/27801).

19. Józef Marszałek, *Obozy pracy w Generalnym Gubernatorstwie w latach 1939–1945* (Lublin: Państwowe Muzeum na Majdanku, 1998), 139–56. Ilya Altman's more recent publication gives the number of just ninety-four ZALfJs in Distrikt Galizien; see Il'ja Al'tmann, *Opfer des Hasses: Der Holocaust in der UdSSR 1941–1945* (Zurich: Gleichen, 2008), 222. Due to the establishment of barracks camps at their workplaces, in some towns there were as many as six or seven separate ZALfJs.

20. Excellent local maps of Greater Poland from the 1920s and 1930s can be found on the Mapster Polish website Przeglądarka skorowidzów, http://igrek.amzp.pl/mapindex.php?cat=WIG100.

21. Gavriel Lindenberg, ed., *Sefer Tlustah* (Tel Aviv: Irgun yots'e Telustah veha-sevivah be-Yirsra'el uve-Artsot ha-Berit, 1965), 133. See also Tatiana Berenstein, "Praca przymusowa ludności żydowskiej w tzw: Dystrykcie Galicja (1941–1944)," *Biuletyn Żydowskiego Instytutu Historycznego* (*Bulletin of the Jewish Historical Institute*), no. 69 (1969): 14. On the establishment and organization of the estates until the summer of 1943, see especially the detailed statement of Ehrhart Hanf, BA-L, B 162/5186, 7460–65.

22. BA-BL, NS 19/3921, p. 7, Vermerk, Jagielnica, April 29, 1943.

23. Ibid., p. 4, Feld-Kommandostelle, June 12, 1943.

24. Pohl, *Nationalsozialistische Judenverfolgung*, 345.

25. Aleksandr Kruglov, *Katastrofa ukrainskogo evreistva 1941–1944 gg.: Entsiklopedicheskii spravochnik* (Kharkov, Ukraine: "Karavella," 2001), 201, 274 (Milowce and Rożanówka); and AŻIH, 301/4990, testimony of Max Schmerer (Milowce); VHA, # 5991, testimony of Zofia Pollack. See also the testimony of her brother Carl Berkowitz, VHA, # 13144 (Trawna and Szulganówka).

26. Lindenberg, *Sefer Tlustah*, 133.

27. BA-L, B 162/5186, pp. 7384–7385 (statement of Mendl Wein-

stock, November 10, 1969) and pp. 7540–41 (statement of Ernst Paukstatt, March 13, 1970).

28. Lindenberg, *Sefer Tlustah*, 208–9.

29. VHA, # 32925, testimony of Michael Schiller.

30. Kruglov, *Katastrofa*, p. 274, gives the date of July 17; VHA, # 32925, testimony of Michael Schiller, who gives the date of the *Aktion* as July 20, 1943.

31. VHA, # 5991, testimony of Zofia Pollack, and # 13144, testimony of Carl Berkowitz.

32. Kruglov, *Katastrofa*, 201; AŻIH, 301/4990, testimony of Max Schmerer.

33. VHA, # 32925, testimony of Michael Schiller; Lindenberg, *Sefer Tlustah*, 168–69, 209.

34. VHA, # 27287, testimony of Michael Hirsch.

35. Avraham Beker, *Kehilatayim (Husiatin ve-Kopitsintsah)* (Tel Aviv: Hutza La-'Or ay Irgun Yotsei Husiyatin Ha-Galitsayit Be-Yisra'el, 1977), 262–63; VHA, # 27287, testimony of Michael Hirsch.

36. ITS, 6.3.3.2, T/Ds 211345, 563292–93, and 573382.

37. Aleksandr Kruglov, *Entsiklopediia kholokosta: evreiskaia entsiklopediia Ukrainy* (Kiev: Evreiskii sovet Ukrainy, Fond "Pamiat′ zhertv fashizma," 2000), 163; VHA, # 46576, testimony of Rachel Kriegel. Morgenstern, *Chortkov Remembered*, 81–83, notes that sixty people were shot.

38. Lindenberg, *Sefer Tlustah*, 235.

39. VHA, # 9422, testimony of Samuel Kleiner.

40. AZIH, 301/3882, 3883, 3884, 3888, 3889, and 38890.

41. Prifer, "My Walk through Seven Levels of Hell," translated by Harvey Buchalter, in Sh. Meltzer, ed., *Sefer Horodenka* (Tel Aviv: Former Residents of Horodenka and Vicinity in Israel and the USA, 1963), 275–85.

42. Ibid.

43. Ibid.

44. Nachum Blumental, ed., *Sefer Borshchov* (Tel Aviv: Association of Former Residents of Borszczów in Israel, 1960), 303–8.

45. See, for example, Jan Grabowski, *Hunt for the Jews: Betrayal and Murder in German-Occupied Poland* (Bloomington: Indiana University Press, 2013).

46. Israel Gutman et al., eds., *The Encyclopedia of the Righteous Among the Nations: Rescuers of Jews during the Holocaust—Europe (Part II)* (Jerusalem: Yad Vashem, 2011), 308–9.

47. Bella Gutterman, *A Narrow Bridge to Life: Jewish Forced Labor and Survival in the Gross-Rosen Camp System* (New York: Berghahn, 2008), 5–6. Albrecht Schmelt was the German official in charge of all the labor camps for "foreign workers" in Silesia.

48. Adam Tooze, *The Wages of Destruction: The Making and Breaking of the Nazi Economy* (New York: Penguin, 2006), 528.

49. VHA, # 3728, testimony of Chaim Roessler; see also the account of Berl Yakubowicz in A. Wolf Yasni, ed., *Sefer Klobuck* (Tel Aviv: Former Klobuck Residents in Israel, France, and Australia, 1960), 276–77, who describes the "Gintebrick" camp as a "paradise."

50. VHA, # 3728, testimony of Chaim Roessler. I am grateful to Andrew Kloes for this analysis of Roessler's testimony and other evidence regarding ZALfJ Güntherbrücke.

51. USHMM, RG-41.014M (NIOD), Folder 6, pp. 126–29, Levie Barmhartigheid; see also pp. 131–34 and 138–40, RG-41.010M (NIOD), Reel 368, Verklarung Abraham Jonas Walg, which states that he left ninety-three or ninety-four dead comrades in Seibersdorf.

52. Christopher Browning, *Remembering Survival: Inside a Nazi Slave-Labor Camp* (New York: W. W. Norton, 2010), 76–77.

53. Felicja Karay, *Death Comes in Yellow: Skarzysko-Kamienna Labor Camp* (Amsterdam: Harwood Academic Publishers, 1996), 141–61. Karay notes the comparatively favorable conditions in the farm section of Werk B, for example.

54. Browning, *Remembering Survival*, 296–97.

55. Jack Zaifman (as told to Deanna Bosco Sass), *Tailor-Made for Life: The Story of Jacov "Jack" Zaifman, Holocaust Survivor* (Breinigsville, Penn.: D. Sass, J. Zaifman, 2010), 30–31; VHA, # 9216, testimony of Carl Rosenberg.

56. Raul Hilberg, *Die Vernichtung der europäischen Juden* (Frankfurt am Main: Fischer, 1982), 566–67.

57. David Silberklang, *Gates of Tears: The Holocaust in the Lublin District* (Jerusalem: Yad Vashem, 2013), 430–34.

58. Grabowski, *Hunt for the Jews*, 237–39 (Appendix, Table 9). Searches for survivors of this region conducted using the ITS digital archive, however, do reveal the names of additional Jews, some of whom survived in camps.

59. Dieter Pohl, "The Holocaust and the Concentration Camps," in *Concentration Camps in Nazi Germany: The New Histories*, ed. Jane Caplan and Nikolaus Wachsmann (London: Routledge, 2010), 149–166. Pohl refers here primarily to the concentration camps, but many Jews were transferred from ZALfJs into the concentration camp system in 1943 and 1944.

60. Blumental, *Sefer Borshchov*, 304.

Jan Grabowski

A Study in the Microhistory of the Holocaust: The *Liquidierungsaktion* in Węgrów Ghetto

THIS ARTICLE IS A SMALL PART OF A LARGER, ONGOING PROJECT entitled "Jewish Survival Strategies in Occupied Poland, 1939–1945," led by several members of the Polish Center for Holocaust Research in cooperation with the Yad Vashem Institute for Advanced Holocaust Studies in Jerusalem. The goal of this effort is to conduct an inquiry into the survival strategies of Jews who went into hiding in four preselected, rural counties of the Warsaw, Kraków, and Lublin Districts of occupied Poland (reorganized by the Germans into a rump state known as the Generalgouvernement, or in English, General Government), as well as in one county of the Bezirk Bialystok.[1] While our knowledge of the fate of the Jews hiding in the urban centers of the General Government is significant, much less is known about the survival strategies pursued by the Jews in the countryside. The project is innovative on many levels, but its focus on the victims and on their survival strategies as well as the focus on rural areas needs to be pointed out.

The first step in our work involves reconstructing in as much detail as possible descriptions of the liquidations of the ghettos located on the territories of each researcher's chosen county.[2] These so-called *Liquidierungsaktionen*, which involved an unprecedented level of violence and brutality, are difficult to describe and even harder to imagine. Nevertheless, to understand what the factors were which determined who lived and who died, including Jewish survival strategies and the relations among the Jewish victims, their Polish neighbors, and the Germans, an in-depth examination of these "Actions" (*Aktionen*) is necessary. The present article is an attempt to describe the destruction

Figure 1. Map of Węgrów County, Poland

of the Jewish community of Węgrów, a small town located some fifty miles northeast of Warsaw, in Węgrów County (figure 1).

JEWS IN WĘGRÓW AND THE WĘGRÓW GHETTO PRIOR TO THE *LIQUIDIERUNGSAKTION*

Jews had lived in Węgrów and in the area for hundreds of years. Although they were concentrated, for the most part, in the city of Węgrów and in the smaller towns of Stoczek and Łochów, Jewish communities existed in all of the rural communes (*gminy*) which made up the county.[3] The 1931 Polish national census reported the following population counts for Węgrów County:

Roman Catholics	76,511 (86.2%)
Protestants	1,483 (1.7%)
Jews	8,888 (10.0%)
Mariavites*	1,608 (1.8%)
Greek Catholics	83 (0.1%)

*A sect, an offshoot from the Catholic Church, formed at the turn of the twentieth century in central Poland.

The count based on religious affiliation is much more reliable than responses based on nationality, a term which, for many inhabitants of the county in the prewar period, was still rather elusive. While the overall number of Jews reflected the Polish "average" of 10 percent, the situation in Węgrów was also very different. In 1921, the city had 8,522 inhabitants, among them 5,148 Jews and 3,276 Christian Poles. In the 1930s, the Jewish population stagnated and the Polish population grew considerably, but in terms of numbers, the Jews still formed the largest community in the city.

The outbreak of war brought immediate and dramatic changes to the living conditions of all inhabitants of the area, but from the first days of occupation, Jews were singled out for particularly harsh measures. One of the first victims of terror was Ezechiel Szatensztajn, one of the wealthiest people in town, whose property was stolen by the German officials immediately after his execution. A few days later, on Yom Kippur, September 23, 1939, the German soldiers tortured and later murdered Jakub Mendel Morgenstern, the rabbi of Węgrów. The brutal and public execution of Morgenstern was to serve—according to the Germans—as a "lesson to the Jews."[4] Acts of terror against the Jewish elites went hand in hand with brutal campaigns directed at the Jewish community as a whole, with all men being regularly forced to perform hard, unpaid, and often humiliating labor.[5] Some Jews decided to flee to the east under Soviet occupation, but the vast majority of deeply religious people feared Soviet Communism more than the Germans, whose goals were still very much a mystery. Even though some left Węgrów, many more Jews were resettled there from the former Polish territories now incorporated directly into the Reich (known as *Eingegliederte Ostgebiete*). According to the Polish mayor of Węgrów, due to these migrations, the number of Jews living in the city soon reached eight thousand.[6] The German counts seem to confirm his estimate.[7]

In mid-October 1939, the Germans reorganized the administration of the General Government. One of the changes they made was the dissolution of counties and their transformation into much larger jurisdictions known as *Kreishauptmannschaften*. Węgrów county was thus abolished and fused together with parts of the neighbouring Sokołów county into the new Kreishauptmannschaft Wengrow-Sokolow, with the administrative center located in Sokołów Podlaski, ten miles away from Węgrów. In May 1940, Ernst Gramss, a fanatical Nazi and a murderer of Jews,[8] became *Kreishauptmann* (County Chief) in Sokołów and held the office until the end of the German occupation, in August 1944. In one of the letters to his wife, Gramss wrote, "soon I will be introduced into my new office and I will salute my people. . . . I have here a beautiful house, two horses, a car and I can live like a 'little governor.' There is a swimming pool in the park, we can build a sauna . . . here, I am a king."[9] The arrival of the new "king" meant more misery for the local Jews.

Three ghettos were created: in Węgrów, Łochów, and Stoczek, and Jews living in villages were gradually resettled into the three designated areas. The ghettos had their own Jewish councils, and Jewish police were responsible for maintaining order within the ghettos.[10] The ghetto in Węgrów was rather unique because—due to the large concentration of Jews—the entire city was initially designated as a ghetto.[11] On September 13, 1940, Gramss officially restricted the right of residence for Jews to the indicated areas and, one month later, imposed a curfew for the "non-Aryan" population.[12] In 1941, a string of new regulations made life for the Jews of Kreishauptmannschaft

Sokolow-Wegrow even more difficult. Further restrictions on their freedom of movement brought about famine followed by epidemics of typhus. The final separation of the Jewish population was ordered in March 1942, when the previously open ghettos (including the ghetto in Węgrów) were closed.[13] And in this manner the stage was set for the implementation of the "final solution."

THE PERPETRATORS

We do not know much about the policemen from the Węgrów area, and the little we do know needs to be described in some detail. The main detachment of Schutzpolizei[14] was based in Węgrów itself and—at least until the end of 1942—was placed under the command of one Müller, a tall and strong man in his mid-forties. Sometime at the end of 1942 (or in early 1943) Müller was replaced by Oberleutnant Diestelhorst. Among his subordinates were one Brenner and his colleagues Giler and Langner.[15] Giler has been described by one of the witnesses as "the worst of all gendarmes and whenever he failed to kill a Jew, he would take it out on us, Poles."[16] In the area of our interest there were two other Order Police detachments, one in Sokołów (from which the officers were often despatched to Węgrów) and another in nearby Budziska.[17] Among the officers stationed in Sokołów, many hailed from the former Czechoslovakia and, not infrequently, were able to communicate with the locals in broken Polish.[18]

In July 1940, the Budziska/Łochów police detachment received a new commander, Lieutenant Karl Tedsen.[19] In his new role, Tedsen also became the commanding officer of the Polish "blue" police in Łochów. If one were to trust Tedsen's postwar testimony (and there is no reason to doubt him in this particular matter), his tasks included supervising all Polish police detachments across Węgrów County. His own police force in Budziska included twelve gendarmes, among them Rudolf Pietsch (from Potsdam), the local *Volksdeutscher* Friedrich Hartmann, and officers Oprisnik, Schmidt, and Kögel. Tedsen's deputy, *Gendarmeriemeister* (Chief of the Gendarmerie) Wilhelm Pross, soon acquired notoriety as a murderer of Jews. According to Tedsen, he and his policemen were charged only with fighting common criminality. The rare occasions when his men had to assist their colleagues from the Security Service of the SS, the Sicherheitsdienst (SD), involved the arrests of Poles denounced by other Poles to the

Security Police. Otherwise, maintained Tedsen, his gendarmes were never involved in any "illegal" activities. Karl Kurnig, a gendarme from Sokołów, lied with equal aplomb as his colleague from Budziska: "among my friends, we heard rumors that there were some actions against the Jews, but we had no concrete information. I can state with full responsibility that my colleagues from Sokołów never took part, and in no form," in any such action.[20] According to Kurnig, the forces responsible for the liquidations of the ghettos were recruited from among the unspecified "Finnish troops," SD officers, and the members of the Sonderdienst led by Kreishauptmann Grimss.[21] In reality, however, the involvement of Tedsen and his people in the establishment of the German system of terror in Węgrów County was infinitely more important than one could judge on the basis of their self-serving testimonies. In the summer of 1942, for instance, Tedsen personally conducted the mass shooting of more than seventy Jews in Budziska, next to the police station,[22] and two of his officers, Volksdeutsche Hübscher and Hoppe, belonged to the so-called *Ghettokommando*, or gendarmes who were most often deployed in the Węgrów and Sokołów ghettos.

The second force involved in the implementation of the local *Judenpolitik* was the Security Police, most often referred to simply as the Gestapo. The External Detachment of the Warsaw Commander of the Security Police and SD in Sokołów (Außenstelle des Kommandeurs der Sicherheitspolizei und des SD Warschau in Sokolow) was led by SS-Sturmscharführer and Criminal Secretary Friedrich Schröder. His subordinates included SS-Scharführer Uwe Karsten, SS-Rottenführer Gustav Friedrich, Criminal Commissioner Kurt Nicolaus, and SS-Obersturmführer Rudolf Weber, who replaced Schröder as commander in 1943. Other members of the Gestapo in Sokołów included one Schweitzer, a driver, and Hirsekorn, a local *Volksdeutscher* and interpreter.[23] It is worthwhile to keep their names in mind, since these were the people who were given the overall responsibility for coordinating the liquidations of the ghettos on the territory of Kreishauptmannschaft Wengrow-Sokolow.

In addition to the Gestapo, the local Security Police also included the Polish Criminal Police (*Polnische Kriminalpolizei*, or Kripo) with its headquarters located in Sokołów, headed by the previously mentioned Schröder, the chief of the Gestapo.[24] The German Order Police and the Security Police were further reinforced by the Polish "blue" police (*Polnische Polizei*)—an essential element of the police presence in Węgrów County. The local "blue" police had more than 130 officers on duty, working out of eight stations. The stations of the "blue" police were located in Bojmie, Miedzna, Węgrow, Wyszków, Łochów, Sadowne, Stoczek, and Grębków. The names of most of the Polish officers were long forgotten, and most of the relevant police documentation was destroyed either during or after the war. Some of them, however, can still be identified, and they are also definitely worth mentioning, since their role in the liquidation of the ghettos and the subsequent hunt for the fleeing Jews became all-important.[25] Last but not least, the forces which were soon to be used in the destruction of the local ghettos included the Ukrainian auxiliaries (the so-called *Trawniki-Männer*)[26] led by SS-Sturmbannführer Theodor van Eupen, commander of the notorious Treblinka I labor camp. Van Eupen was in charge of the liquidation *Aktion* in Sokołów Podlaski and, according to numerous witnesses, personally tortured and murdered Jews in the streets of the city.[27]

AKTION IN WĘGRÓW

One needs to begin the description of the liquidation of Węgrów and other nearby ghettos by acknowledging the extent of our ignorance. To start with, the evaluation of the number of Jews killed during the *Aktionen* is nothing more than a guess. Sometimes, as is the case with smaller locations, even the dates of deportations and liquidations cannot be firmly established. Finally, we know precious little about the people involved in the destruction of the ghettos and about their tactics. Bearing this in mind, we can start to analyze the drama that culminated on August 22–24, 1942.

Shortly before the deportation, the German authorities decided to concentrate all Jews living around Węgrów in the city. Many were seized and forcibly relocated; some agreed to move without the use of force. Nehama Rotbart and her family, for example, were forcibly removed from their home village of Bojmie and—having been given just thirty minutes to pack up their possessions—were shipped off to Węgrów.[28] With the influx of deportees, the living conditions in the already overcrowded ghetto deteriorated further, exposing the Jewish inmates to starvation and typhus. In the same period, in the spring and early summer, terrifying news began circulating in the ghetto, news about the deportations and liquidations of more and less distant ghettos. In July 1942, the Jews of Węgrów became aware of the gravity of their situation: two main railway lines carrying death transports to Treblinka (the Warsaw-Tłuszcz-Małkinia and the Siedlce-Sokołów-Małkinia lines) crossed the borders of Węgrów County not far from the city. In July 1942, the death trains to Treblinka carried, for the most part, Jews from the liquidated Warsaw ghetto. In many cases, the desperate Jews tore away the wooden planks of the wagons, or tore away the barbed wires that covered the windows, and attempted to flee. Some were shot by the guards stationed on the roofs of the wagons, some were killed during the jump, and some were later killed by the locals. There were some, however, who managed to reach one of the nearby ghettos, such as Węgrów, and gave accounts of the tragedy unfolding in Warsaw.[29]

"THAT NIGHT WE COULD NOT SLEEP"—WĘGRÓW-SOKOŁÓW, SEPTEMBER 21, 1942, MONDAY, 11:00 P.M.

The "Great Action" in Warsaw overshadowed the tragedy of the smaller ghettos located in the vicinity. In some cases, the liquidation commandos led by the notorious Hermann Höfle took advantage of short "interruptions" in their work in Warsaw to liquidate the nearby ghettos. The Jewish inhabitants of Falenica, Otwock, Rembertów, Jadwisin, Radzymin, Wołomin, Jadów, and Parczew were herded to the death trains August 19–20. The next day it was the turn of the large ghetto in Mińsk Mazowiecki, and then August 22–24, the Kommando arrived in Siedlce, Łosice, and Mordy. Höfle's people then returned to Warsaw to finish their murderous job in the Polish capital. The last transport from Warsaw, consisting of 2,100 Jews—Jewish policemen for the most part—left the ghetto for Treblinka on September 21, 1942.[30] After the "Great Action" in Warsaw was completed, some of Hofle's people were ordered eastward, to the area of our immediate interest, to the Kreishauptmannschaft Wengrow-Sokolow. Once in place, they were reinforced by the local police forces: Schutzpolizei (Schupo), gendarmerie, and the Polish "blue" police.

Rumors about the impending liquidation had run rampant in the Węgrów ghetto for quite some time, at least since late spring. In the course of August and early September, the rumors were confirmed by the refugees fleeing the liquidated ghettos in Warsaw and Siedlce, and in nearby Mińsk Mazowiecki. The desperate Jews in flight shared the stories of unspeakable cruelties committed by the Askars—a name given to the feared and notorious Ukrainian auxiliaries—and their German masters. Norma Przepiórka, a Jewish inhabitant of Węgrów, recalled that on the eve of deportation, all local Jews were fully aware of what was awaiting them in Treblinka.[31] With mounting panic, people started to prepare themselves for a siege. They built ingenious hideouts to make it possible for them to survive the initial German fury. Few were ready to accept that the "final solution" was going to be, indeed, final. At the same time, many Jews started to seek out contacts on the Aryan side of the city, looking for help among the Poles, including former neighbors, sometimes friends, and business partners. Leaving the ghetto was not really a problem, but avoiding capture and finding help on the other side of the fence was an altogether different matter. There is no doubt that, for the Jews crossing to the Aryan side, the greatest danger was associated not with the Germans but with the Poles. Unlike the former, Poles could easily tell a Jew from a non-Jew by their accent, customs, or physical appearance.[32]

The first signs of the impending liquidation reached the office of the *Kreishauptmann* a day or two before the planned *Aktion*. We can pinpoint precisely this moment because that is when wives of German officials began to recover in haste the previously ordered shoes, dresses, and other items they had ordered from the Jewish artisans. The day before the *Liquidierungsaktion*, Polish "blue" police were placed on alert, and local *voits* (commune chiefs) and village elders were ordered to prepare an adequate number of people, horses, and carts for the operation.[33] According to several testimonies, the local Polish volunteer firefighters were also placed on alert. Finally, on September 21, 1942, the Ukrainian Askars and two German "liquidation units" known as *Liquidierungskommando*, one from Warsaw and one from Treblinka, arrived in Sokołów.

At the same time, on September 21, 1942, the Jews started to prepare for the observance of Yom Kippur, or the Day of Atonement, which was about to begin. One of the few Jewish survivors recalled:

> We began our prayers early on Yom Kippur, so that if the Germans caught us and dispersed us, we would have at least finished the *shaharis* [first morning service]. Shmuel Moncarz was the cantor for *shaharis* and Yitzhak Szydlowski for *musaf* [second service]. He

> reached the *Unesaneh Tokeh*, which reads: "Who shall live and who shall die, who shall come to a timely and who to an untimely end, who shall perish by fire, and who shall perish by water, who by the sword and who by wild beast, who by hunger, and who by thirst, who by earthquake and who by plague, who by strangling . . ." When he came to this point, we all envisioned "strangling" as referring to having our lives snuffed out at Treblinka. We all wept so loudly that the cantor had to hold his chanting and could not proceed. After 700 years, this would be one of the final services in Węgrów.[34]

A similar scene took place in the house of another man who eventually survived; he recounted how, right after the common prayer, he was informed that allegedly somewhere in the ghetto guns were being readied and people were bracing for battle.[35]

While most of the Jews of Węgrów were praying in preparation for Yom Kippur, the cordon of German and Polish policemen and their Ukrainian helpers was rapidly encircling the city. On September 22, 1942, between 4:00 and 5:00 A.M., the ring finally closed. Węgrów, Sokołów, and Stoczek were cordoned off in such a way that the policemen taking part in the *Aktion* were spread apart at intervals of no more than one hundred meters. On September 22, the sun rose at 6:15 A.M., but the sky started to brighten around 5:00 A.M. so that the members of the *Liquidierungkommando* could see one another. Yet the cordon closing around Węgrów was not impermeable: although no one could leave the city, people could gain access from outside (see figure 2). This outside access was of particular importance for the peasants who, that very day, brought their products to the weekly market.

The sequence of events in Węgrów resembled closely that of the liquidations conducted in other towns and hamlets across the Warsaw and Lublin Districts of the General Government. The only change in the strategy was that, while in the spring and early summer of 1942 the ghettos were being liquidated in a haphazard way, without a clear geographic pattern, now the Germans adopted a more systematic approach. The liquidations henceforth were conducted in one sweep, with the *Aktion* striking simultaneously all Jewish communities located on the territory of the same *Kreishauptmannschaft*.[36] One could even venture a guess that the liquidations were conducted according to one master script which was applied with a macabre regularity and discipline all over Poland beginning in the spring and continuing on

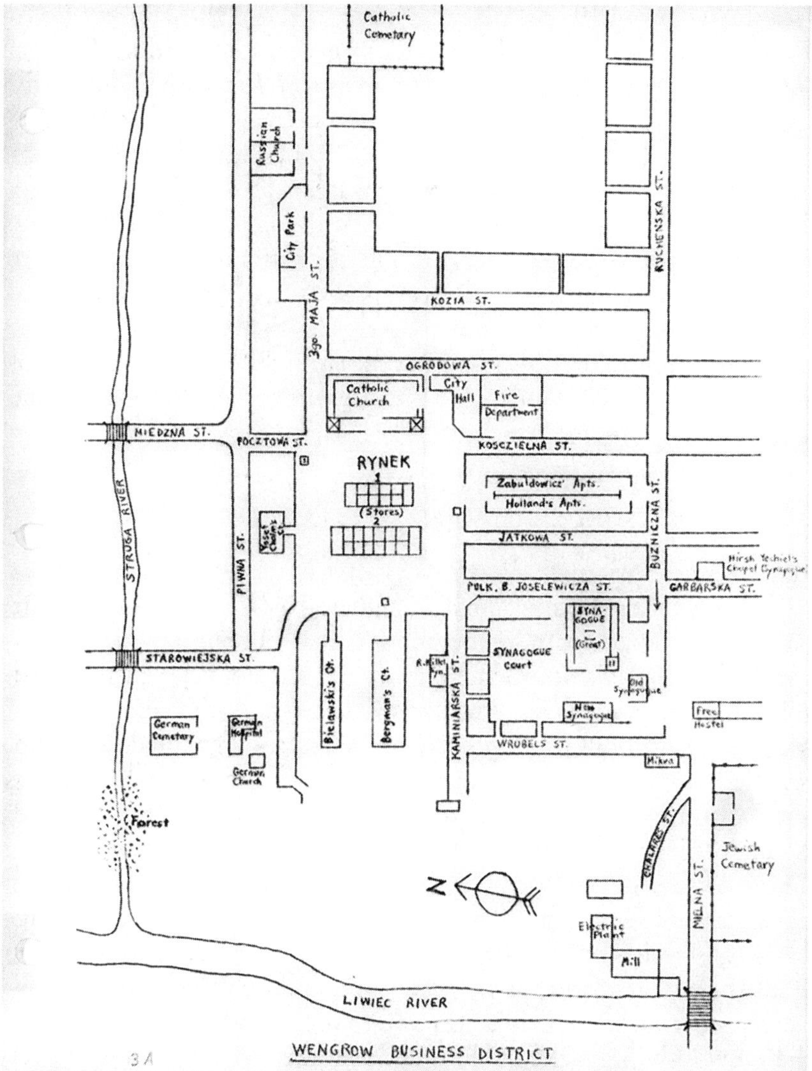

Figure 2. Map of Węgrów, drawn by Shraga Feivel Bielawski, courtesy of his son, Stanley Biel

into the winter of 1942. In larger ghettos, such as those in Lublin or Tarnów, the liquidation process was more complex and multistage, and it included dividing the Jewish areas into sections A and B (for "working" and "nonworking" Jews, respectively) and distributing special passes (known as "stamps of life"). In the end, however, the sole purpose of these additional measures was to facilitate further deportations and the implementation of the next stage of the "final solution."[37] On the eve of deportation, a German officer was said to have made a brief appearance in the ghetto, assuring the members of the Judenrat (Jewish council) that no *Aktion* was planned. It is hard to say whether it was just gossip, a sign of wishful thinking, or a conscious attempt made by the Germans to confuse their victims even further.

WĘGRÓW-SOKOŁÓW-STOCZEK, TUESDAY, SEPTEMBER 22, 6:00 A.M. TO NOON

Harry Miller (originally known as Hersz Meier), who had to move to Węgrów from Jarnice, a small village nearby, learned about the approaching soldiers from his neighbor, just before 5:00 A.M. on September 22. By that point, the ghetto had already been surrounded, and some armed men were strolling the streets.[38] At the same time that Miller learned about the approaching Askars, a man named Rotsztajn, resettled to Węgrów from his native Grębkowo three weeks before, was witness to the growing panic of the Jewish inmates of the ghetto.[39] Facing the imminent *Aktion*, the Jews tried desperately to find shelter on the Aryan side, among the Poles. Most often the Jews pleaded with peasants from the nearby villages for help, knowing that finding refuge in the city itself would be practically impossible. Usually the children would be sent first, and parents, if still able and welcome, would follow.

At dawn, when the first shots were fired, Jews started to hide in the previously prepared hideouts and bunkers. The members of the Judenrat made an attempt to convince people to report to the main market square "to go to work," but their appeals fell on deaf ears. Even the Jewish police (a small force of two dozen) were unable to force the Jews into the open, as few people doubted that the final destination was the death camp at Treblinka.[40]

Hiding in the cellars, in the attics, and in the bunkers was, in most cases, a short-term solution that ended in tragedy. It was at this stage that the Germans and the Ukrainians gained a powerful ally in the form of many Polish inhabitants of Węgrów, who joined the *Liquidierungskommando* in the search for hidden Jews. According to Efraim Przepiórka, Christian neighbors were additionally motivated by the Germans with the promise of a quarter kilo of sugar as a prize for every Jew delivered to the authorities.[41]

Just after 6:00 A.M., the Germans reached the house in the attic of which Shraga Feivel Bielawski hid himself and his family. The Germans were not alone: "We heard the voice of our 'friend' Maniek Karbowski [Polish neighbor of the Bielawski family] saying: 'I'll bring an axe and chop it down.' A moment later, an axe was hacking at the door. Maniek told the Germans, 'These bastard Jews are still sleeping.' When the door yielded, Maniek and the SS troops entered. The soldiers yelled: 'Raus!' ['Come out!'] as they scoured the store and the cellar. They pounded at the floor boards but found no one. The Germans left. We lay still as if dead."[42] Eighteen-year-old Cyla Rubenfeld described these moments in similar terms: the town had been surrounded by the Gestapo, the Ukrainian police, and the Schupo. Many Jews hid in the bunkers that, one after another, were being discovered by the German and Polish search parties.[43] The searches were conducted with extreme brutality and violence, and the streets were soon filled with crowds of Jews being driven toward the market square, which the Germans had transformed into a holding pen for thousands of the ghetto inmates. "Jews, who woke up to the terrible news, ran like mad around the city, half-naked, looking for shelter," wrote Władysław Okulus, the mayor of Węgrów. Most of the people taken to the market square were those who were deemed (or: who were judged to be) able to withstand the ordeals of further travel. Others—small children and the elderly, for the most part—were either killed in the streets or executed in the nearby Jewish cemetery. The sixteen-year-old son of Müller, the chief of the Węgrów Schupo detachment, also took part in the *Aktion* and, dressed in his Hitlerjugend (Hitler Youth) uniform, helped his father kill Jews.

The same day, at the same time, around 6:00 A.M., another *Liquidierungskommando* struck the ghetto in Sokołów Podlaski, ten miles east of Węgrów. The pattern was the same: thousands of Jews were driven from their houses straight to the main square, and special search teams looked for the hideouts, killing those who offered any resistance. Paul Thurm, the director of the District Office for Commerce in Agricultural Products (*Kommissar der landwirtschaftlichen Kreis-*

handelgenossenschaft) in Sokołów, was on his way to work as usual.[44] He was driven by his Polish chauffeur, one Raciborski. They reached the city shortly before 7:00 A.M. Thurm recalled, "When I asked him 'what's new in town,' Raciborski said to me: 'Oh, yes, today they are shooting all over the place, they want to kill all the Jews.' On the way I saw soldiers shooting the Jews who tried to flee by jumping from one roof to another. From the windows of my office, which was located just 100 metres from the ghetto, I saw Jews being driven into the main square. They stood there, at the so-called Market Square, the whole day. Those who tried to flee were killed. From what I know the old and the infirm were executed in their beds."[45] According to Thurm, the *Kreishauptmann*, SS-Obersturmbannführer Ernst Gramss himself, was involved in the *Aktion*, and he was "working" hand in hand with his deputy, Dr. Klaus Hermann, and Schröder, the chief of the Gestapo. Szabtaj Grünberg, whose entire family was killed that day, witnessed the destruction of the Sokołów ghetto. He wrote that "the place was surrounded by the SS, Schupo and the Polish 'blue' Police. Shortly before 7 am they started to drive everybody toward the central square."[46]

WĘGRÓW—NOON TO 5:00 P.M.

We do not know exactly what the situation was in the market square, the assembly point for Jews in Węgrów. No Jewish testimony survives, and the Germans and Poles who were present in the area preferred, for obvious reasons, to keep their memories to themselves. We have, however, the testimony of Aaron Elster, a ten-year-old boy who, together with thousands of other Jews, waited in horror at the market square in nearby Sokołów:

> A woman escapes from the ghetto, and two Poles violently drag her back to the Market Place as she fights for her life. Though trying to cover my face, I watch as the woman attempts resistance, grabbing at the ground as she kicks and punches the Poles in vain. The female victim is turned over to the Gestapo guard who has been holding the machine gun pointed at all of us. Standing in his black boots and dark uniform, he grabs the woman by her dark hair and tells her she must choose if she wants to be shot or be sent to Treblinka. The woman falls to the ground and begs for her life. The guard's head tilts back, and with a loud bellowing laugh he tells the

> woman she has taken too long to make the decision. He pushes the woman away by kicking her and shoots her in the head. As this happens, the Market Place is filled with screams as the Ukrainian lackeys and the Gestapo guard laugh.[47]

The situation in Węgrów, on the main square, around noon, seems to have been no different. Władysław Wójcik, an inhabitant of Liw (a village situated four miles south of Węgrów) who was later recognized by Yad Vashem as Righteous Among the Nations, observed the unfolding events from "the front row," as he wrote later. Having heard about the ongoing liquidation, Wójcik set off to Węgrów early in the morning. He describes what he found:

> Around noon I finally reached the market square, in the center of the city. I was able to see for myself that getting to the center was not a problem, so that the sidewalks were filled with the [Polish] population living on the Aryan side of town. In order to gain a better view, I climbed the stairs of a building situated opposite the church. The place resonated all the time with rifle and revolver shots coming from the Jewish quarter, and I could hear the cries and moans of dying people. The market was right next to the ghetto, so that the shootings and the moans drove us, spectators, to despair. As soon as I arrived at the market I saw that the whole area had been surrounded by the gendarmes and their Ukrainian lackeys. In the middle of this ring I could see a few thousand Jews, men, women and youth, sitting on the stones or on their luggage. All the time more Poles of Semitic descent[48] were being marched into the circle from the ghetto.[49]

According to Wójcik, the children, the elderly, and pregnant women were murdered in the Węgrów Ghetto, or in the Jewish cemetery. Zygmunt Klem, another Pole watching the unfolding massacre, noted:

> On the small square the Germans held a group of about 400 Jews and on the large square in front of the synagogue a larger group of about 1000 people was being guarded by the gendarmes. I could clearly see an officer holding his pistol and staring at a young Jew. The Jew, gesticulating, tried to explain something to the German, but the officer raised his weapon and killed him. The Jew fell down and we [the author and his friend] went on our way, to the nearest bar. We sat there until later in the afternoon, when we learned that the Poles were again allowed to leave the city.[50]

Henryka Grabowska, a young woman at the time, saw the masses of Jews being marched toward the market square. She recalled the terrible scenes that occurred in plain sight of all the inhabitants of the city: "I went out to fetch water from the well. Gendarme Gil [most likely officer Giler from the Schupo detachment in Węgrów] and two Ukrainians led a woman with a little child. With the mother watching, they took the baby by the legs, impaled it on a bayonet, and later shot the woman. I will never forget her horrible screams. . . . Nearby, I saw another dead woman; she was lying in the street and next to her there were two children. One of them had its head smashed, and it cried: 'Mama!' "[51]

Shraga Feivel Bielawski also had something to say about Giler and his role during the liquidation:

> In the course of the day, we heard Fishel Chudzik's family. They were our nearest Jewish neighbors and the proprietors of a restaurant that Maniek Karbowski had stolen. They had three daughters, Bracha, age eleven, Chaya, nine, and Hinde, five. The Germans had often come to eat in his restaurant. The commander of the German forces here, Herr Giller, also frequented the restaurant. He had befriended the children and brought them chocolates every day. Frequently, they crawled onto his lap, and he played with them. They liked him and greeted him by name. . . . Fishel had hollowed out a hiding place under the floor boards of his house for his family. When it became too difficult and crowded, he stole away in the night to a nearby village to search for a new hideaway. . . . Before Fishel could return, Poles scoured the home and found his wife, Toibe, and the girls. They summoned Giller, who came and hauled the four to the front of the building. It was near our store, and we could hear every word. The children begged Giller: "Herr Giller, let us live! You know us. You used to bring us chocolate. You used to play with us. You used to love us! Let us live, please let us live!" Giller yelled, "Faster, faster!" The oldest of the girls said to her mother, "I want to live a little longer." Her mother answered bitterly, "No, you will not live because the world has no room for you!" The children screamed and cried as they were herded into the market square. A few seconds later we heard some shots, and then it was quiet.[52]

According to Mayor Okulus, during these tragic moments, the Polish population of the city splintered into three "nearly hostile" groups: "The first group, the most numerous one, not only sympathized with the Jews, but offered shelter and provided [Jews] with food, even though it was a capital offense. The second group were the fascists who expressed their joy and satisfaction [with the German actions] but did not cooperate with the enemy." The third group of the Polish citizens of Węgrów, described Okulus, became directly involved in the extermination of the local Jewry.[53] It must have been this third group of local citizenry whose role prompted Bielawski to note, "On the street, the cries of Jews mixed with the shouts of the Germans and with the laughter of the Poles. Throughout the day the *SS-Männer*, with the eager assistance of the Poles, loaded the Jews on open lorries, which left for Treblinka."[54] The search for hidden Jews was spearheaded by young teenage boys, who scoured the city looking for new victims whom they promptly delivered to the Germans. Twenty-year-old Renia Lipski, who desperately tried to leave the city to seek refuge in one of the Julags (*Judenlager*, or labor camps for Jews), was caught by a group of Polish boys. She was saved from the hands of the teenage hunters by the local teacher, who convinced the boys that the girl was actually a Pole. Nevertheless, she had to flee because her tormentors went to look for the police.[55]

Some teenagers not only tracked the Jews but also murdered them. Seventeen-year-old Edward Witecki helped the gendarmes locate the Jewish hideouts. Sometime around 2:00 P.M., a gendarme known as "Hans" shot a fleeing Jew in the groin and then handed his rifle to Witecki to finish off the wounded man lying in the street. One of the Polish witnesses recalled after the war, "Witecki wanted to shoot him through the head, from the front, but the Jewboy couldn't stand it and kept writhing on the ground so that finally Witecki grew bored of the dance and shot him through the head, from behind. . . . I saw all of this with my own eyes, because it happened right in my backyard."[56] Sevek Fishman, one of the Jewish survivors, also commented on the efficiency and brutality of "bystanders" who, with no warning, became associates in murder. A few of them trapped his wife and, when she failed to take off her gold earrings as promptly as demanded, tried to cut off her ears together with the prized jewelry. Fishman was particularly bitter when talking about these helpers full of zeal, but he also stressed the importance of voluntary firefighters and of the Polish "blue" police, who enabled the Germans to complete the sweep of the ghetto.[57]

By early afternoon, shortly after 2:00 P.M., the majority of Jewish inhabitants of the Węgrów Ghetto had been rounded up and delivered to the market square. While the roving squads of Germans, Ukrainians, and Poles continued to search the houses for bunkers and hideouts, some members of the *Liquidierungskommando* began mass executions of the elderly in the Jewish cemetery. The victims were being delivered to the site on carts commandeered from the locals, and the shootings took place over the shallow pits dug out earlier by the specially assembled Polish workers. Also in the early afternoon, Polish city officials were ordered to remove the bodies that littered the streets and the sidewalks of the ghetto and to prepare additional carts for the evening. The Polish mayor set out with trepidation to follow up on the German orders, worried that it would be difficult at best to find anyone ready to do the awful work. He was wrong: "Before I was able to leave my office in order to assess the situation and to issue orders, the removal of the bodies had already started. There were carriages and people were ready—they volunteered for the job without any pressure. Our hyaenas were after Jewish clothes, footwear, and the cash which could be found on the dead."[58] While some were robbing the bodies left behind in the ghetto, others were busy at the execution site in the cemetery. Wójcik recalled, "My friends who found themselves at the cemetery had tears in their eyes when they told me about the wounded being buried alive together with the dead, and with the grave diggers finishing-off some of the Jews with spades and stones."[59] For the Jews, Okulus later wrote, the liquidation was a "biological tragedy. For the Poles, it was a moral one. The extent of this moral tragedy was, of course, impossible to measure, but its consequences—were frightening."[60]

The "hyenas" took their clues from their peers, most of all from the Polish "blue" police and from their neighbors, members of the firefighting brigades. The firefighters, led by Wincenty Ajchel, their chief, showed up in the liquidated ghetto and, as Ajchel later testified, "they threw themselves [on the Jews] like hunting dogs on their prey. Henceforth, they 'worked' hand in hand with the Germans and—as locals and firefighters—did it much better than the Germans." Chief Ajchel carried around a briefcase into which his men deposited precious objects taken from the Jews. Their plan was to pool their resources and then split the loot in the evening, after "work." Müller, the chief of the Węgrów Schupo, recognized the contribution made by the Polish firefighters and met with some of them in the evening in a local restaurant. According to Ajchel, "He pulled out from his case a wad of money, and gave it to them saying 'here, this is for your good work.'"[61]

Some bystanders who morphed into perpetrators volunteered to help with the removal of bodies from the streets, in the process absconding with the clothes and shoes of the dead. As Mayor Okulus observed, "they even pulled out golden teeth with plyers. That's why people in Węgrów called them 'dentists.' The 'dentists' sold their merchandise through fences and go-betweens. When I mentioned to one of them (he was a court clerk) that this gold was soaking in human blood, he told me: 'impossible, I personally washed this stuff.'"[62]

RESISTANCE

It is not easy for a historian to establish how the Jewish inhabitants of Węgrów reacted to the liquidation of the ghetto. Although one cannot generalize, survivors recalled feeling widespread fear and horror, mixed with individual acts of desperate and hopeless defiance. The "hundreds of revolvers" in the possession of Jews, as mentioned in the Węgrów Memory Book, can be dismissed as a fairy tale. Nevertheless, as much as the cowed, defenseless, and disorganized Jewish people were no match for the German, Ukrainian, and Polish police and their civilian helpers, their struggle to survive, which started well before the *Aktion*, lasted until the very end of Jewish Węgrów. The bunkers and hideouts were the first (and often the last) line of defense. In many cases the hideouts allowed the Jews to weather the first few days, or even weeks, of the hunt and, later, to take advantage of the cover of night to leave the ghetto and slip away from the city. Surviving on the Aryan side was difficult, but many people who had hesitated initially, later, during the *Aktion*, made up their minds to attempt it. Some parents sent their children ahead, hoping to join them in due course.

At least one group of Jews decided to break out together and charged the police. Wrote Węgrów Mayor Okulus, "on the way [to Sokołów] a group of young Jews and Jewesses, at a pre-arranged signal, scattered, and started running away. The Germans started shooting and killed a few people, but many Jews reached the forests and some of them even survived until the liberation."[63] There were also instances of hopeless and desperate resistance, always ending in a tragedy. Several such cases have been reported in the Memory Book of Węgrów, although it is difficult to find corroborating evidence in other sources.[64] Michal Izbica and his wife are said to have barricaded themselves in their house and opened fire on the Germans. In response, the Germans set fire to the house and burned it down together with all of its occupants. Shmuel Halbersztat also resisted the *Liquidierungkommando* and was shot on the spot. A similar fate befell the members of the Naparstek and Steinberg families, who were all shot for resisting the police.

Some Jews were delivered to the station in horse-drawn carts that were earlier requested by the Germans from the nearby villages. The carts started arriving in Węgrów in the afternoon, and the cart drivers, Polish peasants, were told to load young children first.[65] One of these cart drivers testified after the war, "I drove them [to the Sokołów station] just once. They were crying the whole way; they knew they were going to their death."[66] The final acts of defiance were reported from the death trains headed for Treblinka. The Jews of Węgrów, after a few hours' march, reached Sokołów, where they were loaded into the cattle cars that had been waiting for them at the railway station. One of the survivors, twelve-year-old Dina Rubinstein, wrote later about the horrific scenes she had witnessed while being loaded into the train and, later, inside the wagon when people started to suffocate: "and the train stood, and stood and stood. Only the next day it started to move. We were all dying of thirst."[67] As soon as the train had left the station, some men began to tear away the wooden planks on the sides of the wagons and tried to escape, jumping onto the tracks.

In the aftermath of the *Aktion*, surviving inmates of the ghetto were systematically plucked out, one after another, from their hideouts and killed in the Jewish cemetery. Some, however, who were able to slip out of the city and reach the dubious safety of the nearby woods, would often flee to one of the *Restghettos* (remnant, or secondary ghettos)[68] and Julags located in the area. According to many postwar testimonies, the Julags afforded a degree of security impossible to find "on the Aryan side." The camps were located in Karczew, Ostrów Mazowiecka, Mordy, and Mrozy, all within a radius of thirty miles from Węgrów. This option, for obvious reasons, was available only to strong men and women; others would be turned away or shot on the spot by the guards.[69]

WĘGRÓW, SEPTEMBER 22, EVENING

On September 22, 1942, late in the evening, Jewish Węgrów ceased to exist. After the mass shootings in the Jewish cemetery and the departure of the column of Jews forcibly marched to Sokołów, there were perhaps six or seven hundred Jews remaining, hidden in various bunkers and hideouts. Nearly all of them were later discovered by the Polish "blue" police, by the firefighters, and by the locals, and delivered into the hands of the Germans for execution. According to several testimonies, close to two thousand Jews (or nearly 20 percent of those "deported") were murdered in the city during the first day of liquidation alone.[70] Bielawski, hidden in the attic of his house, recalled the end of the day of the *Aktion*: "Dusk brought calm and quiet. Frost formed on the tin roof. We shivered, but I am not sure if we did so from the cold or because of what we had heard all that day. No one slept the entire night. We thought only of what the next day would bring. Our thoughts were interrupted only by the sound of German soldiers entertaining women and laughing loudly. Next door, we could hear Maniek bragging to his customers in the restaurant: "We sent away a lot of Jews today!" He exalted. "A lot of Jews! Then the men in the restaurant cheered."[71] This was only the first day of the *Aktion*. The following days, filled with methodically conducted searches, were to result in hundreds of fresh victims. The whole town took part in the horrible spectacle. Mayor Okulus recalled, "All those who had been found, were later brought to the Jewish cemetery, shot and buried in mass graves. The killings took place in broad daylight, in public view. Our youth watched it and our children watched it too."[72]

NOTES

1. The four counties in question are: Miechów (studied by Dariusz Libionka); Bielsk Podlaski (Barbara Engelking); Biłgoraj (Alina Skibińska); and Węgrów (Jan Grabowski). In addition, a group of scholars working in association with the members of the Polish Center for Holocaust Research undertook similar studies of several other areas, such as Mielec (Tom Frydel); Złoczów (Anna Zapalec); Bochnia (Dagmara Swałtek); and Nowy Targ (Karolina Panz).

2. The methodological frame of this work has been, to an extent, inspired by the recent progress in Holocaust studies related to microhistory.

See Nicolas Mariot and Claire Zalc, *Face à la persécution: 991 Juifs dans la guerre* (Paris: Éditions Odile Jacob, 2010). A selection of recent contributions to the microhistory of the Shoah has been published in English: Claire Zalc and Tal Bruttmann, eds., *Microhistories of the Holocaust* (New York: Berghahn, 2017).

3. Skorowidz miejscowości Rzeczpospolitej Polskiej (Census of Polish Cities), v. IV, Lublin district, Warsaw, 1924, pp. 111–16.

4. Shraga Feivel Bielawski, *The Last Jew Out of Wegrow: The Memoirs of a Survivor of the Step-by-Step Genocide in Poland* (New York: Praeger, 1991).

5. Visual History Archive, University of California, San Diego (hereafter cited as VHA–UCSD), testimony of Najman Natan, 14739.

6. Archive of the Jewish Historical Institute in Warsaw (hereafter cited as AŻIH), collection 301/6043, testimony of Władysław Okulus, p. 1.

7. Based on the following: for 1939–1940, Regierung des Generalgouvernements. Abteilung Ernährung und Landwirtschaft. Statistiche Amt. Die Ernährungs-u. Landwirschaft im Generalgouvernement Polen. Reihe B. Statistische Zusammenstellungen, Heft 6, Krakau 1940, p. 47; for 1943, s. Amtliches Gemeinde- und Dorfverzeichnis für das Generalgouvernement auf Grund der Summarischen Bevölkerungsbestandsaufnahme am 1. März 1943, Krakau: Burgverlag, 1943.

8. Markus Roth, *Herrenmenschen: Die Deutschen Kreishauptleute im besetzten Polen-Karrierwege, Herrschaftspraxis und Nachgeschichte* (Göttingen: Wallstein Verlag, 2009), 443.

9. Ibid., 50.

10. Tadeusz Wangrat, *Polska i Powiat Węgrowski w Przededniu i w czasie II Wojny Swiatowej* (Węgrów, Pol.: Swiatowy Związek Żołnierzy AK Obwód "Smoła," 2010), 100.

11. Public Library in Węgrów, access code 16 (6), Order no. 42 dated July 24, 1941.

12. T. Szczechura, "Życie i zagłada społeczności żydowskiej w powiecie węgrowskim w latach 1939–1944," *Biuletyn Żydowskiego Instytutu Historycznego w Polsce*, no. 1 (1979): 44.

13. Public Library in Węgrów, access code 16(4), Bekanntmachung, Sokolow-Wengrow, March 3, 1942.

14. The Schutzpolizei operated in the cities, while the Gendarmerie detachments were located in rural areas. Both forces together formed the ORPO (*Ordnungspolizei*, or the Order Police).

15. The Polish and Jewish witnesses made no distinction between the "Schupo" (Schutzpolizei) and the Gendarmerie; in their eyes all of them were the feared "gendarmes" (żandarmi). See the testimony of Cyla Rubenfeld from Węgrów, Bundesarchiv Ludwigsburg, BAL, B 162/ 6843, pp. 61–64.

16. Instytut Pamieci Narodowej (IPN, Institute of National Remembrance) GK 317/144, testimony of Edward Feliński, pp. 25–25v.

17. A village situated two miles east of Łochów.

18. Until the summer of 1940, the Sokołów detachment was commanded by the Führer des Gendarmeriezuges Sokolow Franz Kessler, a former Czechoslovak citizen (from Hohenstadt-March). Kessler was fluent in Czech and therefore could communicate with the Polish population and with the members of the Polish "blue" police. His successor, Lieutenant August Piotrowski, arrived in Sokołów in July 1940, and his subordinates included Karl Tedsen, Erich Rieger, Karl Oberhofer, Pfützner Reuke, Josef Preiner, Friedrich Ahlers, and several others for whom first names are missing: Draxler, Maurer, Juch, and Krebs.

19. BAL, B 162/6843, interrogation of Karl Tedsen, March 7, 1968, pp. 193–203.

20. BAL, B 162/6843, deposition of Karl Kurnig, July 19, 1967, pp. 121–25.

21. Sonderdienst (Special Service) was a paramilitary organization created in 1940 in the General Government and composed of ethnic Germans (*Volksdeutsche*) living in occupied Poland.

22. BAL B 162/6846, deposition of witness Stanisław Onisk, May 7, 1947.

23. BAL, B 162/6843, interrogation of Rudolf Weber, June 26, 1967, p. 72.

24. Ibid., pp. 75–76. Schröder's Polish underlings included chief Józef Kosmala and two prewar undercover police agents, Marian Nowakowski and Jan Biługa. The Węgrów detachment of the Polish Kripo reported directly to the local chief of the gendarmerie and, indirectly, to the Gestapo in Sokołów. Józef Dominak headed the Polish Kripo in Węgrów, and his men included Edward Podgórniak, Tadeusz Figiel, (Tolek?) Jarosz, Władysław Kuriański, Ryszard Cymerman, Stanisław Lange, and one Gorzoch. Podgórny, Dominiak, and Kuriański were stationed permanently in Węgrów, while other plainclothes officers were called into town whenever needed.

25. Policemen Stanisław Kanciała, Czesław Sałek, and Józef Guzek were stationed in Węgrów; IPN, GK 318/568, p. 3. Piotr Grochal, Władysław Królik, Władysław Babulewicz, and Władysław Sałek—in Bojmie IPN, GK 318/460 vol. 1, pp. 304–6. Sergeant Czesław Krukowski, Corporal Józef Pawlak, Franciszek Barbasiewicz, Kazimierz Ajchel, and Wincenty Jankowski were attached to the Miedzna station—AAN, AK 202-III-115, pp. 17 and 17a, State Archive in Siedlce, Sąd Okręgowy w Siedlcach, Dossier 652, p. 144. Czesław Kurkowski was commanding the Grębkowo Polish "blue" police detachment—IPN GK 318/29, p. 3. Sergeant Wojciech Styperek,

platoon leader Bolesław Wolanin, and officers Kazimierz Skok and Jan Chojecki were based in Sterdyń, on the northern border of the county; and Sergeant Marian Wilczewski, Franciszek Witkowski, and Antoni Kobryński were serving in nearby Prostyń—AAN, AK 202-III-115, pp. 17, 19–21.

26. Arbeits Erziehungs Lager (AEL) Treblinka I, not to be confused with the extermination camp Treblinka II, located in the vicinity.

27. BAL B 162/ 6843, pp. 53–56: Witness Ruwen (Romek) Figowy, Jewish policeman from Sokołów, describes the murders committed by van Eupen.

28. VHA–UCSD, interview with Nellie Kaptsan.

29. Dawid Nowodworski, one of the Jews deported from Warsaw, survived a day in the death camp itself, later smuggled himself out of Treblinka, and returned to the Warsaw Ghetto to inform the people about the real fate of those "evacuated to the East." His testimony has been preserved in the Oneg Shabbat archive as well as in the diary of Abraham Lewin.

30. The quoted phrase "that night we could not sleep" in the head of this section is from Bielawski, *Last Jew from Wegrow*, 47.

31. United States Holocaust Memorial Museum (USHMM), transcript of interview with Norma Schneidermann.

32. VHA–UCSD, testimony of Harry Miller from Jarnice.

33. AZIH, 301/ 6043, testimony of Władysław Okulus.

34. Bielawski, *Last Jew Out of Wegrow*, 55.

35. *Kehilat Wegrow; sefer zikaron* [Memory Book] (Tel Aviv: self-published, 1961).

36. David Silberklang, *Gates of Tears: The Holocaust in the Lublin District* (Jerusalem: Yad Vashem, 2014), 308.

37. Descriptions of the sequence of *Aktionen* in the neighboring Lublin district of the General Government can be found in: Silberklang, *Gates of Tears*, 281–85, 306–10.

38. VHA–UCSD, testimony of Harry Miller.

39. *Kehilat Wegrow; sefer zikaron*, Tel Aviv, 1961.

40. Ibid.

41. Ibid.

42. Bielawski, *The Last Jew Out of Wegrow*, 58.

43. VHA–UCSD, interview with Perla Orenstein [Perla Bruner].

44. BAL, B162 Dossier 6843, pp. 48–52, Vernehmungsniederschrift, June 8, 1967. Thurm was appointed a Kreisstellenleiter, with a "political" rank (*politische Dienstgrad*) of SS-Oberscharführer.

45. BAL, B162 Dossier 6843, pp. 48–52.

46. BAL, B162 Dossier 6843, Thurm deposition of March 28, 1962, pp. 32–33.

47. Aaron Elster, *I Still See Her Haunting Eyes* (Evanston, Ill.: BF Press, 2008), 56.

48. This awkward term was sometimes used in the Communist propaganda in the 1940s and 1950s.

49. YVA, O.33/1066, testimony of W. Wójcik. After the war, Wójcik came into the possession of several parts of Chaim Kaplan's diary from the Warsaw Ghetto. In the 1960s, he tried to sell the diary to the highest bidder.

50. Zygmunt Klem, *Listy Węgrowskie*, 2 vols. Wegrow, 1991, 2:42–44.

51. Ibid., 2:33, testimony of Henryka Grabowska. Her other account can be found ibid., 1:29–34.

52. Bielawski, *Last Jew out of Wegrow*, 61.

53. AZIH, 301/6043, testimony of Władysław Okulus.

54. Bielawski, *Last Jew Out of Wegrow.*, 62.

55. VHA, interview with Renia Lipska-Mecznik.

56. IPN GK 317/144, deposition of Stanisław Raczko, May 23, 1949, pp. 26–27.

57. VHA, interview with Sevek Fishman.

58. AZIH, 301/6043, testimony of Władysław Okulus.

59. YVA O.33/1066, testimony of W. Wójcik, p. 32.

60. W. Okulus, AŻIH, 301/6043, Największa tragedia w dziejach Węgrowa, p. 3.

61. State Archive in Siedlce (APS), SOS, Dossier 652, deposition of Aleksander Ajchel, April 2, 1947, pp. 5–6.

62. W. Okulus, AŻIH, 301/6043, Największa tragedia w dziejach Węgrowa, p. 6.

63. W. Okulus, AŻIH, 301/ 6043, p. 8.

64. *Kehilat Wegrow; sefer zikaron*, Tel Aviv, 1961: chapter "Holocaust."

65. Testimony of Henryka Grabowska, *Listy Węgrowskie*, 2:42.

66. Stanisław Roguski, "Tę piłę, to ja rzeczywiście mam do dziś," *Listy Węgrowskie* 2:19–20.

67. Dina Rubinstein, YVA, M1E 2450: "dabei stand der Zug und stand und stand. Erst nach einem Tage setzte er sich in Bewegung. Der Durst quälte uns alle." She added, "Juden wurden weiter gesucht und weiter wie Wild gejagd . . . nie hätte ich geglaubt, dass Menschen einander so grundlos hassen können." ["Jews were further searched for and hunted like animals . . . never would I have believed that people could hate each other so baselessly."]

68. There were two "remnant ghettos" which had been created, in November 1942, in the area, one in Kossów Lacki and another, unofficial, one in Węgrów. The ghetto in Kosów Lacki had been liquidated in February 1943 and the one in Węgrów on April 30, 1943.

69. For more information about the camps, please see the preceding chapter by Martin Dean.

70. BAL, B 162/ 6843, pp. 61–64. AŻIH, 301/6043 Okulus, Cyla Rubenfeld put the number of dead as high as three thousand.

71. Bielawski, *Last Jew Out of Wegrow*, 58–59.

72. AŻIH, 301/6043 Okulus, p. 7.

II.

R • E • P • R • E • S • E • N • T • A • T • I • O • N

Simone Gigliotti

Home Seeking: Cinematic Geographies of Displacement in Meyer Levin's *The Illegals*

THIS CHAPTER EXAMINES THE REPRESENTATION OF JEWISH DISPLACED persons in flight from post–World War II Europe to Palestine as portrayed in Meyer Levin's docu-fiction film *The Illegals* (1947/48).[1] The film was, along with *Lang ist der Weg* (*Long is the Road*),[2] one of the earliest films in the postwar period to depict the movement of Holocaust survivors along the *Brichah*, the Hebrew term for the flight and organized illegal immigration of Jews from Europe to Mandatory Palestine in the postwar period. It is easily the more forgotten. Funded largely by Americans for Haganah, one of the groups responsible for organizing the *Brichah*, *The Illegals* follows the fictional journey of Sara and Mika Wilner and sets it against the backdrop of actual Jews along the *Brichah*. Sara and Mika are Holocaust survivors, recently married and expecting a child. Mika is from Poland, and after seeing the ruins of the Warsaw ghetto and his home town of Strykow, they are compelled to seek a new life in Palestine for their unborn child. They move across towns and countries, on trains, trucks, and on foot, all the while evading capture by border officials. Even more restricted is their intended final destination of Palestine, under the control of the British, who set strict quotas that limited the entry of Jewish immigrants. Having survived more than ten years of war and displacement, Sara and Mika put their fate in the hands of Haganah and the highways. Fearful yet determined, they must become empowered activists in the search for home and homeland. They will become "illegals," eventually travelling along with approximately 850 actual refugees on board the ship *The Unafraid*. Prevented from settling in Palestine, the refugees on the ship are then taken to Cyprus, a temporary detention from which, the voice-over promises, "they would soon return and live in their own land as a free people."

Levin hoped the film would make a serious political statement about obstructed Jewish immigration in the wake of the ill-fated *Exodus* voyage of July 1947. This was not to be. The film's topical irrelevance (it was released after the state of Israel was created in May 1948) and lukewarm reception immediately diminished its impact. Levin's ambition was further cast asunder after the December 1960 release of Otto Preminger's blockbuster film *Exodus*, which became the de facto story of the *Brichah*. This article argues that Levin's film remains an enduring document of the *Brichah*; it foregrounded what I call the cinema of the displaced. This cinema, whether in newsreels, feature films, documentaries, or fund-raisers, depicted the Jewish homeseeker of the Nazi and postwar eras as its principal narrator, one who used the highway as home, navigated forbidden borders, and experienced life as luggage. The chapter proceeds by outlining first a brief overview of home seeking and the Holocaust, then Levin's motivations for making *The Illegals*, the film's premise and ambition of "writing with a camera,"[3] its critical reception, and finally its articulation of cinema of the displaced.

HOME SEEKING AND THE HOLOCAUST

To be a homeseeker during the Holocaust was to be a refugee, hiker, cave dweller, mountain climber, ship passenger, death marcher, detainee, transmigrant, displaced person, asylum seeker, settler-colonist, and new immigrant. During the 1930s and early 1940s, homeseekers moved across Europe to leave it. After enduring or anticipating persecution, they explored new towns, cities, and places; trekked across mountains; wrote touristic accounts; and waited for months in various cities hankering after transit visas.[4] Once arranged, they took these visas, their luggage, and their memories to ports such as Hamburg, Trieste, Marseille, Bari, and many others, and also along rivers, such as the Danube, and the Mediterranean Sea. Their journeys from and across Europe received widespread multilingual coverage in newspaper reports, radio, and newsreels from the time. There were, in addition, many eyewitness reports from refugees en route, humanitarian organizations, private volunteers and philanthropists, nongovernment organizations, and those in newly resettled countries that accepted new refugees.[5] Some of the most well-known transnational crossings include the Kindertransports of children from Central Europe (Germany, Austria, Czechoslovakia, and Poland) that began in December 1938; the ill-fated voyage of the *St. Louis* from Hamburg, Germany, to Havana, Cuba, in May 1939; and the Haganah ship, *Exodus*, which sailed from Sète, France, to Palestine, alongside other doomed wartime ship voyages with the Aliyah Bet; and rescue attempts on foot, ship, and train.

The home-seeking vocation of displaced Jews persisted in the postwar era when several hundred thousand Jews from wartime concentration camps, forced labor camps, and places in the former Soviet Union feared a return to their home countries. In the displaced persons (DP) camps across Europe, which were particularly densely populated in the U.S. Zone of occupied Germany, conditions for Jews were dire. The insistence that Jews were no different from other victims of Nazism (such as slave laborers, political prisoners, and other victims of ethnic violence) prevailed in initial Allied attitudes and policies. In the U.S. Zone, the release in September 1945 of Earl Harrison's report, *The Plight of the Displaced Jews in Europe: A Report to President Truman*, signaled a major shift in Allied and United Nations Relief and Rehabilitation Administration (UNRRA) policy toward the Jewish DPs. Harrison's recommendations included separate camps for Jews; an improvement in living conditions, clothing, and nutrition; and the immediate resettlement of one hundred thousand Jews to Palestine. The report contributed to what Dan Diner and Gerard Daniel Cohen each have interpreted as "subjectification" moments in the recognition of Jews as a national entity worthy of their own political state and physical home.[6] Others included the 1946 Anglo-American Inquiry Committee on Palestine (calling for one hundred thousand emigration certificates to be issued to Holocaust survivors), which sought territorial solutions for this newly recognized displaced national entity; the resurgence of antisemitism in Eastern Europe in mid-1946;[7] the return of Polish Jewish survivors from hiding in the former Soviet Union to DP camps;[8] and the rapid uptake of Jewish youths in Zionist training and other activities, especially in the U.S. Zone of Germany.[9]

The main territorial and political issue for Jewish DPs in postwar Europe was emigration, most notably to British-controlled Palestine. The British Mandate in Palestine, in force since 1920 and ending in

September 1947, limited Jewish emigration during the "illegal" period from 1945 to 1947, which were the most intense years of Zionist activism in the DP camps in Europe, and also for a shorter period among detainees in DP camps in Cyprus.[10] Between 1934 and 1948, approximately 85,000 immigrants left for Palestine on the *Brichah* route on more than one hundred ships that departed from ports in Italy, Greece, France, Romania, Yugoslavia, Belgium, and Bulgaria; between 1934 and 1939, approximately 15,000 immigrants traveled on forty-three ships;[11] and from mid-1945 up to the creation of Israel in May 1948, approximately 70,000 immigrants traveled on sixty-six ships.[12] Much of this illegal immigration was organized under the auspices of the Haganah, the underground paramilitary organization of the Jewish Agency in Palestine.[13] The Jewish Brigade, formed as part of a special unit of the British Army in September 1944, participated covertly and extensively in the movement of Jews along the *Brichah*, particularly in Italy.[14] Because it was British policy to deport immigrants who attempted illegal entry to Palestine, the Jewish DPs from Europe intercepted on ships were detained beginning in August 1946 in camps in Cyprus before eventually gaining admission to Palestine at the rate of 750 per month from November 1946 until May 1948. This intake was half the total monthly quota.[15] The most well-known illegal journey was that of a Haganah ship, the *President Warfield* (renamed the *Exodus 1947*), which carried approximately 4,500 Jewish DPs from France to Palestine in July 1947. The ship was intercepted as it tried to enter Haifa harbor, which produced a scuffle that claimed passenger lives and turned international opinion against the British. The ship then returned to Marseille, but the passengers refused to disembark, nor did the authorities force them to do so. The British government had no choice but to send them to the British Zone of Germany, to be detained anew in DP camps in Lübeck, an hour northeast of Hamburg. Historians such as Aviva Halamish have noted the political opportunism of Zionist policy in the face of such intransigence: "The idea was to keep the plight of the Jewish DPs, languishing in Europe so many months after the war, alive in the newspaper headlines, and to drive home the fact that they were yearning to come and settle in Palestine. . . . Illegal immigration had the potential to embarrass the British for callously preventing the entry of Jewish survivors of the Holocaust into their homeland, and thus making full use of the moral force of the Zionist cause."[16] These refugee and displacement crises of prewar, wartime, and postwar Europe were heavily documented by aid workers, reporters, photographers, filmmakers, military film crews, and journalists.

CINEMA OF THE DISPLACED

Cinema of the displaced collates techniques of documentary, fiction, fund-raising, or incentive film, and it advances a geographic archive of the home-seeking itineraries of Jews on the move, on foot, in the crowd, on ships, and in detention and displacement locations in Europe and around the world. I do not offer this cinema as a coherent or discrete archive of displacement but rather as a European and international visual map of Jewish refugees and DPs' movements induced by Nazi persecution and which continued in the postwar era. Cinema of the displaced depicts people on the move, usually from conflict or persecution, sleeping in makeshift accommodation with limited material resources and whose fates are in the hands of impersonal bureaucracies. It is an inherently transnational cinema: the mobility is dangerous, the journey perilous, and the destination often unknown. This cinema has some affinity with the Iranian scholar Hamid Naficy's notion of "accented cinema," of the political and exiled filmmaker who chronicles journeys and struggles of identity, of home seeking, of deterritorialization and reterritorialization. In accented cinema, "the representation of life in exile and diaspora . . . tends to stress claustrophobia and temporality and it is connected to sites of confinement and control and to narratives of panic and pursuit."[17] The narrative forms of cinema of the displaced evolved over time, expanding from the short English and foreign-language newsreels of the 1930s to longer-form featurettes in the 1940s that reused this earlier footage.[18] This temporal focus reflected not only the changing producers of clips and fragments and their intended messaging but also the bureaucratic regulation of a displaced life. Longer periods of resettlement in designated settler colonies such as the Dominican Republic were underwritten by an unthreatening and well-developed visual representation of the Jewish refugee in *Sosúa: Haven in the Caribbean* (1941) as a productive and universal "settler colonist" who had been promised reterritorialization in the host country provided that they fulfill the terms of their settler agreements.[19]

These representations continued in the postwar period. With the disclosure of Nazi atrocities, the portrayal of the homeseeker was premised on recovery and productivity. Jewish and Zionist organizations based in Europe, the United States, and Palestine, such as the American Jewish Joint Distribution Committee, ORT (Obchestvo Remeslenogo Truda / Association for the Promotion of Skilled Trades), Hadassah, the Hebrew Immigrant Aid Society, and the Jewish Agency, among others, undertook a cinematic mission to document the surviving remnant (*She'erith Hapletah*) of Holocaust survivors and Jewish DPs who converged on DP camps in Allied zones of occupied postwar Germany and Austria, and in France, Switzerland, and Italy. Filmmakers who were recruited by these organizations showcased DPs as actively upskilling and improving their worthiness as immigrants in gender-based activities such as cosmetics, aviation, sewing, textiles, and metalwork, among others. They documented what scholars have discussed as political territorialization practices in the form of youth training farms, Zionist activism, and places of protest.[20] This messaging showcased DP camps as the clustered homelessness of Europe's Jews. Within these clusters or zones, they raised families, organized political associations to liaise with the allied authorities and UNRRA, and introduced measures to reinvigorate cultural life and memory of the Holocaust, as shown in *These Are the People* (1946).[21] Postwar films also documented the more painful and inconvenient aspects of life and dependence on bureaucracies: ongoing challenges of adjustment, mental health traumas, and the futureless world of the DP family. For example, the United Jewish Appeal's fund-raising film *We Must Not Forget* (1947) presented displacement as a violation of human liberty and pleaded for the recognition of Jews as worthy of empathy and financial commitment.[22] As its purpose was to raise money, the homeseeking desperation was unsurprisingly prominent, but of interest was its curation of motifs that would signify Holocaust and post-Holocaust suffering: tattooed arms, shoeless children, and nomadism. These DP films were frequently amateur and quickly produced, and they were recorded, perhaps due to technical difficulties, without sound. Filmed on 16mm stock, the footage was sent to production houses in the United States, where it was edited, revoiced and refashioned into political, if not highly persuasive, "message" films to raise funds for the Zionist cause. It is to this context that *The Illegals* corresponds, with Levin as its principal correspondent, a self-styled liberator of displaced Jews.

Levin was a passionate Zionist, a prolific novelist and critic, and a war correspondent for the Overseas News Agency and the Jewish Telegraphic Agency, having covered the Spanish Civil War and the liberation of Nazi concentration camps. He later became the first writer to dramatize *The Diary of Anne Frank*, though not without battles with Anne's father, Otto, over the dilution of Jewish meaning from the translated text.[23] He also went on to write several novels about Jewish life and the Holocaust as well as the best seller *Compulsion* (1956), about the Leopold and Loeb murder trial of the 1920s.[24] Levin claimed other firsts before *The Illegals*. The earliest was a screenplay for the first full-length feature produced in prestatehood Israel, *My Father's House* (1947), which was adapted from his novel of the same name. The film depicted a Jewish war orphan's search for his father in Palestine. Premiering in New York in late September 1947, just a few months after the drama of the *Exodus* ship and a few months before the UN resolution to partition Palestine, the film, according to Bosley Crowther in the *New York Times*, was composed of moving subject matter that was deeply affecting though technically flawed in its telling. Crowther noted that the film's homeland politics were overly dramatized, contrary to the filmmakers' intentions to present a story of the people of Palestine: "The implication is plain that Palestine is the Jewish 'homeland,' that illegal entry is justified and that the Arabs, represented by several classes, are profuse in their friendships with the Jews."[25] The cheery relations between the "people" (not peoples) conveniently minimized the historical friction and displacements that preceded and followed illegal Jewish immigration.

The theme of home seeking in Levin's work and life converged in the story for *The Illegals*. In it he saw elements of his own war story that had taken him from Chicago to Europe and Palestine many times before filming began. The idea for *The Illegals* fermented while he was working on *My Father's House* and witnessed the drama of the *Exodus* ship. Levin's biography unfolded in his approach to filming Jewish DPs in flight and would conclude his own war story. He believed, in a rather bombastic way, that the Haganah could be the present-day Moses, and he urged Americans for Haganah to let him film "the secret route,"[26] relocating to the ruins of postwar Europe the archetypal biblical journey of Moses leading the Jews from Egypt: "It seemed to me that under our very noses, in our own time, there was an exodus as difficult and stirring as the first exodus was from Egypt. How could it be left unrecorded? Suppose there had been cameras in the time of Moses, and it had been neglected to film the Exodus?"[27] Levin portrayed *The Illegals* as a homecoming: "I had to go there, to touch Poland before I was free. Perhaps, too, I had to re-enact for myself the exodus. Then my own journey would be rounded and complete."[28]

THE ILLEGALS: PLOT AND ITINERARY

Levin filmed *The Illegals* between October 1947 and March 1948 in the occupied zones of Germany and Austria, and in Poland, Czechoslovakia, France, and Italy on what he described as a "world's record low budget of $25,000."[29] He captured footage of groups of actual Jewish refugees and DPs making perilous journeys on foot through the Austrian Alps and at British naval interceptions near the Haifa coast and then set them against the home-seeking aspirations of the fictional characters of Sara and Mika Wilner. The film's plot from Poland to Palestine follows a southwesterly direction beginning in Strykow and then, for dramatic purposes, following divergent trajectories near Prague due to Mika's arrest for carrying false papers. Sara's route to Italy is via Austria and France, while Mika's after his release is via Czechoslovakia, Austria, and Germany. They look for each other, retracing steps and making enquiries with the *Brichah* Headquarters, though to no avail. They press on, fearing that they will miss the boat. Ultimately, they each independently reach Rome and their ship. Sara and Mika are finally reunited on the boat that is bound for Palestine. From there, the film's dialogue is largely unscripted, and the fate of the passengers on board is unknown. Levin's insistence that he captured a temporally authentic document or archive of the *Brichah* is, therefore, valid.

It is amazing that the shoot was actually completed. It covered many countries of divided and occupied postwar Europe. Although the plot was planned, the actual film shoot of six months was much more chaotic. Levin and his crew traveled eighteen thousand miles, crisscrossing the underground routes of various groups of refugees on the *Brichah*. Refugees moved from and between DP camps, kibbutzim (such as Kibbutz Buchenwald), hospitals, and transit stations to waiting trucks and trains. Levin notes that "our confused wandering back and forth between Poland, Austria, Hungary, Czecho-Slovakia, might seem a strange way to present a route through Europe, but in itself this was typical of the way of the people."[30] Traversing the distances between DP camps and so-called Brayha [*sic*] bridges often took days and weeks, and it did not follow the geographic route presented in the film.[31] Visas had to be obtained for Levin and his multinational crew in each location, which often meant backtracking and leaving at a moment's notice. The cast included Tereska Torrès playing Sara Wilner[32] and Yankel Mikalovitch as Mika Wilner.[33] Mikalovitch was a Holocaust survivor and gym instructor Levin had found through Torrès at a refugee orphanage in Paris. At various points along the route, Levin employed three people behind the camera: André Cauvin, Jean-Paul Alphen, and Bertrand Hesse. Cauvin was a famous Belgian cameraman who pulled out of the filming since he thought Levin lacked objectivity and was conducting a pilgrimage. He was replaced by Alphen, an active member of the French Resistance and a survivor of the Buchenwald concentration camp who had previously worked with the renowned French director Jean Renoir.[34] Hesse, a German Pathé News cameraman, came on board when Alphen had to leave due to other filming commitments. Hesse filmed the route from Italy to Palestine.[35]

The high point of the film involved the strenuous crossing of the Krimmler Tauern in southern Austria into Italy. At an altitude of 2,634 meters, the refugees gathered at Sammy's Place, a Tyrolean resort not far from Innsbruck, and were then driven three hours to the beginning of the crossing. With blankets and a food parcel each, the refugees made the slow trek up and over the Alps, while their belongings were driven to the Brenner Pass.[36] After the crossing, *Brichah* trucks collected the refugees and drove them inside South Tyrol in northern Italy to the next "Brayha [*sic*] post, a hotel in a small town."[37] This difficult crossing is captured in a still from the film (figure 1). It exemplifies the aspiration of Levin's cinematic enterprise, to document a historic travelogue of flight as if he were "writing with a camera." Levin used that phrase to describe reporting with urgency: the narrative voice of the war reporter in the field. He noted that this method was used by Ernest Hemingway, John Dos Passos, and André Malraux during their coverage of the Spanish Civil War. This visual travelogue of "writing with a camera" captured the "real places" that had to be endured and mastered by home-seeking Jews. The Alpine image captures multiple levels of witness: the physical strain of the refugees is the core narrative story of people as spatial activists; the white wilderness frames their desperate and clandestine movement and also conceals them from

Figure 1. An unidentified cameraman films refugees crawling across the Alps. Film still from *The Illegals* (1947/48), directed by Meyer Levin Courtesy of Deutsches Filminstitut, Frankfurt.

discovery; and the photographer documents the achievement. After crossing the Krimmler Tauern, the refugees arrived at the Cinecittà DP camp on the outskirts of Rome and from there were transported to Civitavecchia, where the ship awaited them for the voyage to Palestine.[38] The ship departed on December 11, 1947.

Levin spoke about the difficulty of filming the voyage to Palestine. He noted in the voice-over how "each embarkation was perilous with the dangers of wind, sea and discovery," while the most difficult problem was not having sufficient lighting to capture the faces of refugees then and also on the ship. The claustrophobic conditions on the ship optimized the drama on camera: "Again, the very limitations had to be utilized for effectiveness—the meagre light had to be concentrated on cramped shots, on closeups, on details, or rayed through in beams to render the gloomy murky depths, with parts of faces, eyes, picked up far in the gloom."[39] The emotional high point comes when Mika finally finds Sara sleeping below the deck (figure 2). The center right of the image depicts a makeshift light that Levin used to illuminate their emotional reunion in the cramped, dark quarters.

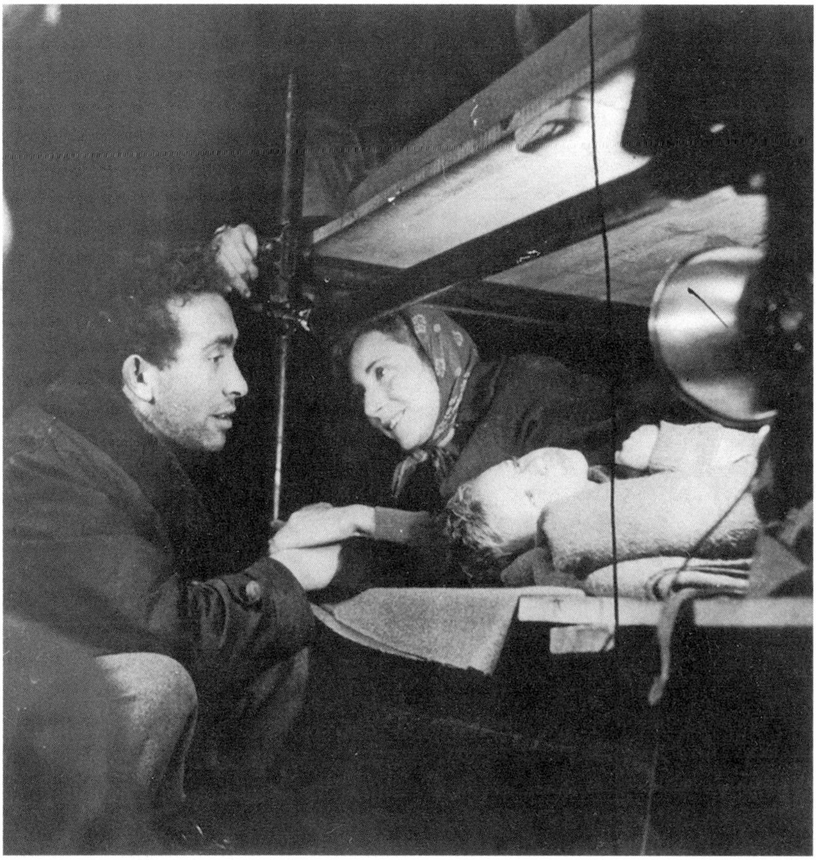

Figure 2. Mika and Sara's reunion on board *The Unafraid* (*Lo Tafchidenu*) in the film *The Illegals*. Courtesy of Deutsches Filminstitut, Frankfurt.

The difficulties during the sea crossing were more than technical. With 853 people on board, among them 112 pregnant women and 150 children younger than three years old, it took almost two weeks to make the journey to Haifa, as it was delayed by rough seas.[40] Not unlike the renaming of other Haganah ships, the passengers named the ship *Lo Tafchidenu—Haganah Ship Unafraid*. These words were draped from the upper deck in the closing scenes of the film (figure 3). The ship was towed into Haifa harbor on December 23, 1947, after having been escorted by several British ships from around ninety miles off the coast.[41] Except for about thirty immigrants who were sent to

Figure 3. Bertrand Hesse filming the journey on board *The Unafraid* (*Lo Tafchidenu*) in the film *The Illegals*. Courtesy of Deutsches Filminstitut, Frankfurt.

an infirmary in Athlit, the refugees were sent to the British colony of Cyprus.[42] The island was a temporary way station for the refugees, as the voice-over declares defiantly that they would "soon return and live in their own land as a free people." Levin and his crew were also treated as "illegals," though not as severely as the actual immigrants. They were detained by the Palestine Police Force for several days in a Haifa jail, their cameras and film sequestered, and some of the remaining reels were stolen from the ship while under police guard.[43] Levin returned to Europe shortly thereafter to collect the film footage he had stored with friends along the route and commenced work on postproduction.[44]

The film's abrupt end on the shores of Palestine promoted a seamless transition from home seeking to homecoming, with all of its overt Zionist inferences. Unsurprisingly, Levin does not seem interested in exploring in the film, and nor does he hint at, the many problems that new Jewish immigrants faced in Palestine, the many cultural and linguistic divides between Diaspora and Palestinian Jews, or the feelings of nonbelonging and negation of Holocaust survivors in Israel's early years.[45] The film suppresses the chaos of its own cinematic geography of displacement and the challenges of Arab–Jewish relations in British Mandate Palestine that preceded and followed waves of postwar immigration along the *Brichah*.

THE ILLEGALS: RELEASE AND CRITICAL RECEPTION

The Illegals premiered in a seventy-seven-minute print in New York City on July 14, 1948, at the Ambassador theater on Broadway (figure 4),[46] and also in Paris, where it enjoyed a two-month release. Levin marketed the authentic personality of his film at its New York premiere with slogans such as "the real places!, the real people!, and the real story!"[47] When Pathé News released a short newsreel capsule of the voyage to Palestine in 1948 following the overseas release of *The Illegals*, Levin recalled that he and Torrès (who was by then his wife) "went to several theaters to watch the audiences. The effect was overwhelming. . . . That five minutes on the screen did more to explain the Jewish problem than years of talk. At last the public saw the faces of the people, at last they witnessed the exodus itself."[48] His euphoric reaction was short-lived. He embarked on a two-year journalistic campaign to have the film screened in Israel and went further in editing customized versions of *The Illegals* for specific audiences. Those versions included a twenty-minute short, *The Voyage of the Unafraid*, which he placed in libraries including the Americans for Haganah Film Library in New York in 1949, and screenings for students at the Balfour School in Tel Aviv in 1950.[49] What was a profoundly moving and international human drama had hardly any critical impact or commercial success. Why was this so? Fast-moving political events, bureaucratic stumbling blocks, and the film's release two months after the creation of Israel all deprived *The Illegals* of the impact it deserved.

Reviews of *The Illegals* suggested that its problem was poor editing and underplaying of the real-life drama of the DPs. Robert Warshow,

Figure 4. Premiere of *The Illegals* at the Ambassador theater, New York City, 1948. Courtesy of Deutsches Filminstitut, Frankfurt.

managing editor of *Commentary Magazine*, wrote, "but a camera automatically records what is before it, and in this case, it is the record that counts most—the faces and bodies of the Jews who survived: it is impossible to watch them in even their most commonplace actions without feeling the presence of events to which they testify."[50] Warshow applauded the visual document and yet bemoaned its slow, steady pacing, writing that it "is like a travelogue made in a tunnel: no scenery, no incidents, only a destination."[51] He praised the film for having been made from the perspective of refugees but also questioned its one-dimensionality, particularly Levin's overuse of children and family to mask the traumas of survival: "In the context of the events that stand behind this film, is a picture of a baby at its mother's breast *necessarily* a symbol of hope?"[52] The *New York Times* commented that the film "gains in impact with English narration and understatement," although it was undermined through editorializing when Levin portrayed the insensitive British navy in Haifa.[53] The American Jewish Committee's annual roundup of *Films on Israel* noted, with a presumably intentional pun, that the "film missed the boat. The story is basically good but is confused in the telling and is underplayed dramatically, thereby losing much of its potential impact."[54]

Levin's strongest and most bitter reaction to the displacement of *The Illegals* from cinematic recognition and critical glory was reserved for *Exodus*, Otto Preminger's 1960 film based on Leon Uris's novel. Its box office success around the world meant that Preminger's film became the de facto story of illegal immigration to Palestine. Levin insisted that *The Illegals* was more real than Preminger's fictionalized account, noting that it was a film about "real refugees shot with their real Haganah guides, on the underground route to Israel."[55] To restore *The Illegals'* historical and geographic "realness," Levin hastily released a new fifty-five-minute version of the film and dubbed it in four languages: Hebrew, English, French, and Spanish. It contained several new details, cutting out most of the enacted scenes and leaving only the thread of the story of a couple trying to reach Palestine in time for their baby's birth. Attempting to account for its obscurity, Levin remarked that *The Illegals* was ahead of its time, and for that reason, it had been a struggle to find a distributor.[56] Yet *The Illegals'* footage of the home-seeking Jews on the *Brichah* continues to feature in well-known documentary, feature films, and television miniseries about the history of Israel's founding.[57] For example, the Israeli filmmaker Amos Gitai's feature film *Kedma* (2002), about the founding of Israel and the war of 1948, based its opening scenes on *The Illegals*.

CINEMATIC GEOGRAPHIES: EXILE AND AUTHENTICITY

The Illegals' depiction of the postwar Jewish survivor as alpine trekker, border crosser, and ship passenger are key spatial mobilities in cinema of the displaced. Though not a unique exemplar of cinema of the displaced, *The Illegals* documented the reality that homeseekers had to adopt a range of spatial initiatives and strategies that would propel, though not guarantee, their arrival close to Palestine.[58] The visual language of bypassing Europe's forbidden borders through Jewish heroism and the mastery of bureaucracy and landscape, including the Alpine crossings, was eminently suited to the early goals of national cinema in Israel.[59] Early Israeli cinema dates back to the late 1940s, following the defeat of Nazi Germany, and went on into the 1950s, when hundreds of thousands of displaced European Jews flocked to the newly born State of Israel. Several post–World War II films portray young survivors in agricultural boarding schools; after undergoing training, these youngsters join pioneer groups to set up a new Jewish settlement. While the survivors are coping with their memories, their instructors and peers help them heal their fraught psyches and prepare for their active participation in the Zionist enterprise in British Palestine. The climax in the young survivors' drama occurs when they yearn for a new life through joining pioneer activities or enlisting in the emerging defense forces.[60] These films, including Levin's *My Father's House*, were produced to serve national goals as defined by the Yishuv leadership and its political agencies that commissioned these films.

Levin contributed to postwar Holocaust and Jewish cinema an image of the Jew as a heroic territorial activist, which was to some extent an appropriation and a refutation of the long-standing image of the "Wandering Jew." That negative trope has featured extensively in studies of exile and homecoming in modern Jewish culture, and it has also been used in different and complicated ways by Zionists, Nazis, and antisemites variously to narrate and degrade the condition of Jews in the Diaspora. While an extensive analysis of the "Wandering Jew" is not possible within this article, Sidra DeKoven Ezrahi's comment that the "struggle to realize the utopian vision of a sovereign Jewish place under the sun gives rise to a new chapter in the poetics of exile and return" provides a pathway into exploring how Levin appropriates and subverts this motif in visual form.[61] *The Illegals*, furthermore, exemplifies a real-time visual chapter of post-Holocaust exile and challenge to it. The filming of Holocaust survivors en route to Palestine was a resistance to ongoing displacement and a rebuttal of the visually contaminated image of "the Jew" from years of abuse. As Robert Shandley notes, "filmmakers in the postwar period had the aesthetic problem of creating a new image of 'the Jew' that would signify Jewishness in the wake of vulgar filmic language of Nazi cinema."[62] In doing so, Levin records a defiant spatial behavior of Jews as embodied homeseekers, which contrasts with the depiction of passivity so readily ascribed to

Jewish behavior during the Holocaust and also in pogroms preceding them. To be on the move was an act of political and territorial resistance. Levin's depiction of the roving Jewish homeseeker, rather than the confined Jewish displaced person, represented a political and physically embodied spatial act and promised the passage from home seeking to homecoming. Yet, the docu-fiction form, where fictional elements are interspersed with actual persons and locations, was to the detriment of the film's spoken-word potential, for Levin effectively disembodied the refugees from their voices by including dubbed English-language dialogue and advancing Sara and Mika as principal ventriloquists of the Jewish home-seeking experience.

Levin's coverage of real-time movements and the physical topography of the *Brichah* route in *The Illegals* contributes several innovations to studies of post-Holocaust geographies on film. The merging of the fictionalized Sara and Mika Wilner with real-life refugees produced a type of "road" movie that is by now a pronounced feature in Holocaust cinema. To film historian Ariel Schweitzer, *The Illegals* blurs the boundaries between the feature film and the documentary and thus aligns with the genre of docu-fiction film. At a screening in Israel in early 2012 to mark the film's original version, he commented that "I don't know of any other cinematic project that has such an ambivalent, disturbing and paradoxical character. The relations between reality and fiction in this film stir questions that are very current in contemporary cinema, which is constantly working to undermine the traditional distinction between the two genres."[63] Schweitzer notes that Levin might have been influenced by Italian neorealism and Roberto Rossellini's wartime trilogy of *Rome, Open City* (1945), *Paisan* (1946) and *Germany, Year Zero* (1947). *The Illegals* takes the DP camp as the cinematic geography of the 'zero hour' and relocates it to the highway. Other films of the postwar era also experimented with blending documentary and fiction, such as Robert Flaherty's *The Louisiana Story* (1948) and *The Big Lift* (1950). The fluid form of cinematic narrative in the postwar era is echoed in other analyses of documentary films in Britain and the United States. Betsy McLane notes that "post-war films were freer and more varied in their techniques than were the earlier documentaries. More nonactuality was employed—fictional and dramatic elements—and structurally they tended to be organized as narrative or drama."[64]

The second innovation was to document contemporaneous evidence of the *Brichah* as a liberation-from-Europe narrative that moved visually beyond liberations from camps. Recent studies in film scholarship related to the Holocaust have seen a bookending theme: analyses of early or first-wave Holocaust films in national cinemas in Poland, the Soviet Union, and the United States,[65] juxtaposed with studies of twenty-first-century documentary cinema, aesthetics, and a rethinking of the applicability of the term "genre" to systems of image creation and circulation that spur ongoing filmmaking about the Holocaust.[66] Meyer Levin anticipated these debates about authenticity, the unattributed use of photographic stills from documentary and liberation films, and often their deliberate negation (as in Claude Lanzmann's *Shoah* [1985]) and extensive dependence (Yael Hershonski's *A Film Unfinished* [2010]), in his comments about how *The Illegals* was first seen and then repurposed after its release. Lawrence Baron noted that Orson Welles's *The Stranger* (1946) was the first American film to employ footage from the liberation of the camps, a directorial choice that would be impossible to track in subsequent feature and documentary films since that time, given their ubiquity and the array of (by now) familiar physical and emotional tropes (barbed wire, camps, trains, ghettos, and family separations).[67] *The Illegals* can also be read in this way; it did for postwar films about the *Brichah* what Soviet, Polish, and Allied liberation footage from 1944 and 1945 did for postwar feature and documentary films, such as *Death Mills* (1945) and *Night and Fog* (1955), and many others. Whereas films about camp liberations focused on the discovery of Nazi atrocities and the reckoning with what could be shown, Levin's travelogue showcased the visual evidence of the despair and displacement among Europe's Holocaust survivors. His intention was to portray a transnational cinematic geography of Jewish DPs' necessary liberation from hostile Europe.

The final innovation of *The Illegals* is that it offers a Jewish Diasporic twist to the genre of *Heimat* cinema, with its veneration of roots, blood, soil, and belonging. Levin's inclusion of ruined landscapes in Poland (such as Strykow and the Warsaw Ghetto) evokes the "rubble film" (*Trümmerfilm*) of early postwar German cinema. To Robert Shandley, "these films took the '*mise-en-scene*' of destroyed Germany as a background and metaphor of the destruction of Germans' own sense of themselves."[68] But unlike in rubble films, Levin traveled from the destroyed cityscape to towns, highways, and mountain crossings, and with the Jewish DPs, writing their history with a camera. The cinematic geography that displaced persons had to move through was a transnational spatial network lined with corridors of interrupted and clandestine movements and physical endurance as well as careful improvisation between border officials, the Haganah, the Jewish Brigade, and other agencies.

For all of his bitterness about other directors' uses of *The Illegals*, it is clear that Levin wanted it to endure through his editorial viewpoint. He continued to advocate for *The Illegals* as the preeminent reality narrative of the *Brichah* and revisited the topic in a thirty-minute documentary in December 1977, *The Unafraid*, which included interviews with refugees who had made the voyage in 1947 and the ship's captain, Gad Lasker. That film has also disappeared into obscurity. It is unfortunate that Levin's great ambition with *The Illegals* was not achieved. He had to make do with seeing snippets of it here and there, in newsreel fragments, and in films that reimaged his coverage of boat crossings and Alpine treks as their own.

Levin's portrayal of the Jews as homeseekers on an exodus from postwar Europe resonates in ongoing practices of *Brichah* pilgrimage and place making. From the writer Leon Uris, who offered *Exodus* tours of the "highways of history, the roads of glory followed by the heroes and heroines" in the early 1980s,[69] to young students making documentaries of the escape route, to commemorative treks of the Alpine Peace Crossing in Austria, to news that the *Exodus 1947* ship is getting a Hollywood update,[70] the fascination is unabated. The intergenerational attention to the *Brichah*'s physically embodied place making asserts an alternative geography of memory that is somewhat out of place with the boom in the so-called dark tourism to ghettos and camps. The rise of pilgrimage activities, or routes tourism, suggests that the flight of DPs in postwar Europe to Palestine has become spatially relived and physically endured anew, re*emplaced* through commemorative routes as dialogues with contemporary displacement of war victims, detention, and refugees. Indeed, this dialoguing is not unique to the memory of the Holocaust.

In conclusion, the visual evidence of *The Illegals* and from many other newsreels, ship films, memoirs, and histories about refugees and their journeys on boats such as the *St. Louis*, the *Patria*, the *Struma*, or the *Exodus 1947* suggests that Holocaust survivors were boat people before and after they were victims in ghettos and camps; they were seekers of asylum, leaving countries that held no future for them and which had actively advertised this fact as early as 1933, if not before. They sought asylum in countries near and far, their entry regulated by strict immigration quotas, racism, and fear mongering. This movement and the legacies it has produced have not received their due in contemporary debates about boat people, undocumented and illegal immigrants. The study of the Holocaust as a migration and displacement narrative in relation to the European refugee crisis is, therefore, valid and overdue. *The Illegals* is a bridge connecting both displacements. Media coverage in news agencies, social media, and short films about the mass flight of traumatized refugees, particularly since mid-2015 from North Africa and Syria in the Middle East to Europe via Mediterranean and Balkan countries revive *The Illegals* on a daily basis. This ongoing flight reveals the permanence of the mobile condition of asylum seekers and boat people during the twentieth century, particularly those displaced during and after the First World War, continuing during the interwar and postwar periods in Europe, and also in massive internal and cross-border displacements in Asia. The proposed building of walls across the European Union and Turkey, for example, reveals the lack of coordinated humanitarian solutions and a crisis of European solidarity. Who will provide homes for these new "illegals"? It is to Levin's credit that he captured on film what has now become an all-too-familiar image, that of the homeseeker.

NOTES

1. *The Illegals*, directed by Meyer Levin (Palestine, 1947; U.S., Americans for Haganah, 1948), 77 min. The film was previously available online, but has been removed from YouTube. Readers should be able to purchase a copy on DVD.

2. *Lang ist der Weg*, directed by Herbert B. Fredersdorf and Marek Goldstein (Germany, 1947–1948). I use the translation *Long Is the Road*, which is also used in Robert R. Shandley, *Rubble Films: German Cinema in the Shadow of the Third Reich* (Philadelphia: Temple University Press, 2001). The film is available on DVD.

3. See Levin's discussion on the making of *The Illegals*, from the Jewish Welfare Board (JWB) Lecture Bureau, typescript, 2 pp. marked, Box 37, Meyer Levin Collection, Howard Gottlieb Archival Research Center, Boston University. The JWB was located at 15 East 26th Street in New York City.

4. See Marion Kaplan's article in this volume, which is centrally concerned with the experiences of Jewish refugees in limbo in Portugal.

5. See, for example, Margarete Limberg and Hubert Rübsaat, eds. *Germans No More: Accounts of Jewish Everyday Life, 1933–1938*, trans. Alan Nothnagle (New York: Berghahn Books, 2006).

6. Earl G. Harrison, *The Plight of the Displaced Jews in Europe: A Report to President Truman.* The report's original title is recorded as Report, Earl G. Harrison's "Mission to Europe to inquire into the condition and needs of those among the displaced persons in the liberated countries of Western Europe and in the SHAEF area of Germany—with particular reference to the Jewish refugees—who may possibly be stateless or non-repatriable," undated [c. August 1945] [Dwight D. Eisenhower's Pre-Presidential Papers, Box 116, Truman Harry S. (4); NAID #12007695]. Dwight Eisenhower Presidential Library: https://www.eisenhower.archives.gov/research/online_documents/holocaust.html (Accessed February 12 2018). Dan Diner, "Elemente des Subjektwerdung: Juedische DPs in historischem Kontext," *Jahrbuch zur Geschichte und Wirkung des Holocaust* (1997): 22–48; Gerard Daniel Cohen, "The Politics of Recognition: Jewish Refugees in Relief Policies and Human Rights Debates, 1945–1950," *Immigrants and Minorities* 24, no. 2 (July 2006): 125–43.

7. On antisemitism in postwar Poland, see, for example, Jan T. Gross, *Fear: Anti-Semitism in Poland after Auschwitz; An Essay in Historical Interpretation* (Princeton, N.J.: Princeton University Press, 2006).

8. On this topic, see Laura Jockusch and Tamar Lewinsky, "Paradise Lost? Postwar Memory of Polish Jewish Survival in the Soviet Union," *Holocaust and Genocide Studies* 24, no. 3 (Winter 2010): 373–99.

9. The best recent analysis of youth activism (in English) is Avinoam Patt, *Finding Home and Homeland: Jewish Youth and Zionism in the Aftermath of the Holocaust* (Detroit: Wayne State University Press, 2009).

10. Except for Dalia Ofer's "Holocaust Survivors as Immigrants: The Case of Israel and the Cyprus Detainees," *Modern Judaism* 16, no. 1, (1996): 1–23, the years of detention in Cyprus are still underexamined by scholars, despite the documentation of transmigration and camp life in photos and memoirs. For example, in August 2012, Yitzhak Teutsch, director of the American Joint Distribution Committee in Jerusalem, began an effort to document more than two thousand babies born to Jewish refugees interned in camps in Cyprus between 1946 and 1949. See Ofer Aderet, "Archivist Tracks Down the 'Lost Babies' of Cyprus' Jewish Refugee Camps," *Haaretz*, August 24, 2012, http://www.haaretz.com/news/israel/archivist-tracks-down-the-lost-babies-of-cyprus-jewish-refugee-camps-1.460401. In his follow-up film to *The Illegals*, called *The Unafraid* (1977), Levin returned to Israel to find out what happened to the refugees he had filmed, some of whom had been interned on Cyprus.

11. The data on ship numbers and passengers are taken from

"Ha'Mossad Le'Aliya Bet," accessed July 8, 2017, http://www.palyam.org/English/HaMossad/mainpage. See also Dalia Ofer, *Escaping the Holocaust: Illegal Immigration to the Land of Israel, 1939–1944* (New York: Oxford University Press, 1990). Artur Patek has written an excellent history of the 1934–1944 phase: Artur Patek, *Jews on route to Palestine: Sketches from the History of Aliyah Bet—Clandestine Jewish Immigration*, trans. Guy Russel Torr and Timothy Williams (Kraków: Jagiellonian University Press, 2012).

12. Aviva Halamish, "American Volunteers in Illegal Immigration to Palestine, 1946–1948," *Jewish History* 9, no. 1 (Spring 1995): 91.

13. Much English-language literature on the Haganah examines the voyage of *Exodus 1947*, the overloaded Haganah ship that prompted Levin to push forward his plans to make *The Illegals*. There are, however, studies that look at the Haganah in terms of histories of militarism in Palestine and Israel, such as Uri Ben-Eliezer, *The Making of Israeli Militarism* (Bloomington: Indiana University Press, 1998). On the operations of Haganah in Europe, particularly in Austria, see Thomas Albrich and Ronald W. Zweig, *Escape Through Austria: Jewish Refugees and the Austrian Route to Palestine* (London; Portland, Ore.: Frank Cass, 2002), and Susanne Rolinek, "Clandestine Operators: The Bricha and Betar Network in the Salzburg Area, 1945–1948," *Journal of Israeli History: Politics, Society and Culture* 19, no. 3 (1998): 41–61.

14. Hanoch Bartov's *The Brigade*, trans. David S. Segal (New York: Holt, Rinehart and Winston, 1968) is the classic fictionalized account based on Bartov's experiences in the Jewish Brigade. There remains no academic monograph in English on the topic of the Jewish Brigade, although Howard Blums's *The Brigade: An Epic Story of Vengeance, Salvation, and World War II* (New York: HarperCollins, 2001) is a good introduction. See the film Chuck Olin, *In Our Own Hands: The Hidden Story of the Jewish Brigade in World War II* (USA, 2000), 85 min., http://www.olinfilms.com/brigade/index.htm, for oral history interviews with former soldiers, including Hanoch Bartov. In terms of local histories, one can refer to the brigade's operations in particular countries, such as Italy. See Bruno Archi, *Storia generale della Brigata ebraica: 1939–1945, verso la proclamazione dello Stato d'Israele* (Rome: Aracne editrice S.r.l., 2014); Primo Fornaciari, *I ragazzi venuti dalla terra di Israele: Luoghi e storie della Brigata ebraica in Romagna* (Ravenna: Longo, 2011).

15. Ofer, "Holocaust Survivors as Immigrants," 3.

16. Aviva Halamish, *The Exodus Affair: Holocaust Survivors and the Struggle for Palestine*, trans. Ora Cummings (Syracuse, N.Y.: Syracuse University Press, 1998), xx. See also Ellen Jenny Ravndal, "Exit Britain: British Withdrawal From the Palestine Mandate in the Early Cold War, 1947–1948," *Diplomacy and Statecraft* 21, no. 3 (2010): 424.

17. Hamid Naficy, *An Accented Cinema: Exilic and Diasporic Filmmaking* (Princeton, N.J.: Princeton University Press, 2001), 5.

18. See the newsreels of British Pathé, Fox Movietone, and Universal, for example.

19. Dominican Republic Settlement Association, *Sosua: Haven in the Caribbean* (1941), 18 min., posted to YouTube January 30, 2016, https://www.youtube.com/watch?v=WvzpjQoIFVU. On the topic of Jewish settlers in the Dominican Republic, see Simone Gigliotti, "Acapulco in the Atlantic: Revisiting Sosúa, a Jewish Refugee Colony in the Caribbean," *Immigrants and Minorities* 24, no. 1 (2006): 22–50; Marion A. Kaplan, *Dominican Haven: The Jewish Refugee Settlement in Sosúa, 1940–1945* (New York: Museum of Jewish Heritage, 2008).

20. See Patt, *Finding Home and Homeland*; Ze'ev Mankowitz, *Life between Memory and Hope: The Survivors of the Holocaust in Occupied Germany* (Cambridge: Cambridge University Press, 2007).

21. See the link to *These Are the People* in the Spielberg Jewish Film Archive: https://www.youtube.com/watch?v=9ZtZhpihRn8.

22. See the link to *We Must Not Forget* in the Spielberg Jewish Film Archive: https://www.youtube.com/watch?v=F27nDTmVV7o.

23. On this topic, see Lawrence Graver, *An Obsession with Anne Frank: Meyer Levin and the Diary* (Berkeley: University of California Press, 1995).

24. For a brief biography of Levin, see *Encyclopaedia Judaica*, 2nd ed., vol. 12, s.v. "Levin, Meyer," by Sol Litzpin, accessed August 15, 2013, *Gale Virtual Reference Library*, Gale Document Number GALE|CX2587512285.

25. Bosley Crowther, review of "My Father's House," *New York Times*, September 26, 1947, http://www.nytimes.com/movie/review?res=9804EFD71731E13BBC4E51DFBF66838C659EDE.

26. Meyer Levin, "The Illegals: Clandestine Israel Documentary Long Before Uris and Preminger," *Variety* 224, no. 7 (January 10, 1962), 35, 57.

27. Meyer Levin, *In Search: An Autobiography* (Paris: Authors' Press, 1950), 358.

28. Ibid., 359.

29. Meyer Levin, "Repatriation Epic Going Unrecorded," *Palestine Post*, November 21, 1949, 2.

30. Levin, *In Search*, 401.

31. Levin made this point repeatedly in his memoir, *In Search*.

32. Levin and Torrès married in 1948, and she became an established writer in her own right. They divided their time among Europe, the United States, and Israel. Torrès's family had escaped from France just as the Nazis occupied it.

33. His name has been recorded also as Yankel Mikalowitz. I use the

spelling Mikalovitch, although it contrasts with Levin's spelling, Mikalowitch, in *In Search*.

34. See Ronny Loewy, "Vom Geschichtenerzählen und Staatgründen," in *Unerschrocken: Auf dem Weg nach Palästina; Tereska Torrès' Filmtagebuch von 1947*, ed. Ronny Loewy (Berlin: Jüdisches Museum, 2004), 23.

35. Levin notes that Mikalovitch survived the Holocaust on "false papers and luck and swift legs." Quoted in Levin, *In Search*, 360.

36. Levin's account of the trek is quite fascinating. See Levin, *In Search*, 408–12.

37. Ibid., 409.

38. Cinecittà is a famous film studio outside of Rome, which still functions today. Part of it had been converted to a DP camp. See Noa Steimatzky, "The Cinecittà Refugee Camp, (1944–1950)," *October* 128 (Spring 2009): 23–50.

39. Levin, *In Search*, 419.

40. As noted in Tereska Torrès's diary of the journey, "Filmtagebuch 1947," in Loewy, *Unerschrocken*, 82.

41. See British Pathé footage of the ship's arrival, with some of the footage that was possibly shot by Bertrand Hesse: "Illegal Jewish Immigrant Ship, 1940–1949," http://www.britishpathe.com/video/illegal-jewish-immigrant-ship-1/query/illegal+ship.

42. Judith Avrunin, "No Change in Deportation Routine: 880 to Cyprus," *Palestine Post*, December 24, 1947, 1.

43. Meyer Levin, "The Saga of the Stolen Film," *Palestine Post*, December 31, 1947, 4.

44. For the exact details of how this was planned with his cameraman, Bertrand Hesse, see ibid.

45. On this topic, for example, see Tom Segev, *The Seventh Million: The Israelis and the Holocaust* (New York: Hill and Wang, 1993); Hanna Yablonka, *Survivors of the Holocaust: Israel after the War*, trans. Ora Cummings (New York: New York University Press, 1999); Idith Zertal, *From Catastrophe to Power: Holocaust Survivors and the Emergence of Israel* (Berkeley: University of California Press, 1998).

46. "Film Depicting Flight of Displaced Jews to Palestine to Open in New York," *Jewish Telegraphic Agency*, July 9, 1948, http://www.jta.org/1948/07/09/archive/film-depicting-flight-of-displaced-jews-to-palestine-to-open-in-new-york.

47. As seen in marketing material for the film's premiere in New York City in July 1948, and also in subsequent articles such as Levin, "Illegals: Clandestine Israel Documentary."

48. Quoted in Nirit Anderman, "Jewish Film That History Over-

looked," *Haaretz*, January 20, 2012, http://www.haaretz.com/jewish/the-jewish-film-that-history-overlooked-1.408306.

49. "Educational Films Shown in Tel Aviv," *Palestine Post*, January 26, 1950, 2.

50. Robert Warshow, "The Flight from Europe," *Commentary Magazine*, October 1948, 369.

51. Ibid.

52. Ibid., 371.

53. T.F.B., "How Displaced Jews Get to Palestine," *New York Times*, July 15, 1948, 26.

54. Film Division of the American Jewish Committee, *Annual Review of Films from Israel*, January 1949, 11.

55. Meyer Levin, "The Illegals; Clandestine Israel Documentary Long Before Uris & Preminger," *Variety* 225, Issue 7 (Jan 10, 1962), 35, 57.

56. Levin complained about the lack of distribution networks on several occasions. He wrote, for example, "But then as a result of what I claim to be a lack of proper distribution organization the film did not, in my opinion, reach five percent of its potential audience. Few Jewish communities in the United States have had the opportunity to see it. Not a single copy has been sent to Europe." Meyer Levin, "Repatriation Epic Going Unrecorded," *Palestine Post*, November 21, 1949, 2.

57. Additionally, scenes from *The Illegals* can be found in several documentaries including *The Last Sea* (1979), *Pillar of Fire* (1981), and *The Long Way Home* (1997). See Anderman, "Jewish Film That History Overlooked."

58. See Tim Cole, '(Re)placing the Past: Spatial Strategies of Retelling Difficult Stories,' *Oral History Review* 42, no. 1 (2015): 30–49.

59. On this topic, see Judd Ne'eman, "The Tragic Sense of Zionism: Shadow Cinema and the Holocaust," *Shofar: An Interdisciplinary Journal of Jewish Studies* 24, no. 1 (2005): 22–36; Ella Shohat, *Israeli Cinema: East/West and the Politics of Representation* (Austin: University of Texas Press, 1989).

60. For a good discussion of these films, see Ne'eman, "Tragic Sense of Zionism."

61. Sidra DeKoven Ezrahi, *Booking Passage: Exile and Homecoming in the Modern Jewish Imagination* (Berkeley: University of California Press, 2000), 3.

62. Shandley, *Rubble Films,* 78.

63. Anderman, "Jewish Film That History Overlooked."

64. Betsy A. McLane, *A New History of Documentary Film*, 2nd ed. (London: Bloomsbury, 2013), 176.

65. On Poland, see Marek Haltof, *Polish Film and the Holocaust: Politics and Memory* (New York: Berghahn Books, 2012); Stuart Liebman, "Docu-

menting the Liberation of the Camps: The Case of Aleksander Ford's Vernichtungslager Majdanek—Cmentarzysko Europy (1944)," *Lessons and Legacies: the Holocaust in International Perspective*, ed. Dagmar Herzog (Evanston, Ill.: Northwestern University Press, 2006), 333–51. On the Soviet Union, see Olga Gershenson, *The Phantom Holocaust: Soviet Cinema and Jewish Catastrophe* (New Brunswick: Rutgers University Press, 2013); Jeremy Hicks, *First Films of the Holocaust: Soviet Cinema and the Genocide of the Jews, 1938–1946* (Pittsburgh: University of Pittsburgh Press, 2012). On the United States, from a large literature, see Lawrence Baron, "The First Wave of American 'Holocaust' Films, 1945–1959," *American Historical Review* 115, no. 1 (February 2010): 90–114.

66. Brad Prager's *After the Fact: The Holocaust in Twenty-First Century Documentary Film* (New York: Bloomsbury Academic, 2015) is a must-read on the dissonance between history and images.

67. Baron, "First Wave of American Films," 95.

68. Shandley, *Rubble Films,* 2.

69. See Leon Uris Papers (1939–1999), Box 25, Folder 7, Information Folder on Exodus, "Exodus Tour," Harry Ransom Humanities Research Center, University of Texas, Austin. See also M. M. Silver, *Our Exodus: Leon Uris and the Americanization of Israel's Founding Story* (Detroit: Wayne State University Press, 2010).

70. James White, "Chris Columbus Leads Exodus 1947," *Empire Online*, August 25, 2014, last updated October 9, 2015, http://www.empireonline.com/movies/news/chris-columbus-leads-exodus-47/.

Pedro Correa Martín-Arroyo

"Franco, Savior of the Jews"? Tracing the Genealogy of the Myth and Assessing Its Persistence in Recent Historiography

THE LEGEND BY WHICH THE FRANCOIST GOVERNMENT CLAIMED TO have saved the lives of thousands of European Jews from the Holocaust constitutes one of the largest and most successful rescue myths in Holocaust historiography. The Spanish myth of the rescue is the result of a decades' long propaganda campaign that was initiated by Franco's government toward the end of World War II and culminated with the public canonization of General Francisco Franco as rescuer and benefactor of Jews. The first time the regime utilized this propaganda was in the early postwar years, in the belief that presenting Franco's Spain as rescuer of Jews would help overcome the international isolation that the United Nations (UN) had imposed on the dictatorial regime for its fascist nature and unconcealed support of Nazi Germany during the war. Although Spain's reconciliation with the Western democracies was ultimately the consequence of the Cold War game of alliances, the propaganda concerning Franco's alleged mass rescue of Jews from the Holocaust certainly had a redemptive effect for the Spanish dictatorship. In fact, the myth of the rescue was not just spread by Franco's regime but also by foreign, mostly right-wing commentators in the West who saw in Franco's ultraconservative regime a useful ally in the global conflict with the Soviet Union. But far from being extinguished, the whitewashing potential of this propaganda continued to be exploited by Francoist Spain's Right until the death of the dictator in 1975. In fact, the myth of the rescue is still present today in Spain's official discourse in more concealed and sophisticated ways, evidencing the myth's resilience and its capacity to adjust to the growing historiography on Spain and the Holocaust.

Unfortunately, most of the earliest historical accounts on Franco's Spain and the Holocaust were deeply influenced by the regime's propaganda. When Israeli historian Haim Avni published his pioneering monograph on *Spain, the Jews, and Franco* in 1974, he was quite right to say that "no study published so far has brought to light all the facts in their true perspective."[1] Avni's authoritative study was the first to approach the historical record without a political agenda, and it devoted a whole chapter to distinguishing "facts from fantasy" within the official mystified discourse. The fact that it was translated into English only in 1982, coupled with the slow opening of Spain's archives, was perhaps the reason why it took so long until the next scholarly study on the subject. Published in 1987, the book by Antonio Marquina Barrio and Gloria Inés Ospina, *España y los Judíos en el siglo XX* (*Spain and the Jews in the Twentieth Century*), made an even harsher assessment of Francoist Spain's treatment of Jews during the war.[2] It was not until 2001, however, that the position of the Franco government toward the Spanish Jewish community living in countries under Nazi occupation was subject to thorough analysis. Grounding his research on German as well as Spanish diplomatic sources, Bernd Rother in his *Franco und der Holocaust* (*Franco and the Holocaust*) evidenced Spain's reluctance to repatriate its Jewish colony abroad in the context of the "repatriation campaign" (*Heimschaffungsaktion*) that Nazi Germany had offered to the neutral governments.[3] More recently, several other publications have added to our understanding of more specific research areas such as Spanish modern antisemitism and the transit of refugees through Spain.[4] Despite the consensus achieved by this historiography, there are still important gaps that merit further research. This is particularly the case for Franco's policies during the early years of World War II, when the Spanish dictatorship was still negotiating Spain's entry in the war alongside Nazi Germany, which it followed closely.

In April 1940, the chair of Lisbon's Comissão Portuguesa de Assistência aos Judeus Refugiados (COMASSIS), Augusto d'Esaguy, reported that "the situation of the Jews in Spain, as well as in Spanish Morocco, is getting worse every day"; and that the Spanish minister of interior—"an open advocate of racial and Nazist doctrine"—was preparing several police measures directed against Jews that would be "carried out secretly" in order not to "alarm public opinion."[5]

D'Esaguy's predictions were confirmed in May 1941, when the minister of interior commanded the Spanish police to register all Jews in Spain in the so-called Archivo Judaico (Jewish Archive), a police file index created to that end.[6] In October 1941, and with the same secrecy, the Ministry of Commerce and Industry ordered Spanish shipping companies not to allow "the undesirable" Jews aboard Spanish vessels.[7] Other anti-Jewish policies included the government's general mistreatment of Spanish Jews, whom it stripped of their Spanish nationality, as well as the irregular returning of refugees to the French border. When contextualized, the Spanish anti-Jewish stance of the early war years clearly calls into question the image of philosemitism and humanitarianism that the Franco regime started to profess even before the end of World War II.

THE WARTIME ORIGINS OF THE SPANISH RESCUE MYTH

The Francoist pro-Jewish propaganda had started already during 1943, when the downfall of Mussolini and the shifting balance of power in favor of the Allies obliged the Franco government to review its foreign policy approach. At that time, Madrid's propaganda targeted mainly American diplomatic circles and aimed to contest the claims that Spain was ill-treating refugees and cooperating with Nazi Germany in the persecution of Jews. Interestingly, the stimulus to spread such propaganda did not come only from within the Franco regime. In March 1943, Rabbi Maurice Perlzweig, who headed the British wing of the World Jewish Congress (WJC), met with the Spanish ambassador in Washington, D.C., Juan Francisco de Cárdenas, to make two requests to the Spanish government: to authorize the Jewish communities of South America to send parcels to the European Jewish refugees stranded in Spain, and to negotiate with Germany the transit through Spain of Jewish children in Nazi-occupied Europe to avoid their deportation. Convinced that this was the perfect opportunity to alleviate the growing opposition to Franco's regime in the United States, Ambassador Cárdenas tried to persuade his superiors that these initiatives would bring good publicity for the regime, and at virtually no cost.[8]

Madrid's refusal to cooperate with the WJC did not stop Rabbi Perlzweig from mentioning in a May 1943 radio broadcast across the United States that "some twenty thousand refugees have found both a temporary haven and security in Spain, and they have found these things in circumstances which would have denied them entrance into many other countries."[9] This was also the case of the American Joint Distribution Committee (JDC), which on repeated occasions thanked Ambassador Cárdenas for the "sympathetic attitude of your government in Madrid in behalf of the refugees who have come to Spain."[10] Given that the Franco government had the last word regarding Spain's immigration and refugee policies, the powerless Jewish organizations had no alternative but to praise the government and hope for Spain's cooperation in the refugee crisis. However, as the JDC representative in Barcelona, Samuel Sequerra, reported in October 1942, the reality of the refugee situation in Spain was far from ideal:

> A large percentage of those trying to cross the border are being arrested by the Spanish authorities . . . the Spanish police demands of us that we give them the names of those who seek our help. If we so denounced them, they would be immediately arrested. . . . In spite of the fact that they know of the humanitarian work that we do, they do not stop torturing us. During the month of August they took away all our files and papers and returned them only after almost a month, and then only a part. . . . I should also mention the anti-Semitic campaign which the Spanish press is conducting. . . . The Jewish organizations in Portugal are simply admitted to function, and we are barely tolerated. . . . We must keep our problems of assistance very quiet in order to avoid difficulties with the authorities.[11]

The Spanish government's first tangible propaganda efforts occurred in February 1944, when the Spanish Ministry of Foreign Affairs (MFA) spread news throughout the Americas concerning the repatriation to Spain of 365 Sephardic Jews from Greece, "to counter the anti-Spanish campaign which insinuates that we follow a racist policy."[12] What this propaganda did not mention was the fact that these Sephardim had Spanish citizenship and that the Spanish government had tried to avoid their repatriation for more than a year. Moreover, these Spanish Jews were only admitted into Spain on condition that American and Jewish relief groups would organize and cover the cost of this whole operation, which Madrid made conditional on the Sephardic refugees' prompt evacuation from Spain.

Another important piece of propaganda was deployed during the WJC's November 1944 annual convention in Atlantic City, New

Jersey. The WJC had invited the Jewish community of the Spanish Protectorate of Morocco to participate in the international meeting by sending a spokesperson. After some hesitation, the Spanish government understood that the conference was the perfect opportunity for "perplexing our enemies and earning many sympathies without compromising our position with anyone."[13] In an attempt to disseminate the regime's propaganda within the American Jewish community, Minister Jordana gave orders to find a spokesman—"as fond of the regime as possible"—and to give him "precise instructions" regarding what to say concerning Francoist Spain's attitude towards Jews: "The Spanish legislation discriminates in no way whatsoever against them [Jews]. They receive absolutely the same treatment as the rest of the Spanish citizens in relation to their political and civil rights, without any limitation of access to public positions and official functions."[14]

Meanwhile, in Washington, Rabbi Perlzweig continued to work toward ameliorating Francoist Spain's image in the United States. This time, the rabbi requested from the Spanish government a list of all Spanish rescue efforts up to that date for publicity purposes. Three days later, the Spanish ambassador in Washington received a memorandum from Madrid in which the Spanish activities in favor of Jewish refugees had been multiplied and exaggerated to suggest a large rescue program orchestrated by the government.[15] The memorandum suggested, for instance, the alleged Spanish evacuation of Jewish children from Shanghai and Czechoslovakia, negotiations on behalf of Jews interned in Auschwitz-Birkenau, and the protection of Sephardic Jews held in concentration camps. Despite the fact that most of these claims were either unsubstantiated or misrepresented, the WJC issued a resolution thanking Spain for having protected many persecuted Jews.

In addition to the American Jewish organizations, the Franco regime's propaganda also found its way into the U.S. printed media. In July 1944, for instance, the *New York Times* also praised Spain's efficient role in "aiding European refugees from several nationalities, most of them Jews, proving wrong the defamation campaign of the left that assured that the Spanish government hindered these evacuations."[16] Evidently, this idea was repeated to exhaustion in the Spanish media. In July 1945, the head of the Representation in Spain of American Relief Organizations (RSARO) sent the Lisbon JDC office "a sample of how screwy the [Spanish] press can make things"—namely, a Spanish newspaper article claiming that Barcelona was to be "one of the chief transit centres for the repatriation of thousands of civilians liberated from German concentration camps."[17]

Rather than questioning this propaganda, the U.S. State Department made at least two public declarations flattering Spain's cooperation in the evacuation of Jewish refugees. On one occasion, for instance, Assistant Secretary of State Breckinridge Long claimed that Spain had given shelter to no fewer than sixty thousand Jews: "[Spain was] one of the countries that contributed the most to alleviate the Jewish exodus during the war. Spain, despite not being a rich country, gave refuge to sixty thousand people who crossed the Pyrenees clandestinely, fleeing from German occupation. The Franco Government efficiently cooperated with the United States ambassador in Madrid and the Jewish Committee for Refugee Relief [*sic*], supplied them with food and money."[18] As opposed to the Jewish relief organizations' attempts to engage Spain's support in the refugee crisis, the motivations behind the State Department's declarations seem to be of a different kind. One possibility is that, by exaggerating the number of those allegedly rescued in cooperation with the Franco government, Breckinridge Long—who as head of the State Department's Visa Division had been severely criticized for his obstructionist policies—was trying to exonerate its own controversial refugee and immigration policies.[19] It is also possible, however, that the U.S. State Department was simply paving the way for a future alliance with Franco's government, the fervent anticommunism of which rendered it a most convenient ally in the ever-increasing competition against the Soviet Union.

THE POSTWAR PROPAGANDA CAMPAIGN IN THE CONTEXT OF THE COLD WAR

As a consequence of the defeat of its former Italian and German homologues, Franco's dictatorship entered a period of international isolation and economic autarky that severely threatened the stability and survival of the regime. On December 12, 1946, the UN General Assembly excluded Franco's Spain from membership in any UN-related agency on the basis of its fascist "origin, nature, structure, and general conduct," until a "new and acceptable government" was formed in Spain.[20] In an attempt to reverse the UN declaration, the

Franco regime implemented a series of reforms with the aim of improving the regime's image in the West.

The most urgent matter for the Spanish dictatorship was to free itself from the burden of the Axis stigma. Given that the persecution and extermination of Jews were among the defining characteristics of the vanquished Axis powers, the Franco government focused on further expanding its previous propaganda. Only a few days after the UN anti-Franco declaration, the Spanish MFA requested from all its legations in countries formerly occupied by Nazi Germany any information regarding aid given to Jews during the war. Despite the near lack of positive responses, the MFA prepared a report describing "the very ample protective efforts realized by Spain in favor of the Sephardi," and forwarded it to Washington, D.C., and London.[21]

In the following months, this report grew into two propagandistic brochures. The fifty-page brochure *Spain and the Jews* (1949) was widely distributed by the MFA in Spanish, English, and French.[22] Simultaneously, the Spanish embassy in Washington published its own *Spain and the Sephardi Jews*, which synthetized the same theses in just five pages.[23] In addition to shamelessly misrepresenting Spain's humanitarianism and attitude toward the refugees more generally, this propaganda insisted on the regime's deeply Christian mores in an attempt to distance itself from "totalitarian materialism"–a term skillfully designed to conflate the Nazi regime with the Soviet Union: "Considered as a whole, the action taken by Spain to protect the Sephardi Jews during World War II is one of which Spain is justly proud. Such diplomatic protection of defenceless persons is not only one of the highest missions of the diplomatic purpose but also that of Christian charity to a neighbour who had been caught up in the ruthless wheels of totalitarian materialism."[24] In addition to whitewashing the regime's past record, the Spanish government also enacted a decree that granted the vague status of "Spanish subjects abroad" (*súbditos españoles en el extranjero*) to a limited number of Sephardic Jews "whose love for Spain made them worthy of such honor."[25] In practice, the regime was just playing to the gallery, for most potential "citizens abroad" had perished during the Holocaust and, in any case, this citizenship status was merely symbolic. Furthermore, this decree entered in clear contradiction with two circular orders issued secretly in the early postwar years "to avoid at all cost the entry and settlement in Spain of those Sephardic Jews who previously lived in a foreign country."[26] Despite the regime's hypocrisy, Franco's new decree proved quite successful in the Western media. The morning after the decree was officially enacted, the *Washington Post*'s front-page headline announced Franco's determination to invite some one hundred thousand Sephardic Jews to return to Spain.[27] Jerusalem's daily, the *Palestine Post*, followed soon after with the simple and yet powerful headline of "Franco Invites Jews to Return."[28]

These initiatives signal the peak of the Spanish government's propaganda efforts, and they paved the way for Spain's reconciliation with the Western democracies, as tensions between the Western and Communist blocs escalated significantly. Following the Communist invasion of South Korea in June 1950, many anti-Franco commentators in the West started to see General Franco's militant anti-Communism as a lesser evil than the feared spread of Communism. This was notably the opinion of former U.S. ambassador to Spain Alexander W. Weddell, who unapologetically defined Franco's fascist regime as "bad, unqualifiedly bad, and one which I abhor" and yet was convinced that any attempt to overthrow the Franco government would result in another civil war that would open the gates of the Iberian Peninsula to the Soviet Union: "of the two evils, I prefer the former."[29] This position was also shared by the State Department, whose first director of policy planning and Cold War policy, George Kennan, saw it as in the U.S. national interest to establish political and economic relations with Spain, "irrespective of wartime ideological considerations or the character of the regime in power."[30]

The American pro-Franco shift ultimately led, in November 1950, to the abrogation of the UN's 1946 anti-Franco declaration, which allowed for the progressive reestablishment of diplomatic relations between Spain and the West and put an end to the regime's international isolation. This call to realpolitik, however, became particularly problematic for Israeli officials, who until then had been punitive of Franco's fascist regime in international forums. In the midst of heated debates concerning Israel's stance in the global conflict, an increasing number of right-wing Knesset members campaigned in favor of Spain's joining the war against Communism. From early 1951 onward, the Israeli right-wing party Herut published a series of articles that capitalized on the Spanish myth of rescue to gain support for their cause. This was notably the case for Knesset member Benjamin Arditti, who in May 1951 published several articles claiming that Jews were indebted to General Franco for his wartime rescuing of Jews of Spanish citizenship in Bulgaria. Later that year, Arditti represented the Bulgarian community of Israel at the World Congress of Sephardic Jews in Paris, during which he also publicly thanked Franco for the aid given to Jews during the war.[31]

But it was not just the Israeli right wing that propagated the myth of rescue as a means to enlist Franco in the war against Communism. Such was also the case with Richard Pattee, former assistant chief of the Division of Cultural Relations at the U.S. State Department, and director, since 1946, of the Latin American Bureau at the National Catholic Welfare Conference's Social Action Department. As he stated in his visibly pro-Franco monograph, *This Is Spain* (1951):

> Spain can indeed be proud of this page in her contemporary history, for the evidence reveals that the Madrid government utilized every avenue and took advantage of every channel to render aid to the Jews. . . . Within Spain, the religious, military, and civil authorities were generous to a fault in offering a sanctuary to those fleeing the concentration camps of Nazi Europe. . . . In the social field, the Spanish authorities have been spending upward of a million pesetas a year on behalf of the Jewish communities for such things as free school lunchrooms, clothing for those in distress, medical aid, and special donations for Jewish religious festivities.[32]

Despite the fantastic nature of these claims, Pattee's book sold fifteen editions in just five years and was translated into three languages. The most hyperbolic representation of the Spanish propaganda, however, was printed in January 1953 by Norway's right-wing and highest-circulated newspaper *Aftenposten*, which claimed that General Franco had saved the lives of more than three hundred thousand Jews from the gas chambers.[33]

FRANCOIST SPAIN'S PHILOSEMITISM: THE LEGITIMIZATION OF THE RESCUE MYTH

The relative success of the Spanish propaganda efforts was to a large extent dependent on the regime's ability to adjust the Spanish dictatorship's internal structure and political culture to Western democratic values. To this end, General Franco had appointed the monarchist and leader of the Spanish organization Acción Católica (Catholic

Action), Alberto Martín-Artajo, as minister of foreign affairs in 1945. The choice of a technocrat—rather than a high-ranking army official or a Falangist, a member of Spain's fascist political party—for such a crucial post was in tune with the regime's broader reform program, aimed at the defascistization of the Spanish dictatorship.[34] The single most essential piece of legislation from this period was the July 1945 Fuero de los Españoles (Spaniards' Charter of Rights), a pseudoconstitution that theoretically guaranteed the Spaniards' most basic civil liberties. In the words of British historian Paul Preston, the sole purpose of such "empty legislation" was "to give the impression that the Caudillo presided over a *sui generis* democracy and was not a dictator."[35] Nonetheless, the 1945 Fuero de los Españoles was instrumental to the support for Franco's pro-Jewish claims, insofar as it supposedly introduced religious freedom in Spain. Until then, National Catholic Spain had been rather hostile to the Spanish Jewish community, but this situation was no longer compatible with the regime's postwar propaganda. In this context, the Spanish government initiated a second line of propaganda aimed at presenting Franco's Spain as a tolerant and multicultural state with an interest in Sephardic culture. In addition to improving the regime's image in the West, this new philosemitic facade would give credibility to the regime's propaganda, retroactively legitimizing the government's allegations regarding the rescue of Jews during the Holocaust.

First and foremost, the regime needed to give some proof, even symbolic, of the implementation of religious freedom. As stipulated in the Fuero de los Españoles of 1945, religious practices other than the state-official Roman Catholic would be tolerated conditionally, as long as they did not threaten the "spiritual, national, and social integrity of Spain" (art. 33).[36] In January 1946, the Barcelona synagogue was authorized to hold Jewish prayers for the first time after being closed down by the rebel army back in 1939. This was accomplished thanks to the intercession of the WJC representative in Lisbon, Isaac Weissman, since the Franco government had initially opposed the petition of the Barcelona Jewish community.[37] The Jewish community of Madrid, however, had to wait until January 1949 for the government's sanction to establish a synagogue in the country's capital. Even then, the Barcelona and Madrid synagogues were in private houses and had no outward signs that defined them as places of worship, since only Catholics were allowed to make public exhibition of their faith.[38] After a 1951 visit, Rabbi Ephraim F. Einhorn reported that Jews in Spain made "every effort to hide their identity" and that, realizing the fact that criticism was not a useful form of resistance against the Franco government, Spanish Jews had become accustomed to the regime's "psychological and refined form of anti-Semitism, [which] finds its expression in an under-the-surface discrimination."[39]

During the 1950s and 1960s, Francoist Spain's rescue myth was put to the test when Spain was asked to assist the Jews of Egypt and Morocco, who were in distress due to the escalating Arab–Israeli conflict. Compelled by the regime's own propaganda, Madrid authorized the issuing of documents and travel tickets to Jews wishing to leave these countries. As argued by Israeli historian Raanan Rein, there are many parallels between Spain's reaction to the 1956 and 1967 wars in the Middle East and the World War II experience. As had happened during the Holocaust, humanitarian aid was in most cases restricted to Jews of Spanish citizenship, and the Spanish government was determined to avoid at any rate the resettlement of Jews in Spain. Additionally, this assistance owed once again to the initiative of Spanish diplomats abroad rather than to any consistent policy shaped by Madrid, which exaggerated these actions to further legitimize the rescue myth and improve its image in the West.[40]

As Danielle Rozenberg points out, this was a way to make symbolic gestures directed to the Jewish world without the need to establish formal diplomatic relationships with the state of Israel, which would have had a deleterious effect on Spain's good diplomatic relationships with the Arab countries. In January 1960, for instance, the MFA met with diplomatic representatives of the Arab countries in Madrid to assure them that the Spanish government's pro-Jewish initiatives were based on long-standing cultural bonds with the Sephardic community and had nothing to do with the conflict in the Middle East. The former head of Arab and Middle Eastern political affairs, who was at the time serving as Spanish Ambassador to Cairo, captured the government's cautious and cynical treatment of the Jews when he said that "the Sephardic soul has always been a double-edged sword that should be used only when there is certainty that it will not fall into foreign hands."[41]

One unintended consequence of the Spanish assistance to the exodus of Moroccans Jews to Israel during the 1956 Suez Crisis was the private audience that took place between General Franco and

Solomon Gaon, a prominent Sephardic rabbi and hakam of the Sephardic communities of the British Commonwealth. As future founder of the Sephardic Studies program at New York's Yeshiva University and promoter of the journal *The American Sephardi*, Rabbi Gaon soon became an essential link between the American Sephardic community and Spain.[42] Upon his request, the World Sephardi Federation (WSF) appointed Yair Behar as WSF representative to Spain in 1957. In the years following, Behar made an effort to increase the visibility of Sephardic Jewry, but aware of the delicate situation of the Jews in Spain, he opted for cultural and educational initiatives in cooperation with the Spanish Ministry of Education. The most important outcome of this collaboration was the World Sephardic Bibliographical Exhibition that took place at Madrid's National Library toward the end of 1959. The WSF had proposed that the Spanish government take this exhibition on a traveling tour to various European and American capitals, but the MFA rejected the plan, arguing that Jewish-Zionist propaganda would exploit this event to weaken Spain's position in the Arab world. After all, the Madrid exhibit had been authorized by the ministry on condition "that this exaltation of one facet of our own culture does not degenerate into a glorification of those aspects of Sephardic thought which are fundamentally antagonistic to the spiritual concept of the authentic Spain."[43]

Overall, the 1959 Sephardic exhibition in Madrid was a success that perfectly fit into the regime's propaganda efforts and political agenda. Among the attendees were the representatives of the World Jewish Congress, the World Zionist Organization, the Hebrew University of Jerusalem, and the Alliance Israélite Universelle, as well as president of the WSF, Denzil Sebag-Montefiore, and the hakam of the British Sephardim, Solomon Gaon, to whom General Franco then bestowed the order of Alfonso the Wise, one of Spain's highest honors. As reported by *The American Sephardi*, Rabbi Gaon gave a speech in the Sephardim's Judeo-Spanish language at the close of the exhibit that touched General Franco himself, who "wiping away his tears, declared: 'the Spanish Government is proud to have been able to save Jewish lives during the Second World War and wishes to do everything possible to develop cultural bonds between the Sephardim and Spain.'"[44]

From that moment forward, the Franco regime's gestures toward the Sephardim in particular, and the Jews more generally, became more common and publicly visible. In 1961, the government established the Instituto de Estudios Sefardíes (Institute of Sephardic Studies), a joint initiative with the WSF to encourage research on the Judeo-Spanish language and the cultural heritage of the Spanish Jews. A direct consequence of this cooperation was the First Symposium of Sephardic Studies, which took place in Madrid in June 1964 and led to the publication of a 781-page volume at the Spanish Government's expense.[45] Also in 1964, the government unveiled a monument to Maimonides in the city of Córdoba, and the Caudillo authorized the establishment of a museum and a library devoted to Spanish-Jewish culture at Toledo's legendary El Tránsito synagogue.

It is no coincidence that the peak of Francoist Spain's pro-Jewish initiatives occurred in parallel with the reformist Second Vatican Council (1962–65). A self-defined loyal follower of the Roman Catholic Church, Franco's Spain could not ignore the church's formal acquittal of the Jews as murderers of Jesus Christ (*Nostra Aetate*, October 1965), nor its recognition of religious freedom as a fundamental right (*Dignitatis Humanae*, December 1965).[46] In 1965, General Franco had an audience with the heads of the Madrid and Barcelona Jewish communities, Alberto Levy and Max Mazin, respectively, which resulted in the formal recognition of Spain's four major Jewish communities of Madrid, Barcelona, Ceuta, and Melilla. Then came the Law of Religious Freedom of June 1967, by virtue of which the Spanish Jewish community was finally enabled to practice Judaism both in private and in public. This allowed, on December 16, 1968, for the inauguration of a synagogue in Madrid with the government's sanction. During the ceremony, the congregation also read a text prepared by the Spanish Ministry of Justice by which the 1492 Alhambra Decree was officially abrogated.[47]

The legal emancipation of the Jews of Spain toward the late 1960s constituted, in the eyes of many observers, the ultimate proof of the regime's sympathy toward Jews. Promoted by more than two decades of propaganda and unchallenged by the absence of a more nuanced analysis of the Spanish role in World War II, the government's claims of rescue and assistance to Jews during the war continued to be taken at face value. Upon General Francisco Franco's death in November 1975, the editors of *The American Sephardi* made an offering before the ark of New York's historic Sephardic synagogue in New York City "for the repose of the soul of Generalissimo Francisco Franco" and thanked him for having helped the Jews during the war. The obituary concludes, "Putting to one side any other considerations, Jews should honour and bless the memory of this great benefactor of the Jewish people . . . who neither sought nor reaped any profit in what he did."[48]

THE ROLE OF HISTORIANS: THE CONSOLIDATION OF FRANCO'S PROPAGANDA

Despite the gratitude shown by the American Sephardic community, Franco's canonization as benefactor of Jews toward the end of his life would not have been possible without the endorsement of historical research. Unfortunately, the impossibility of accessing Spain's archives, in contrast to the widespread availability of mystified publications, resulted in the consolidation and diffusion of Franco's rescue narrative by a whole generation of historians. Moreover, there were at least three occasions in which the Spanish government, and even Franco himself were involved in the writing process.

This was the case, for instance, of one of Franco's earliest and best-selling biographers. Quoting the government's propaganda pamphlet *Spain and the Jews* (1949), Australian historian Brian Crozier stated that Franco "gave refuge to thousands of Hitler's Jewish victims" and "made repeated efforts to get local Sephardic Jews to register as Spanish citizens" in France, Romania, Greece, and French Morocco. Crozier, who maintained correspondence with General Franco and was given advice by him during the writing process, also mentions that Franco "revived citizenship rights for the Sephardic Jewish community of Salonika to save it from Nazi persecution" [49]—a claim that is difficult to believe given the nearly complete annihilation of Salonika's Jews during the Holocaust. Published in sixty-seven editions and translated into five different languages, Crozier's biography of Franco became a powerful channel for the regime's propaganda. British historian George Hills, who published his Franco biography the same year as Crozier, also accepted the regime's propaganda at face value and noted that "Franco described with unusual sensitivity the plight of the Jews."[50] This remark is illustrative of the near-legendary fascination that the regime's propaganda created around the Caudillo, which produced all sorts of speculations regarding his personality and his reasons to aid the Jewish people. Harry S. May, for instance, hypothesized that it was due to the dictator's concealed Jewish origins that he showed "humanism and compassion" toward Jews and defended the Sephardim's "inalienable right" to reclaim their Spanish citizenship.[51]

The second example of the Spanish government's involvement in the writing process is Federico Ysart's *España y los Judíos en la Segunda Guerra Mundial* (1973), the first monograph entirely devoted to the subject of Franco's Spain and the Jews during the Second World War.[52] Commissioned by the Spanish MFA, this publication was clearly a premeditated attempt to legitimize the regime's propaganda discourse. In addition to supplying its author with a selection of sources from its archives, the ministry also made several suggestions on Ysart's initial draft to adjust it to the regime's line of thought and insisted that it should be published by an independent press under the appearance of an independent academic publication.[53] Being one of the most widely cited publications on the subject, Ysart's *España y los Judíos en la Segunda Guerra Mundial* has contributed greatly to the spread of the regime's fabrications within the scholarly community.

A third publication that contributed to the propagation of the Spanish rescue myth is *Franco, Spain, the Jews and the Holocaust*, written by the American Rabbi Chaim U. Lipschitz during the 1970s but published only in 1984.[54] In January 1970, the MFA heard of Lipschitz's research project and invited the rabbi to conduct research in Madrid and Barcelona, put an official car at the rabbi's disposal, and paid all his accommodation expenses. More important, the ministry also supplied Rabbi Lipschitz with a selection of archival sources that were later translated and sent to Washington for the author's convenience.[55] The resulting monograph, which was printed by one of the most influential publishers in the field of Judaica and Jewish studies, also includes the transcript of Rabbi Lipschitz's interview with General Franco, in which the dictator commented on his rescue of Jews during the war and on the current situation of the Jewish community in Spain. The rabbi concluded that Franco "did, in fact, pull tens of thousands of Jews from the clutches of the Nazi juggernaut of genocide" and highlighted "the uniqueness of his humanitarian work as compared to the intransigence, deliberate stalling, and, in some cases, downright anti-Semitism" of the Allied democracies.[56]

The impact of these mystified publications on later historical research is difficult to measure. Shortly after General Franco's death, Caesar C. Aronsfeld, Holocaust researcher and promoter of the Wiener Library in London, made one of the earliest attempts to write an impartial narrative of the Spanish Jewish community's recent history. Unfortunately, Aronsfeld's *The Ghosts of 1492* (1979) was grounded on the limited and mystified available literature and was unable to discern between the actions of the individual Spanish diplomats who assisted Jews in countries under Nazi occupation and the policy of the government. As a result, Aronsfeld attributed the saving of thousands of Jews to Franco's personal initiative.[57] Similarly, Italian historian Enrico Deaglio also believed that the Spanish efforts to rescue European Jews from the Holocaust were driven by the "specific and energetic request of the *Generalísimo*" and that Spain's balance of rescue was "certainly superior to that of the anti-Nazi democracies."[58] A last example is that of Spanish historian Juan Antonio Cabezas, who, based on Lipschitz's theses, suggested a hypothetical "movement of redemption" carried out jointly by the Franco regime and the Vatican.[59]

In recent years, as a consequence of the growing scholarship on Francoist Spain, the quasi-legendary role of General Franco as savior of Jews has been slowly replaced by more articulated interpretations of the rescue myth. An illustrative example of this trend can be found in the work of American historian Willian D. Rubinstein, who considered Spain "a country whose policies were philosemitic, despite its fascist regime headed by Franco." Even though it represented the shift away from a Francocentric rescue narrative, however, Rubinstein still claimed that Spain willingly changed its immigration policies on two occasions, so that "*all refugees without exception* [*sic*] would be allowed to enter and remain."[60] In reality, Spain's refugee policy was significantly less welcoming, and not even the Sephardic Jewish refugees who had Spanish nationality were allowed to remain in the country. A second example of this phenomenon can be found in Wayne H. Bowen's recent work on Spanish collaborationism with Nazi Germany. According to Bowen, it was thanks to "the strong efforts of [wartime Foreign Affairs Ministers] Jordana and then Lequerica in Madrid" that the Spanish diplomats abroad "managed to save thousands of Jews by the end of the war."[61]

In terms of historiographical output, the subject of Franco's Spain and the Holocaust has been significantly more popular among non-Spanish than Spanish scholars. This situation has gradually shifted since the Spanish transition to democracy of the late 1970s, but especially during the widespread revisiting and revaluation of the Spanish Civil War and the Francoist dictatorship during the early twenty-first century in Spain.[62] Unfortunately, a significant amount of this historical production has been driven by right- and left-wing political affiliations rather than by a scholarly interest, resulting in simplistic readings of the subject with a clearly teleological intent.[63] On the Right side of the political spectrum, the politicization of the rescue myth has adopted the form of counterrevisionist publications that aim at reinvigorating the notion of a comprehensive rescue campaign "*In the name of Franco*"—such is the title of Arcadi Espada's monograph.[64] On the Left, the hyperbolic distortion of historical evidence with political aims has gone in the opposite direction, as illustrated by Eduardo Martín de Pozuelo's book *Francoism, Accomplice of the Holocaust* (2012).[65]

Finally, it is worth analyzing the shifting attitudes of the Spanish MFA in regard to the Francoist myth of rescue, as exemplified by the following four initiatives. The first of them is the ministry-sponsored academic monograph *Spain, the Sephardic Jews, and the Third Reich: The work of Spanish Diplomats against the Nazi genocide* (1997), which deliberately disregarded a portion of the available historiography as well as key archival documentation in a last attempt to prove the Francoist government's supposed zeal in protecting the European Sephardic communities abroad.[66] Despite being severely criticized by the scholarly community, this publication marked the beginning of a new official discourse that focuses on highlighting and celebrating the "heroic" actions of Spanish diplomat-rescuers over the more controversial role of Madrid's central government.[67]

The exhibition *Spanish Diplomats and the Holocaust: Visas for Freedom* (2000), which toured Spain and some of the Balkan countries where Sephardic communities had been located prior to the Holocaust, is illustrative of this shift in narrative.[68] Through this exhibition, the MFA acknowledged for the first time a more evidence-based interpretation of Francoist Spain's treatment of Jews during World War II. Paradoxically, the exhibition's greater emphasis on the actions of the few Spanish diplomats who intervened on behalf of Jews resulted—in spite of the apparent break from the former propaganda—in a self-congratulatory narrative that is, in essence, a modernized version of Franco's long-standing myth.

Recently, this attempt to establish a "hall of fame" of national diplomat-rescuers crystallized in a second exhibition held on the very premises of the MFA in Madrid under the revealing title of *Beyond Duty: The Foreign Service's Humanitarian Response to the Holocaust*

(2014).[69] This exhibition evidenced the ministry's determination to reduce a complex and unpleasant national reality of Spain's recent history into a self-congratulatory narrative gravitating around "those members of the Foreign Service who, from their European destinations, and with exemplary courage, saved thousands of Jews from a certain death under the sole protection of the Spanish flag."[70] This new official narrative was consolidated in a book published by the ministry itself shortly after the exhibition, which highlights the "outright, decisive, and proactive" attitude of the vaguely termed "Spanish Foreign Service," in an attempt to revive for the Spanish democracy the myth once propagated by Franco, now without the dictator.[71]

CONCLUSION

As recalled by *Jewish Digest* founder Bernard Postal following Francisco Franco's death in November 1975, the fact that the last-standing fascist dictator in Europe had rescued thousands of Jews during the war remained "one of the great ironies of 20th century history."[72] But far from merely anecdotal, the myth of the rescue's redemptive potential constituted a crucial asset for General Franco's fascist dictatorship, which carefully cultivated and disseminated it for decades. This redemptive quality was first put into practice toward the second half of World War II as a means to readjust the regime's image to the shifting balance of power. After the war ended, Franco's former sympathies toward the defeated Axis powers drove the regime into a period of international isolation and economic autarky that severely threatened the survival of the regime. It was then that the propaganda regarding Franco's alleged mass rescue of European Jews was presented to the West as a token of the regime's charitable nature, and, more important, as a vital point of divergence with Nazi Germany's antisemitic policies. With the escalating Cold War, the fear of Communism led many in the Western hemisphere to echo the regime's propaganda in their public appeals, calling to recruit Franco's fervent Catholicism and anti-Communism in the conflict against the Soviet Union. Despite attaining its desired reconciliation with the Western democracies in the early 1950s, Franco's government continued to nurture the myth of the rescue through cultural initiatives, as a means to authenticate its professed religious tolerance and interest in Sephardic Jewish culture. Pleased with the dictator's increasing concessions toward Jews, both the Spanish Jewish community and certain sectors of the American Jewish community became increasingly supportive of the regime, thus contributing to the further legitimization of the Spanish rescue myth. The galvanizing factor of the legend, however, was the perpetuation of the myth in publications by a number of independent scholars, who, due to both the Spanish government's interfering and the unavailability of archival material, validated Franco's propaganda as historically factual.

NOTES

I wish to thank the editors of this volume, Alexandra Garbarini and Paul Jaskot, for sharing their very useful comments and ideas with me during the writing of this chapter.

1. Haim Avni, *Spain, the Jews, and Franco*, trans. Emanuel Shimoni (Philadelphia: Jewish Publication Society of America, 1982), 3. First published in Hebrew in 1974.

2. Antonio Marquina Barrio and Gloria Inés Ospina, *España y los Judíos en el siglo XX: La Acción Exterior* (Madrid: Espasa Calpe, 1987).

3. Bernd Rother, *Franco und der Holocaust* (Tübingen: Max Niemeyer Verlag, 2001). I will be citing the Spanish translation, *Franco y el Holocausto* (Madrid: Marcial Pons, 2005); English translations from this edition are mine. On this topic, see also Bernd Rother, "Spain and the German Repatriation Ultimatum 1943/44," in *Bystanders, Rescuers or Perpetrators? The Neutral Countries and the Shoah*, ed. Corry Guttstadt et al. (Berlin: Metropol, 2016), 169–79.

4. On Spanish antisemitism, see Isabelle Rohr, *The Spanish Right and the Jews, 1898–1945: Antisemitism and Opportunism* (Brighton, U.K.: Sussex Academy Press, 2007). On the matter of refugees, see Rosa Sala Rose, *La penúltima frontera: Fugitivos del nazismo en España* (Barcelona: Papel de Liar, 2011); Josep Calvet, *Huyendo del Holocausto: Judíos evadidos del nazismo a través del Pirineo de Lleida* (Barcelona: Milenio, 2015).

5. Augusto D'Esaguy, COMASSIS Lisbon, to HICEM Paris, April 5, 1940, YIVO Archives, RG 245.4, Series I, File XII, MKM-13.36#3. The minister of interior to whom D'Esaguy refers in this letter is José Finat, Count of Mayalde.

6. Jacobo Israel Garzón, "El Archivo Judaico del Franquismo," *Raíces: Revista judía de cultura* 84 (2010): 51–55.

7. Jesus María de Rotaeche, Ministry of Commerce's Director General, to MFA, October 23, 1941, United States Holocaust Memorial Museum (USHMM), RG-36.001M, R-1190-83-6.

8. See Bernd Rother, "Myth and Fact—Spain and the Holocaust," in *The Holocaust in Spanish Memory: Historical Perceptions and Cultural Discourse*, ed. Antonio Gómez-Quiñones and Susana Zepp (Leipzig: Leipzig Universitätsverlag, 2010), 53.

9. Rother, *Franco y el Holocausto*, 384–85.

10. JDC secretary Moses A. Leavitt to Ambassador Cárdenas, December 30, 1943, JDC Archives, AR193344, Reel 69, Folder 916.

11. Sequerra to JDC Lisbon, October 2, 1942, JDC Archives, AR193344, Reel 69, Folder 914.

12. MFA memo to all Spanish Embassies in the Americas except Washington, La Habana, and San Salvador, February 19, 1944; cited in Rother, "Myth and Fact," 55.

13. Javier Martínez de Bedoya, press attaché of the Spanish Embassy in Lisbon, to Minister Jordana, April 11, 1944, Archivo del Ministerio de Asuntos Exteriores (hereafter cited as AMAE), R-1716, Folder 4. My translation.

14. Cited in José Antonio Lisbona: *Retorno a Sefarad: la Política de España hacia sus Judíos en el Siglo XX* (Barcelona: Riopiedras ediciones, 1993), 123–24. My translations.

15. See letter exchange between Ambassador Cárdenas and the MFA, November 14 and 21, 1944; cited in Rother, "Myth and Fact," 56.

16. As reproduced by the Spanish media: EFE, "España ha ayudado a la Evacuación de Refugiados Europeos," *ABC Andalucía*, July 23, 1944, 9. My translation.

17. Robert L. Briggs, RSARO Madrid, to JDC Lisbon, July 22, 1945, YIVO Archives, RG-335.5, Reel 68, Folder 727. Briggs's own translation.

18. Breckinridge Long's declaration first appeared in New York's *Daily News* on June 14, 1946, and was reproduced in the Spanish press the following day. The two articles referred to are EFE, "España ha ayudado a la evacuacion de refugiados europeos," *ABC Andalucía*, July 23, 1944, 9; EFE, "España Protegió a Sesenta Mil Judíos," *ABC Madrid*, June 15, 1946, 7–8. My translations.

19. For greater insight into Breckinridge Long's personality and the debate around his controversial refugee policies at the U.S. State Department, see Rebecca Erbelding, "About Time: The History of the War Refugee Board" (Ph.D. thesis, George Mason University, 2015), 40–42.

20. UN General Assembly, Resolution 39/I. Relations of Members of the United Nations with Spain (December 12, 1946), *Fifty-ninth Plenary Meeting of the General Assembly of the United* Nations. https://documents-dds-ny.un.org/doc/RESOLUTION/GEN/NR0/032/83/IMG/NR003283.pdf?OpenElement.

21. MFA to Spanish Legation in London, July 24, 1948, and MFA to

the Spanish Legation in Washington, D.C., July 26, 1948; cited in Rother, "Myth and Fact," 59.

22. MFA, *Datos sobre la protección a los judíos sefarditas* (Madrid, 1948), AMAE, 2996/1; MFA, *Spain and the Jews* (Madrid, 1949), in Leo Baeck Institute, DS-135.S7.S72. The brochure's French translation is cited in Avni, *Spain, the Jews and Franco*, 179.

23. MFA, *Spain and the Sephardic Jews* (Washington, D.C.: Spanish Embassy, 1949), in American Jewish Historical Society Archive, DS-135.S7.S7.

24. Ibid., 5.

25. Francisco Franco, "Decreto-ley de 29 de Diciembre de 1948 por el que se reconoce la condición de súbditos españoles en el extranjero a determinados sefadíes, antiguos protegidos de España," *Boletín Oficial del Estado* 9 (January 9, 1949). My translation.

26. Circular Orders number 2083 and 2088 "Sobre Nacionalidad de Sefarditas y su Entrada en España," July 24 and October 10, 1945, respectively, AMAE, R-1672, Folder 1; Cited in Lisbona, *Retorno a Sefarad*, 123–24. My translation.

27. Associated Press, "Sephardic Jews Invited Back by Spain: Franco Decree Involves Descendants of About 100,000 Ousted in 1492," *Washington Post*, January 10, 1949, 1.

28. Associated Press, "Franco Invites Jews to Return," *Palestine Post*, January 12, 1949, 2.

29. Editor, "Sound Advice on Franco from Mr Weddell," *Richmond News Leader*, June 11, 1946.

30. Keenan to State Department, October 24, 1947; cited in Raanan Rein, *Shadow of the Holocaust and the Inquisition: Israel's Relations with Francoist Spain* (London: Routledge, 1997), 83.

31. *Herut*, May 11, 1951; cited in Rein, *Shadow of the Holocaust*, 120.

32. Richard Pattee, *This Is Spain* (Milwaukee: Bruce, 1951), 396–404.

33. Previously, on May 7, 1945, *Aftenposten* had published the Nobel laureate Knut Hamsun's infamous obituary of Adolf Hitler, causing great controversy. Synnøve Stray Fischer, "Los 'judíos españoles' han escapado de las cámaras de gas de Hitler" (Spanish translation), *Aftenposten*, January 15, 1953; cited in Orti, *Spanish Perception*, 82–84.

34. In the aftermath of World War II, the Francoist regime got rid of some Falangist symbols such as the fascist salute, which had been the compulsory national salute since April 1937. Enrique Moradiellos, *La España de Franco (1939–1975): Política y sociedad* (Madrid: Síntesis, 2000), 106.

35. Paul Preston, *Franco* (London: Basic Books, 1994), 537–39.

36. Cited in Danielle Rozenberg, *La España Contemporánea y la*

Cuestión Judía: Retejiendo los hilos de la memoria y de la historia (Madrid: Casa Sefarad-Israel/Marcial Pons, 2010), 45.

37. Isaac Weissman to Maurice L. Perlzweig, "Our work for free exercise of religion in Spain," December 31, 1945, USHMM, RG-67.014M, Reel 314, 10.027–8.

38. Rein, *Shadow of the Holocaust*, 16.

39. AJP, "Spain's Jews Try to Hide Identity as Anti-Semitic Tension Flourishes," [Barcelona] *Sentinel*, September 20, 1951, 3.

40. Raanan Rein, "Diplomacy, Propaganda, and Humanitarian Gestures: Francoist Spain and Egyptian Jews, 1956–1968," *Iberoamericana* 6, no. 23 (2006): 21–33.

41. José Felipe de Alcover to Fernando María Castiella, Minister of Foreign Affairs, January 26, 1960, AMAE, R-5965, Folder 40; cited in Rozenberg, *La España Contemporánea*, 198–99.

42. Although politically independent from the Franco regime, the *American Sephardi* (published by the Sephardic Studies Program of Yeshiva University between 1966 and 1978) celebrated each of its pro-Jewish initiatives with reverence and dedicated an extensive and laudatory obituary to General Franco in its last issue of 1978. See, for instance, Maír José Benardete, "Spain Grants Freedom of Religion to the Jews: An Excursion into the Realms of the Imagination and Vision," *American Sephardi* 1, no. 2 (June 1967): 26–30; Richard D. Barnett, "Sephardi Museum Inaugurated in Toledo, Spain," *American Sephardi* 5, nos. 1–2 (1971): 143–45.

43. Rein, *Shadow of the Holocaust*, 184–85.

44. Herman P. Salomon and Tomás L. Ryan de Heredia, "In Memoriam: Francisco Franco (1892–1975), Benefactor of the Jews," *American Sephardi* 9 (1978): 216.

45. Iacob M. Hassán et al., eds., *Actas del Primer Simposio de Estudios Sefardíes* (Madrid: Instituto Arias Montano, 1970).

46. The *Ley de Principios del Movimiento Nacional* (May 17, 1958) declared the Spanish nation as subordinate to the "Law of God," meaning that Spanish legislation should be inspired by the doctrine of the Roman Catholic Church.

47. "Spanish Government Formally Rescinds 1492 Decree Ordering Expulsion of Jews," *Jewish Telegraphic Agency*, December 17, 1968.

48. Salomon and Ryan de Heredia, "In Memoriam," 215–18.

49. Brian Crozier, *Franco* (Boston: Little, Brown, 1967), 7, 388. First published in 1949.

50. George Hills, *Franco: The Man and his Nation* (New York: Macmillan, 1967), 408. First published in 1949.

51. Harry S. May, *Francisco Franco: The Jewish Connection* (Washington, D.C.: University Press of America, 1977), 13–28.

52. Federico Ysart, *España y los Judíos en la Segunda Guerra Mundial* (Barcelona: Dopesa, 1973).

53. The assessment of Ysart's and Lipschitz's monographs is consensual among scholars of Francoist Spain and the Holocaust. See, for instance, Marquina and Ospina, *España y los Judíos en el siglo XX*, 222–24; Lisbona, *Retorno a Sefarad*, 120–21; Rother, "Myth and Fact," 51–63.

54. Chaim U. Lipschitz, *Franco, Spain, the Jews, and the Holocaust* (New York: Ktav Publishing House, 1984).

55. See Marquina and Ospina, Lisbona, and Rother, as cited in note 53 above.

56. Lipschitz, *Franco, Spain, the Jews, and the Holocaust*, 168.

57. Caesar C. Aronsfeld, *The Ghosts of 1492: Jewish Aspects of the Struggle for Religious Freedom in Spain, 1848–1976* (New York: Columbia University Press, 1979), 47–55.

58. Enrico Deaglio, *La Banalità del Bene: Storia di Giorgio Perlasca* (Milan: Feltrinelli Editore, 1991), 125.

59. Juan Antonio Cabezas, *Madrid y sus Judíos* (Madrid: Avapiés, 1987), 175. My translation.

60. William D. Rubinstein, *The Myth of Rescue: Why Democracies Could Not Have Saved More Jews from the Nazis* (London: Routledge, 1997), 146.

61. Wayne H. Bowen, *Spaniards and Nazi Germany: Collaboration in the New Order* (Columbia: University of Missouri Press, 2000), 164–65, 205.

62. See chapter 7 in Helen Graham, *The War and Its Shadow: Spain's Civil War in Europe's Long Twentieth Century* (Brighton: Sussex Academic Press, 2012).

63. For an analysis of the politicization of the rescue myth in Spain, see Alejandro Baer and Pedro Correa, "The Politics of Holocaust Rescue Myths in Spain: From Francoist Humanitarianism to the Righteous Diplomats," in *Bystanders, Rescuers or Perpetrators? The Neutral Countries and the Shoah*, ed. Corry Guttstadt et al. (Berlin: Metropol Verlag, 2016), 205–16.

64. Arcadi Espada, *En Nombre de Franco: Los Héroes de la Embajada de España en el Budapest Nazi* (Barcelona: Espasa, 2013).

65. Eduardo Martín de Pozuelo, *El Franquismo, Cómplice del Holocausto: Y otros Episodios Desconocidos de la Dictadura* (Barcelona: La Vanguardia, 2012).

66. David Salinas, *España, los Sefarditas y el Tercer Reich (1939–1945): La Labor de Diplomáticos Españoles contra el Genocidio Nazi* (Valladolid: MFA and Universidad de Valladolid, 1997).

67. Baer and Correa, "Politics of Holocaust Rescue Myths," 210.

68. Alejandro Baer et al., *Diplomáticos Españoles ante el Holocausto: Visados para la Libertad* (MFA and Casa Sefarad-Israel, 2000). Exhibition catalog.

69. *Más Allá del Deber: La respuesta humanitaria del Servicio Exterior*

frente al Holocausto (Madrid, November–December 2014). Exhibition catalog.

70. Excerpt from the commemorative plaque unveiled during the exhibition's inauguration at the MFA's premises in Madrid. Cited in Baer and Correa, "Politics of Holocaust Rescue Myths," 214.

71. José Antonio Lisbona, *Más Allá del Deber: La respuesta humanitaria del Servicio Exterior frente al Holocausto* (Madrid: MFA, 2015), 41. My translation.

72. Bernard Postal, "How Spain's Franco Saved 12,000 Jews," *Sentinel*, March 25, 1976, 27.

Jonathan Druker

Tadeusz Borowski, Walter Benjamin, and the "Real State of Emergency"

ANGLOPHONE READERS OF HOLOCAUST LITERATURE NEED LITTLE INtroduction to Tadeusz Borowski (1922–1951), the author of several canonical stories set in Auschwitz and first published as early as 1946. They were later translated from Polish into English and collected in a volume titled *This Way for the Gas, Ladies and Gentlemen.*[1] Arrested by the Gestapo at age twenty-one, Borowski spent more than two years in various prisons and camps, including Auschwitz and Dachau, where he was liberated in April 1945. As a non-Jewish Pole not slated for automatic extermination by the SS, he received regular food packages from his family and was assigned lighter work duties than those performed by common inmates. While Borowski's stories are told in the first person by a narrator known as Tadeusz or Tadek and convey the authority of testimony, their genre remains stubbornly ambiguous. Are they memoir or historical fiction? Do the author and his deeply cynical narrator share the same point of view, let alone the same experiences?

Rather than force the stories into one category or another, the most fruitful interpretive strategy is to embrace their hybridity.[2] As texts operating within the conventions of memoir, they are genuinely marked by the suffering that Borowski witnessed personally. They also acknowledge the author's relative privilege, which condemns him to what Primo Levi called "the gray zone," in which victims were drawn into a web of complicity with the SS and became, to varying degrees, the oppressors of their fellow victims.[3] Borowski believed that the level of privilege he experienced, which afforded him a broad panorama of Auschwitz, enabled him to come to a profound and immediate understanding of its historical significance. In its structure, he perceived the recurring traumas that shaped Europe. He learned, wrote Jan Kott, that "history is a sequence of Auschwitzes, one following the other."[4] Moreover, the camp experience confirmed his troubling suspicion that history is so repeatedly catastrophic that the suffering of others, which ought to rouse our deepest empathy and moral outrage, seems normal and tolerable.

As a writer of historical fiction, Borowski deploys an array of literary devices that make his stories among the most compelling in Holocaust literature. Satire, irony, and the disparity between content and tone are among his most important techniques. When, for example, Borowski's narrator maintains the pretense of normality in the face of extremely abnormal events—a stance that would undermine the ethical credibility of a memoirist—it is clear that the author does not share this craven perspective. Instead, he employs this strategy to make a larger point: where other texts underscore its unique horror, Borowski's domesticates Auschwitz to reveal its filiations with both past history and the seemingly tranquil Polish countryside that surrounds the camp. To do so, his narrator largely maintains a flat, unemotional tone that normalizes the abnormal violence he witnesses, a technique that runs the risk of making both the author and the reader complicit in the erasure of the victims' suffering. However, Borowski's personal point of view seems aligned with the narrator's when, at a few key moments, the narrator disavows his nihilism and ironic detachment and sounds an alarm of moral outrage. In these crucial passages, I argue, Borowski declares the literary equivalent of what Walter Benjamin called "a real state of emergency." This is a call for a revolutionary caesura, a kind of temporal standstill capable of "blast[ing] open the continuum of history," which, Benjamin believed, otherwise leads to repeated catastrophes, such as those brought on by Nazism.[5]

Benjamin's best-known representation of the relentless "continuum of history" occurs in his "angel of history" allegory. The angel, the figural embodiment of true historical consciousness, would like to halt history's disastrous rush forward, deceptively called "progress." The angel would, in other words, like to declare "a real state of emergency." Instead, the silenced messenger, who represents the traumatized subject, can only stare in mute shock—and in amazement—at the accumulating ruins of the past. "The angel would like to stay, awaken the dead, and make whole what has been smashed. But a storm is blowing from Paradise. . . . This storm drives him irresistibly into the future, to which his back is turned, while the pile of debris before him grows toward the sky. What we call progress is *this* storm" (*SW*, 392).[6]

Benjamin's longed-for caesura, a transcendent suspension of time he calls "now-time" (*Jetztzeit*; *SW*, 395), which posits all of history as one single event, seems to mark the return of a secular messiah and the genuine end of history. This chance for redemption, however slight, provides solace to victims and witnesses of catastrophe who are forced to confront the possibility that history is indeed a sequence of Auschwitzes. Moreover, an artist or writer who sees history as clearly as Benjamin's angel does, and then invokes "a real state of emergency," takes a stand against "the continuum of history" by introducing historical contingency and offering some hope that history's damaging course may not be fully determined in advance.

This article seeks insights into Borowski's Auschwitz stories through the lens of Benjamin's innovative philosophy of history. Although Benjamin's life ended before the advent of Auschwitz as we know it, his final writings anticipate with great acuity the extent to which the Holocaust would render untenable positivist notions of history and progress.[7] In a similar vein, the relationship between Auschwitz and history, broadly conceived, is a pressing concern in *This Way for the Gas*. These two writers, whose very lives were overturned by the Holocaust, seem to have concluded that history is inherently traumatic and that the tormented past lives on in the present. Consequently, they see historical events as a premonition of the present catastrophe, and they view Nazism as the latest iteration in an extended sequence of traumatic violence that is difficult, although not impossible, to interrupt. This kind of thinking links historical development with Freudian trauma theory, especially with the notion that collective traumas return belatedly in symptomatic form to haunt communities and nations.[8] The two writers may be called anti-Hegelians: both are alert to the residues of past traumas that cannot be synthesized into a positive result.[9] Unlike Marxists convinced that history moves in a positive direction, both are pessimistic about its course and therefore skeptical of the prospects for social progress. Moreover, they seem to suspect that history is more mythic and archetypal than dialectical.

Despite the many parallels, Benjamin and Borowski have never been brought together in an extended critical dialogue like the one staged here. This article offers a comparative analysis of these two important Holocaust authors who developed their analogous ideas in relative isolation from each other. While they both suffered in the encounter with the brute force of Nazism, there is no provable common intellectual culture shared by Benjamin and the younger Borowski, apart from a kind of apocalyptic nihilism pervading Europe in the years following World War I.[10] Nevertheless, Benjamin, by means of brilliant philosophical aphorisms, and Borowski, with a harshly realistic literary style, both meditate on the consequences of building a new civilization on the haunted ruins of an unacknowledged, traumatic past.

Benjamin's career and development as a thinker are well known.[11] The course of Borowski's life and intellectual formation make it unlikely that he knew anything about Benjamin's work before writing the stories under study here. However, even before his stay in Auschwitz, Borowski had reason to view the concentration camp as a paradigmatic institution of modernity. He was born in Ukraine in 1921 to Polish parents, both of whom were later incarcerated in labor camps by the Soviets.[12] Borowski attended high school in Warsaw at the time of the Nazi invasion. During the oppressive occupation and dismemberment of Poland, he began to write poetry, self-publishing his first volume clandestinely in 1942. Titled *Wherever the Earth*, it "predicted in classical cadences the extermination of mankind. Its dominant image was that of a gigantic labor camp."[13] Despite these early indications of Borowski's pessimistic notion of history, it is important to remember that he had not completed a university education before arriving in Auschwitz. According to Borowski scholar and translator Tadeusz Pióro, "only after he found himself in Auschwitz did his literary, ethical and psychological development begin."[14] This seems to be confirmed by the narrator of one of Borowski's Auschwitz stories, who states, "only now [in the camp] do I realize what price was paid for building ancient civilizations" (*TWG*, 131). What Auschwitz taught the young man—and what Benjamin had already learned—is that the price for the edifice called civilization was, and will always be, the oppression and suffering of the weakest among us.

The specific task of this article is to interpret Borowski's stories with concepts developed by Benjamin in "On the Concept of History," written a few weeks before his desperate suicide in September 1940. This philosophical text attempts to reconceptualize historical time by combining a secularized theology of messianism with a particular version of historical materialism that rejects Marxism's investment in the idea of progress.[15] Its eighteen theses are informed by the Nazi oppression and violence that hounded Benjamin out of Germany, but not by the attempted genocide of Europe's Jews and the wholesale massacre of the Poles, events Borowski experienced intimately. Borowski's fictions, like Benjamin's theses, probe the connection between state violence and the long history of Europe. So far, critics have not made much of this important thread in Borowski's work, and none of them has argued, as this article does, that his literary style is crafted to represent his negative conception of history in which catastrophe is the norm and Auschwitz is the paradigm.[16] Like Benjamin, Borowski believed that barbarism lurks within civilization and is an essential part of it. An important distinction is that, as an inhabitant of "the gray zone," Borowski had more personal experience to support this conclusion than Benjamin had. "I saw the death of a million people—literally, not metaphorically," he wrote in one of his letters.[17] The two writers' analytical frameworks are remarkably similar, and this makes their divergences instructive, too.

It is not the case that Borowski specifically dismissed the historically unique aspects of the Holocaust, or the unprecedented extremes of Nazi racial ideology, or the particular suffering of the Jewish people. However, as a Holocaust writer, he was most interested in understanding malevolent historical and cultural continuities over the long term. He wrote in *This Way for the Gas* that Auschwitz, the very paradigm of state barbarism, revealed to him the dark underside of civilization, which built its glorious monuments on the backs of the oppressed (and on his own back) and then systematically obscured their suffering. This historical process, through which the extreme violence of the Holocaust was destined to be normalized and ultimately forgotten—at least if Germany won the war—was also what shaped his personal history and became central to his storytelling. Borowski's stories recount learning how to live amid terrible suffering and, in pursuit of self-preservation, to ignore it. Yet his strongest writing explores the moral crisis the narrator experiences on account of what he witnesses and can do little to prevent: the brutalization and death of the ordinary inmates, mostly Jews. Shame and guilt, while often masked by an offhand tone, are palpable sensations in nearly all of the stories. In one instance, for example, women in several trucks roll slowly past, pleading, "Save us! We are going to the gas chambers!" Among "the ten thousand silent men," the narrator remarks flatly, and in the first-person plural, "not one of us made a move, not one of us lifted a hand" (*TWG*, 116).

CIVILIZATION AND BARBARISM

In the well-known seventh thesis of "On the Concept of History," on the inherent links between civilization, culture, and barbarism, Benjamin notes that naive "historicist" narratives, always intent on affirming social progress, remember and sympathize "with the victor." As a corrective, Benjamin deploys his theologically inflected historical materialism to uncover the violence—and the "horror"—that insinuates itself into public art and culture, whether it is erected on the backs of the weak or, as spoils of war, looted from vanquished peoples soon to be forgotten:

> Whoever has emerged victorious participates to this day in the triumphal procession in which current rulers step over those who are lying prostrate. According to the traditional practice, the spoils are carried in the procession. They are called "cultural treasures," and the historical materialist views them with cautious detachment. For in every case these treasures have a lineage which he cannot contemplate without horror. They owe their existence not only to the efforts of the great geniuses who created them, but also to the anonymous toil of others who lived in the same period. There is no document of civilization which is not at the same time a document of barbarism. (*SW*, VII, 391–92)

Benjamin asserts, as did Theodor Adorno and Max Horkheimer a few years later in *Dialectic of Enlightenment*, that civilizations have always been built on the oppression of the nameless crowd and that officially sanctioned culture, held to be the highest expression of a people, is at the same time inextricably linked with expropriation, subjugation, and violence.[18] Benjamin's point is that documents pertaining to culture, as well as those of governance and efficient bureaucracy, camouflage the brutality that engendered them.

One of the main themes in Borowski's famous story "This Way for the Gas, Ladies and Gentlemen," conveyed with razor-sharp irony by its title, is the way that the form and substance of civilization, and culture itself, mask impending violence.[19] Borowski's descriptions of the SS men at the railroad ramp simultaneously convey civility and menace as they manage the newly arrived victims who have already been profoundly brutalized by the train journey. "There is an SS man behind your back, calm, efficient, watchful. '*Meine Herrschaften*, this way, ladies and gentlemen, try not to throw your things around, please. Show some good will,' he says courteously, his restless hands playing with the slender whip" (*TWG*, 38). The ever-present threat of violence is softened momentarily by a veneer of orderly calm and genteel civility. "*Ordnung muss sein*" ("There must be order"), the narrator states repeatedly, so as to satirize German fixation with order, one of the hallmarks of civilization that enabled the Nazis to murder so many so efficiently. "Nearby stands a young, clean-shaven 'gentleman', an SS officer with a notebook in his hand. For each departing truck he enters a mark; sixteen gone means one thousand people more or less. The gentleman is calm, precise. No truck can leave without a signal from him, or a mark in his notebook: *Ordnung muss sein*" (*TWG*, 39). Here, as in other passages, Borowski dramatizes Benjamin's observation that suffering is the subtext of official documents. In this case the orderly tallies, an apparently bloodless abstraction, testify to the violence that founds impressive empires. In this concise narrative, Borowski achieves a miniaturized literary evocation akin to the Protocol of the 1942 Wannsee Conference, with its bureaucratic euphemisms—the highly educated attendees discuss "the Final Solution of the Jewish Question"—and its matter-of-fact toting up of the number of Jews in Europe (eleven million) that, we understand in reading between the lines, still need to be annihilated.[20]

Benjamin's concepts are further exemplified in Borowski's "Auschwitz, Our Home (A Letter)," his longest story. The prisoner-narrator speaks from the position of the toiling slave who only now understands that his suffering is woven into every cultural monument, work of art, and philosophical dialogue of every century:

> We carry huge sacks of cement, lay bricks, put down rails, spread gravel, trample the earth. . . . We are laying the foundation for some new, monstrous civilization. Only now do I realize what price was paid for building the ancient civilizations. The Egyptian pyramids, the temples and Greek statues—what a hideous crime they were! How much blood must have poured on to the Roman roads, the bulwarks, and the city walls. Antiquity—the tremendous concentration camp where the slave was branded on the forehead by his master, and crucified for trying to escape. (*TWG*, 131)

This passage shows that, beyond its own historical reality, Borowski understands the Holocaust as the latest expression of long-repressed memories of disaster, and that the traumatic space and time occupied by Auschwitz is contiguous with other forgotten sites of imperial slavery and mass murder. Moreover, he clearly thinks his perilous concentration camp sojourn conferred on him an awful knowledge that illuminates the present and the past, too. By using the terminology of the present—the concentration camp—to describe the past, Borowski posits a mythic form of history that does not truly evolve toward liberation but only repeats its repression. Long before the widely read Giorgio Agamben stated, drawing heavily on Benjamin's thinking, that the concentration camp is "the hidden matrix and *nomos* of the political space in which we still live," Borowski arrived at a similar conclusion.[21] In a later story, set in the immediate postwar period, Borowski's narrator describes himself as a pessimist whose Auschwitz experience had taught him "that the whole world is really like the concentration camp [where] the weak work for the strong" (*TWG*, 168).[22]

Once again sounding like Benjamin, the narrator of "Auschwitz, Our Home" tells us that official histories forget the victims and the horrors inflicted on them but remember the victors, whose achievements are memorialized in "cultural treasures": "If the Germans win the war, what will the world know about us? They will erect huge buildings, highways, factories, soaring monuments. Our hands will be placed under every brick, and our back will carry the steel rails and the slabs of concrete. They will kill off our families, our sick, our aged, they will murder our children. And we shall be forgotten, drowned out by the voices of the poets, the jurists, the philosophers, the priests. They will produce their own beauty, virtue and truth" (*TWG*, 132). Borowski's devastating sentences offer a forceful literary evocation of Benjamin's civilization-barbarism dyad and of the essential "horror" that he locates within high culture. Together, the two writers show us how civilization and culture not only memorialize but also obliterate memory.

WRITING IN AMAZEMENT

Benjamin thought that true philosophy, art, and literature should register the traumatic shocks of one's time.[23] It is for this reason that the

Benjamin-like aspects of Borowski's literary techniques are revealed by focusing on his use of language associated with "amazement" or "shock," and the opposite terms "habituation" or "accustomedness," along with other important binaries such as abnormal/normal and exception/rule.[24] "This Way for the Gas, Ladies and Gentlemen," opens as follows: "All of us walk around naked" (*TWG*, 29). Instead of easing the reader's entry into the world of Auschwitz by explaining that thousands of prisoners are having their uniforms deloused, which we learn eventually, Borowski means to shock and amaze us with this panoramic image of people robbed of all dignity, of all signs of their seemingly civilized nature. The narrator is on a labor crew tasked with expanding Birkenau, the women's camp, which is in close proximity to the unloading ramps as well as the gas chambers and crematoria. He continues, "The heat rises, the hours are endless. We are without even our usual diversion: the wide roads leading to the crematoria are empty. For several days now, no new transports have come in" (*TWG*, 30). We are shocked yet again by the blasé tone and the unsympathetic, callous choice of the word "diversion."[25] The text requires us to become habituated to the narrator's blunt, pitiless utterances and to accept that living in a place like Auschwitz for any length of time results in the normalization of the abnormal. Moreover, our new knowledge is not merely a by-product of our reading but one of the author's chief purposes: to force the reader to become aware of the iniquitous process, functioning to varying degrees in all civilizations, by which the suffering of the vanquished is forgotten.

The four longest of Borowski's many remarkable Auschwitz stories were first published in 1946, along with the stories by former camp internees Janusz Nel Siedlecki and Krystyn Olszewski, in a book translated as *We Were in Auschwitz*.[26] In his preface to the collection, publisher Anatol Girs, another non-Jewish Polish survivor of Auschwitz, states that the book is meant to counter "the naïve amazement that a person forced to live in a criminal system can become so base, an amazement with which we are still filled."[27] Positing a kind of "gray zone," Girs suggests that by reading this book about Auschwitz, we might overcome our initial shock and recognize the coercive effects of all malevolent institutions on human character—extermination camps most of all—and understand how such institutions distort the parameters that define normal behavior. While Borowski took seriously the importance of helping his readers overcome their "naïve amazement," he also tried to bring his readers *back* to a state of amazement with respect to Auschwitz, one based on historical knowledge and experience, in which what is abnormal and morally unacceptable is reclaimed from the insidious effects of normalization. The passage from innocent amazement to jaded familiarity to a wiser amazement involves a layered rhetorical strategy that resembles Benjamin's critique of Nazism and the concept of progress.

In his eighth thesis, Benjamin states, "The current amazement that the things we are experiencing are 'still' possible in the twentieth century is *not* philosophical. This amazement is not the beginning of knowledge—unless it is the knowledge that the view of history which gives rise to it is untenable" (*SW*, VIII, 392). Benjamin counters those who wonder: How is Nazi violence and inhumanity "still" possible in the middle of civilized Europe, in the middle of the twentieth century? The word "still" is in quotations to indicate its omnipresence in the discourse of those who uncritically accept extravagant claims made for the efficacy of progress. It is evident to Benjamin that the state-sponsored racism and violence that persist ("the things we are experiencing") are not amazing historical exceptions but all too expected among advanced civilizations and cultures: the apparent "state of exception" is revealed to be the rule. Seeming to offer a qualification on Aristotle's claim in *Metaphysics* that philosophy begins out of wonder, Benjamin suggests that only those with a naive theory of history continue to be amazed by Nazi violence and inhumanity.[28] When human-made disasters are the norm, as they are for Benjamin, history has a negative teleology. However, he does not reject the value of shock and amazement per se. Like Borowski, he charts a course away from it only to reclaim it, suggesting that a wise amazement is an appropriate affective and intellectual response to the realization that the traumatic histories of the past and present undermine our unexamined faith in progress.

The eighth thesis suggests a fruitful path for encountering Borowski. Each story in *We Were in Auschwitz* has a brief preface that was not included in *This Way for the Gas, Ladies and Gentlemen*, and there is reason to believe that Borowski wrote these short texts.[29] The preface to the story "This Way for the Gas, Ladies and Gentlemen" anticipates some of Primo Levi's most important observations in *The Drowned and the Saved* about the *Sonderkommandos*, the paradigmatic figures of "the gray zone" who truly became "accustomed" to atrocity.[30]

Using similar language, the preface to the ironically titled "Auschwitz, Our Home (A Letter)" describes the perspective of that story's narrator: he is "an 'accustomed' one, to whom the techniques of the camps, the crematoria and the orchestra, X ray and gallows, duplicity and betrayal, are no longer alien" (*TWG*, 116, quotation marks in the original Polish as well).[31]

The narrator, previously assigned to Birkenau, has now been sent to Auschwitz I to train as a medical orderly. (By the end of the story he has returned to Birkenau.) The nine-part letter that constitutes "Auschwitz, Our Home" is ostensibly addressed to the narrator's fiancée, still detained in Birkenau. However, it is clear that the "you" the narrator addresses directly is also the reader who, knowing nothing about the camp, is stunned by every horror recounted. Part 4 of the story addresses directly the need to set aside our amazement, as Benjamin recommends, if we are to understand Auschwitz as clearly as "an 'accustomed' one" does. Here, Borowski's narrator describes the arrival of some local Poles, under investigation for black marketeering, who "gazed in horror at the prisoners in stripes." These inexperienced visitors act as stand-ins for the uninitiated reader:

> They are really quite amusing, these civilians. They react to the camp as a wild boar reacts to firearms. Understanding nothing of how it functions, they look upon it as something inexplicable, almost abnormal, something beyond human endurance. Today,—having become totally familiar with the inexplicable and the abnormal; having learned to live on intimate terms with the crematoria, . . . having, so to say, broken bread with the beast—I look upon these civilians with a certain indulgence, the way a scientist regards a layman. . . . Try to grasp the essence of this pattern of daily events, discarding your sense of horror and loathing and contempt, and find for it all a philosophic formula. For the gas chambers and the gold stolen from the victims, for the roll-call and for the Puff [the brothel], for the frightened civilians and for the "old numbers" [veteran prisoners]. (*TWG*, 111–12)

As is often the case, Borowski's narrator employs black humor and irony (imagine, Auschwitz, *almost* abnormal!) to bring his reader up short and then continues in a witty yet serious vein. Positioning himself as a scientist, he suggests that our civilian shock and amazement impedes knowledge. Only by overcoming "horror and loathing" and thinking rationally (or even philosophically) can we understand how it is possible to kill millions and enslave hundreds of thousands (*TWG*, 112).

For Borowski, "ordinary," another antonym of amazing, is the key term, since the combined elements of the process that enabled genocide were indeed ordinary—not the result of radical evil but of "the banality of evil."[32] His narrator explains that "this is how it is done: first just one ordinary barn, brightly whitewashed—and here they proceed to asphyxiate people. Later, four large buildings, accommodating twenty thousand at a time without any trouble. No hocus-pocus, no poison, no hypnosis. Only several men directing traffic to keep operations running smoothly, and the thousands flow along like water from an open tap. All this happens just beyond the anemic trees of the dusty little wood. Ordinary trucks bring people, return, then bring some more" (*TWG*, 112). The mention of "the anemic trees," which shield the gas chambers from the approaching victims, emphasizes the apparent banality of the setting. Auschwitz-Birkenau, neither shocking nor horrible in this passage, is described as a giant objectifying factory that dehumanizes the victims through an impersonal, bureaucratic "operation." (A few years later, Hannah Arendt would produce a similar analysis in *The Origins of Totalitarianism*.[33]) For Borowski, focusing on the unique aspects of Auschwitz keeps us from seeing what is truly amazing about the camp: that it is built out of ordinary, preexisting elements, which show that the camp is not truly "out of this world," but *of* this world—a point Primo Levi also makes, though less forcefully.[34]

At the close of this letter, Borowski's narrator imagines that his fiancée's bunkmates are surprised by the blunt candor and lack of compassion in his letter. "And probably they are a little bit shocked. But I think we should speak about all the things that are happening around us. We are not evoking evil irresponsibly or in vain, for we have now become a part of it" (*TWG*, 113). Acknowledging his difficult position between victim and victimizer, which makes him a most extraordinary witness from "the gray zone," the narrator, now speaking for Borowski, testifies to the normalization of atrocious violence and his role in it.

STATES OF EMERGENCY

It is striking that Borowski reverses his course at the end of "Auschwitz, Our Home." After having indicated how quickly one becomes habituated to the horrors that surround one, and that Auschwitz is nothing more than the product of many small, ordinary elements, the narrator will effectively throw off the dulled conscience of "an 'accustomed' one" to recover his moral outrage. This is revealed clearly in the ninth and final part, in which the reader is led back to a wiser form of amazement or, what Benjamin called in his eighth thesis, a willed encounter with a "real state of emergency," a concept previously mentioned.

Late in the day, the narrator sees a *Sonderkommando* "returning from the cremo." (The use of the insider term "cremo" marks the narrator as "an 'accustomed' one.") As a habituated inmate, he is not alarmed to observe that these men are "black with smoke" (*TWG*, 141), having incinerated the asphyxiated bodies of today's victims, their fellow Jews. Among the group is a prisoner named Abbie, whom the narrator describes as "an old pal." Exchanging warm greetings and conversing casually, as if they were on the main street of any town, Abbie describes a new, horrible method for burning children's bodies, a most vile example of progress. Sensing the narrator's disapproval, although delivered in a flat, ironic style ("'Congratulations,' I said dryly and with very little enthusiasm"), Abbie defends himself: "Here in Auschwitz we must entertain ourselves in every way we can. Otherwise, who could stand it?" It is at this crucial moment, as Borowski's longest story comes to an abrupt conclusion, that, in anger and with a renewed astonishment after so much emotional paralysis, the narrator explodes the notion that we can tolerate a world where such aggression against the oppressed is "still" conceivable, where the extraordinary violence of Auschwitz can be produced by ordinary means and ordinary people, where we become habituated to such violence and immune to its horror. Now addressing the reader in this present moment, rather than speaking to Abbie in the recollected past, the narrator states emphatically that "this [process of normalization] is a monstrous lie, a grotesque lie, like the whole camp, like the whole world" (*TWG*, 142).[35] Borowski seems to entreat the habituated reader to resist his numb familiarity with Auschwitz and, along with the narrator, to reclaim his outrage and to renew his amazement in the face of this real emergency we now call the Holocaust.

As the great disparity between the flattened tone of "Auschwitz, Our Home" and its horrifying content comes to a crashing halt, Borowski signals the end of his past-tense narrative and the entry into a heightened present that makes ethical claims on us by calling our attention to suffering. Of the end of the story, Lawrence Langer wrote, "The 'monstrous' and 'grotesque lie' that Borowski denounces, abruptly compels us to face the horrible fact that we too may have been seduced into accepting the abnormal as normal, . . . abruptly we are wrenched from the detachment of contemplating a narrative, to an awareness of the narrative's [particular] roots in history."[36] While Langer speaks persuasively to the importance of recovering our sense of shock and breaking with insidious narratives that domesticate and normalize Auschwitz in all its particularity, this present article contends that, for Borowski, it is also a "monstrous lie" to claim that the Holocaust arose from wholly exceptional or abnormal circumstances which are now and forever in the past. By unmasking the link between the violence of the camp and the violence prevalent to all corners of the world and in all epochs, Borowski affirms the tenets of Benjamin's philosophy of history, which traces the endemic recurrence of despotic state violence.

At the opening of his eighth thesis Benjamin states, "The tradition of the oppressed teaches us that the 'state of emergency' in which we live is not the exception but the rule. We must attain to a conception of history that accords with this insight. Then we will clearly see that it is our task to bring about a real state of emergency, and this will improve our position in the struggle against fascism. One reason fascism has a chance is that, in the name of progress, its opponents treat it as a historical norm" (*SW*, VIII, 392). In theory, sovereign governments seldom invoke "states of emergency" or states of exception, the legal means to allocate extraordinary powers to the state while depriving citizens of their rights. To Benjamin, however, a fuller understanding of the history of oppression shows that states, especially authoritarian ones, *always* claim to be under mortal threat, just as the Nazis did in 1933.[37] When the state of emergency is permanent, it means that catastrophic state-authored violence is normal and that the concentration camp is not an exceptional space in history and politics but a paradigmatic one. With full knowledge of the Holocaust and the wisdom of hindsight, Agamben carried Benjamin's analysis to its logical conclusion: "The camp is the space that is opened when the state of exception begins to become the rule."[38] This is surely a valid reading of Benjamin's work and, this article has argued, it is also a concept that deeply informs Borowski's Auschwitz stories.

However, Benjamin's view of history and politics is not entirely pessimistic. His solution for overcoming the traumatic nature of history is phrased in the language of messianism: "it is our task to bring about a real state of emergency" which would unmask tyrannical sovereign power and interrupt conventional narratives that see fascism as a regrettable but necessary stage toward the future. Elsewhere in his "On the Concept of History," Benjamin exhorts us to be alert to moments of revolutionary possibility (i.e., real states of emergency) "in which time takes a stand and has come to a standstill," when it is feasible "to blast open the continuum of history" (*SW*, XVI, 396) that goes under the name of progress and to recover knowledge of "the oppressed past" (*SW*, XVII, 396). Otherwise, progress marches on in "homogeneous, empty time," a form of continuous history, linear and irretrievable, that actively works against the backward gaze of remembrance (*SW*, XIII, 395). This conventional time is homogeneous and empty because every hour and day is the same in relation to the unrealized project of human liberation. As an alternative to historicism, which "contents itself with establishing a causal nexus among various moments in history," Benjamin asserts that every traumatic history's essential discontinuity is visible in "the sign of a messianic arrest of happening" (*SW*, XVII, 396).

Likewise, in leading his reader back to amazement through indifference, Borowski's narratives produce the literary equivalent of a "real state of emergency" or, in other words, an abrupt and shocking intervention in the amnesiac course of "official" history that resembles Benjamin's call to bring time to a standstill. Since Benjamin and Borowski wrote their texts at a moment of extreme hopelessness, it is not surprising that they share an apocalyptic sensibility. Yet they also hope that a more perceptive philosophy of history, although unlikely to mend the world, might properly remember historical traumas that are otherwise repressed and might open a narrow path to a more livable future, what Benjamin called "the small gateway in time through which the Messiah might enter" (*SW*, XVIII, 397).

But how well do Benjamin and Borowski's overall pessimism vis-à-vis the future serve us now, seventy years after the Holocaust? Not well, according to Amir Eschel, who argues persuasively that many of our best contemporary writers, "instead of waiting for the coming of a Messiah or waiting for a 'real state of emergency' . . . seek to maintain the idea of the future as a viable aspect of everyday human life, one we need to pursue actively if we are to have a future at all."[39]

NOTES

This article was made possible (in part) by funds granted to the author through a fellowship at the Jack, Joseph and Morton Mandel Center for Advanced Holocaust Studies, United States Holocaust Memorial Museum. The statements made and views expressed, however, are solely the responsibility of the author.

1. Tadeusz Borowski, *This Way for the Gas, Ladies and Gentlemen*, trans. Barbara Vedder (New York: Penguin, 1976; hereafter cited in text as *TWG*). The first English edition was published by Viking in 1967. The stories it contains were collected from two volumes: *Farewell to Maria* (*Pożegnanie z Marią*, 1947) and *A World of Stone* (*Kamienny świat*, 1948).

2. Rachel Feldhay Brenner confirms the relevance of the hybrid approach: "Borowski represents perhaps the most tragic meeting of autobiography and fiction: his suicide cannot surprise a close reader of his Holocaust fiction; it seems that Tadek's despair directly reflects Tadeusz's loss of hope" (138). Rachel Feldhay Brenner, "The Final Solution in Early Polish Testimonial Fiction: The Impact of the Holocaust on the Witnessing World," *Dapim* 28, no. 2 (2014): 121–38. However, Czesław Miłosz attributed Borowski's suicide to his regret for having made artistic and political compromises when working as a propagandist for Poland's postwar Communist regime. Czesław Miłosz, *The Captive Mind* (New York: Vintage Books, 1981).

3. Primo Levi, "The Gray Zone," in *The Drowned and the Saved*, trans. Raymond Rosenthal (New York: Random House, 1989), 36–69.

4. Jan Kott, introduction to Borowski, *This Way for the Gas*, 25.

5. Walter Benjamin, "On the Concept of History," in *Selected Writings: 1938–1940*, vol. 4, ed. Howard Eiland and Michael W. Jennings (Cambridge, Mass.: Harvard University Press, 2003), 389–400; VIII 392, XVI 396 (hereafter cited in text as *SW*; the Roman numerals refer to the eighteen numbered theses that constitute the text). Even though it does not capture the sense of the original German title, "Über den Begriff der Geschichte," this work is also known as "Theses on the Philosophy of History."

6. There is not sufficient space in this chapter for a full discussion of "The World of Stone," the final story in *This Way for the Gas*, which describes a catastrophic scene resembling what Benjamin's angel of history sees. Borowski's narrator gazes downward on the storm-tossed, destroyed world at his feet, just as the angel does; the past is in ruins and the future fills the narrator "with frightened foreboding" (*TWG*, 177).

7. Sigrid Weigel, *Body-and Image-Space: Re-Reading Walter Benjamin*, trans. Georgina Paul with Rachel McNicholl and Jeremy Gaines (London: Routledge, 1996). According to Weigel, Benjamin's "On the Concept of History" "not only pinpoints the limits of a concrete conception of history—for

example, a concept of progress—but at the same time points up the limitations of any fundamental conception of 'history' as a meaningful process that unfolds over time, that is, a conception on which all such philosophies of history are based . . . be it the Christian doctrine of salvation, or Kant, Hegel, Marx, or Löwith" (149).

8. "Freud attempted a theory of trauma that would account for the historical development of entire cultures. Especially valuable in this work is Freud's elaboration of the concept of 'latency,' of how memory of a traumatic event can be lost over time but then regained in a symptomatic form when triggered by some similar event. In this way, each national catastrophe invokes and transforms memories of other catastrophes, so that history becomes a complex entanglement of crimes inflicted and suffered, with each catastrophe understood—that is, misunderstood—in the context of repressed memories of previous ones." James Berger, *After the End: Representations of Post-Apocalypse* (Minneapolis: University of Minnesota Press, 1999), 22–23.

9. In Hegel's dialectical system, in which "the wounds of the Spirit heal, and leave no scars behind," negative experiences are redeemed and synthesized by the positive forces that move nations forward historically. G. F. W. Hegel, *The Phenomenology of Spirit*, trans. A. V. Miller (New York: Oxford University Press, 1979), 407. However, in the aftermath of the Holocaust, such writers as Theodor Adorno, Benjamin, and Borowski, too, suggest that traumatic wounds borne by the victims of history do not heal; instead, their unheeded screams are silenced and repressed.

10. Benjamin and Borowski were not the only European intellectuals of the time engaged in apocalyptic and messianic thinking. Before the war, scholars including Albert Schweitzer and Gershom Scholem wrote, respectively, about Christian eschatology and Jewish Messianism. For more on wartime apocalypticism in Poland, see Bożena Shallcross, *The Holocaust Object in Polish and Polish-Jewish Culture* (Bloomington: Indiana University Press, 2011), 71–95.

11. Two definitive sources on Benjamin's intellectual milieu and life are Martin Jay, *The Dialectical Imagination: A History of the Frankfurt School and the Institute of Social Research, 1923–1950* (Berkeley: University of California Press, 1996); and Howard Eiland and Michael W. Jennings, *Walter Benjamin: A Critical Life* (Cambridge, Mass.: Harvard University Press, 2014).

12. Kott, introduction to Borowski, *This Way for the Gas*, 12. His father, who had fought with the Poles in World War I, against the Soviets, was sent above the Arctic Circle in 1926 and released in 1932. His mother was sent to Siberia in 1929 and released in 1934.

13. Ibid., 14–15. The original title is *Gdziekolwiek ziemia*. Kott adds, "Already, in the first volume of poetry, there was no hope, no comfort, no pity."

14. Antony Rowland, "Interview with Tadeusz Pióro (re Tadeusz Borowski's Selected Poems)," in *Critical Survey* 20, no. 2 (2008): 43–52, at 46.

15. See note 5. "Debate over Benjamin's conception of history was for many years preoccupied with the question of whether it is essentially 'theological' or 'materialist' in character (or how it could possibly be both at once), occasioned by the conjunction of Benjamin's self-identification with historical materialism and his continued use of explicitly messianic motifs. . . . Yet the question is badly posed if it is framed within received concepts of 'theology' and 'materialism' (the paradox becomes self-sustaining), since it was Benjamin's aim radically to rethink the meaning of these ideas, on the basis of a new philosophy of historical time. This new philosophy of historical time is the ultimate goal of Benjamin's later writings. . . . And it culminates in a quasi-messianic conception of revolution as an 'interruption' of history or an 'arrest of happening.' . . . [Benjamin concluded that] the concept of progress is demobilizing; and Marxism had become infected by the ideology of progress." Peter Osborne and Matthew Charles, "Walter Benjamin," in *Stanford Encyclopedia of Philosophy* (Stanford University, Fall 2015), article published January 18, 2011; last modified July 22, 2015, http://plato.stanford.edu/archives/fall2015/entries/benjamin/.

16. While Borowski's appraisal of European history has often been overlooked, or was simply not central to the many otherwise valid interpretations of his stories proposed so far, some scholars have recently commented on it without, however, linking his critique of civilization to a particular literary style that expresses a particular philosophy of history. For example, Shallcross, in *The Holocaust Object in Polish and Polish-Jewish Culture*, notes that Borowski "negatively appraises Western civilization and past empires, which he compares to the Third Reich in terms of the mechanism of power and slave labor employed by all of them" (124). Christopher Bigsby, in *Remembering and Imagining the Holocaust: The Chain of Memory* (Cambridge: Cambridge University Press, 2006), writes that Borowski "professes to distrust and even despise a history of civilisation which forgets the many who were enslaved, tortured, and worked to death, and celebrates those who earned time and privilege to write poetry and plays" (352). Daniel R. Schwarz, in *Imagining the Holocaust* (New York: St. Martin's Press, 1999) states, "Auschwitz is a kind of parody of Western history and culture that [Borowski] evokes only to remind us that ancient cultures too had a human cost and might be more of a foreshadowing than we would admit of the current terrors" (139). See also Andrzej Werner, *Zwyczajna apokalipsa: Tadeusz Borowski i jego wizja świata obozów* (*An Ordinary Apocalypse: Tadeusz Borowski and His Vision of the World of the Camps*) (Warsaw: Czytelnik, 1971).

17. Tadeusz Borowski, *Postal Indiscretions: The Correspondence of Ta-*

deusz Borowski, ed. Tadeusz Drewnowski, trans. Alicia Nitecki (Evanston, Ill.: Northwestern University Press, 2003), 73.

18. Max Horkheimer and Theodor W. Adorno, *Dialectic of Enlightenment: Philosophical Fragments*, ed. Gunzelin Schmid Noerr, trans. Edmund Jephcott (Stanford, Calif.: Stanford University Press, 2002).

19. His skepticism about the function of culture was widely shared among writers and poets in Poland during World War II, who, according to Czesław Miłosz, "perceived Europe sinking in consecutive stages into inhumanity—as the end of all European culture, and its disgrace. The main reproach to culture, a reproach at first too difficult to be formulated, and then finally formulated, was that it maintained a network of meanings and symbols as a façade to hide the genocide underway. By the same token, religion, philosophy, and art became suspect as accomplices in deceiving man with lofty ideas, in order to conceal the truth of existence." Czesław Miłosz, "Ruins and Poetry," in *The Witness of Poetry* (Cambridge, Mass.: Harvard University Press, 1983), 81. Yet it seems that Borowski, more than others, was intent on linking this violence to "the continuum of history" and on seeing suffering as a perpetual effect of civilization.

20. Yale Law School, "Wannsee Protocol, January 20, 1942," accessed January 22, 2018, http://avalon.law.yale.edu/imt/wannsee.asp.

21. Giorgio Agamben, *Homo Sacer: Sovereign Power and Bare Life*, trans. Daniel Heller-Roazen (Stanford, Calif.: Stanford University Press, 1998), 166.

22. He continued, "We [survivors] believe neither in the morality of man, nor the morality of systems. In German cities the store windows are filled with books and religious objects, but the smoke from the crematoria still hovers above the forests" (*TWG*, 168).

23. This belief is exemplified by the "angel of history" and is also discussed elsewhere in Benjamin's oeuvre. See, for example, "On Some Motifs in Baudelaire," where Benjamin invokes Freud's *Beyond the Pleasure Principle*, in which trauma is defined as a shock to the psyche, in relation to Baudelaire, who, according to Benjamin, "placed shock experience at the very center of his artistic work" (*SW*, 319).

24. My critical approach is borrowed from Weigel, *Body-and Image-Space*, particularly chapter 4, "Non-philosophical Amazement—Writing in Amazement: Benjamin's Position in the Aftermath of the Holocaust," 146–61. Weigel provides one of the best commentaries on thesis VIII and shows how his concepts are useful for interpreting post-Nazi literature, specifically in regard to Ingeborg Bachmann.

25. *Rozrywki* in the original Polish, a form of *rozrywka*, is typically rendered in English as "entertainment."

26. 6643 Janusz Nel Siedlecki, 75817 Krystyn Olszewski, 119198 Ta-

deusz Borowski, *Byliśmy w Oświęcimiu* (Munich: Oficyna Warszawska na Obczyźnie, 1946); trans. Alicia Nitecki, *We Were in Auschwitz* (New York: Welcome Rain, 2000).

27. Anatol Girs, preface to *We Were in Auschwitz*, 1. Girs was a graphic artist before the war; afterward, in Munich, he established the Family Tracing Service to help the families of Polish refugees reunite. For more on Girs, see Alicia Nitecki, "Making Connections," in *Beyond the Archives: Research as a Lived Process*, ed. Gesa E Kirsch and Liz Rohan (Carbondale: Southern Illinois University Press, 2008), 37–43.

28. Aristotle wrote that "it was because of wonder that men both now and originally began to philosophize. To begin with, they wondered at . . . events connected with the sun and stars and about the origin of the universe. And the man who is puzzled and amazed is thought to be ignorant." Aristotle, *The Metaphysics*, trans. Hugh Lawson-Tancred (London: Penguin, 2004), 7.

29. Ruth Franklin, *A Thousand Darknesses: Lies and Truth in Holocaust Fiction* (Oxford: Oxford University Press, 2011), 37.

30. The 1946 preface to the story states: the work of the *Sonderkommandos* "was hard, physically exhausting, and psychologically not to be endured by the occasional actor. The work continues without a break for several hours, several days, several years. . . . However, those who loaded them into the gas weren't bad people. They were Jews whose families were also burned. They weren't bad people, they were simply accustomed" (*TWG*, 83). Forty years later, in 1986, Levi arrived at a similar conclusion about how the *Sonderkommandos* managed to carry out their work. "One of them declared: 'Doing this work, one either goes crazy the first day or gets accustomed to it.'" Levi, *Drowned and Saved*, 53.

31. In the Polish, *"złagrowany" człowiek*, "the 'accustomed' one," is a neologism meaning, literally, "a Lagered-in man"—that is, a man who has consciously and thoroughly submitted to the "Lager" or "camp" mentality. My thanks go to Professor George Gasyna of the University of Illinois for clarifying the significance and etymology of this specialized term.

32. The widely used term "the banality of evil," coined by Hannah Arendt, would certainly figure in a longer discussion on how the normalization of violence made the Holocaust possible. See Hannah Arendt, *Eichmann in Jerusalem: A Report on the Banality of Evil* (New York: Viking, 1963), 252.

33. Hannah Arendt, *The Origins of Totalitarianism* (New York: Harcourt, Brace and World, 1951).

34. Levi, *Drowned and Saved*, 40, 42, 49.

35. The English translation accurately reflects the temporal shift from the past to the present in the original Polish. See "U nas, W Auschwitzu . . . ," in *Wybór opowiadań* (Warsaw: Państwowy Instytut Wydawniczy, 1964), 138.

36. Lawrence L. Langer, *The Holocaust and the Literary Imagination* (New Haven, Conn.: Yale University Press, 1975), 90–91.

37. An example of the "state of emergency" as the permanent rule: after the 1933 Reichstag fire, Adolf Hitler declared a state of emergency, and then had President von Hindenburg sign the Reichstag Fire Decree, which suspended the Weimar Constitution for the duration of the Third Reich. The Weimar Constitution was never actually repealed by Nazi Germany but indefinitely suspended.

38. Agamben, *Homo Sacer*, 168–69.

39. Amir Eschel, *Futurity: Contemporary Literature and the Quest for the Past* (Chicago: University of Chicago Press, 2013), 259.

Brad Prager

Testimonial Performances on Screen: From the Eichmann Trial to *Kitty: Return to Auschwitz*

ANNETTE WIEVIORKA'S STUDY *THE ERA OF THE WITNESS*, FIRST PUBlished in French in 1998, presents an account of the history of Holocaust testimony and pinpoints Adolf Eichmann's trial in Jerusalem as a foundational moment.[1] Although much in her book is new, this particular claim is hardly groundbreaking. Many observers agree that Holocaust witnesses were for the first time given pride of place at that trial.[2] A majority of the prosecution's 112 witnesses were Holocaust survivors who testified at length about what they endured. The trial was videotaped, distributed to broadcast networks, and then aired by stations around the world. Enormous numbers of viewers and listeners in the United States, Europe, and Israel tuned in to the footage, monitoring the trial in various forms, sometimes as part of nightly news programs and occasionally interrupted by commercials.[3] If the 1950s was a decade in which the Holocaust past was put in the past, then the Eichmann trial, in 1961, carried it to the surface. It succeeded in redefining the Holocaust, not only by broadcasting it into living rooms but also by bringing the survivors' individual traumas into the foreground.

There are other indications that greater attention was being paid to survivor testimony at the beginning of the 1960s. Although production on Stanley Kramer's *Judgment at Nuremberg* (1961) began long before the Eichmann trial, the preeminence of witness testimony in that film parallels the importance it was later given in Jerusalem. It is generally held that witness testimony was not the primary strategy for prosecuting war criminals at Nuremberg in 1945 and 1946 and that the prosecutors preferred to highlight the surfeit of incriminating documentation as a means of obtaining conviction. Lawrence Douglas points out that the "representational logic" at Nuremberg differed dramatically from that of the Eichmann trial: "Whereas the witnesses at Nuremberg played a largely supplementary role to the evidence supplied by document, the opposite was the case in Jerusalem: documents were used to establish a tight criminal case against the accused, but it was the words of the survivors that provided the dramatic focus of the trial."[4] Most who saw Kramer's *Judgment at Nuremberg*, however, do not recall documents but rather the Academy Award–nominated performances of Montgomery Clift and Judy Garland playing German witnesses testifying emotionally about their personal experiences of persecution. When that film premiered in New York and in West Germany in December 1961, viewers were likely to think not of what really happened at Nuremberg but rather of the similarities between the fictional portrayals of witnesses and those real survivor-witnesses on the stand in Jerusalem, whom they had recently seen on their televisions.

Approximately fifteen years after World War II, there was a shift in the cultural valuation of testimony. Wieviorka's analysis follows the trajectory of Holocaust testimony subsequent to 1961, starting with the Eichmann trial and culminating in Claude Lanzmann's *Shoah* (1985). She sees Lanzmann's epic nine-and-one-half-hour Holocaust documentary as a watershed, observing that Lanzmann, in his film, invented "a new form of testimony," staging and enacting it, "revolutioniz[ing]" it, and "turning it into a work of art."[5] Most interpreters trace this history similarly, moving from 1961 to 1985, from the courtroom in Jerusalem to Lanzmann's transnational journey, which included sites in Israel, France, Poland, Germany, and elsewhere. Like Wieviorka, Douglas traces this same connection: "By privileging the testimony of the survivor, the Eichmann trial anticipated the documentary idiom of Claude Lanzmann's *Shoah*," a film that "abandons the representational logic of most documentaries by wholly eschewing the use of archival footage."[6]

The connections made by Wieviorka and Douglas, each of which emphasize the primary role Lanzmann gives to testimony, are suggestive, but work remains to be done. Much has been written about *Shoah*, but less about how the performances of testimony at the Eichmann trial function as a precursor to that film and how that earlier filmed testimony can be linked to Lanzmann's strategies. In this article, I first explore the testimony that was taped at the Eichmann trial and attempt to account for its role in the history of testimonial performance. The trial's witnesses were at that point already engaged with the audience and the camera; they were participating in the documentary representation of their traumatic experiences. This participation, itself a symptom of a larger cultural turn toward placing greater emphasis on witness testimony, had begun to alter the shape of Holocaust documentaries. Accordingly, there were other films and filmmakers, prior to Lanzmann, who placed witness accounts in the foreground.[7] For this reason, I also analyze the feature-length documentary *Kitty: Return to Auschwitz* (1979), which was released prior to *Shoah*, and I examine that film's place in Holocaust documentary history, paying particular attention to its heavy reliance on testimonial performance. Filmed Holocaust testimonies such as those examined here are mediated and presented to us in a range of historically determined and specific ways. The transformation from the Eichmann trial to Lanzmann's film can be charted through analyzing the characteristics of testimonial performances as well as the parts played by the films' languages, their camera positions, and the filmmakers' uses of mise-en-scène.

FROM EICHMANN TO LANZMANN

Together with the French film historian Sylvie Lindeperg, Wieviorka has examined Leo Hurwitz's footage of the Eichmann trial and scrutinized it with an eye to his editorial decisions.[8] Hurwitz, an American filmmaker, had been a director of television news at CBS from 1944 to 1947, and he was blacklisted during the McCarthy era. In 1956, he made *The Museum and the Fury*, an intense documentary relying on Polish archival footage about the Holocaust and the Second World War, one that also included images of the Nuremberg trial. Perhaps for this reason, Capital Cities Broadcasting Corporation, the company the Israelis contracted to film the trial, entrusted Hurwitz with filming the Jerusalem courtroom.[9] Prior to the trial's start, Hurwitz settled on four camera positions (figures 1 and 2), which included a camera pointed at the witnesses, located behind Eichmann's glass cage; a second at the judges; a third at the galley; and a fourth directly in Eichmann's line of sight.[10] Hurwitz issued directions from the control room, and although he had no influence over the trial, he shaped its depiction through decisions about camera distance, camera angle, and montage.

Figures 1 and 2. Two of the four camera angles at the Adolf Eichmann war crimes trial in Jerusalem, as filmed by Leo Hurwitz and produced by Milton Fruchtman. Accessed at the United States Holocaust Memorial Museum, courtesy of The Steven Spielberg Jewish Film Archives of the Hebrew University of Jerusalem.

He employed shots and reverse-shots, and he also included cutaways to the public in the gallery. According to Wieviorka and Lindeperg, Hurwitz was "producing a drama of testimony, and constructing the confrontation between accused and witnesses."[11] Although it now appears fragmentary, more as a series of testimonies than a single work, the trial footage was shot, organized, and preserved in accord with Hurwitz's perspective and instincts.

But to control the camera angle, camera distance, and montage is not the same as controlling the proceedings. When historians write about the trial's orchestration, they usually refer to the prosecutors. Wieviorka writes about the prosecutor Gideon Hausner's memoirs, which were published in 1966 and in which he "explains at length his conception of the trial." She summarizes, "To tell this story, to draw a lesson from it, Hausner decided to place testimonies center stage."[12] Hannah Arendt, the trial's most famous spectator, wrote about the trial in terms of the spectacle and mise-en-scène presented by the prosecution, famously observing that whoever designed the Jerusalem courtroom conceptualized it as a theater, "complete with orchestra and gallery, with proscenium and stage." Arendt continues, "Clearly, this courtroom is not a bad place for the show trial David Ben-Gurion . . . had in mind when he decided to have Eichmann kidnapped in Argentina and brought to the District Court of Jerusalem to stand trial for his role in the 'final solution of the Jewish question.' And Ben-Gurion, rightly called the 'architect of the state,' remains the invisible stage manager of the proceedings."[13]

The complementary yet distinct perspectives of the cameraman and the prosecutors each claim a controlling role in eliciting witnesses' performances and presenting them to the public. Wieviorka writes that the trial's testimonies "were not to be written down and read on the witness stand but rather uttered aloud by men and women of flesh and blood. 'The only way to concretize it,' according to Hausner, 'was to call surviving witnesses, as many as the framework of the trial would allow, and to ask each of them to tell a tiny fragment of what he had seen and experienced.' "[14] How does this observation, which proclaims Hausner the trial's director, square with Wieviorka's later claim that the trial "constituted a new staging that Hurwitz took upon himself—a staging that contributed to accentuating the primacy of image over sound"?[15] The prosecution placed witness testimony at center stage, yet Hurwitz, the documentarian, was responsible for the trial's representation. Hausner could be considered the producer and stage manager, yet the documentarian who determined how the world perceived these proceedings was Hurwitz. The prosecution, composed of Hausner and Ben-Gurion, on the one hand, and the filmmaker Hurwitz, on the other, can each be said to have exerted partial control over what has become our contemporary cultural memory of the Eichmann trial. How did these twin standpoints come to inaugurate the era of the witness?

There is, of course, a third party involved in these representations: the witnesses. In documentary film, subjects make decisions about their performances, a fact that renders such films terrains of contestation. Documentary theorist Bill Nichols points out that a basic tenet of documentary is that subjects are assumed to be presenting themselves to the camera *as* themselves.[16] But even if one agrees that performance is part of life, individuals surely alter their behavior in the presence of cameras. In front of the Jerusalem court and on camera before the world, the trial's witnesses act out scenes, dramatizing their traumatic memories in various forms. Their voices, languages, and gestures are all part of that performance. The role of the camera is thus never purely observational; to varying degrees witnesses cooperate with the cameras, performing their personal stories with an eye to public presentation. Although the witnesses are not documentary participants in the strictest sense (that is, they did not actively plan the film's content in conjunction with Hurwitz), they are neither oblivious to the audience nor to the cameras. Their testimony is thus not transparent; it is not truth but is a performative presentation of truth, and persons testifying are engaged in a "performance of memory."[17] The survivors' memories have been framed and presented in accord with the intentions of the prosecution and the filmmaker. These witnesses tell their stories, but the display is coordinated and mediated by others, each of whom has his or her own visions and aims.

The idea that testimony is not transparent but is rather a performance that changes in accord with circumstances is discussed in *Approaching an Auschwitz Survivor: Holocaust Testimony and its Transformations*, in which Jürgen Matthäus recounts the story of the testimony of the survivor Helen "Zippi" Spitzer Tichauer. Despite the widely held assumption that little testimony was taken in the war's immediate aftermath, there were in fact numerous early efforts to record Jewish survivor testimonies in the mid-1940s at various displaced persons camps.[18] Tichauer's story is particularly informative insofar as her testimony was given on several occasions. She was interviewed by David Boder, a psychologist who went to Europe in 1946 to interview displaced persons (DPs) about their experiences. Visiting France, Switzerland, Italy, and Germany, he interviewed 130 DPs, recording them on a wire recorder, a precursor of magnetic tape recording that was state-of-the-art in the 1940s. *I Did Not Interview the Dead*, the book of interviews that grew out of Boder's project, appeared at the end of 1949.[19] The interview with Tichauer was conducted in German, and Matthäus asserts, "For many, including a linguistically trained scholar like David Boder . . . German sounded similar to Yiddish, the language of destroyed Eastern European Jewry. For remembering the dead, Elie Wiesel claims, 'there is no language like Yiddish.'"[20] Matthäus asks, "How do we deal with those survivors who—like [Tichauer]—were brought up in the language of the perpetrators and use it to communicate their experiences?"[21] German is the language of the persecutor. Speaking in German was most likely Tichauer's decision, but Boder may have encouraged her. Matthäus observes that in light of its "Nazi-invented euphemisms and camp jargon," many survivors who had "experienced terror mostly in camps run directly by Germans" preferred to testify in that language rather than others.[22] An interviewer would only create the awkward spectacle of someone testifying in a language other than their preferred one if they deliberately wanted to make their subjects self-conscious. Some survivors preferred to speak German, but to encourage them to testify in German was to request or insist on a certain kind of performance.

The most famous testimonial performance during the Eichmann trial is that of the Jewish author and Holocaust survivor Yehiel De-Nur, who is better known by the pen name Ka-Tsetnik 135633. At his trial testimony on June 7, 1961, De-Nur made an opening statement after which he collapsed. The Israeli Journalist Haim Gouri describes the scene, writing that De-Nur fainted, "as if unconsciously trying to step out of his body and his life in order to reach the things he wants to say. . . . His desperate attempt to break away from the courtroom formalities and return to the planet of ashes, so that we, too, could see what it had been like, had been too terrible for him to bear."[23] Shoshana Felman wonders whether his fainting is "relevant . . . to the legal framework of the trial" and asks, "Under what circumstances and in what ways can the legal default of a witness constitute a legal testimony in its own right?"[24] According to Cathy Caruth, "Felman recasts Ka-Tsetnik's collapse not as a theatrical staging of woundedness (as Arendt would have it) but rather as a moment of actual retraumatization. . . . The sudden fainting of Ka-Tsetnik on the witness stand, his collapse from speech to silence, is, for Felman, not a staging of what is known, but rather the re-enactment of a moment that cannot be known."[25] Most contemporary interlocutors agree that De-Nur's fainting spell was probably not a deliberate, cynical performance but that it was more likely a bodily reenactment of a trauma. Few would maintain that he was being purposefully theatrical. But seeing Hurwitz's footage as documentary footage—as footage constructed with a consciousness of the camera and with an eye to its viewers—permits us to describe the scene in theatrical terms: the effects of trauma, or the visible signs of memory as they emanate from the witness's body, are reproduced as a performance for the court and the cameras.

The witness plays a role in the transmission and preservation of his or her testimony, as does the documentarian. In the minute following De-Nur's collapse, Hurwitz's footage contains nine separate camera shots, including a medium shot of the collapsed witness, aided by bailiffs; a medium close-up of the bailiffs lifting him from the floor of the courtroom; a wide shot of the courtroom in disarray, taken from in front of the gallery; a medium shot of De-Nur's concerned wife among the spectators in the gallery; and a medium close-up of De-Nur's wife coming to her husband's aid. This is an especially dramatic sequence, but to whom do we attribute authorship? Is it De-Nur, who theatrically presents his woundedness? Is it Ben-Gurion and Hausner, who have stage-managed the proceedings as part of the project of nation building? Or, is it Hurwitz, whose editing moves rapidly between medium close-ups of key players and wider shots of the frenzied arena? Owing to the many standpoints and the numerous participants involved in shaping the story that is communicated to the spectator, the final product is hardly unmediated and is far more than a mere transcription of events.

Less frequently discussed than De-Nur's testimony is that of Simon Srebnik, one of the few survivors of atrocities at Chełmno. Srebnik's testimony is a key link between Eichmann's trial and Lanzmann's *Shoah*.[26] His family members were murdered—his father in Łódź and his mother in Chełmno—and, after surviving a death camp's work detail, he was, in 1945, shot in the back of the head and left for dead. As Srebnik tells the Jerusalem court his story (figures 3 and 4), he approaches the bench to show the judges his wound. He is asked whether this wound still bothers him and whether he has managed to forget what he went through. He answers that he cannot and does not sleep at night and that he is constantly haunted. If one only reads the trial transcript and does not watch Hurwitz's footage, one misses much of Srebnik's performance: he approaches the bench to show the place where the bullet passed through his neck, entering the nape and coming out through his mouth. During the course of the testimony, as tears appeared in his eyes, he found himself wiping his face with a handkerchief. To only read the text of the testimony, one would see neither of the key documentary aspects: neither the performative aspect, including how Srebnik leans against the armrest for support and how he displays his wounds; nor the directorial choices, including the over-the-shoulder shot of Hausner, as he asks Srebnik whether his wound still hurts him, and Hurwitz's cross-cutting from the survivor, who is having his day in court, to Eichmann, with his infamous sneer, receiving his comeuppance.

Srebnik's account is gripping, and it is no surprise that he is Lanzmann's first witness in *Shoah*. Today, it would be wrong to describe Lanzmann's film merely in terms of its nine-and-a-half hours, because more than two hundred additional hours of interview material now sit archived at the United States Holocaust Memorial Museum (USHMM) and at Yad Vashem, and the director himself has produced four additional films based on those outtakes.[27] The massive amount of testimony Lanzmann recorded from survivors, bystanders, and perpetrators are themselves an archive for historians. Lanzmann's interviews elicit new information, and in Wieviorka's narrative, his work would not have come into being were it not for the Eichmann trial. Not only was the trial a key moment in making witness testimony central to Holocaust history, but, because of the links between the trial's performances and the performances in *Shoah* (and other documentaries), the footage recorded in Jerusalem was significant in shaping the trajectory of Holocaust documentaries. It represents a turning point in how testimony was performed and communicated on screen.

Wieviorka explores explicit connections between the testimonies at the trial and *Shoah*, noting that "three figures in Claude Lanzmann's *Shoah*—Simon Srebnik . . . and Mordechai Podklebnik, two of only

Figures 3 and 4. Simon Srebnik testifies at the Eichmann trial in Jerusalem, as filmed by Leo Hurwitz and produced by Milton Fruchtman. Accessed at the U.S Holocaust Memorial Museum, courtesy of The Steven Spielberg Jewish Film Archives of the Hebrew University of Jerusalem.

three people to survive Chełmno; and Itzhak Zuckermann, a hero of the Warsaw ghetto uprising—had all previously served as witnesses in the Eichmann trial."[28] She continues, "I had thought to compare the testimonies of Simon Srebnik and Michael Podklebnik during the Eichmann trial and in Lanzmann's film. But this comparison proved almost impossible. . . . [O]nly stenographic transcripts and no film of the Eichmann trial were available to me at the time. The voices and faces were missing."[29] This footage is now available from several sources, including the USHMM. Lanzmann has since revealed that he was, when he made his film, thinking along lines that confirm Wieviorka's suspicions. He was in his midthirties in 1961, and he would surely have seen parts of the trial on French television. In his autobiography *The Patagonian Hare*, Lanzmann recalls reading through the transcripts from the Eichmann trial in preparation for the filming of *Shoah*: "It became clear to me that the trial had been conducted by ignorant people: the historians at the time had done too little research, the president and the judges were poorly informed; Hausner, the chief prosecutor, thought that pompous moralizing flights of rhetoric compensated for what he lacked in knowledge—he made hundreds of mistakes." Lanzmann then adds that "the tearful witnesses gave a kind of show, making it impossible to recreate what they had truly experienced."[30]

The testimonies in Lanzmann's films can be distinguished from the ones at the trial through comparing the two testimonies of Ada Lichtman, another trial witness who, like Srebnik, Podklebnik, and Zuckermann, was also among Lanzmann's subjects.[31] Lichtman, who was first imprisoned in the Kraków Ghetto and was then one of only three survivors from her original transport to Sobibor, kept herself alive by working as a washerwoman for the SS. She was the first survivor to take the stand in Jerusalem, and Wieviorka notes the profound impact of her Yiddish-language testimony: "[Lichtman's] testimony marks a rupture in the trial. This was a linguistic rupture first of all, for when the presiding judge asked her if she spoke Hebrew, she replied that she didn't 'speak well' and that she would prefer to speak in Yiddish. The court took her preference into account and decided that questions would be put to her directly in Yiddish." Wieviorka then cites Douglas: "'As one observer commented, 'You shivered on hearing the words of the language of the slaughtered and the burned.'"[32] Lichtman testifies with her sunglasses on and, despite an offer from the court that she take her seat, she opts to remain standing (figure 5). She is not the only witness to have done this, but here one can understand her decision as a posture of defiance—a function of her desire to confront her tormentor. Douglas writes that "[Lichtman's] voice remained firm throughout. Though she struggled to control her emotions, she did not weep . . . ; she did not stammer or wander, yet during her entire time on the stand her eyes remained concealed behind dark sunglasses. She appeared, then, to be blind (though she was not), an impression made all the more striking as the dramatic force of her testimony found focus in the words 'I saw everything.' Her presence in the courtroom suggested a latter-day Tiresias, or rather a witness who has been blinded by what she has seen."[33]

Wieviorka likely was unaware that Lanzmann interviewed Lichtman approximately twenty years later, and that they conducted that interview in German.[34] In the earlier instance, Lichtman is stalwart, neither hesitating nor straying from the point. Her eyes shielded by her dark glasses, she testifies in a language in which she is comfortable. By contrast, her German-language interaction with Lanzmann is halting and tentative. She once stood in the Jerusalem courtroom, facing her accuser, but here she is seated in front of Lanzmann and sewing dolls' clothes (figure 6), which is a deliberate reperformance of the duties she performed—repairing expropriated Jewish toys so they could be given to perpetrators' children—in exchange for her survival. Lanzmann may have chosen the German language because it was a language that they had in common, but he may have also had another rationale: German was the language of the perpetrators, and it was the language of Lichtman's persecutors. Lanzmann may have wanted her to feel challenged: the dolls and the decision to use German are calculated to produce an effect; they are elements of mise-en-scène. One needs to watch both testimonies, the Eichmann trial *and* the Lanzmann interview, if one wants to understand the transformations of her testimonial performance and how different documentarians, from Hurwitz to Lanzmann, shape testimony, providing the performances with a range of new dimensions.

Figure 5. Ada Lichtman testifies at the Eichmann trial in Jerusalem, as filmed by Leo Hurwitz and produced by Milton Fruchtman. Accessed at the United States Holocaust Memorial Museum, courtesy of The Steven Spielberg Jewish Film Archives of the Hebrew University of Jerusalem (*top*).

Figure 6. Ada Lichtman as interviewed by Claude Lanzmann in outtakes from the film *Shoah*. Created by Claude Lanzmann during the filming of *Shoah*. Copyright © The United States Holocaust Memorial Museum and Yad Vashem, the Holocaust Martyrs and Heroes' Remembrance Authority, Jerusalem (*bottom*).

BEFORE THERE WAS *SHOAH*: PETER MORLEY'S *KITTY: RETURN TO AUSCHWITZ*

From Wieviorka's perspective, Lanzmann was revolutionary: in encouraging survivors and perpetrators to return to sites of memory in Eastern Europe, he invented a new form of testimony. This article challenges this claim on two levels. First, as I have argued, there was *already* documentary performance in Hurwitz's film of the Eichmann trial. Lanzmann's approach represents an extension of this same process. The second level on which I wish to challenge this assertion concerns the extent to which the British documentarian Peter Morley developed a style that anticipates Lanzmann's when he filmed a survivor's testimonial performance in the 1970s.

In November 1978, Auschwitz survivor Kitty Hart returned to the site of the camp to which she had been deported in April 1943, when she was sixteen years old. Hart traveled to Auschwitz-Birkenau together with Morley, and his film, *Kitty: Return to Auschwitz* (1979), is an early example of testimonial Holocaust documentary. It was released six years before Lanzmann's *Shoah*, while Lanzmann was still conducting interviews, and this particular style of nonfiction filmmaking—bringing traumatized subjects to the scene of the crime—had not yet coalesced into the widely recognized form one frequently sees today.[35] Although many similar films have been made since then, Morley's documentary was revolutionary in that he placed Hart in a situation in which there was the possibility that she would reexperience traumatic events. Morley was aware that he was making great demands on his subject, yet his film—or, one should say, *their* film—perhaps as a consequence of those very demands, highlights and thematizes its subject's resilience.

The centerpiece of Morley's film is the camp at Auschwitz-Birkenau, which is treated as the metonymic equivalent of the Holocaust. Hart, however, had many other experiences related to her persecution, starting in August 1939, when she fled her hometown for Lublin, all the way to April 1943, when she was deported. Very little of that makes it into Morley's work, which likely had something to do with the centrality of Auschwitz in the Anglophone world's knowledge of the Holocaust. In England in the 1970s, most of those who were familiar with the Holocaust knew it from the television show *The Final Solution: Auschwitz*, originally planned as an episode of the series *World at War* and broadcast in 1975.[36] The American network NBC's 1978 miniseries *Holocaust*, a depiction that went beyond only the death camps, attracted an audience in England, but Andy Pearce observes that "it was very difficult to sustain intrigue in a topic which many saw as having little to do with Britain."[37]

Morley was born in 1924 and is thus only two years older than Hart, which means they were part of a generation who were teens or adolescents during the war. They were definitely old enough to process consciously their experiences. He was German-born and fled Germany as a nine-year-old child, along with his elder siblings. Like Hart, he ended up in England. According to his own memoirs, "This 90-minute film, shot in 1978, differs from others dealing with the Holocaust because of its style, [which is] best described as 'observational.' I did not speak to Kitty once during the three days we were filming—she was oblivious of the camera. We simply followed her. With memories flooding back she impatiently described to her son every minute detail of what happened to her thirty-five years earlier. Time and again she surprised him, and us, with the most dreadful revelations. The raw and uncompromising style of this . . . film established a cruel truth about Auschwitz-Birkenau which is unchallengeable."[38]

Morley's use of the term "unchallengeable" indicates that he meant to address questions about Holocaust denial. Arthur Butz's *The Hoax of the Twentieth Century* was published in 1976, and in the years 1978–1979, Robert Faurisson began to garner public attention for propagating the claim that the gas chambers did not exist. Morley expressed concern about sequences in which Hart and her son stumbled first upon a prisoner's shoe and then upon some bone fragments at Auschwitz, and he worried that people would think that these things were planted there for the sake of the film.[39] He responds to the anxiety about falsification in a number of ways. The narrator, for example, details Hart's school reports, which both serve as documentation and provide viewers with a feel for the fabric of her prewar life. We see Hart's last set of grades, from Poland at the end of the summer term in 1939, and the narrator informs us that this is "the only documentary evidence remaining that the Felix family had ever lived in Bielsko." Morley's documentary thus also serves an evidentiary function, aiming to present itself as documentation.

Equally noticeable in Morley's remarks is his reference to the "three days we were filming," by which he means the time he, Hart, and the film crew spent in Poland. This was, for Morley, evidently the core of the film.[40] His memory excludes the material at the film's margins, particularly its introductory minutes, in which we learn who Hart is. These ostensibly marginal scenes are important, however: they establish the film's terms, particularly with respect to gender. The documentary's first image is of the facade of the Safeway grocery store in Birmingham, England, where Hart shops. For many viewers, the first association with concentration and death camps is the image of hunger and starvation, but here Hart is seen living in a commercialized world in which food products in colorful packaging are abundant and easily available. Even the name "Safeway" is a not-so-subtle joke with which to begin a film about the perils of Auschwitz. The camera slowly zooms in on Hart, culminating in a freeze-frame. Her first name, "Kitty," then appears on the lower right in all caps, and the background then dissolves into the pinstripes generally associated with concentration camp uniforms (figures 7 and 8). This introduction, placing us on a first-name basis with her, presages the level of familiarity the film hopes to achieve. It invests the viewer in the intimate story Hart has to tell, one that is going to involve her losses, her struggle to survive, and even how she used the toilet in her years of internment at Auschwitz and Gross-Rosen. The intimacy presumably opens us up to alternate narratives about her experience, countering the gendered presuppositions that overdetermine the reception of women's testimonies. As Zoë Waxman observes, testimonies are often employed "to make sense of a difficult subject in an easy manner." She adds, "Using a familiar, gendered conceptual framework, women's testimonies are often used to show us what we already want to see. . . . [A]ssumptions about appropriate gender behavior obscure the diversity of women's Holocaust experiences."[41] Because of the relative rarity of testimony from female prisoners who survived by handling and disposing of victims' corpses, as Hart ultimately was forced to do, we may be inclined to preempt her testimony; we may miss key details owing to our expectations about women's attitudes and fates.

Morley claims that his film is largely "observational," a term now associated with Bill Nichols's typology.[42] That term describes documentaries in which a director presents events as they would have transpired irrespective of the presence of the filmmaker and his or her crew. Along these lines, Aaron Kerner writes, "characteristic of the personal documentary employing the observational mode, Hart and

Figures 7 and 8. The first images of Kitty Hart Moxon in *Kitty: Return to Auschwitz* (1979). Directed by Peter Morley and produced by Yorkshire Television (YTV).

her son arrive at the front gate of Birkenau in a taxi. Prior to their arrival the pair was wired with radio-microphones so that Morley could capture Hart's initial candid reaction to the camp, and follow them unobtrusively from a distance."[43] Although the distance taken by the camera facilitates intimacy, Hart would not have taken this trip had it not been for Morley, and it is unlikely that she and her son were ever truly unaware of the camera. In the sense that the film's subject is performing her trauma, the film is more of a participatory documentary, marked by the active input and involvement of the film's subjects. A trademark of the participatory mode is that the participant becomes a *cocreator* of the film; his or her decisions and comportment contribute to dictating its tone. As in Lanzmann's *Shoah*, the director has a level of input, framing and stylizing the work in accord with a particular vision; here, Morley makes decisions about camera distance, camera angle, and montage, and Hart shapes and steers the film's overall tenor.

The film is thus not entirely observational; that is only one mode among many at work here, and in this respect one can also speak of this documentary's reliance on mise-en-scène. The colorful grocery store facade at the film's beginning is not only a far cry from a concentration camp but also a foreshadow of a story Hart later tells about the liberation, when she fed herself with a store of bread kept by the Germans at Salzwedel. Other uses of mise-en-scène are equally interesting. At the time of filming, Hart was working as a radiographer, and images of her in the workplace are used to recall Nazi medical experiments. The inclusion of the medical images serves as an indirect echo, one that relates her present existence to the violations of prisoners in the camps. The scenes do not guarantee but rather suggest certain historical associations. Images of evil medical experiments were well known at that time: for example, *Marathon Man*, with its fearsome Nazi dentist, was released in 1976, and *Boys from Brazil*, a feature film about SS physician-experimenter Josef Mengele's manias, was released in 1978.

Morley's use of mise-en-scène extends to the sequences on the grounds of the camp, and here one gets the most profound impression of the extent to which Hart's exceptional and unsentimental testimony sets the film's tone. Some long shots depict Hart and her son, David, entirely alone, crossing a startlingly empty green landscape at Birkenau. She tells her story without much prompting; although David occasionally interjects, no filmmaker, reporter, or television personality is asking questions. Eliciting specific information is not really the aim, and the particular spaces are not clearly identified for the viewer. The film's two subjects move like dark silhouettes from block to block. It is hard not to see these long shots of their diminutive profiles as stylizations meant to underscore Hart's story: her tale of a thousand women vying for a single drop of water and of a stench so foul that one could smell it all through the camp. In these sequences, she shares with her son the fact that one of the best things to do was to carry bodies, because dead bodies had rations of food and changes of clothes, all of which was no longer any good to them, and she explains with remarkable clarity a point similar to one made by Primo Levi, about how the camps forced the prisoners to look out for themselves, behaving in ways they would never have behaved outside of the camp's gates.[44] She concludes with the rhetorical question, "I don't have to feel guilty about this, do I?"

To this question David responds laconically, "that's true," and his economical replies are consistent throughout the film. He does not perform empathy but is instead calm and sober, making no attempt to provide his mother with comfort. Either he is attempting to be strong for her or, more likely, he does not believe she needs his support. Hart, for her part, reflects on why it is important that they return, which has to do with the survivors dying out. She observes, "Soon there will be no one like me alive. . . . I have seen one, two, three million people die. My mother was there . . . . It is my duty to go back, even though I am psychologically not ready for it." At points, she struggles to "find [her] bearings," yet each and every one of her son's comments, by contrast, is cool. As she asserts, "I owe this to all the people who died. Thirty members of your family. . . . All my school friends," he replies simply, "um-hum."

At one point, while walking close to the ruins of the crematoria, Hart unearths what appears to be a bone fragment. She pokes in the dirt near a puddle, and the camera follows her gaze so closely that it is difficult to believe Morley's camera crew was at a wholly unobtrusive distance. Viewers will recognize that this is an alarming find; it is the remains of an unmourned victim and a synecdoche for the massive numbers who died in that place. Hart's role as a metaphorical excavator of the past here becomes literal; the survivor is an inadvertent archeologist. Her response to her discovery is avowedly unsentimental ("I can't cry over this anymore"), yet she is pretending not to be saying precisely what she means. Rather than becoming sentimental, she counterintuitively announces that she is *not* becoming sentimental. This puts David in a difficult situation: what is the right thing to say in such circumstances? His clinical response—he assures his mother that it is, in fact, a bone fragment, remarking on the visible trabeculation—is hardly commensurate with Hart's assertion that he could be holding in his hands the remains of his murdered grandparents.

Kitty: Return to Auschwitz is deliberately framed as a provocation, particularly with respect to conventional expectations about women's testimonies and the sentimentality viewers expect to find in them, but it is Hart herself who is provocative. To refer to the film as "observational" shortchanges the subject's role in shaping it. This survivor's resilient testimonial performance exerts a powerful influence, interpreting her own visit and occasionally steering the camera's gaze. Hart has returned to the camp for the sake of the film; the documentary is a synthesis of her memories and the director's choices.

Hart participated in a Survivors of the Shoah Visual History Foundation interview on June 9, 1998, nearly twenty years after her excursion with Morley.[45] It is difficult to describe such a video as documentary; those videos are testimonies. She offers a good deal of information, in some ways more than in Morley's film: Hart goes into detail about how she was brought up speaking German in her home because of Silesia's inclusion in the Austro-Hungarian Empire. She explains that they spoke Polish at school and that her mother had introduced her to the English language early on. She quite fascinatingly details her early encounters with antisemitism as an adolescent on her school's swim team, when she was twelve, not to mention the family's persecution in Bielsko during the war and prior to her deportation. As with most such testimonies, there is no variation in camera angles and camera distance, and, because it is composed of a series of lengthy, uninterrupted single takes, as is standard for this type of testimony, the testimonial footage can hardly be called montage in the traditional cinematic application of that term. Although Hart is still performing her testimony, which is unavoidable insofar as she has emotions and a body, and because there is still, at least occasionally, what Renov would describe as "the kernel of trauma," erupting as a sign of bodily distress, the goal of this form is to reduce its filmmakers' impact to a degree of zero.[46] She is engaged in a testimonial performance, but here the camera and editing work produce a different kind of relationship between survivor and filmmaker; the filmmaker neither intends to manipulate the viewer's response nor to be present on the screen, as was Lanzmann. The interview's success in doing so only highlights the extent to which Hurwitz's 1961 footage of the Eichmann trial, which was creatively and dramatically edited, and Morley's 1979 documentary, which drew Hart back to the scene of the crime, each follow their own path. Watching this Visual History Foundation interview, we may miss the montage, the mise-en-scène, and the presence of other interlocutors. Where such interventions do appear, they too provide us with important information about the filmmakers' intentions and about the historical moment when the testimony was taken. They are the hallmarks of documentary film—not exclusively of Lanzmann's *Shoah*—and they are present in the Eichmann footage as well as in *Kitty: Return to Auschwitz.*

NOTES

1. Annette Wieviorka, *The Era of the Witness*, trans. Jared Stark (Ithaca, N.Y.: Cornell University Press, 2006).

2. See Jeffrey Shandler, *While America Watches: Televising the Holocaust* (New York: Oxford University Press, 1999), 83–85. See also Christian Delage, *Caught on Camera: Film in the Courtroom from the Nuremberg Trials to the Trials of the Khmer Rouge*, ed. and trans. Ralph W Schoolcraft and Mary Byrd Kelly (Philadelphia: University of Pennsylvania Press, 2014), 198.

3. See Shandler: "According to Milton Fruchtman, an executive producer with Capital Cities, footage of the trial was used by thirty-eight countries, and an estimated 80 per cent of the world's viewers have seen shots of the trial" (*While America Watches*, 91).

4. Lawrence Douglas, *The Memory of Judgment: Making Law and History in the Trials of the Holocaust* (New Haven, Conn.: Yale University Press, 2001), 104–5.

5. Wieviorka, *Era of the Witness*, 82.

6. Douglas, *Memory of Judgment*, 109.

7. Another early example: Michael Rothberg and Joshua Hirsch each take note of Edgar Morin and Jean Rouch's documentary *Chronicle of a Summer* (1961), which was filmed shortly before Eichmann's trial. Although Morin and Rouch's film is hardly centered on the Holocaust, it features the extended first-person testimony of Marceline Loridan-Ivens, who recalls her experiences in Auschwitz-Birkenau. See Michael Rothberg, *Multidirectional Memory: Remembering the Holocaust in the Age of Decolonization* (Stanford, Calif.: Stanford University Press, 2009), 180–98; Joshua Hirsch, *After-*

image: Film, Trauma, and the Holocaust (Philadelphia: Temple University Press, 2004), 67.

8. See Sylvie Lindeperg and Annette Wieviorka, "The Two Stages of the Eichmann Trial," in *Concentrationary Memories: Totalitarian Terror and Cultural Resistance*, ed. Griselda Pollock and Maxim Silverman (London: I. B. Tauris, 2014), 59–81.

9. See Shandler, *While America Watches*, 91. See also Delage, *Caught on Camera*, 167–69. For contemporaneous reporting on this, see Lawrence Fellows, "TV Makes its Israeli Debut with a Tragedy," *New York Times*, July 2, 1961, X9.

10. Lindeperg and Wieviorka, "Two Stages of Eichmann Trial," 67. See also Delage, who provides an especially detailed description (*Caught on Camera*, 172).

11. Lindeperg and Wieviorka, "Two Stages of Eichmann Trial," 79.

12. Wieviorka, *Era of the Witness*, 66.

13. Hannah Arendt, *Eichmann in Jerusalem: A Report on the Banality of Evil* (New York: Penguin Books, 2006), 4–5. Shandler echoes much of this sentiment (*While America Watches*, 88–89). Shandler draws from Gideon Hausner's own memoir *Justice in Jerusalem* (New York, Harper and Row, 1966).

14. Wieviorka, *Era of the Witness*, 69.

15. Lindeperg and Wieviorka, "Two Stages of Eichmann Trial," 79.

16. See Bill Nichols, *Introduction to Documentary*, 2nd ed. (Bloomington: Indiana University Press, 2010), 8–9.

17. Noah Shenker, "Embodied Memory: The Institutional Mediation of Survivor Testimony in the United States Holocaust Memorial Museum," in *Documentary Testimonies: Global Archives of Suffering*, ed. Bhaskar Sarkar and Janet Walker (New York: Routledge, 2010), 47. Shenker employs the term "testimonial performance" in "Embodied Memory," 44.

18. For an account of these early testimonies, see Laura Jockusch, *Collect and Record! Jewish Holocaust Documentation in Early Postwar Europe* (New York: Oxford University Press, 2012).

19. David P. Boder, *I Did Not Interview the Dead* (Urbana: University of Illinois Press, 1949). Boder's collection does not contain the Tichauer interview, but the audio of that interview has been digitized and is archived online: "David P. Boder Interviews Helen Tichauer; September 23, 1946; Feldafing, Germany," Voices of the Holocaust, http://voices.iit.edu/audio?doc=tichauerH.

20. Jürgen Matthäus, "Displacing Memory: The Transformations of an Early Interview," in *Approaching an Auschwitz Survivor: Holocaust Testimony and its Transformations*, ed. Jürgen Matthäus (Oxford: Oxford University Press, 2009), 56.

21. Ibid., 56.

22. Ibid., 57.

23. Haim Gouri, *Facing the Glass Booth: The Jerusalem Trial of Adolf Eichmann*, trans. Michael Swirsky (Detroit: Wayne State University Press, 2004), 128–29.

24. Shoshana Felman, *The Juridical Unconscious: Trials and Traumas in the Twentieth Century* (Cambridge, Mass.: Harvard University Press, 2002), 131.

25. Cathy Caruth, "Trauma, Justice, and the Political Unconscious: Arendt and Felman's Journey to Jerusalem," in *The Future of Memory*, ed. Richard Crownshaw, Jane Kilby, and Antony Rowland (New York: Berghahn Books, 2010), 215. The spelling of Ka-Tsetnik's name has been amended for consistency.

26. Wieviorka takes note of the fact that Lanzmann twenty-four years later opened his film with an interview with this same witness (*Era of the Witness*, 82).

27. The four films are: *A Visitor from the Living* (1999), *Sobibor, Oct. 14, 1943, 4* P.M. (2001), *The Karski Report* (2010), and *The Last of the Unjust* (2013).

28. Wieviorka, *Era of the Witness*, 81.

29. Ibid.

30. Claude Lanzmann, *The Patagonian Hare: A Memoir*, trans. Frank Wynne (New York: Farrar, Straus and Giroux, 2012), 425.

31. Generally referred to as Ada Lichtman, she is referred to as Eda Lichtman in her 1992 oral history interview, archived by the USHMM: http://collections.ushmm.org/search/catalog/irn502769.

32. Wieviorka, *Era of the Witness*, 78. She is citing Douglas, *Memory of Judgment*, 103. The quotation is attributed to the Israeli poet and playwright Nathan Alterman.

33. Douglas, *Memory of Judgment*, 104. The Jewish-Lithuanian poet Abraham Sutzkever similarly insisted on standing when he testified in Nuremberg in 1946. Sutzkever had originally hoped to testify in Yiddish but was told he had to testify in Russian. On his testimony, see Christian Delage, "Bringing History into the Present through Film: An Historian in the Archives of Nuremberg," *Cineaste* 37, no. 1 (2011): 34–39.

34. Lanzmann's sessions with Lichtman landed on the cutting room floor, omitted wholesale from the final version of the film, and they are only now available, preserved by the USHMM and Yad Vashem. At the time she wrote *The Era of the Witness*, Wieviorka would not have had access to them.

35. Examples of films in which the subjects return to the camps include James Moll's *Inheritance* (2006) and Tzipi Baider's *Just the Two of Us* (2011). On *Inheritance* and other return documentaries, see Brad Prager, *After the*

Fact: The Holocaust in Twenty-First Century Documentary Film (New York: Bloomsbury, 2015), 73–90.

36. See Michael Darlow, "Baggage and Responsibility: *The World at War* and the Holocaust," in *Holocaust and the Moving Image: Representations in Film and Television since 1933*, ed. Toby Haggith and Joanna Newman (London: Wallflower, 2005), 140–45.

37. Andy Pearce, *Holocaust Consciousness in Contemporary Britain* (New York: Routledge, 2014), 172–73.

38. Peter Morley, *A Life Rewound: Memoirs of a Freelance Producer and Director* (New Romney, U.K.: Bank House Books, 2010), 8.

39. See Morley's comments in "Kitty—Return to Auschwitz," in Haggith and Newman, *Holocaust and the Moving Image*, 158.

40. The visit took place on November 18, 1978. Hart engraved her name in a wall at Auschwitz, and this image of her signature, accompanied by the date, is the last shot of the film.

41. See Zoë Waxman, *Writing the Holocaust: Identity, Testimony, Representation* (Oxford: Oxford University Press, 2006), 124.

42. According to Nichols (*Introduction to Documentary*, 172), the term "observational" applies to documentaries in which the filmmaker attempts to observe aspects of the historical world as they happen, typically without voice-over commentary, supplementary music, or historical reenactments. The subjects, in general, behave as if no filmmakers were there.

43. See Aaron Kerner, *Film and the Holocaust: New Perspectives on Dramas, Documentaries, and Experimental Films* (New York: Continuum, 2011), 213–14.

44. See in particular the chapter entitled "Shame" in Primo Levi, *The Drowned and the Saved* (New York: Summit Books, 1988), esp. 79–82.

45. "USC Shoah Foundation Institute testimony of Kitty Hart-Moxon," VHA Interview Code: 45132, June 9, 1998, Visual History Archive (VHA), USHMM, http://collections.ushmm.org/search/catalog/vha45132.

46. See Michael Renov, *The Subject of Documentary* (Minneapolis: University of Minnesota Press, 2004), 127.

III. T • H • E • O • R • Y

Gershon Greenberg

Jewish Religious Thought of the Holocaust: Through the Lens of Metahistory and History

THE AREA OF MY RESEARCH IS THE HISTORY OF JEWISH THOUGHT, A synthesis between history and systematic religious reflection. I approach religious phenomena from a nonreligious or nontheological perspective. For example, I use the terms "myth," "sacred," "profane," "history," "metahistory," and "metanarrative" as points of entry. At the same time, there is room for theological ideas to be understood in their own, faithful terms.

Beginning in the 1980s, Hebrew and Yiddish sources have been discovered by the scholarly world that evidenced an unbroken line of religious thought during, and in response to, the Holocaust. Here, I will draw from texts that represent its major streams: *Da'at torah*, religious nationalist, Hasidic, Musar, mystical, and apocalyptic. My approach is exegetical, seeking to understand the sources from the authors' perspectives, in historical context. My working premise is that internal coherence existed. The lives of these individuals blended with their faith, and they did so to the point of staking life itself on the words they expressed. They sought to console their communities as their followers faced torture and death, directing them through the chaos—whether actually in Europe or spiritually in the Land of Israel and the United States. For some, the words constituted final, personal addresses to God and to those of their religion who might succeed them in life. Given the weight of their verbal expression, it was imperative that they be inherently cohesive.

The terms "Holocaust" and "genocide" of the Jewish people, going back to their use, respectively, in Yiddish by 'Eliezer Silver in August 1942, and in Hebrew by Mosheh Prager in 1943, have referred to the unprecedented reality of the destruction of the Jews through World War II.[1] That reality was the encounter between those who came to be known as "perpetrators," the actors, and those upon whom the category of "victim" has been imposed, those acted upon—although from the perspective of Jewish thinkers of the time, the "perpetrators" were but actors in a higher drama scripted by God, staged by God, and for the sake of Israel.

The encounter's truth was contained in the moment of meeting—rather than in the actor or those acted upon, or even in one and the other. As the Holocaust was both unprecedented and unrepeated, it remains impossible to get to the truth of the encounter directly. Moreover, the sanctified universe in which the texts appeared has been eclipsed by the Nazi universe and the profane world left in its wake. Yet, the study of religious thought can direct us to it and provide a sense of the mystery and the sanctity hidden behind the eclipse, for religious thought speaks the language of myth and mystery. It penetrates through empirical data and overcomes the limits of rational language.

The Jews of the catastrophe were predominantly religious, by today's standards, "Orthodox." Despite the enormous amount and great breadth of research about the Holocaust, study of the religious mind has largely eluded the discipline of Holocaust studies. The elusion has been circumstantial, not a matter of substantive methodological issues as has been the case with historical studies of the Jews with regard to the Holocaust.[2] The neglect (not in Israel, but in the United States and Europe) has been rather a function of linguistic limitations and secularist exclusionism on the part of Holocaust scholars. The obliviousness has been consequential. It has meant tacit support for a posthumous triumph of the perpetrator's universe, for it has emphasized and lent credence to that world to the point of eclipsing the religious dimension of Judaism and its salience for understanding the Holocaust.

For decades, Jewish-focused scholarship assumed that the Holocaust brought paralysis to real-time Jewish thought during the 1938–1945 period.[3] When sources began to come to light in the 1980s, the historians of Jewish thought often neglected them—seemingly content to leap over the wartime era. Or theological systems about the Holocaust that emerged following the 1967 Six-Day War became the lens through which to view wartime thinkers—setting aside their literature in itself while deceptively measuring them against the standards and values of later thought. A chronological division between "post" and "pre" was mistakenly imposed, for real-time thinkers did not understand reality in such sequential terms. Rather, they thought in terms of planes of being that succeeded and/or preceded one another—notably destruction, atonement, morality, unity, and redemption, which were outside the calendar. For example, when the war ended and the expected and promised redemption did not come, it was explained that redemption was a function of repentance or of ascent to the Land of Israel that was indifferent to temporal categories. Or, to take another example, while post-1967 theologians assumed it was valid to ask whether God existed during the Holocaust, real-time thinkers did not. God existed for them, preempting the later question. In recent years, however, there have been positive changes. Led by the work of 'Eliezer Schweid of Jerusalem, the leading historian of Jewish thought of our era, Jewish thought's wartime path has been delineated and increasingly illuminated.[4]

EMANCIPATIONIST METAHISTORY INTO THE HOLOCAUST

In the wake of the emancipation of the Jews in Western Europe beginning at the end of the eighteenth century, a new body of Jewish thought emerged from the territory that opened up between the enclosed traditional Jewish community as it entered non-Jewish society and the Christian world that participated in the enlightenment. Thinkers stretching from Moses Mendelssohn of Dessau at the end of the eighteenth century to the neo-Kantian Marburg University professor Hermann Cohen, who died at the end of World War I, formulated metahistories with positive views of Jewish emancipation and assimilation into Western European society. Most assumed that, by its very nature, history progressed culturally, intellectually, and ethically. They also took for granted that human beings were naturally moral and rational. Under the leadership of the people of Israel, they maintained, humankind would usher the world into the stage of redemption.[5]

I will use the term "metahistory" to refer to narratives that are bordered below by spatiotemporal history and above by eternity and apocalyptic drama. It consists of a sacred process, administered by God, that advances from creation to redemption and correlates heaven (as eternal) and earth (as temporal). It narrates the role of what, in 1841, the Jewish philosopher of Galicia Nahman Krokhmal called the

"Absolute Spirit." This spirit enabled the nation of Israel to rise again after historical decline, in contrast to all other nations, which grew up, flourished, declined, and then passed forever from the arena of history.[6]

The Holocaust challenged Jewish emancipationist themes of universal moral values and historical progress; of seeking a modus vivendi for the people of Israel in Western European society; and of Israel's leading role in guiding humankind toward an ethical and spiritual future. Nevertheless, a thin thread did make its way into and through the catastrophe, and then into the immediate postwar years. Rabbi 'Aharon Kaminka, who fled his post at the University of Vienna for Palestine following the Anschluss, brought the motifs of natural and universal morality, with the nation of Israel as paradigm, forward. In his 1940 essay "Why Did the Way of the Evil Ones Succeed?" he extended the principle to the point of holding the Jewish people responsible for the unfolding tragedy. Had they developed the moral paradigm for which they were chosen by God with enough strength, he held, morality would have been instilled so broadly among the nations as to have precluded the disastrous outbreak.[7]

Leo Baeck, the head of the Reichsvertretung der deutschen Juden (Reich Representation of German Jews) who survived Theresienstadt later to become president of the Council of Jews in Germany (London) and professor at the Reform movement's Hebrew Union College in Cincinnati, also carried those themes forward. In his postwar work, he brought his earlier writings to the fore, still committed to the theme of historical progress toward a universal moral idea. He spoke of God's electing the people of Israel to receive God's revelation of morality and then serve as mediator between their moral essence and the world. This obliged the people simultaneously to maintain a particular identity and to universalize themselves with the inevitably painful integration into other cultures that it entailed. Progress toward ethical ideals and, finally, redemption was, however, certain—and even the caesura of the Holocaust could not stop it.[8] In the United States, beginning in 1938 and continuing through the war, modern Orthodox rabbi David Shapiro of Milwaukee maintained that although man's animal soul reigned during the Holocaust, the divine soul within, with its quest for justice and righteousness, remained intact. As God brought Noah out of the flood, he would bring humankind out of the Holocaust.[9]

But the thread of emancipationist thought both during and immediately following the war remained thin. The movements associated with it were constrained by their own grounding principles from responding theologically to the catastrophe. Reform Judaism's premise of universal, metaphysical morality lost value in the face of Hitler's evil. Conservative Judaism's axiom of an evolving chain of Jewish tradition over the generations lost meaning in the face of the mass slaughter of the bearers of that tradition. Mordecai Kaplan, founding leader of the Conservative-associated Reconstructionist movement, who was born in Lithuania where the Jewish population was now being targeted for extermination, published nothing either during or immediately after the war about the Holocaust.

Religious thought at the eve of, during, and in the immediate aftermath of the Holocaust was, in effect, the province of the Haredi (ultra-Orthodox) world. As 'Eliezer Schweid has observed, the very Orthodox Jews whose established strongholds were thoroughly destroyed, whose masses were almost entirely annihilated along with most of their rabbinic leadership, were the ones to provide the dominant stream of religious thought through the Holocaust.[10] Haredi thinkers related to the Holocaust as onlookers and participants simultaneously. They reflected on it (as subject) while they also belonged to the world on which they reflected (as object). This was true whether they were physically located within war-torn Europe, or in Palestine and the United States, where the sense of Jewish unity and shared *Torah* (divine instruction as it came to expression over the ages) identified them with their European brethren. Their religious reflections blended with their very selves and were ultimately addressed to God. They served both as consolation for their respective audiences and as lasting testaments to any Jews who might remain alive after their own deaths.

AT THE PERIPHERY: SILENCE, DEFLECTION, AND BLAME

If seen from a distance, religious thought of the Holocaust appears to coalesce into a sphere with a periphery consisting of silence, deflection, and blame. These were immediate reactions. They delineated Jewish consciousness from the world around it and provided a moment in which thinkers could collect themselves and begin a process of deeper reflection. Some considerations were either at the periphery or at the center. Others began at the periphery and then moved toward the center. Silence and incomprehension formed a periphery around the collective whole of reflection about the Holocaust. At the time of

Kristallnacht, 'Elhanan Wasserman of Baranowicz, Poland, wrote that any attempt to understand and verbalize the events rationally could make a person insane.[11] Bentsiyon Halberstam, the *'Admo"r* (a Hasidic acronym for "Our Master, Teacher, and Rabbi") of Bobov, issued an open letter saying that it was impossible to comprehend such horrendous events, especially in the face of an era of supposed enlightenment.[12] When the catastrophe was fully under way, on April 17, 1943, Rabbi Shelomoh Zalman Ehrenreich of Simleul-Silvaniei, Transylvania, admonished those Jews who were demanding to know where God was and why God was doing this: "We can only be silent. We will be able to answer such questions only when God in His mercy will send our redeemer and end our dark exile."[13] Over the course of the war, the head of the Merkaz harav yeshiva in Jerusalem, Ya'akov Mosheh Harlap, recalled the silence of ancient Israelites in the face of daunting encounters. After escaping Egypt, they became silent before leaping into the Red Sea to experience the divine presence.[14]

In the wake of the war, the Hasidic rabbinic scholar Simhah 'Elberg, who had escaped Warsaw in August 1939 for Shanghai, wrote in the *Binding of Isaac in Treblinka* (1946) that there were no words in the human language for the destruction (*Hurban*). Indeed, any words about it would desecrate the tragedy.[15] In 1947 in Tel Aviv, the Hasidic rabbi Hayim Yisrael Tsimerman cited the rabbinic sages to convince his congregants to set their bafflement aside and accede to divine omniscience. He offered an anecdote: A guest who was not honored with a call to bless the Torah on a particular Sabbath complained to the sexton that his priorities were wrong. The sexton rejected the guest's pretension to know the proper order: "I have been in charge for forty years and know everyone personally. I know who should be called for the first, second, and third blessings. So don't give me any advice! Whatever you might know, I know already. Besides, it's none of your business."[16] Yehiel Meir Morgnshtern, a great-grandson of the founder of the Kotsk Hasidic dynasty Menahem Mendel Morgnshtern, fled Poland in summer 1939 for London with the hope—in vain—of securing visas for the rest of his family. In his 1947 treatise, he cited Israel's sins against the Torah as a reason for the tragedy. He also pointed to internal frictions of the interwar period, noting that enmity persisted between Jewish groups, parties, and nationalities, making Israel vulnerable. To the enemy, Jews were one in life and death, and it drew no distinctions among professions, status, religious inclination, or nationalities. For their part, Jews criticized one another, failed to protest the sin of the other, and treated each other unequally, Morgnshtern contended. But then he stopped abruptly: "My brethren, children of Israel, we are to accept the decree of the Blessed One in silence." They were to stay silent, just as the priest Aaron was silent when his sons Nadav and Abihu took their censers, put fire to the sacrificial altar, and were inexplicably devoured by flames that issued from God (Lev. 10:1–3).[17]

The periphery also consisted of deflection, turning from direct confrontation with the theological crisis to refer the dilemma to God. At a communal fast on March 12, 1942, held as a means of trying to halt deportations to the labor camps, Shelomoh Zalman Unsdorfer, the de facto chief rabbi of the Bratislava Orthodox Jewish community, concluded that God alone could have brought such suffering. He then challenged him: "God, You are pious and redemptive. What do You want from us? Penitence, charity, shattered spirit? You already have all these. What will You achieve by our blood, should You slaughter us?"[18] In a sermon of July 11, 1942, which was salvaged from the Warsaw Ghetto ruins and published under the title *Sacred Fire*, the Piaseczner Hasidic rabbi Kalonymous Kalman Shapira explained that the people of Israel were suffering because they were perceived by the enemy to be God's proxy. The enemy was really after God but attacked the Jews because God was untouchable. Shapira demanded from God to release the Jews from this role.[19]

Haredi thinkers were locked into the covenantal relationship between a just God and his people Israel. Given this framework, they found themselves probing Israel's behavior toward God to explain the tragedy. An initial and (subsequently) peripheral reaction was to blame other Jews. The motives remain uncertain. Perhaps a motive was to bring others into the fold and unify the nation in anticipation of redemption. Or, in keeping with the principle as stated in the Torah that "All Israel are a surety for each other" (Numbers Rabbah, Parashah 10, Siman 5), accusers felt obliged to attend to the faults of others. Possibly, a sense of self-righteousness led to the blame. Or, blame was tied to hope: if a human cause could be found for the catastrophe, identifying and dealing with it could prevent its repetition. Those who sought blame belonged primarily to the *Da'at torah* school of thought, where Torah was the foundational reality of the universe that encompassed everything one needed to know, the essence of the Jewish people and internal to every Jew; or to the religious national school, identified with the Mizrahi movement, which advocated Jewish settlement in the Land of Israel on the basis of Torah principles and laws.

In the wake of Kristallnacht, 'Eliezer Gershon Fridenzon of Warsaw, editor of the *Beit Ya'akov* journal, declared that God was punishing the people of Israel collectively on account of those Jews in particular who had immersed themselves into German society and culture.[20] 'Elhanan Wasserman held that the loss of Torah had allowed the essence of Amalek, the paradigmatic enemy of Israel, to enter inside the Jew through secularism and nationalism. This interior Amalek became projected outward, where it assumed the form of persecutor.[21] Also in the wake of Kristallnacht, 'Aleksander Zisha Frydman of Warsaw, secretary general of 'Agudat yisrael in Poland, explained that by removing the barrier between the Jews and non-Jews, assimilationists let the chronic hatred of the world toward Jews explode unimpeded.[22] Similarly, during the war years, Tel Aviv Chief Rabbi Mosheh Avigdor Amiel accused those who followed in the footsteps of Moses Mendelssohn and moved away from revealed Torah of breaching the divide between Israel and the nations and releasing an underlying contempt for the Jewish people and their religion.[23]

Adherents of religious nationalism blamed those who resisted ascent to the Land of Israel (Aliyah). In Budapest between 1942 and 1943, Yissakhar Taykhtahl wrote that God brought suffering on Jews to turn exilic Jews from their assimilation and their indifference to the Land of Israel. When this was not effective, God brought the Holocaust and closed off every refuge except the land. Taykhtahl held to account for the blood that was being poured those Haredi leaders who insisted on waiting for divine, heavenly action before ascending.[24] In Palestine in 1947, Hayim Yisrael Tsimerman wrote that the failure to recognize the signs of imminent redemption that appeared in the interwar years (the fruited mountains, the vineyards, fields and settlements in the land, as in Ezekiel 36:8) and to ascend resulted in the destruction of a third of world Jewry. In ancient times, he explained, God had the older males who left Egypt die off because their slavery was internalized to the point of their being unable to conquer Canaan. Now, God let the interwar generation that failed to ascend be removed, so a fresh generation could take over, one capable of returning to, and restoring, the land.[25]

CENTRAL EXPLANATIONS AND DECENTRALIZED HISTORY

The silence, incomprehension, deflection, and blame that avoided direct confrontation with the theological crisis were, however, part of the larger process. They served to objectify the tragedy and clear the way for direct, substantive reflections. In speaking of the sixteenth century, Shalom Rosenberg of the Hebrew University identified a change from a community of believers united by their faith, sanctity, and destiny in the context of a hierarchical cosmos to a community that belonged to the historical order, intertwined with natural laws.[26] The same change, but in reverse, took place in the transition from emancipationist to Holocaust-era thought. Thinkers of the Holocaust regarded the historical emancipation, with its assimilation, as a tragic error. To them, the Europe into which emancipationist thinkers had entered hopefully, as an arena of religious, cultural, and social opportunity, turned out to be a Jewish cemetery. Aside from pointing out that the Jewish tragedy was unprecedented, the category of history per se had lost value. History needed to be correlated with, or absorbed into, metahistory—or else it would be left to descend as a whole into oblivion. Progress in historical terms was an illusion; it was to be found rather in metahistory, in the nonchronological movement from one plane of being—that is, creation, repentance, redemption—to another. Holocaust thinkers rejected the premise that morality was inherent to human nature; it existed only in the people of Israel. They abandoned the view that Israel was to enter the world of nations and lift it toward moral ideals, and instead they held that the people of Israel belonged to its own, isolated sphere. Finally, they lost trust in reason as a source of truth. Instead, truth belonged to revelation, to pious experience, and to apocalyptic vision.

Correlating History and Metanarratives: Da'at torah

'Agudat yisrael, the international organization of halakha (Jewish law)–grounded rabbis, founded in Kattowicze in 1912, had two wings, one centered on *Da'at torah*, the other Hasidic. The leading figure of the *Da'at torah* world into the war was 'Elhanan Wasserman of Baranowicz. His known writings, which extended into the summer of 1940, a year before he was killed, correlated historical data with metahistory—with metahistory as the moving force. In his *Treatise on the Footsteps of the Messiah*, a classic in the postwar Haredi world, Wasserman depicted the universe in terms of *Da'at torah* versus chaos. He personalized chaos as Amalek and the existence of the people of Israel a function of the presence or absence of *Da'at torah*. Amalek and the Amalekites had attacked the children of Israel in the wilderness after they left Egypt; they were later totally obliterated physically (1 Samuel 15:2), but eventually Amalek and the Amalekites became transmuted into a mythic antiethical entity, with historical forms such as Haman, Chmielnicki, and finally Hitler. Failure of Torah in recent years left the world to Amalek. Amalek became instilled within Israel as irreligiosity and manifest outside as persecution. At the same time, the outer Amalek neutralized the inner Amalek, clearing away chaos for the return of *Da'at torah*. Wasserman correlated specific historical events with the mythic displacement. The dynamic was measure-for-measure. Thus, the assimilation that took place as part of the Berlin-centered enlightenment (*Haskalah*) that accompanied Jewish emancipation in Germany induced pushback by non-Jews, and the deeper the penetration, the harsher the repulsion. The failure to observe kashruth, the Jewish pure food laws, yielded the counterforce of laws enacted against kosher slaughter. When Jews filled places of amusement instead of houses of study, they were chased away as lepers. In response to Jewish nationalism and socialism, there was National Socialism. Wasserman predicted that in the years to follow, Jews would be scattered like kernels of wheat being sifted, not a one remaining in its original place. Families would be split apart, there would be no refuge from the persecution, and there would be a level of poverty heretofore unknown.[27]

Isaac Breuer correlated history and metahistory as well, but he joined the theme of *Da'at torah* to that of settlement in the Land of Israel. He left Germany in 1936 for Palestine, where he founded the ultra-Orthodox workers political party, Poalei 'agudat yisrael, which sought a messianic Torah state. Breuer counterposed metahistory with general history: the one the sacred realm of Israel, the other the profane realm of sovereign nations. When the Jews were emancipated, they entered a profane universe filled with danger. Self-defining nationalism was reaching its peak, made extreme by the inclusion of racism. The world of *Da'at torah* under God eventually collided with race-based sovereignty, specifically Nazism. To retrieve its metahistorical integrity and position as grounded in *Da'at torah*, the people of Israel needed their own land, the Land of Israel. Breuer foresaw the possibility that once there, metahistory and history could be correlated, or even synthesized, with a land whose historical reality was conducive to sacred metahistory.[28]

CONGRUENCE OF COSMIC METAHISTORY AND HISTORY

Whereas the *Da'at torah* response correlated the events of history with metanarrative, other religious responses to the Holocaust synthesized metanarrative (or myth) and historical activity to the point of congruence. Chief rabbi of Tel Aviv Mosheh Avigdor Amiel's *To the Perplexed of Our Time* (1943), bringing Nahman Krokhmal's *Guide for the Perplexed of Our Time* forward, scripted a metanarrative that began with Absolute Spirit. God, as Absolute Spirit, expressed himself in Torah—to which the metahistorical, indeed metaphysical, entities of the Land of Israel and the people of Israel were joined. The revelational event at Mount Sinai gathered the people of Israel into a distinct spiritual and sacred realm, one infused with a separate and racialist culture. Amiel spoke of Israel's having its own set of Nuremberg Laws. This realm was opposed to the profane, material realm of the world's nations, which harbored a pathological hatred toward the Jews. The hatred could be contained, but only if the two realms remained apart. When the enlightenment generated by Moses Mendelssohn and the secular Zionism generated by Theodor Herzl removed the separation, the hatred reached Israel, eventually as the Holocaust. At the same time, the Holocaust was intended by God, who directed metahistory, to restore the division. To this end, it was up to the Jewish people to return as a collective body to the Land of Israel, in terms of Torah, to establish a spiritual center nourished by Absolute Spirit. The historical development of the land coincided with resolving the metanarrative tension of sacred Israel vis-à-vis the profane nations.[29]

The congruence between metanarrative and historical layers of reality also appeared in the 1942–1943 work of Yissakhar Taykhtahl in Budapest, *The Mother of the Children Is Happy*. In Munkacz, Hungary, Taykhtahl had associated himself with the view that participation in restoring the Land of Israel had to wait for miraculous intervention from above. By the time he made his way to refuge in Budapest, the realities led him to switch from a passive to an active perspective. He now viewed exilic history as a troubled scene in which assimilation and obliviousness to the Land of Israel reinforced each other, whereupon God intervened in history and had the nations punish the Jews back to their true selves, Torah observant and yearning for Zion. Ultimately, the Holocaust, a catastrophe in which the people of Israel had no refuge other than the Land of Israel, became necessary. Taykhtahl reversed his earlier stance to the point of judging a secular Zionist who helped build the Land of Israel as more favored by God than the pious Jew who awoke at midnight to pray to God to intervene. He urged his people to assert themselves and move en masse to Palestine, to take action on the level of history congruent with the metanarrative of the Holocaust that God directed.[30]

ABSORBING HISTORY INTO INTERNAL METAHISTORY: HASIDISM AND MUSAR

Da'at torah–grounded thinkers correlated history and metahistory, while religious Zionists spoke in terms of their congruence. Devotees of the mysticism-turned-ethos movement of Hasidism, founded in the eighteenth century by the Ba'al Shem Tov, and the moralistic movement Musar, founded by Israel Salanter in the nineteenth century, absorbed the external realia of history into internal metanarratives of spiritual character. Hasidic responses dwelled on sacred sparks of light within the individual and the divine, illumined effulgence. Musar responses dwelled on the center between the Jew and God of trust and penitent return.

Here, I will refer to Polish Hasidic thought during the war and its dialectics of illumination. Each Jew contained an inborn, sacred spark of love for, and of faith in, God. The spark had the potential to nourish an illumination of universal cosmic dimensions (the *Shekhinah*—God's illuminated presence) for its advance out of darkness until eventually darkness would ebb from the world and there would be redemption. Simultaneously, the cosmic light nourished the inner spark. Historical events, positioned between individual sparks and cosmic lights, were to be influenced by, and absorbed into, the respective individual and universal spiritual realities.

In his open letter of January 3, 1939, Bentsiyon Halberstam of Bobov concluded that insofar as the cruelties under way were so unnatural as to be beyond comprehension, they had to have come from

God. As God was good, relief was implicit to the cruelties. For Halberstam, whatever transpired outwardly in history was governed by the internal, dialectical metahistory of individual and cosmic light. He anticipated that the darkness would intensify to a point where light would verge on total disappearance. At that moment, the light would burst forth into messianic redemption. Israel's metahistory was grounded in an internal dialectic of illumination, such that Jews recovered from the Crusades and after the Chmielnicki pogroms, and the light of Israel reappeared. Each Jew had to participate in the cosmic progress through acts of piety.[31]

On the other hand, Mosheh Prager, a Gur Hasid who escaped Warsaw for Palestine in summer 1940, drew a dichotomy between sacred light and profane history. His initial scholarship provided early historical accounts of the Holocaust. His work gravitated to mythic and apocalyptic descriptions, which relied on Hermann Rauschning's 1939 account of Hitler's belief that the god of Germany, with his newly chosen barbaric nation, was in combat with the God of Israel and his chosen people the Jews, for rule of the planet. Prager concluded his scholarship with descriptions of a universe divided between the German Amalek of history and the Hasidic Jew. The inner spark of the Hasid, part of the eternity of Israel, adhered him to God. The Hasid overcame history by reaching a stage of sublimity which enabled him to transcend Amalek—and have no reaction to him.[32]

Abraham Heschel, a scion of Hasidic masters and scholar of Hasidism who reached the United States from Poland in 1939 to become a leading theologian of the Jewish people, spoke of the holy spark of the Jews as capable of transforming history with its current tragedy. The objective, empirical evil of the world corresponded with subjective evil, with sin. The war came when humanity as a whole defied and abandoned God and nearly extinguished the inner sacred light. God awaited man to revive the spark, whereupon the objective evils would ebb. Heschel called upon the Jewish people, as "ministers of the sacred," to welcome God back into their lives, to enable the dissolution of the evils of history. While Halberstam's history was enveloped by internal metahistory and Prager transcended history with sublime adherence to God, Heschel looked to internal illumination to transform history.[33]

While Hasidic thinkers subsumed historical activity into a dialectic between the inborn spark and divine *Shekhinah*, Musar thinkers absorbed historical events of the Holocaust into an internal metahistory of trust (*Bitahon*) and penitent return (*Teshuvah*). In summer 1941, the Germans reached Telsiai, Lithuania, home of the Musar yeshiva. They force-marched the Jewish population of 2,500, including that of the yeshiva, to the Rainiai labor camps, from which many were to be killed in nearby death pits. Leading up to the assault, the head of the yeshiva, Avraham Yitshak Blokh, expounded on the a priori, inner point of union between God and man. This point of union came to expression as uninterrupted consciousness of divine presence, as a trust nourished from above and below (*Bitahon*). *Bitahon* ensured that God remained present in historical events, enacting within time and space a metahistorical transition from the bad to the good. This certainty, in turn, enabled the Musar devotee to persevere through the outer ascent and descents, knowing that all was for the best and that redemption would come. Blokh called for *Bitahon* among fellow Jews, citing Psalms 91:2 ("I will say of the Lord, who is my refuge and my fortress, my God in whom I trust"), until moments before he was murdered at the death pits.[34]

When information about the catastrophic turn of events for Hungarian Jews reached the Land of Israel in fall 1944, the Musar community gathered for a day of eulogy and repentance at the movement's central yeshiva in Jerusalem. Wrapped in a tallith, or prayer shawl, the head of the yeshiva, Yehezkel Sarna, rose to speak. He was unable to begin, until it struck him that God had cried at the destruction of the temple in ancient Jerusalem. As God's weeping over tragedy was forever, God was weeping now as well. God's tears released Sarna's, and the tears released words. Sarna articulated an inner metahistory, where internal suffering, *Teshuvah*, and relief below joined a higher metanarrative of *Hurban* (catastrophe), *Teshuvah*, and *Geulah* (redemption). A passage toward *Geulah* was under way above and below simultaneously—with each effectuating the other. Insofar as *Geulah* was inevitable, the *Teshuvah* which was necessary for *Geulah* was as well. The *Teshuvah* overcame the suffering of *Hurban*—itself a necessary dimension of existence. The dual metahistory absorbed and determined external events from within—such that acts of *Teshuvah* below assured that the catastrophe would subside.[35]

BEYOND HISTORY AND METAHISTORY

Da'at torah interpretations correlated history and metahistory, with metahistory as the moving force. Religious nationalists thought in terms of their congruence, with settlement in the land channeling the metahistorical process. Hasidic thinkers internalized metahistory and subsumed historical events into a dialectic of illumination. Musar theologians subsumed the historical reality into *Bitahon* and *Teshuvah*, moving toward redemption. Following yet a different logic, mystical thinkers of the Holocaust abandoned history and its metahistorical dimensions for thoughts of transcendental experience and apocalypse. 'Areleh Roth's apocalypse was about liberating sacred sparks, Yosef Yitshak Schneersohn's about performing *Teshuvah*, and Ya'akov Mosheh Harlap's about obliterating profane nations and the salvation of Israel.

'Areleh Roth ("Reb Areleh") fled Hungary for the Land of Israel in late spring 1939 and published *Guardian of the Faithful*, sectionally, in 1941 and 1942. He described the work as the attempt of a zaddik, or pious leader, to leap into the pit of horrors to help his Hasidim endure spiritually. He urged his followers to identify with the patriarch Abraham, who annulled his personality (*Bitul*) to become filled with God. Adhering to *Devekut* (God), Abraham overcame terrible trials, and doing so enabled him to ascend to God. His life was one of pristine, pure faith (*Emunah peshutah*). The intensity of his faith was such that it overflowed to the generations to come. By identifying with Abraham's *Emunah peshutah*, Hasidim could share in the redemption of the universe. Roth's thinking went beyond both history and metahistory. He envisioned an apocalyptic drama, as scripted by Lurianic Kabbalah, in which cosmic vessels were broken at creation, with the shards and sparks of the cosmic light dispersed across the universe and exiled Israel. The sparks were to be sifted, so as to repair the cosmos (*Tikkun*) for redemption. Those Hasidim of the catastrophe whose souls achieved pristine purity would be included in this *Tikkun*.[36]

The zaddik of Habad Hasidism, the Rebbe of Lubavitch Yosef Yitshak Schneersohn, found refuge in New York in 1940. In his writings through the war, he described the exile of the people of Israel as divine punishment for sin in the ancient Land of Israel, with the intention of evoking *Teshuvah*. *Teshuvah* would lead to supernatural return to the land and redemption. Because suffering over the generations did not bring *Teshuvah*, God was moved to radicalize the choice into a decision by Jews between *Teshuvah* or death: this was the Holocaust. Jews who chose *Teshuvah* would find refuge in a spiritual "Camp of Israel" (*Mahaneh yisrael*), awaiting rapturelike return to the land for the redemption that would join all the pious souls of the past. As with Roth, Schneersohn did not concern himself with changes in history as they correlated with, or became absorbed into, metahistory. His *Teshuvah-Geulah* nexus was of an apocalyptic character, where all those Jews who did not belong to *Mahaneh yisrael* would be left in exile and be destroyed.[37]

Reb 'Areleh's transcending drama was centered around having his Hasidim achieve pure, pristine faith, whereas Schneersohn's focus was on having his Hasidim perform *Teshuvah* and find safety from the catastrophe in anticipation of redemption. The focus of Ya'akov Mosheh Harlap of Jerusalem, head of the Merkaz Harav yeshiva, was on the apocalyptic struggle between the entire people of Israel and the evil nations of the world. Like the others, Harlap was convinced that redemption was imminent, preluded by the tragedies. In its first stage, under the messiah son of Joseph, sacred light entered the universe. It did so only partly, lest it destroy the world by coming totally and all at once. There, it struggled with the darkness of the Holocaust, and the sanctified people were assaulted by the realm of negative being (*Sitra ahra*). The Nazis and their cohorts sensed the imminence of redemption and the collective end of the *Sitra ahra*. They convulsed in the throes of death, destroying everything around them, and especially the people of Israel who served as the vessel of redemption's entry into the universe. Insofar as sacred Israel was the source of all being, including even that of the *Sitra ahra*, the assault on Israel was ultimately self-destructive. Following this self-destruction, the full light of redemption would burst forth, that of the messiah son of David. All of history, filled with Holocaust, would thereupon descend into oblivion.[38]

CONCLUSION

My research quest for the truth within the mysterious encounter between the perpetrators and the Jews of the Holocaust is channeled through Jewish religious thought. Insofar as religious thought moves beyond rationality and empiricism, I believe it is akin to the mystery. Even so, the Nazi world pushed the sanctified arena to the brink of oblivion—taking several of our thinkers with it. In July 1941, Halberstam was killed in the Yanova forest, and Blokh was murdered outside Rainiai. Frydman and Shapira died in the Trawniki concentration camp in 1943. Fridenson died in the Warsaw Ghetto. In January 1945, Ehrenreich and Unsdorfer were murdered at the gates of Auschwitz. That is, the mystery of the encounter has been deepened by the disappearance of the Haredi world of holiness.

I began by speaking of the discovery of that world's texts. I end with the recognition that the further the study proceeds, the deeper the conviction that the researcher of the present can but look in that world's direction—knowing that one will never again be able to grasp it.

NOTES

This article was originally presented as the opening keynote address at the 2014 Lessons and Legacies Conference. I am indebted to Yehudah Bauer, David Silberklang, Dani Michman, and Steven Sage for their insightful suggestions; to John Roth and Steve Katz for their support of my work in this area over the years; and to Ze'ev and Alice Weiss for creating the forum for the presentation. It is dedicated to the memory of Talia Agler, my precious student of the Holocaust in Washington, D.C.

1. The anonymous translation of "holocaust" for Silver's *hurbn un katastrofe* first referred to the entire world, and then to Jews especially. "In opening this special conference of the 'Agudas Israel we are fully conscious of the frightful holocaust (*moradiger tsayt fun hurbn un katastrofe*) that has enveloped the whole world and realize the special grave danger that threatens the whole of our people at the hands of the demon upon the earth." 'Eliezer Silver, *Derefenungs-rede fun hanasi fun 'agudas yisrael in amerika, 7 'Ellul 5702*, August 20, 1942), reprinted in English as 'Eliezer Silver, "Address at the American Conference of the 'Agudas Israel for the Strength of Our Religion," *Jewish Weekly/'Idishe vokhnstaytung* 7, no. 346 (November 13, 1942): 1. Silver was president of the Union of Orthodox Rabbis. Mosheh Prager, *Hashmadat dam*, and *Retsah le'om*, in " 'Al hurban yahadut 'ayropah," *Keneset* 8 (1943–1944): 5–39; Mosheh Prager, "Yahadut 'ayropah 'al hamoked," in *Shenaton davar* (1943–1944). Prager was an early, if not the earliest, historian of the Holocaust.

2. David Engel, *Historians of the Jews and the Holocaust* (Stanford, Calif.: Stanford University Press, 2010).

3. Emil Fackenheim, "The Commanding Voice of Auschwitz," in *God's*

Presence in History (New York: New York University Press, 1970), 70–71; Elie Wiesel, "On Jewish Atheists," *Jewish Advocate*, April 15, 1965, 8–17; Arthur A. Cohen, *Thinking the Tremendum* (New York: Leo Baeck Institute, 1974), 4–5.

4. 'Eliezer Schweid, *Bein hurban liyeshuah: Teguvot shel hagut hareidit lashoah bizemanah* (Tel Aviv: Hakibuts hame'uhad, 1994).

5. See Gershon Greenberg, introduction to *Modern Jewish Thinkers: From Mendelssohn to Rosenzweig* (Boston: Academic Studies Press, 2011), 13–24.

6. Nahman Krokhmal, *Moreh nevukhei hazeman* (Lemberg, Austria: Typis Josephi Schnayder, 1851). Metahistorical considerations continued into the interwar period, with Franz Rosenzweig and Jakob Rosenheim. See Gershon Greenberg, "Franz Rosenzweig's zwiespaeltigen Gottessicht: Von der Zeit und in Ewigkeit," *Judaica* 34, no. 1 (March 1978): 27–34; and *Judaica* 34, no. 2 (June 1978): 76–89; Gershon Greenberg, "Sovereignty as Catastrophe: Jakob Rosenheim's *Hurban Weltanschauung*," *Holocaust and Genocide Studies* 8, no. 2 (1994): 202–24.

7. 'Asaf Yedidyah, "'Why Does the Way of the Wicked Prosper?' 'Aharon Kaminka's Theological Response to the Persecution of the Jews," *Yad Vashem Studies*, 42, no. 2 (2014): 123–54.

8. See 'Eliezer Schweid, "From *The Essence of Judaism* to *This People, Israel*: Leo Baeck's Theological Confrontation with the Period of Nazism and the Holocaust," in *Wrestling Until Day-Break* (Lanham, Md.: University Press of America, 1994), 3–82; Leo Baeck, *Der Sinn der Geschichte* (Berlin: Habel, 1946).

9. 'Ido Pachter, "Hurban be'olam moderni: Hashoah behaguto shel harav david shelomoh shapira," in *'Avodah* (Ramat Gan, Isr.: Bar Ilan University, August 2014).

10. 'Eliezer Schweid, "An Ethical Theological Response to the Holocaust as it was Evolving: The Teachings of Rabbi 'Eliahu 'Eliezer Dessler," *Henoch* 17, nos. 1–2 (1995): 171–96.

11. 'Elhanan Wasserman, *Ma'amar 'ikveta dimeshiha* (New York: [publisher not identified], 1938).

12. Bentsiyon Halberstam, "'Igeret hakodesh me'et kohen kadosh 'admo"r hakadosh maran mibobov shlit"a: Be'ezrat hashem 3 leseder lishuatekha kiviti hashem 5699 bobov," in Hayim ben Shelomoh Czernowitz, *Sha'ar hatefilah*, ed. Hillel Grinfeld (Tel Aviv: H. Grinfeld, 1955), 157–59. See Gershon Greenberg, "Hasidic Thought and the Holocaust, 1943–1947: Optimism and Activism," *Jewish History: Toward a New History of Zionism* 27 (2013): 26–52.

13. Shelomoh Zalman Ehrenreich, *Sefer derashot lehem shelomoh* (Brooklyn, N.Y.: Y. Kats, 1976). See Gershon Greenberg, "The Religious

Response of Shelomoh Zalman Ehrenreich (Simleul-Silvaniei, Transylvania) 1940–1943," *Studia Judaica* 9 (2000): 65–93.

14. See Gershon Greenberg, "The Holocaust Apocalypse of Ya'akov Mosheh Harlap," *Jewish Studies* 4 (2002): 57–66.

15. "*Hilul hakodesh fun hayntigen tragedie.*" Simhah 'Elberg, *'Akedas treblinka* (Shanghai: [publisher not identified], 1946). See Gershon Greenberg, "Myth and Catastrophe in Simhah Elberg's Religious Thought," *Tradition* 25, no. 1 (1991): 35–64.

16. Hayim Yisrael Tsimerman, *Tamim po'alo* (Tel Aviv, 1947). See Gershon Greenberg, "Orthodox Jewish Thought in the Wake of the Holocaust: *Tamim po'alo* of 1947," in *In God's Name: Genocide and Religion in the Twentieth Century*, ed. Omer Bartov and Phyllis Mack (New York: Berghahn Books, 2001), 316–41.

17. Yehiel Meir Morgnshtern, "Hakdamah," in *Bikurei 'avi"v* (London: Y. Naroditski, 1947), 1–3. See Gershon Greenberg, "Jewish Mysticism and Kabbalah through the Holocaust," in *Back to the Sources: Reexamining Perpetrators, Victims and Bystanders*, Lessons and Legacies 10, ed. Sara Horowitz (Evanston, Ill.: Northwestern University Press, 2012), 37–67.

18. Shelomoh Zalman Unsdorfer, *Siftei shelomoh* (Brooklyn, N.Y.: Judaica Treasures, 1996). See Gershon Greenberg, "Shelomoh Zalman Unsdorfer, Disciple of the Hatam Sofer: With God through the Holocaust," *Yad Vashem Studies* 31 (2003): 47–74.

19. Kalonymous Kalman Shapira, "Parashat matot (July 11, 1942)," in *Sacred Fire*, translation of *'Esh kodesh* by Hershy Worch (Northvale, N.J.: J. Aronson, 2000), 333–34.

20. 'Eliezer Gershon Fridenzon, "'Nokh alets farblendinishn," *Beit ya'akov* 16, no. 153 (December 22, 1938—January 20, 1939): 1. See Gershon Greenberg, "*Kristallnacht*: The American Ultra-Orthodox Jewish Theological Response," in *American Religious Responses to Kristallnacht*, ed. Maria Mazzenga (New York: Palgrave Macmillan, 2009), 145–82.

21. 'Elhanan Wasserman, *Ma'amar 'ikveta dimeshihah* (New York: [publisher not identified], 1938).

22. 'Aleksander Zisha Frydman, "Hasinah liyehudim," in *Ketavim nivharim*, vol. 1 (Jerusalem: Moreshet Sofrim, 1960): 51–56.

23. Gershon Greenberg, "Mosheh 'Avigdor 'Amiel's Religious Response to the Holocaust," in *Proceedings of World Congress of Jewish Studies* (1994): 93–100.

24. Yissakhar Taykhtahl, *'Em habanim semehah* (Budapest: Zalman Katsburg, 1943). See Isaac Hirshkowitz, "'Em habanim semehah. Mehibur kanoni liyetsirah dialektit," *'Alei sefer* 22 (2012): 115–27.

25. Tsimerman, *Tamim po'alo*, citing 'Avraham Ibn 'Ezra, *ad Exodus* 14:13. See Gershon Greenberg, "Ultra-Orthodox Jewish Thought about the

Holocaust from World War II: The Radicalized Aspect," in *The Impact of the Holocaust on Jewish Thought and Theology*, ed. Steven T. Katz (New York: New York University Press, 2005): 132–60; Gershon Greenberg, "American Religious Voices and the Holocaust: Mizrahi (religious nationalist) and 'Agudat yisrael (*Da'at torah*) Real-time Responses," in *The Highest Form of Wisdom: A Memorial Publication in Honor of Saul S. Friedman* (New York: KTAV, 2016), 90–118; Gershon Greenberg, "Mordekhai Yeshoshua 'Atiyah's Kabbalistic Response to the Holocaust," *'Iggud* 2 (2008): 72–99.

26. Shalom Rosenberg, "Galut ve'erets yisrael bemahshavah yehudit bameah ha-16th," in *'Erets yisrael behagut hayehudit bi'yemei habeinaim,* ed. Mosheh Halamish and 'Aviezer Ravitzky (Jerusalem: Yad Yitshak Ben-Tsevi, 1991), 166–92, as summarized by David Sorotzkin, "Binyan 'erets shel matah vehurban 'erets shel ma'alah: Harabi misatmar ve'askolah ha'ortodoksit haradikalit," in *'Erets yisrael behagut hayehudit bameah ha'esrim*, ed. 'Aviezer Ravitzky (Jerusalem: Yad Ben Tsevi, 2005), 133–67.

27. See Gershon Greenberg, "'Elhanan Wasserman's Response to the Growing Catastrophe in Europe: The Role of Ha'gra and Hofets Hayim upon His Thought," *Journal of Jewish Thought and Philosophy* 10 (2000): 171–204. On *Da'at torah* and Platonic thought, Benny Brown writes, "*Da'at torah* is arguably not a religious version of Plato's *Republic*, but if we set aside the utopian visions, we may find that *Da'at torah* is the closest model to that of the Platonic ideal ever proposed in Jewish political thought. / If in the Platonic model the community's political leaders are its philosophers, and the masses were not permitted (or unable) to decide who could or could not achieve philosopher status, in the Haredi model this parallel role is held by the Talmudic masters." Benjamin Brown, "Jewish Political Theology: The Doctrine of *Da'at Torah* as a Case Study," *Harvard Theological Review* 107, no. 3 (July 2014): 274–75.

28. Brown, "Jewish Political Theology," 255–89. See Rivkah Horowitz, "Exile and Redemption in the Thought of Isaac Breuer," *Tradition* 26, no. 2 (1992): 77–98.

29. See Greenberg, "Mosheh 'Avigdor 'Amiel's Religious Response to the Holocaust."

30. Yissakhar Taykhtahl, *'Em habanim semehah* (Budapest: Zalman Katsburg, 1943).

31. *Midrash talpiyot* cited Shemuel Fayvish ben Nata Faytil of Vienna, *Tit hayaven* (Venice, 1649/50) incorrectly. See Gershon Greenberg, "Hasidic Thought and the Holocaust (1933–1947): Optimism and Activism," in *Jewish History: Toward a New History of Zionism* 27 (2013): 26–52.

32. Mosheh Prager, "'Al hurban yahadut 'ayropah," *Keneset* 8 (1943–1944): 5–39; Hermann Rauschning, *Hitler M'a Dit* (Paris: Cooperation, 1939). See Gershon Greenberg, "Mosheh Prager's Holocaust Historiogra-

phy: Concrete Data, Inner Faith, and Myth," *Holocaust Studies: A Journal of History and Culture* 21, no. 1 (2015): 54–72. Prager published *Yeven metsulah* in 1941 and *Hurban yisrael be'ayropah* in 1947.

33. Abraham Heschel, "The Meaning of This War," in *Jewish Weekly / Di vokhntsaytung* 8, no. 433 (July 14, 1944): 1.

34. See Gershon Greenberg, "Dying With God: The Paths of Three *Rashei yeshivah* Into and During the Holocaust," in *The Horrific Summer: Seventy Years Since the Destruction of Jewish Communities Across Lithuania*, ed. Mikhal Ya'akov and Sigalit Rosmarin (Jerusalem: 'Efrata College, 2013), 5–27.

35. Yehezkel Sarna, *Liteshuvah velitekumah* (Jerusalem: [publisher not identified], 1944). See Gershon Greenberg, "A Musar Response to the Holocaust: Yehezkel Sarna's *Liteshuvah velitekumah*," *Journal of Jewish Thought and Philosophy* 7, no. 1 (1997): 101–38.

36. 'Aharon Roth, *Shomer 'emunim* (Jerusalem: [publisher not identified], 1942). See Gershon Greenberg, "R. Areleh Roth: Pristine Faith through Holocaust to Redemption," *Journal of Modern Jewish Studies* 14, no. 1 (2015): 72–88.

37. See Gershon Greenberg, "Redemption after Holocaust According to Mahaneh Yisrael-Lubavitch, 1940–1945," *Modern Judaism* 12 (1992): 61–84.

38. See Gershon Greenberg, "The Holocaust Apocalypse of Ya'akov Mosheh Harlap," *Jewish Studies: Journal of the World Union of Jewish Studies* 44 (2002): 57–66.

Lissa Skitolsky

Rethinking the Existential Condition of the *Sonderkommando*

> *An extreme case of collaboration is represented by the Sonderkommandos of Auschwitz and the other extermination camps. Here one hesitates to speak of privilege: whoever belonged to this group was privileged only to the extent that—but at what cost!—he had enough to eat for a few months, certainly not because he could be envied. With this duly vague definition, "Special Squad," the SS referred to the group of prisoners entrusted with running the crematoria . . . our need and our ability to judge falters when confronted by the Special Squad. Questions immediately arise, convulsed questions for which one would be hard pressed to find an answer that reassures us about man's nature. Why did they accept that task? Why didn't they rebel? Why didn't they prefer death? . . . I believe that no one is authorized to judge them, not those who lived through the experience of the Lager and even less those who did not.*
>
> —*Primo Levi, "The Gray Zone,"* The Drowned and the Saved

PHILOSOPHERS AND HISTORIANS WHO STUDY HOLOCAUST VICTIM EXperience have largely suspended moral judgment in relation to the behavior of former Jewish prisoner-functionaries who worked in the *Sonderkommando* unit in the Nazi camps. These men were forced on pain of immediate death to assist in the machinery of mass murder in both the gas chambers and the crematoria. Holocaust scholars feel torn about judging these prisoners as guilty for assisting the Nazis in order to stay alive. They suggest that here moral judgment runs up against an impossible impasse, for, in the words of Christopher R. Browning, one must "navigate the treacherous waters between the Scylla of blanket condemnation and the Charybdis of apologia."[1]

In his essay on "The Gray Zone" that existed in the camps, former victim and writer Primo Levi expresses his own hesitation to blame former members of the *Sonderkommando*; rather, he insists that there is no "human tribunal" to which one could delegate the judgment of their actions.[2] I will argue that the effort to suspend judgment with regard to the moral value (or nonvalue) of the actions performed by these prisoner-functionaries only reinforces the reigning structure for moral evaluation. This structure is based on the Socratic distinction between actions taken on behalf of "life" and those taken on behalf of the "good life," where actions motivated by self-interest are radically opposed to actions meant to address the common good. So, for example, when Levi asks about the condition of the men in the *Sonderkommando*, "Why did they accept that task? Why didn't they rebel?" he contrasts the act of working in the crematoria with true "rebellion" or resistance to the regime. The implication is that "accepting the task" of working in the *Sonderkommando* can only be a sign of collaboration. Already the nature of his questions forecloses the possibility of assigning moral value to the actions and choices of these Jewish prisoner-functionaries. His last question, "Why didn't they prefer death?" also presupposes the Socratic dichotomy between actions taken to preserve one's life and those taken for the sake of "the good life," for it is based on the assumption that these men crossed certain moral limits that allow for a decent and "good life" that is *more important* than "life itself." This assumption forecloses the possibility that the concern for one's mortality can play a role in moral reasoning and the possibility that actions motivated by self-interest are not, for that reason, altogether lacking in moral value.

This dichotomy between self-interest and the common good informs the majority of moral theories in the Western tradition of philosophy, and I will argue that it cannot elucidate the existential and moral position of those forced to work in the Nazi machinery of mass murder. We should not judge the value of our categories in terms of how long they have been operative but instead in terms of their ability to shed light on new forms of life and death that emerged from the genocidal violence of the twentieth and twenty-first centuries. In his work *Negative Dialectics*, Theodor Adorno warns us that "if thought is not measured by the extremity that eludes the concept, it is from the outset in the nature of the musical accompaniment with which the SS liked to drown out the screams of its victims."[3] If we heed his wisdom, we can recognize that victims of genocidal regimes suffer from an *ontological* assault that shatters the relevance of ancient and modern assumptions about freedom, moral agency, and reason. The specificity of genocidal suffering and the position of prisoner-functionaries in the economy of genocide require that we reevaluate the validity of the Socratic mode of moral evaluation through an analysis of the existential condition of the *Sonderkommando*.

The Socratic model of moral evaluation also informed the lens through which Hannah Arendt arrived at her controversial judgments about Jewish victims of the Nazi regime. Although Arendt recognized the specificity of the genocidal assault on human populations (as illustrated in her work *The Origins of Totalitarianism*) as well as how traditional legal and moral categories fell short of representing the nature of this crime against the "order of mankind"[4] itself (as illustrated in her report on *Eichmann in Jerusalem*), she was nevertheless harshly criticized for judging former prisoner-functionaries who worked in the ghetto councils as "cooperating" with the Nazis.[5] Arendt does not adequately draw out the moral implications of her analysis as developed in these two works, or how the structure specific to genocide changes the structure and meaning of ethics within that structure. Although she remarks on the aberrant ontological condition of camp prisoners transformed into "living corpses"[6] or a "bundle of reactions,"[7] she does not comment on the moral agency possible from within this existential condition.

In what follows I will consider the condition of those Jewish prisoners forced to work in the *Sonderkommando* in Auschwitz—often viewed as the most morally problematic type of prisoner-functionary—to expand on the thesis that they are only blameworthy if we assume the Socratic moral worldview that is based on a strict opposition between the selfish concern for "life" and the moral concern for the "good life." If we can argue that this distinction actually blurs the lens through which we can morally and historically analyze the actions of those forced to work in the crematoria, then we need no longer suspend moral judgment of their actions. Closer historical analysis of their behavior in the gas chambers and crematoria reveals that many of these prisoner-functionaries aided others in the camp, took copious notes about the killing apparatus, and formed a resistance movement that was able to blow up a crematorium in 1944.[8] We cannot claim that as a "unit" these men were amoral, preoccupied with "staying alive at all costs." Instead through their actions, many of the men in this unit attempted to live through a genocidal system to defeat its essential function, or the destruction of a population. Sources in rabbinic literature (*Responsa*) written at the time of the Nazi onslaught present an alternative to the Socratic model for moral evaluation, one based on the specific existential condition of genocidal suffering. This alternative model reveals that despite Levi's view and his refusal to judge these prisoner-functionaries, we need not view those Jewish victims who worked in the *Sonderkommando* as having "collaborated" with the Nazis but rather as having resisted them and the logic of genocide.

For when individuals are stripped of their status as individual legal and moral subjects in order to more effectively kill them as a group, we cannot measure their actions in accord with the norms that apply to individuals *as* legal and moral subjects. It is not the case that the traditional (Socratic) moral framework is no longer operative in a genocidal state, or that the distinction between "life" and the "good life" is altogether irrelevant for shedding light on the meaning of individual choices by victims, bystanders, and perpetrators. Rather, it is the case that in a genocidal state *there is more than one moral framework* by which we can judge the behavior of victims, given their distinct ontological and existential position as nonsubjects (excluded from law and moral concern). The point is not to offer a justification for all of the morally compromised decisions made by Jewish victims to stay alive, but instead to encourage a reexamination of the behavior of these particular victims against a different moral framework that better illuminates the value of their actions. There may have been a particular member of the *Sonderkommando* who did not help his fellow victims, who did not take notes on the process, and who inflicted gratuitous abuse on his comrades to court favor with his Nazi overlords. Such an individual may be worthy of some moral blame. But the fact of the *Sonderkommando* as such does not require that we suspend moral judgment of its members. Instead, we must evaluate the moral worth of their individual actions according to a frame made necessary by the specificity of the suffering to which they were subject.

THE SOCRATIC DISTINCTION BETWEEN "LIFE" AND THE "GOOD LIFE"

Socrates's stance toward intent and moral agency is most explicitly illustrated in Plato's dialogue *Crito*, in which he defends his decision to stay in jail and receive his death sentence for corrupting the youth of Athens instead of taking the opportunity to escape an unjust sentence and state violence. The dialogue opens with Socrates's friend Crito creeping into his prison cell early in the morning to wake him and help him escape with the aid of their friends and the prison guard. Socrates refuses to leave until they have rationally examined whether escaping would be the right thing to do, "for the most important thing is not life, but the good life."[9] For Socrates, we should care for our souls more than our lives, for our lives become meaningful to the extent that we organize our actions around our moral values and honor our commitment to them *over* the protection of our physical well-being. He also suggests that the concern for the body precludes the possibility of true moral intent insofar as I privilege my corporeal "life" over my devotion to the ideal of the "good life." The latter requires that I rationally examine my intent *before* I act in order to determine whether it has moral worth, whereas the former only requires the instinct for self-preservation. In Plato's *Apology* he clearly states that "neither I nor any other man should, on trial or in war, contrive to avoid death at any cost."[10] Our efforts to preserve ourselves often coincide with harming others, which then undermines the integrity of our souls and our desire to rationally examine ourselves and our reasons for acting. In this sense, as he famously states in Plato's *Apology*, "the unexamined life is not worth living," as actions that are not guided by the intent to do good do not have any specifically *moral* justification and so lack value and rational sense. Thus, we must always choose death over dishonor, or follow the path of justice even at the cost of our corporeal well-being.[11] Arendt presents a Socratic critique of Adolf Eichmann insofar as she finds him guilty of *thoughtlessness*,[12] or the refusal to evaluate the moral worth of his actions. He was prepared to rise in the Nazi hierarchy and keep his job (for the sake of his "life") at any cost. At the same time, Arendt recognized that the modern conditions of technology and bureaucracy conditioned this sort of thoughtless performance of instrumental tasks, which she termed the "banality of evil," or the modern proclivity of ordinary men to commit extraordinarily evil deeds when sanctioned by the state for the sake of "security" and "duty."[13]

Although Socrates never found a perfect definition of the "good life," the ancient Greeks associated this life with the condition of *arête*, or moral excellence, that allows for a life of specifically human flourishing. So although we may not be able to provide a positive definition of the good life, we know that actions that harm human flourishing are antithetical to the good life. Socrates explains to Crito that "wrongdoing or injustice is in every way harmful and shameful to the wrongdoer," and then he insists, "nor must one, when wronged, inflict wrong in return."[14] Thus, Socrates insists that we should not harm others when they harm us, for we should honor the good above our own pride and desire to stay alive. The fact of our mortality should not play a role in the proper moral evaluation that guides our actions. He reinforces this view in the *Apology* when he states that "death is something I couldn't care less about . . . my whole concern is not to do anything unjust or impious."[15] Our concern for our corporeal well-being precludes our concern for the moral value of our actions and thus the possibility of living a good, meaningful life. When cornered into the position of suffering the injustice of state violence or committing the injustice of breaking the law, Socrates chose the former because, as he states in Plato's *Gorgias*, "it is more shameful to commit than to suffer injustice."[16] We should protect the moral integrity of our souls, rather than the safety of our bodies, "at all costs."

Socrates's worldview is compelling and poignant given that he chose to die rather than to commit the unjust act of breaking the law. In the dialogue Socrates explains to Crito that breaking the law is a type of violence to the state and to the Ideal of Justice itself. In defending his view that we must comply with the law even when unjustly sentenced to death by the state, Socrates assumes the voice of the "Laws" that instruct Crito about the nature of civic responsibility:

> [The Laws]: "Come now, what accusation do you bring against us and the city; that you should try to destroy us? Did we not, first, bring you to birth, and was it not through us that your father married your mother and begat you? Tell us, do you find anything to criticize in those of us who are concerned with marriage?" [Socrates]: And I would say that I do not criticize them. [The Laws]: "Or in those of us concerned with the nurture of babies and the education that you too received? Were those assigned to

> that subject not right to instruct your father to educate you in the arts and in physical culture? . . . and after you were born and nurtured and educated, could you, in the first place, deny that you are our offspring and servant, both you and your forefathers? If that is so, do you think that we are on equal footing as regards the right, and that whatever we do to you it is right for you to do to us? You were not on an equal footing with your father as regards the right, nor with your master if you had one, so as to retaliate for anything they did to you, to revile them if they reviled you, to beat them if they beat you, and so with many other things. Do you think you have this right to retaliation against your country and its laws? That if we undertake to destroy you and think it right to do so, you can undertake to destroy us, as far as you can, in return? . . . Is your wisdom such as not to realize that your country is to be honored more than your mother, your father and all your ancestors, . . . that you must worship it, yield to it and placate its anger more than your father's? You must either persuade it or obey its orders, and endure in silence whatever it instructs you to endure, whether blows or bonds, and if it leads you into war to be wounded or killed, you must obey. . . . It is impious to bring violence to bear against your mother or father, it is much more so to use it against your country.[17]

Although on first reading it appears that Socrates advocates an extremely authoritarian state, he grounds the authority of the "Laws" on the responsibility of the state to nurture and educate its citizens and ensure their ability to flourish. The Laws are also open to persuasion, and a citizen is able to defend himself in a court of law. For Socrates, the law is the vehicle for Justice in the sensible world, and citizens owe their lives—and the possibility for honoring "the good life"—to a society where some sort of justice is possible (however imperfect). If someday the law *were* the perfect embodiment of the Just and the True, then it would deserve the sort of unquestioning obedience that Socrates describes. Socrates is not denying the right for civil disobedience against an authoritarian state, and one could cite the quoted passage to argue that Germans had the moral obligation to resist the Nazi state insofar as it had abandoned entire populations and excluded them from moral consideration. However, there are no resources from within Socratic theory to affirm the right of victims of state violence to prioritize their self-preservation over their fidelity to the laws or traditional values. And in his own time, Socrates did not appear to protest the exclusion of select communities from the rights of citizenship (women, slaves, and foreigners).[18] For these reasons, Socrates's moral theory is inadequate to reflect on the plight of marginalized populations who are excluded from the protection of the law, and it cannot help us evaluate the decisions made by victims of state violence whose very "lives" have been criminalized and judged superfluous to the human community. This is the moral crime that Arendt viewed as unique to genocide and to Nazi policy: the judgment that some communities are superfluous to the world community.[19]

Further, Socrates's view of the mutual opposition between a concern for "life" and a concern for "the good life" is thrown into doubt by a closer analysis of the behavior of those Holocaust victims who were forced to work in the *Sonderkommando*. Members of this "special squad" were usually chosen by the SS from new arrivals of Jewish prisoners to the camp, and if a prisoner refused the initially vague invitation to join the "special squad," he was immediately killed. Georges Didi-Huberman provides a succinct background of their creation and the isolation in which they were kept from the other prisoners:

> The first *Sonderkommando* at Auschwitz was created on July 4, 1942, during the "selection" of a convoy of Slovakian Jews for the gas chamber. Twelve squads succeeded each other from that date; each was eliminated at the end of a few months, and "as its initiation, the next squad burnt the corpses of its predecessors." Part of the horror for these men was that their entire existence, including the ineluctable gassing of the squad, was to be kept in absolute secrecy. The members of the *Sonderkommando* could therefore have no contact whatsoever with the other prisoners, and even less with whatever "outside world" there was, not even with the "noninitiated" SS, who were ignorant of the exact functioning.[20]

Their specific responsibilities included keeping order in the dressing rooms outside of the gas chamber, leading prisoners into the gas chamber and shutting the doors, and dragging dead bodies out of the gas chamber and searching them for gold and other valuables. They also had to cut the hair of women who had just been gassed to death.[21] Last, they transported the bodies to the crematoria and burned them in ovens. Each squad was typically murdered after about six months of work (there were exceptions when individual prisoners survived more than one squad). Each new squad was often initiated with the task of burning the bodies of the members of the former squad. These prisoner-functionaries were not murderers or sadists, and they were conscripted for the most depraved part of the killing apparatus; so depraved, in fact, that even the SS preferred to outsource it to its most frequent victims. Members of the *Sonderkommando* were better fed than the majority of other prisoners, but they suffered from torments unique to their grisly labor.

Yet even in the midst of this ghastly and traumatic work, many of these men still risked their lives to aid their fellow victims in the camp by smuggling food and clothing to them (of which there was an abundant amount in the dressing room of the gas chamber). Many members of the *Sonderkommando* also took copious notes about the killing apparatus and buried them in the ground around the gas chamber and crematoria—both for the historical record and as a warning to future generations.[22] As documented and analyzed in his text *Images in Spite of All*, Didi-Huberman illustrates the significance of four photographs smuggled out of Auschwitz by members of the *Sonderkommando*, taken by a prisoner—whom we know only as "Alex"—while hiding in a crematorium.[23] Didi-Huberman contextualizes these photographs as resistance in light of the aim of Nazis to eradicate evidence of their crime, to render the Jewish people "invisible" by eradicating all witnesses to their destruction: "Indeed 'the forgetting of the extermination is part of the extermination.' The Nazis no doubt believed they were making the Jews invisible, and making their very destruction invisible. They took such pains in this endeavor that many of their victims believed it too, and many people still do today. . . . The archives of the Shoah define what is certainly an incomplete, fragmentary territory—but a territory that has survived and truly exists."[24] In this environment of administrative torture and mass death, the effort to record an image of its horror possesses moral value *in itself* as an effort to resist the obliteration of the record and memory of this moral crime "against humanity" itself.

Didi-Huberman further illustrates the moral weight of this act by describing the conditions of its possibility: "the image was formed by virtue of stepping back: for a few minutes, this member of the *Sonderkommando* set aside the ignoble work that the SS had ordered him to do. By hiding in order to see, the man momentarily delayed the task he had set himself—seizing a unique opportunity—of putting together an iconography. The image was possible because a zone of calm (but achingly limited) had been spared for this act of looking."[25]

By virtue of "stepping back" and interrupting the ghastly routine of "staying alive" in a crematorium in order to take four photographs that are now essential for the historical record of Nazi crimes, Alex and those who helped him created a space for ethics in Auschwitz or a form of moral agency against evil crimes.

In addition to risking their lives to create a historical record of Nazi crimes, members of the *Sonderkommando* also risked their lives to join the camp resistance movement. After the larger resistance movement continually put off the time for a coordinated revolt, members of the *Sonderkommando* initiated the only armed revolt in Auschwitz in 1944.[26] They managed to blow up a crematorium and at least slow down the machinery of death, even though the vast majority of those who participated were killed in the process or in the immediate aftermath of the revolt.[27] So even in the midst of their own supposed moral compromise, Jewish victims who were forced to work in the *Sonderkommando* were able to preserve some space for ethics in the very environment that had laid waste to and eviscerated the possibility of the "good life."

The memoirs of those few former victims who survived working in the *Sonderkommando* do provide evidence for the Socratic view that when we knowingly transgress moral limits, we risk the ruin of our souls and our ability to peaceably commune with ourselves. This view is illustrated in the haunting words of Henryk Mandelbaum, who worked in the last *Sonderkommando* unit in Auschwitz, when he replied to the question posed to him by Igor Bartosik about whether he was ever able to "vanquish the memories of Auschwitz" from his memory: "When children do something wrong, their parents threaten them with hell. 'Don't do that because you'll go to hell,' my mother said. So when I ended up in the *Sonderkommando*, it was as if I had gone to that hell. The burning and the pulling of teeth is with me every day. I walk around, eat, sleep, dance, and sing with those images. It's not something you can erase. It's in my blood, in my whole body."[28] However, though their transgressions may have cost them their spiritual health, the actions taken by these prisoner-functionaries *in the midst of their suffering* still have moral significance, for many of these men-made-into-slaves did not forget about their fellow victims or future generations. They did not forswear their own responsibility to resist the very system they were simultaneously forced to facilitate. Their actions attest to the ability to commit actions that compromise the soul's health for the sake of preserving a space for ethics as such; they also attest to a distinctive situation where we can recognize the moral value of protecting "life itself."

No doubt this situation would be difficult for Socrates to understand, as his right to exist was never thrown into question, nor did he ever witness the systematic, administrative annihilation of entire populations. Thus he counseled Athenians to be preoccupied with the health of their *own* souls as the only path toward properly moral action. The prisoner-functionaries of the *Sonderkommando* did not have the luxury of protecting their spiritual integrity in the face of the existential threat they faced but instead sacrificed their souls' health for the sake of moral action. They did not volunteer to be in the *Sonderkommando*, but their choice or instinct to stay alive was valuable in itself as a moral and political protest to the evil premise of a genocidal state that some populations, as such, are superfluous to the human community. Though Arendt recognized genocide as an ontological assault on humanity itself, her Socratic critique of the Jewish leaders in the *Judenräte* (Jewish councils) as too readily "cooperating" with their Nazi overlords indicates that she did not recognize that this specifically genocidal assault provoked new forms of moral agency that could not be recognized within the traditional philosophical framework for moral evaluation.[29] For as a devout student of Socratic theory, Arendt does not recognize that under specifically genocidal conditions of suffering, the effort to preserve one's life can be coterminous with the effort to preserve the good life.

Our analysis of the condition of those prisoner-functionaries in the *Sonderkommando* illustrates that the rigid Socratic opposition between the concern for self-preservation and the concern for the good life proves to be incapable of providing a model by which to evaluate the moral worth of their actions. Here we glimpse the excess that cannot be represented within traditional moral categories. In response, we should not declare that we will "suspend judgment" of actions that cannot be assessed with traditional moral theories, for this gesture actually reinforces the universal validity of the Socratic worldview through dismissing the condition of the *Sonderkommando* as a mere "exception" in the human world of affairs. Rather, we should recognize the insufficiency of the Socratic worldview to assess the existential condition of those who suffer from genocidal regimes, and we should search for an alternative model whereby we can better judge the moral value of those deeds performed by the *Sonderkommando*.

HOLOCAUST *RESPONSA* ON JEWISH ETHICS UNDER NAZI OPPRESSION

Collections of *Responsa* in the Jewish legal tradition are answers given by authorities in Jewish law to questions that cannot be answered with reference to the Talmud because they arise from new conditions of modern life.[30] The main respondents through the ages still drew on the Talmud and later legal codes to address unprecedented moral questions. At times *Responsa* have served as the source for new legal decisions. According to Rabbi Louis Jacobs, "the Responsa collections (of which around two thousand have now been published) are not only important for Jewish law but serve historians as a rich source for the study of the social life of Jews reflected in them—a particularly reliable source since the details are mentioned in an incidental manner."[31] Thus the *Responsa* delivered by rabbis during the Holocaust to address unprecedented moral conflicts in the ghettos and camps represent a significant source of information about the forms of moral agency that victims could exercise in a genocidal regime.

Compare the Socratic view—that the concern for self-preservation should not play any role in our moral reasoning about what we ought to do—with the sermon given by the Polish rabbi Yitzhak Nissenbaum while he was imprisoned in the Warsaw ghetto in 1942: "It is a time for *Kiddush ha-Hayim*, the sanctification of life, and not *Kiddush Ha-shem*, the holiness of martyrdom. In the past the enemies of the Jews sought the soul of the Jew, and so it was proper for the Jew to sanctify the name of God by sacrificing his body in Martyrdom, in that manner preserving what the enemy sought to take from him. But now it is the *body* of the Jew that the oppressor demands. For this reason it is up to the Jew to defend his body, to preserve his life."[32] Nissenbaum counsels his fellow victims that the moral response to Nazism requires a new orientation for ethical action, one in which the victim's effort to preserve his or her life has moral worth in itself. Socrates was unable to grant moral value to the effort to stay alive, for he died as a martyr of philosophy, or *for the sake of* rational, moral inquiry into the good life (an activity that some Athenians viewed as corrupting the youth). In his martyrdom he was able to secure a legacy for humanity and so attain a meaningful death. On the contrary, Nissenbaum emphasizes that the Nazis' intent to destroy the Jewish people had made martyrdom meaningless, for any death of any Jew only facilitated the Nazis' aims. Instead, the only path of political and moral resistance left to humans who are viewed as "life unworthy of life" (*Lebensunwerte Leben*) was to resist their own deaths and so affirm the value of their existence, their "right" to be alive at all. Unlike previous periods of Jewish persecution, the Jews were not given the option of religious conversion to avoid death. Thus, as Nissenbaum indicates, the Jews did not have anything to fight *for* except their corporeal presence in the world. This, of course, was not the position of Socrates, who was tried in a court of law for illegal actions he was accused of having committed during the course of his life. The fact that he viewed himself as innocent of his charges is not relevant to the fact that he had the moral privilege of dying as a martyr for his beliefs rather than as a number without value or human dignity. The Nazis' judgment that specific populations were "unworthy of life" effaced the significance of individuals as well as the notion of individual responsibility; in this sense, their judgment and the actions that followed constituted a specifically *ontological* attack against the very "being" of individuals and the groups to which they belonged. Arendt also emphasizes the dual nature of this ontological attack on the individual (the "living corpses" of Auschwitz) and on the body of humanity (its "diversity-as-such").[33] Thus any sort of sacrificial "resistance" by victims of genocide is futile against such ontological crimes that threaten the very diversity of human populations.

Nissenbaum recognized that the Nazi onslaught against Jewish existence required that victims regard their lives as inherently valuable and worthy of defense; that indeed, here the effort to stay alive was the only possible way to morally and politically object to a criminal regime. It is not relevant that Nissenbaum did not know the full extent of the Nazis' "final solution"; it was enough to know that the Nazis were destroying Jews without cause or sense. He viewed Nazi policy toward the Jews as an ontological attack against the corporeal existence of the Jewish people well before it was recognized as a genocide aimed at the total destruction of European Jewry. And Nissenbaum understood the importance of forming new *Responsa* in relation to the particular position that his people faced as an enemy population in a criminal regime, *Responsa* that clarified the moral task the Jews faced so that they could receive ethical guidance from their religious authorities that was immediately relevant to the specific catastrophe they suffered. In the Jewish tradition, the *Responsa* have always served as an important supplement to the legal code insofar as they create precedents for action when faced with unprecedented situations and moral dilemmas.[34] Thus Nissenbaum does not offer words of consolation but of religious obligation: "It is a time for *Kiddush ha-Hayim*, the sanctification of life, and not *Kiddush Ha-shem*, the holiness of martyrdom . . . for this reason it is up to the Jew to defend his body, to preserve his life." He does not claim that Jews ought to live "at any cost" but rather enjoins them to view their existence as *worth saving* amid the loss and destruction they could not escape. Here the effort to stay alive is not at odds with the effort to live "the good life" but instead its only real path. Nissenbaum rejects the Socratic dichotomy between self-preservation and moral action and insists that here a concern with mortality has a role in moral reasoning. He does not set up an alternative dichotomy but instead rejects the Socratic view that it is always wrong to inflict violence to save oneself. Because here, saving oneself was the only way to resist the ontological crime of genocide against an entire population.

In the Nazi ghettos and death camps, Jews sought religious advice from rabbis about the "best" course of action given the paucity of their choices and their excessive suffering. In his text *Rabbinic Responsa of the Holocaust Era*, Robert Kirschner records and translates an exchange that occurred when a Jewish victim in Auschwitz sought counsel from his fellow victim, the Rabbi R. Zevi Hirsh Meisels, about whether he had the right to die in place of another who had been marked for death. The young man wished to save a fellow victim who had been "selected" for the gas chamber because this fellow victim was a superior student of Torah. So he had made an arrangement with a guard who would allow the exchange so that he, rather than this superior student, would die in the gas chamber. However, before the exchange took place, he asked the rabbi about whether it was morally justified. Rabbi Meisels counseled the young man to privilege the preservation of his own life over saving the life of the other student: "On the same day, R. Meisels was approached by a boy seeking permission to ransom a young man who was a superior student of Torah. R. Meisels replied that the ransom was forbidden since it would merely condemn someone else.

The boy responded that he wished to offer himself as the substitute. R. Meisels prohibited this also, since in the case of mutual extremity the preservation of one's own life takes precedence."[35] Here, similar to the religious counsel given by Nissenbaum, Meisels emphasizes that in this case of "mutual extremity," the preservation of *one's own life* has moral value and ought to assume an important role in moral reasoning itself. And this reinforces the Jewish view that every single human life has inherent value, and thus to save a single life is akin to having saved the entire world.[36] As a witness to the Nazi genocide, Meisels understood that in this context, the effort to save one's own life may indeed coincide with the effort to save the world of European Jewry, or the Jewish people as such. In an environment of genocidal suffering, the value of an individual life also represents the value of the group to which that individual belongs, and in fighting for one's own life, one is simultaneously fighting for the existence of an entire culture or population.

Here, again, Socrates's strict dichotomy between acting on behalf of self-interest or the common good breaks down in light of the distinct existential condition faced by victims of genocide. We can grasp the moral value of actions performed by the prisoner-functionaries in the *Sonderkommando* through applying the *Responsa* provided by Nissenbaum and Meisels in the midst of their oppression, for those who were forced to work in the *Sonderkommando* were also preoccupied with the effort to stay alive and chose the only means by which this was possible. Their effort to stay alive cannot be separated from the effort to survive the destruction of their people or bear witness to this destruction. Thus simply being a member of the *Sonderkommando*—or having "chosen" to work in the crematoria to stay alive—does not in itself require that we suspend moral judgment of the actions of individuals who worked in this unit. In the midst of this "mutual extremity," the preservation of their own lives was *just as morally important* as the preservation of any other Jewish lives at Auschwitz. As Meisels suggests, there was no moral justification for privileging the preservation of another, particular life over one's own when every single life had been denied existential value. The members of the *Sonderkommando* were not the architects but the slaves of a system that sought to annihilate their people, and their continued existence in that system was a form of moral resistance against its logic and aims. Though individual members may be deserving of moral blame for what they did in that position, we know that many members sustained a commitment to ethics and truth in the midst of their degradation.

For this reason, the effort to stay alive when one has been targeted for elimination in a genocidal regime represents a moral protest to the logic of genocide and an affirmation of an individual's right to exist as well as the value of the group to which one belongs. When he coined the term "genocide" to designate the crime committed by the Nazis, Raphael Lemkin also described the distinct interrelation of the individual and the group in genocidal suffering: "Genocide is directed against the national group as an entity, and the actions involved are directed against individuals, not in their individual capacity, but as members of the national group."[37] An important part of Lemkin's rationale for why genocide represented a crime distinct from mass murder is because it sought to destroy or undermine the foundations of entire national or cultural groups. The recognition that genocide is an international crime is thus based on the moral view that human diversity is a *good* thing and that we *ought* to protect the variety of cultures and religions and ethnic groups that compose the diversity of human experience. And for Arendt, diversity is an ontological condition for the possibility of humanity "without which the very words 'mankind' or 'humanity' would be devoid of meaning."[38] So, again, the very definition of "genocide" indicates that we cannot analytically separate the fate of an individual's life from the fate of the group under attack, and the personal effort to survive genocide coincides with the moral effort to protect the life of a group and the fact of human diversity.

The existential condition of those who suffer from genocide also suggests an alternative form of moral agency than the Socratic model of rational deliberation with its emphasis on intent. Sometimes moral action *is* the result of forming a good intent to respect individual values, but in a condition of "mutual extremity" it may also be the result of honoring the instinct to stay alive amid collective ruin. Thus we can understand the actions of the prisoner-functionaries in the *Sonderkommando* as moral *even* if they lacked the formal intent "to do good" when they agreed to work in the heart of the killing apparatus at Auschwitz to stay alive, for the Nazis unleashed an ontological assault on the body of the Jews that did not always allow individual victims to engage in calm, rational deliberation about means and ends before they acted. Nevertheless, we cannot claim that their efforts to stay alive through moral compromise are devoid of moral value simply because they cannot be properly assessed by ancient and modern models of moral agency. Instead, we must allow that if there are certain conditions under which the effort to stay alive has moral significance *in itself*, then so too do our instincts for self-preservation.

SOCRATIC AND JEWISH ETHICS FOR A GENOCIDAL WORLD

As previously mentioned, several Jewish prisoners who were conscripted to work in the *Sonderkommando* actually risked their lives to take meticulous notes about the Nazi machinery of death, and they buried these notes in the grounds around the crematoria. Among the notes that were found were fragments of a scroll written by Zalman Lewental before he was killed in Auschwitz. An excerpt of these partly illegible fragments states, "The truth as it really exists is immeasurably more tragic and terrible. In the notebook—— dig, to [search]——it is by chance that [this] is buried in several places. Keep looking! You will [still]——find more."[39] In the midst of his acute suffering, Lewental was clearly preoccupied with testifying about Auschwitz for the sake of future generations. He enjoins the reader to "dig, to search" to find the other testimonies, to "Keep looking!" despite, perhaps, a desire to give up. His efforts to survive *even at the cost of his moral integrity and psychological health* cannot be separated from his efforts to repair the world (*tikkun olam*) in the aftermath of the Nazi genocide. In other words, Lewental transgressed his ethics as a member of the *Sonderkommando* for the sake of higher values, or to help rebuild a world in which ethical choice might once again be relevant. His brief life as a member of the *Sonderkommando* thus held moral significance even though it coincided with ghastly actions that he could not reconcile with ethical choices made possible in a different existential condition of agency.

Socrates could not imagine such a condition because his model of moral evaluation depended on a strict dichotomy between the intent to preserve one's life and the intent to respect the good life. This dichotomy was also picked up by Levi and then subsequently assumed by those Holocaust scholars who insist on the need to "suspend judgment" with regard to the actions performed by Jewish members of the *Sonderkommando*. Rather than adopt a Jewish moral framework like that developed by Nissenbaum and Meisels in the context of the ghettos and the camps, they have drawn from or reverted to Socrates.

They do not recognize the possibility that in specific situations when the value of "life itself" has been denied, the effort to stay alive contains moral value in itself. This possibility must be granted to grasp how acts of moral transgression for the sake of survival do not in themselves represent the abandonment of the good life.

To recognize the distinct forms of moral agency possible in a condition of genocidal suffering, or understand the coexistence of moral transgression and fidelity to the good in acts of self-preservation necessary to survive a genocidal regime, we must move beyond this ancient dichotomy toward new models for moral evaluation of victim behavior under ontological attacks. To hear and respect Lewental's insistence that "the truth as it really exists is immeasurably more tragic and terrible," we cannot assume the validity of traditional modes of moral judgment in our effort to evaluate the actions of prisoner-functionaries who faced conditions far more terrible than we can imagine and that threatened the very diversity of human communities. We have seen that in the face of the existential threat posed by genocidal regimes, we cannot make a facile distinction between self-preservation and moral action or exclude the instinct to stay alive from the moral reasoning that precedes and allows for ethical actions.

To adequately confront the genocidal world in which we live, we must recognize that systems of moral evaluation can never be universal but instead—like rabbinic *Responsa*—must emerge from the specificity of the existential conditions with which we are faced. It is not the case that the actions of Holocaust victims—even those of the *Sonderkommando*—lie "outside" the moral universe of values and ideals. Despite the efforts of the Nazis, the prisoner-functionaries who worked in the *Sonderkommando* were not transformed into amoral machines that sought to stay alive at all costs. The only way to recognize this is to grant their efforts to stay alive the moral value they deserve. To do otherwise is to ignore the reality of their condition in the same way that the SS used the orchestras in the camps "to drown out the screams of its victims." Our recognition of unique forms of moral agency that emerge in victim behavior under genocidal regimes requires that we acknowledge more than one framework for moral evaluation. In the *Responsa* developed in the ghettos and camps we can find a model of moral evaluation that offers a viable alternative to Socratic ethics insofar as it is not based on a rigid dichotomy between self-interest and the common good, or between our instincts and our values.

The coexistence of multiple frameworks for moral evaluation of the members of the *Sonderkommando* is poignantly illustrated in the recent Hungarian film *Son of Saul* (*Saul fia*, 2015, directed by László Nemes), which centers around a day in the life of Saul, a member of the *Sonderkommando* in Auschwitz. In the film, as Saul is removing dead bodies from the gas chamber, he believes he recognizes one of the bodies as his own son. He spends the rest of the movie risking his life and the lives of his fellow prisoners to try to arrange proper mourning rites and a real burial for this young boy, amid the industrial burning of Jewish bodies all around him. At some point in the film, it becomes impossible to grasp whether Saul's efforts or the system in which he is forced to operate is the more "irrational" or absurd of the two. Saul is obsessed with finding a rabbi amid the prisoners to properly mourn his son, and it is clear that this one act will allow him to die with some measure of peace. Presumably, his ability to mourn this one child indicates that the Nazis failed to eviscerate the significance and the loss of every single victim they killed. And in that sense, Saul's insistence on mourning for the boy is a profound form of resistance against genocidal practices that inflict social death on populations judged superfluous to humankind. At the same time, after Saul's efforts to find a rabbi to help him mourn lead to one man's death and imperil his fellow prisoners' plans to resist, one of the prisoners chides him, "You failed the living for the dead." For this man, the effort to survive the Nazi genocide was a greater moral priority than the effort to mourn its victims, while for Saul the need to mourn and mark *what was lost* was a greater moral priority than the effort to escape his death. Unless we recognize the coexistence of multiple frameworks for the moral evaluation of actions taken by victims of a genocidal regime, we are forced into the absurd and morally obscene position of judging either Saul or his friend as pursuing the "better" or more "valuable" form of resistance against their spiritual and physical destruction. The aim of this article is not to argue that in the Nazi death camp it was "better" to prioritize living over living well but instead to illustrate that there is moral value in the radical efforts of some victims to stay alive even (and especially) at the cost of their own spiritual health and psychic well-being.

Unfortunately, we still have need for alternative models of evaluation and moral agency in a world in which states continue to target specific populations for destruction in accord with the biopolitics of the modern era. As we face an increasingly devastating environmental crisis that threatens to create a real scarcity of resources for existing populations, it is likely that states will continue to privilege the preservation of some groups at the expense of others. And we must recognize that those who are viewed as the "expendable" populations will engage in forms of moral agency that Socrates could not understand or recognize. However, this does not indicate that their actions will be devoid of moral worth or that we should exclude them from our moral considerations. I am not claiming that Socratic ethics is no longer relevant and, indeed, there are times when we ought to privilege the common good over our selfish desires for power, profit, and pleasure. However, I am claiming that traditional models of moral evaluation cannot illuminate the choices made by Jewish men in the *Sonderkommando* and most likely fail to clarify the moral value of actions taken by other victims of genocidal regimes. To adequately recognize these victims, we must accept the inadequacy of traditional moral theories to assess the unique existential condition faced by victims of ontological crimes that target the very existence of entire human groups so that we may preserve intellectual honesty and moral integrity in a world that ceaselessly, ruthlessly threatens the conditions that make them possible.

NOTES

1. Christopher Browning, "In the Cauldron," *New York Review of Books,* August 2012.

2. Primo Levi, "The Gray Zone," *The Drowned and the Saved*, trans. Raymond Rosenthal (New York: Vintage Books, 1989), 36–69; 44.

3. Theodor W. Adorno, *Negative Dialectics,* trans. E. B. Ashton (New York: Seabury Press, 1973), 365.

4. Hannah Arendt, *Eichmann in Jerusalem: A Report on the Banality of Evil* (New York: Penguin, 1994), 272.

5. Ibid., 125.

6. Hannah Arendt, *The Origins of Totalitarianism* (New York: Harcourt, 1973), 447.

7. Ibid., 441.

8. All general information about the behavior of Jewish prisoners in the *Sonderkommando* units in Auschwitz was derived from five sources: Gideon Greif, ed., *We Wept Without Tears: Testimonies of the Jewish Sonderkommando from Auschwitz* (New Haven, Conn.: Yale University Press, 2005); Schlomo

Venezia with Béatrice Prasquier, *Inside the Gas Chambers: Eight Months in the Sonderkommando of Auschwitz*, ed. Jean Mouttapa, trans. Andrew Brown (Malden, Mass.: Polity Press, 2009); Filip Müller, *Eyewitness Auschwitz: Three Years in the Gas Chambers*, trans. Susanne Flatauer (Chicago: Ivan R. Dee, 1999); Sybille Steinbacher, *Auschwitz: A History* (New York: Harper-Collins, 2005); and Georges Didi-Huberman, *Images in Spite of All: Four Photographs from Auschwitz*, trans. Shane B. Lillis (Chicago: University of Chicago Press, 2008).

9. Plato, *Crito*, trans. Hugh Tredennick, in *The Collected Dialogues*, ed. Edith Hamilton and Huntington Cairns (Princeton, N.J.: Princeton University Press, 1961), 48b.

10. Plato, *Apology*, trans. Hugh Tredennick, in *Collected Dialogues*, 39.

11. My interpretation of Socrates follows the one provided by Hannah Arendt in her essay "Thinking and Moral Considerations," in *Responsibility and Judgment*, ed. Jerome Kohn (New York: Schocken Books, 2003).

12. Arendt, "Thinking and Moral Considerations," 164.

13. Arendt, *Eichmann in Jerusalem*, 276.

14. Plato, *Crito*, in *Collected Dialogues*, 49b.

15. Plato, *Apology*, in *Collected Dialogues*, 32d.

16. Plato, *Gorgias*, trans. W. D. Woodhead, in *The Collected Dialogues*, 474b.

17. *Crito*, in *Collected Dialogues*, 50a–51c.

18. It is clear in Plato's *Euthyphro* that the historical Socrates was not morally shocked by slavery, as he questions Euthyphro's effort to prosecute his own father for killing a slave. Since a slave does not have the same legal rights as a citizen, Euthyphro is going out of his way to prosecute his own father, and it is this insistence on bringing his father to court *on behalf of a slave* that Socrates questions as impious.

19. Arendt, *Origins of Totalitarianism*, 444.

20. Didi-Huberman, *Images in Spite of All*, 4.

21. Steinbacher, *Auschwitz*, 102.

22. The notes that survived have been collected in the volume *The Scrolls of Auschwitz* and have been essential to the historical documentation about the Nazi machinery of mass murder. See Ber Mark, ed., *The Scrolls of Auschwitz* (Tel Aviv: Am Oved Publishers, 1985).

23. Didi-Huberman, *Images in Spite of All*, 11.

24. Ibid., 22–23.

25. Ibid., 39–40.

26. Steinbacher, *Auschwitz*, 119–20.

27. Didi-Huberman, *Images in Spite of All*, 38.

28. Henryk Mandelbaum, *I Was at the Auschwitz Crematorium: A Con-*

versation with Henryk Mandelbaum, trans. William Brand (Oświęcim, Pol.: Auschwitz-Birkenau State Museum, 2011), 87.

29. Arendt, *Eichmann in Jerusalem*, 118.

30. Robert Kirshner, trans., *Rabbinic Responsa of the Holocaust Era* (New York: Schocken, 1985), 6.

31. Louis Jacobs, *The Jewish Religion: A Companion* (New York: Oxford University Press, 1995), 420.

32. Quoted in Abraham J. Edelheit and Hershel Edelheit, *Holocaust: A Handbook and Dictionary* (Boulder, Col.: Westview Press, 1994), 93.

33. Arendt, *Eichmann in Jerusalem*, 269.

34. Kirshner, *Rabbinic Responsa of the Holocaust Era*.

35. Ibid., 113.

36. Jerusalem Talmud, Sanhedrin 4:1 (22a) Mishnah 12: "Whoever destroys a soul, it is considered as if he destroyed an entire world. And whoever saves a life, it is considered as if he saved an entire world." Heinrich W. Guggenheimer, *Tractates Sanhedrin, Makkot, and Horaiot* (Berlin: De Gruyter, 2010), *eBook Collection (EBSCOhost)*, p. 165.

37. Raphael Lemkin, *Axis Rule in Occupied Europe: Laws of Occupation, Analysis of Government, Proposals for Redress*, 2nd ed. (Clark, N.J.: Lawbook Exchange, 2008), 80.

38. Arendt, *Eichmann in Jerusalem*, 269.

39. Mark, *Scrolls of Auschwitz*, 240.

Dorota Glowacka

Gender and the Holocaust: Relational Imagination in the Cul-de-Sacs of Remembrance

> *One can turn a human being into a skeleton gurgling with diarrhea, without time or energy to think. Imagination is the first luxury of a body receiving sufficient nourishment, enjoying a margin of time, possessing the rudiments from which dreams are fashioned.*
>
> —*Charlotte Delbo,* Auschwitz and After

IN *STILL ALIVE*, RUTH KLUGER REMARKS, "WARS, AND HENCE THE MEMOries of wars, are owned by the male of the species. . . . Besides, women have no past, or aren't supposed to have one. A man can have an interesting past, a woman only indecent."[1] In Kluger's view, not only have women's experiences been excluded from official projects of Holocaust remembrance, but also the notions of history and memory have been defined through an androcentric lens.

While research conducted during the war and immediately after showed evidence of interest in women's experiences, these approaches soon disappeared, and the normative Holocaust story that emerged was gender-neutral, although in fact it privileged male experience.[2] The interest in women did not reemerge until the 1970s, when feminist scholarship slowly began to change our understanding of gender-specific experiences and behaviors under extreme conditions. In the mid-1980s and throughout the 1990s, feminist perspectives finally began to rise to prominence in Holocaust studies, resulting in a new conceptual matrix that has recalibrated both the parameters of historical research and the debates about memory and representation.

In what follows, I do not aspire to summarize the prolific contributions by feminist scholars to the field of Holocaust studies or to diagnose their impact on what is today a sui generis discipline of knowledge.[3] Instead, I would like to highlight several areas of conceptual ambiguity that have continued to hinder our understanding of the dynamic of gender under extreme conditions and contributed to the marginalization of women's Holocaust experiences and narratives. I will focus on female sexual shame, interpretations of the psychoanalytic concept of trauma in Holocaust contexts, and visual representations of atrocity. I will then draw on feminist articulations of relational personhood and memory to propose a concept of relational imagination and to argue that it can help us illuminate and recover marginalized areas of experience for the purposes of both history writing and commemorative practices.

Already in the late 1920s, French sociologist Maurice Halbwachs proposed that memory is shaped by social frameworks, such as family, nationality, religion, and language, which determine the content and patterns of recollection: "It is in society that people acquire their memories."[4] In *Shadows of Trauma: Memory and the Politics of Postwar Identity*, German memory theorist Aleida Assmann returns to Halbwachs's pioneering theses and writes, "Memories do not exist as a closed system; they are always already affected, strengthened, inflected, modified, and polarized by other memories and by impulses to forget within the context of a given social reality."[5] What Assmann does not consider, however, is that if socially sanctioned frameworks of meaning dictate which events are worth remembering and count as true and historically significant facts, then experiences that fall outside these schemata may be impossible to articulate. Until relatively recently, many of women's experiences during the Holocaust, especially those related to sexual violence, fell into such a conceptual oubliette.

Women's silence about sexual violence during the Holocaust raises questions not only about social stigma and taboos but also about women's epistemic authority and their status as credible witnesses.[6] As feminist philosophers have argued, within a community of knowledge, our positions as testifiers are distributed in ways that support only certain groups, while marginalizing others. These a priori epistemic advantages may predetermine which facts are selected for investigation, and thus count as evidence, and which lines of inquiry are foreclosed. Since women's knowledge and cognitive abilities in general have been traditionally suspected and distrusted, women suffer epistemic vulnerability, which is also inseparable from their lesser status as moral and political agents. Memory is one of our key cognitive abilities since our self-conceptions and ways of perceiving the world are based on how we remember the past. In *Relational Remembering*, Sue Campbell concludes that the challenge to the competency of women's memory is related to the prevalent view of women as suggestible and emotionally unstable. Memory is "a complex of cognitive abilities and social-narrative activities where one's success and failure as a rememberer are affected by one's social location."[7]

We may infer, therefore, that gender-biased notions of identity and moral personhood, which result in skepticism about women's capacity for accurate recall, have contributed to why stories written by men and about men rose to prominence within the Holocaust canon. An emblematic instance of privileging male testimony in the 1980s was Claude Lanzmann's *Shoah*. As Marianne Hirsch and Leo Spitzer have shown, the French director pruned his footage of women's voices and faces, while simultaneously reinscribing tropes of female passivity, invisibility, and unredeemable death into a supposedly gender-neutral narrative of destruction, as told by male witnesses.[8]

Since *Shoah* outtakes became available on the website of the United States Holocaust Memorial Museum (USHMM), scholars have been able to gain deeper insight into Lanzmann's resolute omissions, of which the exclusion of Czech Jewish survivor Ruth Elias's testimony is especially striking. In an interview that lasted almost three hours, Elias told Lanzmann about her family members' ordeal in Theresienstadt, their deportation to the East and eventual murder, and the horror of arriving pregnant in Auschwitz, giving birth, and then being forced to kill her baby girl. Yet she also recounted happy moments of intimacy with her boyfriend, whom she had married in Theresienstadt to avoid deportation, and emphasized her fierce desire to stay alive: "I wanted to live, nothing else."[9] In the final version of the film, Lanzmann introduces only brief fragments from Elias's testimony, mainly in the form of voice-over that opens the sequence on Auschwitz in the film. Elias is heard saying, "I didn't know anything about Auschwitz," as if she were relinquishing her testimonial agency to male witnesses, who would proceed to give chilling accounts of death, despair, and the annihilation of the Czech family camp.[10] In Markus Zisselsberger's view, Lanzmann's vision of the Nazi camps as the vortex of death, from which only a few (male) witnesses emerged to testify to the atrocities, could not accommodate Elias's simple message of the will to survive. Despite being separated from all of her family members and the despondence she felt after she had lost her child, she continued to affirm that "the will to live was so very strong. We were only thinking of how to live, how to come over all this."[11]

Lanzmann's interview with Elias ends with a literal gesture of silencing the female witness:

> R.E.: I can tell you plenty of it, something more. Did you ask me something more?
>
> C.L.: Don't talk now. Stay like this.[12]

This definitive interruption, the director's "cut" of the original interview, which was then excised almost entirely from the body of the film, indicates that Lanzmann repeatedly failed to hear Elias's testimony not only due to the weight and moral value he attributed to male narratives of death but also because he was at a loss for conceptual structures and meaningful modes of remembrance to interpret and incorporate her searing account.[13] Considering that the figure of the suffering mother is one of the most iconic representations of Holocaust victimhood, Elias would have been perceived as a perverted mother, who sacrificed her child to save her own life.[14] Moreover, she manifested her remarkable will to live through frank expression of her sexual desire for her boyfriend and descriptions of their moments of intimacy in Theresienstadt—that is, through powerful affirmation of her sexual agency.[15]

HOLOCAUST MEMORY AND FEMALE SEXUAL SHAME

Elias's unpretentious assertion of her sexuality and of the ownership of her body, including her reproductive capacity, in disregard of the social norm, is unique. Her inadmissible and therefore unreceived account reveals that the politics of gender, informed by social norms and taboos, often dictate which narratives become part of collective memory and which are airbrushed from accepted Holocaust narratives. Her self-expression in the *Shoah* outtakes contravenes the sanctioned myths of chaste femininity and sacrificial motherhood, which, as Sara R. Horowitz argues, have functioned as privileged tropes of Holocaust memorialization. In her essay "The Gender of Good and Evil: Women and Holocaust Memory," Horowitz scrutinizes the enduring legend of ninety-three Beth Jakov (Beis Ya'akov) Maidens, who poisoned themselves rather than be forced into sexual slavery, and she juxtaposes it with French director Marcel Ophuls's hostile representation, in *Hotel Terminus* (1988), of a French woman who had her head shaved as punishment for having sexual relations with a German soldier.[16] Horowitz's analysis shines light on the pervasiveness of the trope of female sexual shame, premised on the denigration of female sexuality.

The way the fear and disavowal of female agency have informed dominant Holocaust narratives is exemplified in the largely forgotten story of the talented Polish-Jewish singer Wiera Gran (born Dwojra Weronika Grynberg). Before the war, Gran, despite her young age, became a star at Warsaw cafés and cabarets and recorded many popular hits, although, in her own words, she was "pathologically modest and shy."[17] In 1941, Gran, who at the time was married to Kazimierz Jezierski, a Polish physician, decided to move to the ghetto to be with her mother. Between 1941 and 1942, she performed at the ghetto's Café Sztuka on Leszno Street, with the piano accompaniment by Władysław Szpilman, who composed some of the best-known songs in her repertoire. She was also known for her philanthropy, especially on behalf of the ghetto's orphaned children. On one occasion, she performed at a private show for members of the infamous collaborationist Group Thirteen (Das Draitzental), venomously referred to in the ghetto as "the Jewish Gestapo." In 1942 Gran escaped from the ghetto, through the City Court building on Leszno Street, and survived the war on the Aryan side, aided by her husband. After the war, she approached Szpilman, then director of the Polish Radio music department, to seek employment, but he accused her of having been a Gestapo agent and of cavorting with the Germans, and sent her away. In his memoir *Pianista: Warszawskie wspomnienia, 1939–1945*, Szpilman never mentioned Wiera Gran, who was much better known both before the war and in the Warsaw Ghetto than he was and with whom he shared the stage at Café Sztuka, although he did make references to the songs from her repertoire. Gran's character did not appear in Roman Polański's acclaimed film *The Pianist*.[18]

The rumors about Gran seemed to have originated with Jonas Turkow, a well-known actor and artistic director in the ghetto and later a member of the Central Jewish Committee in Poland (CKŻP). Gran was cleared of all suspicion in several postwar trials of collaborators in Poland, including by CKŻP's People's Court, and numerous affidavits of innocence were provided on her behalf (by Irena Sendlerowa, Krystyna Żywulska, and Władysław Bartoszewski, among others).[19] Despite the absence of incriminating evidence, Gran was subjected to public shaming, and she left Poland in 1950. The infamy followed her to Israel, then to Venezuela, and finally to Paris, where she managed to attain a measure of success. On her last visit to Israel, in 1971, her concert was cancelled after a group of Polish-Jewish survivors threatened they would stage a protest at the venue and wear striped concentration camp uniforms;[20] as she later stated in an interview, this was for her "a great tragedy that broke [her]" and she never sang again.[21] She vehemently denied the accusations for the rest of her life and unsuccessfully tried to clear her name, including in a self-published autobiography.[22] Gran died in 2007 in Paris, and the Polish government refused her last wish that her remains be repatriated to Poland. Gran's life was documented in a book by Polish writer Agata Tuszyńska, who conducted a series of interviews with the singer in her Paris apartment shortly before her death. Tuszyńska makes an impassioned case for Gran's innocence and argues that baseless slander ruined Gran's postwar career.[23] Her interviews with Gran describe the tribulations of a woman who, like Elias, was determined to stay alive and yet who was later spurned by the community of survivors and excised from both historical accounts and collective memory of the life and death in the Warsaw Ghetto. In 1970, Yad Vashem refused to receive Gran's testimony on the grounds that it was "irrelevant," although in 1995 she was approached by the Shoah Foundation and gave her deposition there.[24]

The leitmotif in the documentary film about Gran, made in 2012, is the phrase "the lost honor of Wiera Gran."[25] Throughout the documentary, Polish filmmaker Maria Zmarz-Koczanowicz subtly alludes to the root causes of the singer's infamy: her ingenuity in orchestrating her own survival[26] and the envy of her success by the influential members of the ghetto's Jewish community.[27] Gran's supposedly ignominious story stands in contrast with heroic narratives that emerged from the Warsaw Ghetto, such as the selfless death of the ghetto fighter Michał Klepfisz, the sacrifice of Janusz Korczak (a legendary director of the orphanage, who followed his wards to the gas chambers of Treblinka), or the fight to preserve the cultural legacy of the doomed people by Emmanuel Ringelblum and other members of Oneg Shabbat. Considering the vehemence of the judgment against Gran, which, as Kislew observed in his article, only grew as time went by,[28] it seems that the figure of a fallen woman, a beautiful and talented one, has served as a dark screen on which the "unheroic" aspects of the ghetto (collaborators, unscrupulous smugglers, and the Jewish police) have been projected. The motif of Gran's alleged moral and patriotic failure has provided an invisible albeit negative safeguard for the preferred, heroic version of the ghetto's history. The elision of her story from the Holocaust narratives of survival, abated by the enduring misogynist stereotype of female sexual shame, evinces the tragic truth of Kluger's dry comment that the only past a woman can have is "an indecent one."

Based on their depositions, Ruth Elias and Wiera Gran were both eager to bequeath their testimonies, yet their stories were unwelcome in the post-Holocaust community of rememberers (and in Gran's case, excommunicated from that community). Exclusions such as these indicate that reigning Holocaust narratives are imprinted with blanks that conceal experiences marked by social taboos pertaining to the sphere of sexuality—female sexuality in particular. These morally proscribed areas of experience are quarantined in the realm of the unmentionable, undermining women's subject position as historical witnesses and their status as authors of their stories.

Reiterating Annette Wieviorka's seminal theses in *The Era of the Witness* (*L'Ère du témoin*, 2002), Assmann notes that, starting with the Eichmann trial, Holocaust survivors began to gain authority as witnesses, which allowed them to gradually overcome the stigma of degradation, convert shame into a source of pride, and thus regain a sense of self-worth and life purpose. The recognition and even reverence granted survivors by "secondary witnesses" have brought about "the transformation of trauma into *honor*, in the sense of an aspiration and a positive self-worth."[29] It must be noted, however, that this positively transvalued shame emphatically excludes female shame, such as Gran's "lost honor" or Ruth Elias's sorrow stemming from her unmentionable deed of infanticide (especially that, scandalously, her unwanted pregnancy was the result of her joyful sexual encounters with her boyfriend). The persistence of oppressive gender norms, enforced by patriarchal relations of power before, during, and after the Holocaust, not only impacted women's experiences during traumatic events but also shaped the ways these events have been remembered and commemorated.

GENDERED SCRIPTS AND LIMITATIONS OF TRAUMA THEORY AS A CONCEPTUAL FRAMEWORK

In an influential 1995 volume on the subject of trauma, edited by Cathy Caruth, feminist psychoanalyst Laura S. Brown remarked that although victims of traumatic events "are rarely blamed for these events," there is a disparity as to how actions undertaken to avert death are later being judged depending on whether the protagonists are male or female. For instance, rarely do male participants, whether combatants who commit excessive acts of killing or prisoners forced to perform horrific deeds under duress, "come under the sort of scrutiny we find given to battered women or survivors of rape."[30] A striking example from the realm of Holocaust history are the actions of the members of Auschwitz *Sonderkommandos*, with respect to whom, as Primo Levi admonishes the readers of his *The Drowned and the Saved*, we must suspend judgement: "No one is authorized to judge them, especially not those who didn't live through the Lager."[31] Brown pries a concealed gender bias from the narratives of trauma and points out that very different standards are applied to mostly female victims of horrific experiences that transpire in secret, are veiled in shame, and thus never attain the status of events that could be publicly remembered or commemorated. Similarly, no moral dispensation, no grace of "*impotentia judicandi*" (inability to judge),[32] has been accorded to women who, like the *Sonderkommandos*, embraced survival as the ultimate value: in the camps, in the ghettos, or in hiding, at whatever "moral" cost, though in the case of Gran, the allegations of sexual barter and treason were never substantiated. This gender-inflected ambivalence indicates that certain limitations may inhere in the way Holocaust trauma has been conceptualized. In the twenty-first century, experiences of gender-based violence, especially rape and forced sexual labor, have been recognized in Holocaust scholarship, and a body of knowledge on the subjects that used to be cloaked in taboo is growing.[33] Nevertheless, some of the concepts on the basis of which this knowledge is being interpreted still await scrutiny, and this seems to be the case with the way "trauma" has been applied to analyze gender-specific experiences during the Holocaust.

As Ruth Leys reminds us, in her important study *Trauma: A Genealogy*, when the notion of trauma first appeared in the second half of the nineteenth century, it was most often discussed in relation to the diagnoses of female neurosis: "the hysterical female epitomised the shattering effects of trauma on the mind."[34] Increasingly, however, it also became recognized as a male symptom ("male hysteria") in connection with veterans of World War I who were suffering from shell-shock.[35] In the late twentieth century, it was the "male" trauma of Vietnam that prompted the recognition of post-traumatic stress disorder (PTSD) and solidified it as a paradigm to interpret the consequences of catastrophic experiences. Moreover, since at that time American women were not allowed to serve in combat roles, trauma sustained by female support personnel, mainly nurses, was not acknowledged, and they could not access veteran benefits.[36] Paradoxically, it was only in the 1980s, following the diagnoses of PTSD in Vietnam War veterans, that the interest in the Holocaust began to dominate both theoretical and clinical discussions of trauma.[37]

When PTSD first emerged as a diagnostic concept, psychiatric manuals defined it as a response to an event "outside the range of usual human experience," causing the sensation of intense fear, terror, and helplessness.[38] Despite later revisions, which acknowledged the inaccuracy of referring to traumatic stressors as "outside of usual human experience," the expression still functions as a diagnostic and interpretive tool, while conceptualizations of trauma in diagnostic manuals continue to lack specificity.[39] Yet according to what criteria do certain experiences fall within the range of "being outside of usual human experience," while others are simply deemed difficult and therefore do not count as "real" trauma? Brown concludes that "the range of human experience becomes the range of what is normal and usual in the lives of men of the dominant class. . . . Trauma is thus what disrupts these particular lives, but no others."[40] As she knew from her clinical practice, women's experiences of sexual violence had been all too common, and although they resulted in symptoms that should be classified as traumatic, they hardly fell under the rubric of "unusual." In Brown's experience as an expert witness in court, this argument of "commonality" was then used to disprove the claims of irreparable harm made by female victims of sexual abuse.[41] As confirmed by Brown's and Leys's analyses, trauma has always been constructed in terms of gendered juxtapositions.[42] We have reasons to suspect, therefore, that the understanding of Holocaust trauma also aligns with the prevailing norm that privileges male experience.[43]

We may stipulate that "the usual human experience" is the experience that has been validated by dominant systems of knowledge and cultural norms. In that case, certain traumatic experiences, such as women's experiences of sexual violence, "resist understanding" not only because they are so overwhelming that, in Freud's words, they "break through the [psyche's] protective shield,"[44] but also because they do not fit into the socially constructed dichotomy of what constitutes a traumatic experience and what does not. They thus become "doubly unspeakable," to borrow Elizabeth Heineman's expression,[45] and they cannot be mastered not only because they are structurally external to consciousness but also because no social mechanisms and contexts have emerged that would generate the desire to understand and "master" them in the first place. As psychiatrist Judith Herman has argued, destructive, violent behaviors causing trauma must be understood as perpetuating a particular structure of power relations, while shame involved in the experience of victimization is a social mechanism that supports that structure by silencing the disempowered group.[46] In this way, the nonrecognition of women's traumatic experiences and the imposition of shame disqualifies their attempts to bear witness and invalidates their testimony. In other words, it is necessary that we recognize the gendered frameworks within which trauma was experienced and then dealt with; that is, we must account for multiple and intersecting regimes of its unspeakability.

THE HOLOCAUST IN VISUAL ART: PROBING THE (GENDERED) LIMITS OF REPRESENTATION

Women's precarious status as witnesses and gender bias inherent in conceptualizations of Holocaust trauma pertain not only to written and oral sources but also to other forms of testimony, such as visual art. The first comprehensive overview of Holocaust art, *Depiction and Interpretation: The Influence of the Holocaust on Visual Arts* (1993), features only one female artist, Lea Grundig, who, in tandem with her husband Hans Grundig, was also known for her commitment to Communist ideals and her political engagement in the struggle against fascism. In the interpretations of the various artworks, the author, Israeli art historian Ziva Amishai-Maisels, makes several references to female-centered imagery in the drawings and paintings by artists such as Charlotte Burešová and Malvina Schalková (the inmates at

Theresienstadt and members of the famous *Zeichenstube*) and Halina Ołomucka (a survivor of Majdanek and Auschwitz-Birkenau), yet none of their works are included in the book's 99 color plates and 560 black-and-white images. Moreover, Maisels's compendium entirely omits Charlotte Salomon's series of gouaches entitled *Leben? oder Theater? Ein Singspiel* (*Life? or Theater? A Singspiel*), which she made between 1940 and 1942, despite the monumental character of the German Jewish artist's masterpiece.[47] This exclusion, as well as the fact that Salomon's work remained unknown for decades, bears scrutiny, especially if we consider that paintings and drawings by artists such as Marc Chagall, Felix Nussbaum, Bêdrich Fritta, Leo Haas, and Yehuda Bacon were often evoked after the war as authentic documents of the time and called on as witnesses, including during the trials of the Nazi perpetrators. Brief selections (80 panels) of Salomon's oeuvre were first exhibited in 1961 in Amsterdam and then toured Germany in 1965–1967. They bore the title *Charlotte: A Diary in Pictures*; at the time, they were considered a visual equivalent of Anne Frank's *Diary*, which grossly underrepresented their complexity and artistic innovation.[48] In 1971, the entire collection of Salomon's works was bequeathed to the Jewish Historical Museum in Amsterdam, which exhibited a part of the collection in 1980, but it was not shown as a whole until 1998 (at the London Royal Academy), when a complete catalog was also published for the first time and Salomon began to be recognized as an important artist in her own right.[49]

In the late 1930s, Salomon was a student at the prestigious Berlin Academy of Fine Arts, despite restrictions on Jewish admissions. In 1939, she left Berlin for southern France, where she lived with her grandparents in relative safety at a Mediterranean villa, owned by American philanthropist Ottilie Moore, and later in nearby villages and towns. She married Alexander Nagel, another German Jewish refugee, but in October 1943, both were arrested by the Gestapo and sent first to Drancy and then to Auschwitz, where most likely Salomon was killed on arrival (she was five months pregnant at the time).

Salomon's work, which combines image, text, and music, is an artistically innovative and bold critique of the impact of social constructions of gender on her development as an artist under the darkening skies of National Socialism. It alludes to political events through the lens of intimate, personal experiences, intertwining the narrative of the Nazi persecution with family history. In several sequences of

Leben? oder Theater? Salomon reflects on the high incidence of severe depression among women in her family, including her aunt, mother, and grandmother.[50] Refusing to submit to what has been imputed to her as genetic necessity, she unambiguously attributes the prevalence of suicide among female members of her family to overbearing regimes of masculinity, incarnated in the loathsome figure of her grandfather, whom she also accuses of incestuous overtures. In many panels, she also celebrates female eroticism and presents it as the font of her creativity, challenging the Orphic paradigm of artistic creation that negates the feminine. By inventing her own scenarios, Salomon confirms her subjectivity as a woman, an artist, and an agent of history.

It seems that the artist's desire to articulate distinctly female subjectivity, combined with the frankness with which she delved into the socially proscribed subject matter, consigned her oeuvre to the margins of established historical narratives and divested it of testimonial weight. Instead, she was remembered as either "another Anne Frank," a cliché of Holocaust remembrance that neutralized her mature female sexuality and desire that she had explored in her art, or as a woman who was killed in Auschwitz because she was pregnant—that is, in conformity with the trope of the suffering Jewish mother.

According to Federica Clementi, Salomon's art was nourished and inspired by strong female figures in her life, especially her maternal grandmother and her stepmother, both of whom she loved deeply, rather than solely by male mentors (her professors at the academy and her lover Alfred Wolfsohn). Thus, the belated recognition of the artistic merit and novelty of Salomon's project,[51] inaugurated in the late 1990s by Mary Felstiner,[52] and the acknowledgment of its testimonial value as a unique document of the times[53] can be seen as emblematic of a paradigmatic shift in gendered perceptions of Holocaust testimonies as it was precipitated by the advent of feminist epistemic frameworks. Moreover, this celebratory resurrection of the female voice, formerly silenced within presumably gender-neutral Holocaust narratives, might now be propitious in reframing some of the other forgotten stories. For instance, in light of Clementi's compelling description of Salomon's paintings as "a woman's artistic act of defiance vis-à-vis impending catastrophe," Wiera Gran's brilliant performances at Café Sztuka, which drew crowds every night despite the hunger and sense of doom in the 1941–1942 Warsaw Ghetto, could also be recognized and celebrated as a manifesto of self-affirmation, creativity, and resistance rather than as acts of survival at all cost, for which she was subsequently ostracized.[54]

BETWEEN HISTORY AND MEMORY: TOWARD A FEMINIST MODEL OF RELATIONAL IMAGINATION

According to Hannah Arendt, the task of imagination is to open up yet-unrealized possibilities and to allow us to change both ourselves and the external world. National Socialism, however, sought to eradicate in its victims this unique human ability to envisage the future and to create new ways of living; for Arendt, as for Primo Levi, the *Muselmänner* were the extreme embodiment of that collapse.[55] This is why Arendt contends that imagination, with its spontaneity and unpredictability, is "the greatest of all obstacles to total domination."[56] Arendt enjoins us that, after the Shoah, we have an obligation to exercise this faculty to its full potential, so that we will "dread the concentration camp as a possibility for the future."[57] In *The Generation of Postmemory*, Marianne Hirsch ponders the relation between imagination and our ability to remember the past and argues that memory is never a literal transcript of events because its connection to the past is mediated by "imaginative investment, projection, and creation."[58] But if only some experiences are worthy of being preserved in memory while others are evicted from projects of remembrance, then we have to acknowledge an ethical shortcoming of our imaginative faculty. In Immanuel Kant's classical formulation, imagination (*Einbildungskraft*), unlike reason and cognition, is a free power of the mind because it operates without predetermined rules and always reaches for untried possibilities; in transcending existing horizons, imagination makes it possible for new knowledge to emerge.[59]

In *Images in Spite of All*, French philosopher and art historian Georges Didi-Huberman reiterates Kant's apotheosis of imagination in a very different context. He is looking at the eponymic clandestine photographs of the Auschwitz *Sonderkommandos* and states, "In order to know, we must *imagine* for ourselves. We must attempt to imagine the hell that Auschwitz was in the summer of 1944. Let us not invoke the unimaginable. . . . We *are obliged* to that oppressive imaginable."[60] Yet does imagination truly roam free, unconstrained by dominant regimes of knowledge? Can we imagine what we do not know, what does not fit into the socially accepted frameworks? Per-

Figure 1. A group of Jewish women and girls huddle together on a beach near Liepaja on December 15, 1941, prior to their execution by Latvian SD and police. In the background Latvian police are forcing other Jews to undress. Pictured are members of the extended Epstein family: Sorela (10 years old, hiding behind her mother); Roza (age 43); an unidentified friend or relative; Mia (18); and her mother, Emma (47). Photographer: Carl Strott. Copyright © Bundesarchiv, B 162 Bild-02615.

haps the unbridled power of imagination is also subject to epistemic limitations, and it may even secretly collude in reinforcing conservative social norms and taboos.

For over a decade, my own imagination, for example, has been stunted by another iconic Holocaust photograph (figure 1). It shows four Jewish women in their undergarments, as if posing for the camera, shortly before their execution on the dunes of Škēde, near Liepaja, Latvia, on December 15, 1941.[61] The negatives of the photos, most likely taken by SS-Oberscharführer Carl-Emil Strott, were found by David Siwzon, one of the few survivors of the *Aktion* (roundup and mass killing of Jews) in Liepaja. They were deposited in the Soviet Archives, where they were discovered in the 1960s by a German researcher, Gerhard Schönberner.[62] Although I looked at that image many times, I never paid much attention to the fifth figure, of a little girl wearing a frock and a bonnet, pressed against one of the women. It took me even longer to notice the details in the background, one of which is a blurry, pale shape that, on closer scrutiny, appears to be an old woman, uncomfortably bent over and most likely being helped to undress. For years, I was only paying attention to the four partly undressed women in the foreground, seeing a version of a historical event as it had been recorded by the lens of a camera held by a German soldier and then retold at official sites of remembrance.

In her poetic memoir *Auschwitz and After*, Charlotte Delbo enjoins her readers, "Try to look. Just try and see," which conveys the sense that, in order to remember, it is not enough to merely look at the spectacle of suffering: we must look with the intention to break through the crust of unseeing.[63] Looking at the photograph from Liepaja, French historian Nadine Fresco writes:

> These photographs do not say if, even for a moment, there appeared in the minds of the murderers, standing in front of the elderly women, a trace of fear or respect that they would have felt before the bodies of their own mothers. Or if in the minds of the murderers there appeared even the smallest trace of a memory of their own children's little bodies. These photographs do not say whether the people who are trembling from cold, fear and absolute abandonment and whom the murderers are watching as they undress, run and then die, whether these people have, in their eyes, at least a feeble connection with the "sphere of human duties and responsibilities." [64]

Fresco's contemplation of the photograph is a compassionate act of imagining and a commentary on the murderous consequences of the foreclosure of the human power to imagine. She concludes her essay with a sentence that reveals a personal connection to the story of the murdered women of Liepaja: "For me [these photographs] also belong to a different history: David Siwzon, who was born in Liepaja on May 29, 1914, and died on June 18, 1983, was my mother's youngest brother."[65] Fresco's imaginative "seeing" of the details in the photograph, supported with archival research,[66] seeks to pierce the veil of the murderous male gaze that has captured the victims in a grotesque pose of femininity. The image of the women, frozen in time a few minutes before their death, has prompted her to develop the blind spots in the photograph from the negative of the past and to recover life stories that have disappeared from our field of vision.

Philosopher David Hume once wrote that when I see another person's suffering, I can experience her pain through an act of imagination.[67] This means, however, that to respond with empathy, I must first *see* the person who endures the pain. In her imaginative retelling of the events of that day, Fresco follows the women on the agonizing march, in subzero temperatures, from Liepaja to the dunes of Šķēde, and she can see all of them. Then why was the old woman in the background of the photograph absent from *my* field of vision, even though I could also "see" her? As contemporary phenomenologists have argued, our perceptions of the world are influenced by ingrained yet often disavowed epistemic biases, and even basic sense impressions are filtered through interpretive frameworks, which thus undergird everyday habits of being.[68] As a result, the areas of experience that do not appear to us as intelligible never enter into our perceptual field and thus cannot etch themselves in memory, limiting our knowledge of the past and holding us captive to certain ways of remembering the past while excluding others. Yet these everyday acts of perception are also bound up with imagination, coimplicating our own capacity for sentience in "the pain of others."[69]

I would like to propose the term *relational imagination*, which draws on the feminist rethinking of self and memory as fundamentally "relational." We are constituted as persons endowed with cognitive abilities, including the capacity for memory, always in relation to others and with the support of communal practices that foster these abilities. We are shaped through interactions with others, and we live our lives and develop the narratives of our lives within these complex networks. The relational model departs from the traditional Western conception of the autonomous, self-sustaining subject whose memory is unique, unshareable, and fundamentally free of the influence of others. As gender theorist Judith Butler shows in her work on mourning and grievability, our bodies expose us to others before they properly belong to us. Since, through corporeality, our being is shared prior to our proper being in the world, embodied subjectivity emerges relationally, in its vulnerability to violence and its dependence on others. Conversely, we are exposed to the pain and trauma of others that coconstitute us, even of those who do not dwell in our immediate proximity, and we grieve their inevitable loss. Construing imagination as relational takes into account these complex webs of human interdependency. Thus, as Herman argues, breaking through the wall of silence (and, we may add, of blindness) imposed by socially constructed accounts of trauma "always starts relationally with people telling their secrets to someone who listens, who acknowledges and validates."[70] We saw the connection between the transmission of traumatic memory and relational imagination when Nadine Fresco's embodied connection to the women in the photograph prompted her to imagine and to recover the stories of their lives and death. It is in our exposure to the outside, in our indebtedness to others, that we are capable of imagining the shared humanity of others, although, as Charlotte Delbo reminds us, we are also vulnerable to having this ability taken away.

Writing in 1940, Jean-Paul Sartre conceived of imagination as the ultimate locus of man's existential freedom.[71] Relational imagination, however, or coimagining with others, is prior to imagination understood as the highest expression of individual freedom, and it is necessary so that we can conceive of the pain of others and postulate their freedom from suffering as always incumbent on us. In Griselda Pollock's words, the role of imagination is to "potentially create the future . . . by sharing, by recognizing co-humanity rather than anxiously policing the boundaries of difference."[72] In dredging hidden shapes and colors from the crypts of invisibility and unspeakability, relational imagining thus renders us accountable not only for what we have imagined but also for what we have failed to imagine.[73]

If imagination is a primary and indispensable condition of acquiring and transforming knowledge, then acts of imagination can foster our desire to know and to shift the parameters of how we perceive the victims of catastrophic experiences and which victims we perceive at all. Only if we can imagine the victims' existence will we look for their traces in the archives, in the International Tracing Service (ITS) database, or in survivors' oral testimonies. If we are to follow Didi-Huberman's injunction, then the task of imagination is to rewrite history so that the invisible can inscribe itself on its pages. Yet if memory depends on deep-seated habits of knowing and on cultural means of expression, it is also the duty of imagination to break away from the rules that dictate what the content and shape of an appropriate representation should be. Remembering the past requires that we imagine looking in the face of the old woman in the dark background of the photograph, the face that will forever remain invisible, and that we guard the memory of the indignity and injury done to her.

Knowledge about the past, gathered in the archive, must be supplemented with an act of imagination that fills in the objects where previously none could be apprehended, reclaiming them from the void. We need to search for images, and the ways of looking at these images, that will invite and hold those men, women, and children whose traumatic experiences our practices of remembrance have abjected from the realm of the visible. This search is both an ethical imperative and an ontological postulate because if we fail, then the old Jewish woman from Liepaja, cast in the grayish, indistinct background of the photograph, will never have existed.

NOTES

1. Ruth Kluger, *Still Alive* (New York: Feminist Press, 2003), 18.

2. I am referring to, for instance, Emmanuel Ringelblum's project on the experience of the Jewish woman in the Warsaw Ghetto in the Oneg Shabbat archive. See ARG I 597 (Ring. I /49), "Kobieta żydowska w Warszawie od września 1939 do chwili bieżącej [1942]," pp.194–281, and ARG I 506 (Ring. I/158), "Relacje kobiet o pracy społecznej we wrześniu 1939 r. i podczas okupacji: Sylwetki 6 działaczek społecznych, opracowane na podstawie ich własnych wspomnień," pp. 281–91, in *Archiwum Ringelbluma: Konspiracyjne Archiwum Getta Warszawy*, vol. 5, *Getto warszawskie: życie codzienne*, ed. Katarzyna Person (Warsaw: Jewish Historical Institute, 2011). Another example are David Boder's interviews conducted with survivors in 1946 in displaced persons camps. See Alan Rosen, *The Wonder of Their Voices: The 1946 Holocaust Interviews of David Boder* (New York: Oxford University Press, 2010).

3. The Conference on Women Surviving the Holocaust, convened in 1983 by Joan Ringelheim and Esther Katz at Stern College of Yeshiva University, is usually cited as the inaugural event that raised the question of gendered experiences during the Holocaust. For an overview of feminist scholarship in Holocaust studies, see introductions to Carol Rittner and John Roth, eds., *Different Voices* (St. Paul, Minn.: Paragon House, 1993); Dalia Ofer and Lenore J. Weitzman, eds., *Women in the Holocaust* (New Haven, Conn.: Yale University Press, 1998); Sonja M. Hedgepeth and Rochelle G. Saidel, eds., *Sexual Violence against Jewish Women During the Holocaust* (Boston: Brandeis University Press, 2010); and Myrna Goldenberg and Amy Shapiro, eds., *Different Horrors, Same Hell: Gender and the Holocaust* (Seattle:

University of Washington Press, 2013). See also Zoë Waxman's *Women in the Holocaust: A Feminist History* (Oxford: Oxford University Press, 2017).

4. Maurice Halbwachs, *The Collective Memory*, trans. Francis J. Ditter Jr. and Vida Yazdi Ditter (New York: Harper and Row, 1980), 38.

5. Aleida Assmann, *Shadows of Trauma: Memory and the Politics of Postwar Identity*, trans. Sarah Clift (New York: Fordham University Press, 2016), 6.

6. Similar questions emerged in the wake of allegations against American film producer Harvey Weinstein in October 2017, when the hashtag #MeToo spread globally on social media, drawing attention to the prevalence of harassment and sexual assault against women in the workplace.

7. Sue Campbell, *Relational Remembering: Rethinking the Memory Wars* (London: Rowman and Littlefield, 2003), 17. Campbell examines the popularity, in the late 1980s, of attributing the false memory syndrome to female survivors of sexual abuse. See also Miranda Fricker, *Epistemic Injustice: Power and the Ethics of Knowing* (Oxford: Clarendon Press, 2007).

8. Marianne Hirsch and Leo Spitzer, "Gendered Translations: Claude Lanzmann's *Shoah*," in *Gendering War Talk*, ed. Miriam Cooke and Angela Woollacott (Princeton, N.J.: Princeton University Press, 1993), 15.

9. A translation of Lanzmann's original transcript (hereafter cited as Lanzmann translation), Claude Lanzmann's Shoah Collection, Interview with Ruth Elias (1978–1981), p. 20, USHMM Archives, http://data.ushmm.org/intermedia/film_video/spielberg_archive/transcript/RG60_5003/14CD858F-C0D0-4FDC-A0E8-23E9CBF9D9B4.pdf.

10. Markus Zisselsberger, "The Afterlives of Victims as Survivors: Female Voices and Gendered Testimony in the Outtakes of Claude Lanzmann's *Shoah*" (unpublished manuscript, Microsoft Word file, 2015), 55, courtesy of Markus Zisselsberger.

11. Lanzmann translation, 44.

12. Ibid., 57.

13. In his later commentaries on the film, Lanzmann never discussed his interviews with the female witnesses, and he sealed that silence in his autobiography *The Patagonian Hare: A Memoir*, trans. Frank Wynne (New York: Farrar, Straus, and Giroux, 2012). In contrast, he frequently returned to interviews with male witnesses and produced two documentaries based on the unused footage: *The Karski Report* (2010) and *The Last of the Unjust* (on Benjamin Murmelstein, 2013). In October 2017, Lanzmann's most recent project, a four-part TV series, entitled *Les quatre soeurs* (*The Four Sisters*), based on the outtakes of his interviews with Paula Biren, Ruth Elias, Ada Lichtman, and Hanna Marton, premiered at the Jewish Film Festival in New York. It was produced in France by Synecdoche Films and later distributed in

France in January 2018 by Arte TV. The segment with Ruth Elias appears as the first in the series, and it comprises 1.5 hours of the original 2.5 interview.

14. For the discussion of the suffering mother and maternal sacrifice in Holocaust representations see, for instance, Judith Tydor Baumel, *Double Jeopardy: Gender and the Holocaust* (New York: Routledge, 1999); Janet Jacobs, *Memorializing the Holocaust: Gender, Genocide and Collective Memory* (London: I. B. Tauris, 2010).

15. Elias further asserts her sexual agency in a memoir she wrote following the interview with Lanzmann: "The desire for human closeness, for physical love, was especially strong. . . . Love makes you inventive. There were quiet little hiding places in the arcades, and we used every opportunity to make love in these deserted corners." Ruth Elias, *Triumph of Hope* (New York: John Wiley and Sons, 1998), 99.

16. The story of Beth Jakov Maidens was first reported as a factual event in the *New York Times* on January 8, 1943. See Sara R. Horowitz, "The Gender of Good and Evil: Women and Holocaust Memory," in *Gray Zones: Ambiguity and Compromise in the Holocaust and its Aftermath*, ed. Jonathan Petropoulos and John Roth (New York: Berghahn Books, 2005), 165–78.

17. Wiera Gran, interview with Jerzy Płaczkiewicz, Paris, August 1991, posted on YouTube January 1, 2012, http://www.youtube.com/watch?v=xsfWTMjj_m0.

18. Władysław Szpilman's diary, edited by Jerzy Waldorff and entitled *Śmierć miasta* (*The Death of a City*), first appeared in 1946, heavily censored, and for decades remained virtually unknown in Poland. On the initiative of Szpilman's son, it was reissued in 1998 in German as *Das wunderbare Überleben* (published by Ullstag Verlag) and translated into English in 1998 as *The Pianist: The Extraordinary True Story of One Man's Survival in Warsaw, 1939–1945* (Picador, 2000). In Poland, it was republished as *Pianista: Warszawskie wspomnienia, 1939–1945* (Kraków: Wydawnictwo Znak, 2000).

19. Based on the documents from Gran's trials, USHMM, file accession no. 1996.A.0223, RG-15.189M.

20. See a certified Polish translation, entitled "Walka Wiery Gran z cieniami" (Wiera Gran's Struggle with Shadows), of an article in *Haaretz* (December 3, 1971) by Ran Kislew, in which the Israeli journalist defended the singer against a campaign of slander. USHMM, file accession no. 2007/230.

21. Gran interview with Płaczkiewicz.

22. See Wiera Gran, *Sztafeta oszczerców: Autobiografia śpiewaczki* [A relay of slander: A singer's autobiography] (self-pub., 1980).

23. Agata Tuszyńska, *Oskarżona Wiera Gran* (Kraków: Wydawnictwo Literackie, 2010); translated into English as *Vera Gran: The Accused* (New York: Albert A. Knopf, 2013).

24. USC Shoah Foundation Visual History Archive, Interview Code: 8086, Special Collection, accessed at USHMM, https://vha.usc.edu/viewingPage?testimonyID=6999&returnIndex=0.

25. Zmarz-Koczanowicz borrowed the phrase from Kislew's *Haaretz* article.

26. In her interview for the Shoah Foundation, Gran repeatedly emphasizes her feats of survival, ingenuity, and rescue, especially in trying to save her mother's life. She says, "I was always 'a hero'. . . . When I thought of something, it was always well done."

27. *Wiera Gran*, directed by Maria Zmarz-Koczanowicz (Kraków: Studio Filmowe Largo, 2012).

28. Kislew, "Walka Wiery Gran z cieniami," 3.

29. Assmann, *Shadows of Trauma*, 20; emphasis in the original.

30. Laura S. Brown, "Not Outside the Range: One Feminist Perspective on Psychic Trauma," in *Trauma: Explorations in Memory*, ed. Cathy Caruth (Baltimore: Johns Hopkins University Press, 1995), 102.

31. Primo Levi, *The Drowned and the Saved*, trans. Raymond Rosenthal (New York: Vintage Books, 1988), 59. On moral judgment and the *Sonderkommando*, see Lissa Skitolsky's contribution in this volume.

32. Levi, *Drowned and Saved*, 60.

33. See, for instance, Doris Bergen, "Sexual Violence in the Holocaust: Unique or Typical?" in *Lessons and Legacies VII: The Holocaust in International Perspectives*, ed. Dagmar Herzog (Evanston, Ill.: Northwestern University Press, 2006), 179–200; Hedgepeth and Saidel, *Sexual Violence*; Myrna Goldenberg, "Sex-Based Violence and the Politics and Ethics of Survival," in Goldenberg and Shapiro, *Different Horrors, Same Hell*, 99–127; Anna Hájkovà, "Sexual Barter in Times of Genocide: Negotiating the Sexual Economy of the Theresienstadt Ghetto," *Signs* 38 (Spring 2013): 503–33.

34. Ruth Leys, *Trauma: A Genealogy* (Chicago: University of Chicago Press, 2000), 4.

35. In *Hysterical Men*, Paul Lerner describes the appearance of psychosomatic symptoms, akin to female hysteria, in German soldiers returning from the trenches of World War I. Like Leys, he shows that the concept of trauma and the ways it has been interpreted and dealt with are a product of a given historical moment and, in addition to their gendered dimension, are fraught with presuppositions about race, class, and ability. See Paul Lerner, *Hysterical Men: War, Psychiatry, and the Politics of Trauma in Germany, 1890–1930* (Ithaca, N.Y.: Cornell University Press, 2003).

36. Maureen Murdoch et al., "Women and War," *Journal of General Internal Medicine* (March 2006): 5–10; J. Wolfe et al., "Posttraumatic Stress Disorders and War Zone Exposure as Correlates of Perceived Health in Fe-

male Vietnam War Veterans," *Journal of Consulting and Clinical Psychology* 62 (1994): 1235–40.

37. See Dagmar Herzog, "The Obscenity of Objectivity: Post-Holocaust Antisemitism and the Invention of Post-Traumatic Stress Disorder," in *Lessons and Legacies XII: New Directions in Holocaust Research and Education*, ed. Wendy Lower and Lauren Faulkner Rossi (Evanston, Ill.: Northwestern University Press, 2017), 31–63. Herzog argues that, after World War II, "the science of trauma" was initially shaped by the fight—infused with both antisemitism and greed—over financial compensation for mental health damages for Jewish survivors. According to Herzog, the medical and legal recognition of the symptoms of psychic trauma in Vietnam War veterans precipitated "a paradigm shift," bringing post-Holocaust trauma into view and eventually into "cultural dominance" (31–33).

38. Matthew J. Freedman et al., eds., *Handbook of PTSD: Science and Practice* (New York: Guilford Press, 2014), 6.

39. Ibid., 83.

40. Brown, "Not Outside the Range," 101.

41. Ibid.

42. In *Trauma and Recovery* (New York: Basic Books, 2015), feminist psychiatrist Judith Herman distinguishes between specifically male (related to experiences of war combat) and female (usually stemming from sexual violence) types of trauma.

43. Considering the prominence of the Holocaust in interpretations of PTSD, it is unsurprising that female victims of sexual assault sometimes seek comparisons with Holocaust victims to articulate the sense of irreparable harm they have suffered and to ascertain the credibility of their account. For instance, Karyn L. Freedman, a Canadian feminist philosopher, draws on memoirs by Holocaust survivors to develop strategies of working through the trauma of rape; see Karyn Freedman, *One Hour in Paris: A True Story of Rape and Recovery* (Toronto: Freehand Books, 2014).

44. Sigmund Freud, *Beyond the Pleasure Principle*, in *The Freud Reader*, ed. Peter Gray (New York: W. W. Norton, 1989), 607.

45. Elizabeth D. Heineman, "Sexuality and Nazism: The Doubly Unspeakable?" *Journal of the History of Sexuality* 11, no. 1/2 (January–April 2002): 22–66.

46. Judith Herman and Cathy Caruth, "The Politics of Trauma: A Conversation with Judith Herman," in *Listening to Trauma: Conversations with Leaders in the Theory and Treatment of Catastrophic Experiences*, ed. Cathy Caruth (Baltimore: Johns Hopkins University Press, 2014), 134, 138.

47. Salomon left behind 1,325 gouaches, out of which she selected 784 plates that compose the body of *Leben? oder Theater?*

48. The description on the front inside flap of the book jacket for *Charlotte: A Diary in Pictures*, based on the 1961 exhibit of her work, states, "A young girl, passionate, lonely, under threat of death, created this pictorial record of her brief life" (New York: Harcourt, Brace and World, 1963).

49. Charlotte Salomon, *Life? or Theatre?*, trans. Leila Vennewitz (Amsterdam: Waanders Publishers Zwolle, 1998).

50. The excerpts from Salomon's work that focus on mental illness among women in Salomon's family and on her relationship with Wolfsohn are foregrounded in Dutch director Frans Weisz's 1981 film *Charlotte*, which is a cinematographic reconstruction of *Leben? oder Theater?* The same leitmotifs inform a fictional reconstruction of Salomon's life and death in David Foenkinos's novel *Charlotte* (Paris: Éditions Gallimard, 2014). See also Darcy C. Buerkle, *Nothing Happened: Charlotte Salomon and an Archive of Suicide* (Ann Arbor: University of Michigan Press, 2013).

51. See Ernst van Alphen, *Caught by History: Holocaust Effects in Contemporary Art, Literature, and Theory* (Stanford, Calif.: Stanford University Press, 1997); Griselda Pollock, "Theater of Memory: Trauma and Cure in Charlotte Salomon's Modernist Fairy Tale," in *Reading Charlotte Salomon*, ed. Michael P. Steinberg and Monica Bohm-Duchen (Ithaca, N.Y.: Cornell University Press, 2005), 34–72. Pollock describes Salomon's paintings as "one of the twentieth century's most challenging art works: radical in its modernist hybridities, intertextualities, formal daring and diversity" ("Theater of Memory," 34).

52. Mary L. Felstiner, *To Paint Her Life: Charlotte Salomon in the Nazi Era* (Berkeley: University of California Press, 1997).

53. See Monica Bohn-Duchen, "A Life before Auschwitz," in Steinberg and Bohm-Duchen, *Reading Charlotte Salomon*, 21–33; Deborah Schultz and Edward Timms, *Pictorial Narrative in the Nazi Period: Felix Nussbaum, Charlotte Salomon and Arnold Daghani* (London: Routledge, 2009).

54. Federica K. Clementi, *Holocaust Mothers and Daughters: Family, History, and Trauma* (Boston: Brandeis University Press, 2013), 295.

55. In *Survival in Auschwitz,* Primo Levi writes, ". . . their life is short, but their numbers are endless; they, the *Muselmänner*, the drowned, form the backbone of the camp, an anonymous mass, continually renewed and always identical; the non-men who march and labor in silence, the divine spark dead within them, already too empty to really suffer. One hesitates to call them living; one hesitates to call their death death, in the face of which they have no fear, as they are too tired to understand" (New York: Simon & Schuster, 1996), 90.

56. Hannah Arendt, *The Origins of Totalitarianism* (San Diego: Harcourt Brace, 1973), 456.

57. Ibid., 441.

58. Marianne Hirsch, *The Generation of Postmemory: Writing and Visual Culture after the Holocaust* (New York: Columbia University Press, 2012), loc. 156–57, Kindle.

59. Immanuel Kant, *Critique of Pure Reason*, trans. Norman Kemp Smith (New York: St. Martin's Press, 1965).

60. Georges Didi-Huberman, *Images in Spite of All: Four Photographs from Auschwitz*, trans. Shane B. Lillis (Chicago: University of Chicago Press, 2008), 3; emphasis in the original. Didi-Huberman is critical of conceptualizations of the Holocaust as unimaginable and unpresentable.

61. The women in the photograph have been identified as Sorella Epstein (10), her mother Rosa Epstein (43), an unidentified relative or family friend, Mia Epstein (18), and her mother, Emma Epstein (47).

62. Gerhard Schönberner is the editor of *Der gelbe Stern: Die Judenverfolgung in Europa 1933 bis 1945* (Hamburg: Rütten und Loening, 1960), the first well-known album of Holocaust photographs.

63. Charlotte Delbo, *Auschwitz and After*, trans. Rosette C. Lamont (New Haven, Conn.: Yale University Press, 1995), 84–85.

64. Nadine Fresco, *La Mort des Juifs* [The death of the Jews] (Paris: Éditions du Seuil, 2008), 78; translation mine. In *Photographing the Holocaust*, Janina Struk also responds to this photograph (as well as to other photographs of men and women taken at the sites of mass executions) and concludes, "It is apparent that while the Nazis exploited the male Jew in terms of his culture and religion, women were humiliated and exploited entirely in terms of their gender"; Janina Struk, *Photographing the Holocaust: Interpretations of the Evidence* (London: L. B. Tauris), 71. Regarding the gender-specific nature of this photograph, Hirsch takes the view opposite to Struk's (and mine) and argues that "there is no evidence, in anything that I have read about the Einsatzkommando killings in particular, that the killers in any way recognized the victims' sexuality or that there was anything sexual in these murders. In fact, the opposite seems to have been the case: the victims were dehumanized precisely by being desexualized." Hirsch, *Generation of Postmemory*, loc. 2429–32.

65. Fresco, *La Mort des Juifs*, 96.

66. Fresco's account is based on the files from the Einsatzgruppen trials and on her research in the Latvian National Archives.

67. See David Hume, *A Treatise of Human Nature* (Public Domain Books, 1739), book 2, part 2, sec. 7, "Of Compassion." Kindle edition.

68. This discussion is based on Maurice Merleau-Ponty's theses in *Phenomenology of Perception*, trans. Colin Smith, (London: Routledge, 1962), and on feminist philosopher Linda Alcoff's adaptation of the French phi-

losopher's theses in *Visible Identities: Race, Gender, and the Self* (Oxford: Oxford University Press, 2005).

69. I have borrowed the expression "the pain of others" from the title of Susan Sontag's book *Regarding the Pain of Others* (New York: Picador/ Farrar, Straus and Giroux, 2003), in which the American writer revised the theses that she previously developed in her seminal work *On Photography* (New York: Picador/Farrar, Straus and Giroux, 1977).

70. Herman and Caruth, "Politics of Trauma," 145.

71. Jean-Paul Sartre. *The Imaginary: A Phenomenological Psychology of Imagination*, trans. Jonathan Webber (London: Routledge, 2004), 47.

72. Griselda Pollock, "Aesthetic Wit(h)nessing in the Era of Trauma," *EuroAmerica* 40, no. 4 (December 2012): 837.

73. See also Lutz Kaelber's and Gershon Greenberg's articles in this volume, both of which are also centrally concerned with victims who have remained invisible.

Notes on Contributors

Martin Dean, born in London in 1962, received a Ph.D. in European history from Queens' College, Cambridge, in 1989. He worked for the Australian Special Investigations Unit and then as senior historian for the Metropolitan Police War Crimes Unit in London. From 1998 to 2016, he was Applied Research Scholar at the United States Holocaust Memorial Museum. He is the author of *Collaboration in the Holocaust* (2000) and *Robbing the Jews* (2008) and the volume editor of *The USHMM Encyclopedia of Camps and Ghettos 1933–1945*, vol. 2, *Ghettos in German-Occupied Eastern Europe* (2012). He is a member of the Babi Yar Holocaust Memorial Center's Scientific Committee.

Jonathan Druker is a professor of Italian at Illinois State University, where he teaches undergraduate courses on Italian language and culture and graduate courses in literary studies exploring communal trauma, memory, and the Holocaust. His first book, *Primo Levi and Humanism after Auschwitz,* was published in 2009. In 2014, he was a fellow at the United States Holocaust Memorial Museum, where he began research on his current book project, an analysis of Holocaust literature focusing on trauma, history, memory, and time. With Scott Lerner, he edited *The New Italy and the Jews: From Massimo D'Azeglio to Primo Levi* (forthcoming in 2018).

Alexandra Garbarini is a professor of history at Williams College, where she teaches courses on modern Europe, Jewish history, and Holocaust studies. She is the author of *Numbered Days: Diary Writing and the Holocaust* (2006) and the coauthor of *Jewish Responses to Persecution*, vol. 2, *1939–1940* (2011). She coedited a special issue of the journal *Etudes Arméniennes Contemporaines* on "Victim Testimony and Mass Violence" in 2015, and the diary of Lucien Dreyfus (forthcoming). Her research focuses on European Jewish and non-Jewish representations of mass violence in the decades prior to and during the Holocaust.

Simone Gigliotti is based in the Department of History, Royal Holloway, University of London. She is working on a book project, *Home-Seeking and Holocaust Cinema*, from which her chapter in this book is derived. She is also the author of *The Train Journey* (2009) and coeditor of several collections, including *The Young Victims of the Nazi Regime* (2016) and *The Wiley Companion to the Holocaust* (forthcoming).

Dorota Glowacka is Professor of Humanities at the University of King's College in Halifax, Canada, where she teaches classes in Holocaust and genocide studies, gender studies, philosophy of race, and critical theory. She is the author of *Po tamtej stronie: świadectwo, afekt, wyobraźnia* [*On the Other Side: Testimony, Affect, Imagination*, 2017] and *Disappearing Traces: Holocaust Testimonials, Ethics, and Aesthetics* (2012). She coedited *Between Ethics and Aesthetics: Crossing the Boundaries* (2002) and *Imaginary Neighbors: Mediating Polish-Jewish Relations after the Holocaust* (2007), and she edited a special issue on "Community" for *Culture Machine* in 2006. Glowacka has published numerous book chapters, journal articles, reviews, and encyclopedia entries in the area of Holocaust studies and critical theory.

Jan Grabowski is Professor of History of the Holocaust at the University of Ottawa. He has taught at universities in France, Israel, Poland, and the United States. In 2011, he was appointed the Baron Friedrich Carl von Oppenheim Chair for the Study of Racism, Antisemitism, and the Holocaust at Yad Vashem, Jerusalem, Israel. He has authored and edited fifteen books and published more than sixty articles in English, French, Polish, German, and Hebrew. Professor Grabowski's most recent book, *Hunt for the Jews: Betrayal and Murder in German-Occupied Poland*, was awarded the Yad Vashem International Book Prize for 2014.

Gershon Greenberg is a visiting professor in the Department of Jewish Thought at the Hebrew University of Jerusalem, where he offers courses in the history of Jewish religious thought through the Holocaust; and a professor of philosophy and religion at American University in Washington, D.C. His recent publications include *Justice Is of the Great Deep: Orthodox Theological Responses to the Holocaust* (in Hebrew) with Asaf Yedidyah (2016) and "Religion and Violence in Judea, Samaria, and Gaza," in *"Mending the World"? Possibilities and Obstacles for Religion, Church, and Theology* (2017).

Paul B. Jaskot is a professor of art history and the director of the Wired! Lab for Digital Art History and Visual Culture at Duke University. His work focuses on the political history of modern art and architecture, with a specific focus on the Nazi period and its cultural impact over the long twentieth century. Among other scholarship, he is the author of *The Nazi Perpetrator: Postwar German Art and the Politics of the Right* (2012). Jaskot is also a team member of the Holocaust Geography Collaborative, a group committed to using Geographic Information Systems (GIS) and other digital methods to analyze problems in Holocaust studies.

Lutz Kaelber is a historical-comparative sociologist who obtained his doctorate at Indiana University–Bloomington. He is an associate professor of sociology at the University of Vermont. He has published on the politics of memory in Europe, the commemoration of victims of Nazi "euthanasia" crimes, and the status of individuals with disabilities in the Third Reich, with a focus on "children's euthanasia" and Jewish minors.

Marion Kaplan is the Skirball Professor of Modern Jewish History at New York University. She is a three-time National Jewish Book Award winner for *The Making of the Jewish Middle Class: Women, Family, and Identity in Imperial Germany* (1991), *Between Dignity and Despair: Jewish Life in Nazi Germany* (1998), and *Gender and Jewish History* (with Deborah Dash Moore, 2011), as well as a finalist for *Dominican Haven: The Jewish Refugee Settlement in Sosua* (2008). She edited *The Jewish Feminist Movement in Germany, Jewish Daily Life in Germany, 1618–1945* and coedited *Jüdische Welten: Juden in Deutschland vom 18. Jahrhundert bis in die Gegenwart* with Beate Meyer.

Hana Kubátová is an assistant professor at the Charles University, Prague. She has been a research fellow at the Heinrich Heine University, the Slovak Academy of Sciences, Tel Aviv University, and the United States Holocaust Memorial Museum. Her areas of research include majority-minority relations in Slovakia, the social history of the Holocaust, and the relationship between Holocaust memory and wartime robbery. She recently coauthored *The Jew in Czech and Slovak Imagination, 1938-89: Antisemitism, the Holocaust, and Zionism* (2018) and coedited *Jews and Gentiles in Central and Eastern Europe during the Holocaust: History and Memory* (2018).

Pedro Correa Martín-Arroyo is currently completing his Ph.D. at the London School of Economics and Political Science. His Ph.D. dissertation explores the humanitarian work of various relief organizations with Jewish refugees in Spain and Portugal during the Holocaust. Previously, he was the Diane and Howard Wohl Fellow at the United States Holocaust Memorial Museum. He has written a number of articles, including "The Politics of Holocaust Rescue Myths in Spain: From Francoist Legend to the Righteous Diplomats," in *The Politics of the Neutrals during the Shoah* (2016), and has taught at Royal Holloway, King's College, and the London School of Economics.

Brad Prager is a professor of German and film studies at the University of Missouri. He is the author of *After the Fact: The Holocaust in Twenty-First Century Documentary Film* (2015), *The Cinema of Werner Herzog: Aesthetic Ecstasy and Truth* (2007), and *Aesthetic Vision and German Romanticism: Writing Images* (2007). He is the editor or coeditor of several books, including *Visualizing the Holocaust: Documents, Aesthetics, Memory* (2008), and he is currently coediting a volume of essays on the United States Holocaust Memorial Museum's archive of outtakes from Claude Lanzmann's *Shoah*.

Lissa Skitolsky is an associate professor of philosophy at Susquehanna University. Her research in the fields of continental philosophy and genocide studies aims to interrogate our cultural and political responses to mass violence and useless suffering. She has published articles on political theory, rhetoric, and state-sanctioned violence. She is currently working on a manuscript about the role that our notion of the "criminal" has played in genocides in the past and present. As part of this project, she is drawing on hip-hop as testimony to carceral violence and the genocidal wounds inflicted by the U.S. criminal justice system.

DANA SMITH received her Ph.D. from Queen Mary, University of London, where she held a doctoral fellowship with the Leo Baeck Institute. Her dissertation explored the intersection of gender and regionalism in Jewish self-conceptualizations of Jewish art in the Jewish Cultural League in Bavaria from 1934 through 1938. She is currently a postdoctoral research fellow at the Center for Jewish History in New York City.